NO ONE IS ILLEGAL

NO ONE IS ILLEGAL

Fighting Racism and State Violence on the U.S.–Mexico Border

Justin Akers Chacón

Mike Davis

Photographs by Julián Cardona

Updated Edition

Haymarket
Books

Chicago, Illinois

© 2018 by Justin Akers Chacón and Mike Davis
Photographs © 2018 Julián Cardona

First published in 2006 by Haymarket Books in Chicago.
This edition published in 2018 by
Haymarket Books
P.O. Box 180165
Chicago, IL 60618
773-583-7884
www.haymarketbooks.org
info@haymarketbooks.org

ISBN: 978-1-60846-849-2

Trade distribution:
In the US, Consortium Book Sales and Distribution, www.cbsd.com
In Canada, Publishers Group Canada, www.pgcbooks.ca
In the UK, Turnaround Publisher Services, www.turnaround-uk.com
All other countries, IPS International, IPS_Intlsales@ingramcontent.com

This book was published with the generous support of Lannan Foundation and
Wallace Global Fund.

Cover image of a freeway sign near the U.S.-Mexico border in San Diego,
California. Photo © Joe Klein/Zuma Press.
Cover design by Amy Balkin.

Printed in Canada by union labor.

Library of Congress Cataloging-in-Publication data is available.

10 9 8 7 6 5 4 3 2 1

Contents

Trump and the Failure of Neoliberal Immigration Reform

When presidential candidate Donald Trump cast aspersions on Mexicans in the United States as "criminals," "drug dealers," and "rapists," it was not just the noxious ranting of a self-entitled bigot. Renewed attention to Trump and his newfound anti-Latino and anti-immigrant posturing illustrates more than just another perversion of an electoral system long corrupted by wealthy opportunists. Rather, Trump's rhetoric was a political calculation to gain traction for an otherwise an incoherent and uninspiring campaign.[1] Latching onto Mexican and immigrant bashing to leverage support from a shrinking yet well-funded and well-organized base of white conservatives was a strategy designed to recharge the fetid Trump brand, which had become little more than a caricature in popular culture. Latino race-baiting and immigrant-bashing has become a ritualized practice on the conservative circuit and a political get-rich-quick scheme for opportunists seeking traction in the polls through inflammatory incitement. In this, Trump is not a departure but rather a continuation of the politics of his predecessors, both Republican and Democrat.

Trump's antics also reveal more than just the bankruptcy of immigration politics in the U.S., in which the racialized dehumanization of Latino migrants and immigrant workers as "illegals" is normalized in media and political discourse. Rather, it is the latest exhumation of the "Brown Scare," a deeply rooted strain of racism directed toward people of Mexican and Central American origin that has been resuscitated and reimagined in the era of what George Bush declared a generational "war on terrorism." As part of the current phase of U.S. imperialism in the Middle East, immigration has been reframed as a national security threat, conflating refugees and economic migrants with the peril of terrorist activity.

The political dividends of racial scapegoating and fear-mongering were illustrated by the 2016 presidential victory of Donald Trump, who, in his first hundred days in office, made it the priority of his administration to target Muslim and Mexican peoples. One of the first acts of the Trump administration was to issue an executive order that explicitly restricted the entry of Muslim travelers from Iran, Libya, Somalia, Sudan, Syria, and Yemen to the United States, imposing a three-month ban on those seeking to apply for a visa. It also placed a similar four-month comprehensive ban on refugees, by suspending the already woefully inadequate United States Refugee Admissions Program. The rationale for the targeted exclusions was, according to the order, "Each of these countries is a state sponsor of terrorism, has been significantly compromised by terrorist organizations, or contains active conflict zones."[2]

What the order failed to mention is that the U.S. government has already been targeting these predominantly Muslim nations through aerial bombings, proxy war, drone attacks, and other forms of clandestine warfare over the past several years. While claiming that the order was intended to "protect . . . citizens from terrorist attacks, including those committed by foreign nationals," it failed to mention that no citizens from these countries have committed any acts of terrorism on U.S. soil. Rather, this is part of a long tradition in the United States of using immigration policy as another type of weapon in the empire's arsenal.

In practice, the administration's mounting attack on Muslims is not a departure but rather an intensification of the ideological war on people who have been in the crosshairs of U.S. imperialism over the last two decades. Characterizing Yemeni refugees as potential terrorists legitimizes the U.S. government's ongoing drone assassinations in that country and reinforces support for a bloody invasion and sustained war and bombing campaign against the Yemeni population by the U.S.-allied and armed Saudi Arabian government.

Trump's attempted bans on people from countries such as Syria and
Iraq reveal the depths of hypocrisy in U.S. politics, as refugees from these
countries are fleeing U.S.-led wars in their countries. In 2015 and 2016,
according to the Council on Foreign Relations, the U.S. dropped over forty-seven thousand bombs on Syria and Iraq alone, killing untold thousands. On March 17, 2017, for example, a U.S.-led airstrike killed over
two hundred people huddled in a bomb shelter in a residential district in
Mosul, Iraq, after U.S. and British jets bombed the city, allegedly targeting
ISIS positions.[3] Claiming Syrian and Iraqi refugees are therefore a "threat
to U.S. national security" is the ultimate irony, as millions of Syrians and
Iraqis have been displaced as a result of U.S. policies in their countries.

A second front in this attack targets undocumented Mexican and
Central American immigrants within the United States. Again, the executive order falsely characterizes this population as a threat, claiming, "Aliens who illegally enter the United States without inspection or
admission present a significant threat to national security and public
safety. . . . Among those who illegally enter are those who seek to harm
Americans through acts of terror or criminal conduct. Continued illegal immigration presents a clear and present danger to the interests of
the United States." Researchers have long dispelled the notion of the
"criminal immigrant," including researchers that collect crime data for
police departments and the FBI, but that is not the point.

The same executive order rhetorically affirms the continuation of
the trajectory of immigration politics and policy from Reagan to Clinton, and from Bush to Obama: increased militarization of border enforcement and the further expansion of the existing six-hundred-mile
wall; augmentation of enforcement personnel and their authority; police participation in immigration enforcement; and expansion of the
country's detention and deportation capacities. While Congress must
approve the funding for Trump's increased expenditures for the Department of Homeland Security (it approved $65 billion in 2016), the
proposals are based on existing policy statutes that enable such increases. Presidents from both parties have made use of this statute to ratchet
up enforcement over the last generation.

Another act of the Trump administration has been to implement a
series of rule changes known as "guidance memos," that are currently
being implemented by the DHS under executive authority. The memos give a broader mandate for Immigration and Customs Enforcement

(ICE) agents to arrest, detain, and deport undocumented people, as well as authorizing them to act on their own impulses and target people more generally in the course of conducting their "duties" without restriction or checks. Anyone who cannot prove two-year consistent residence can be put into the "expedited removal" process, regardless of criminal record.

It should be noted that the union representing the Border Patrol (along with the National Fraternal Order of Police) officially endorsed the candidacy of Donald Trump, showing the alignment of thinking with the twenty-thousand-member armed border force. In other words, this order is designed to allow more impunity to the federal border police, an agency already accused of widespread human rights abuses. In effect, the Trump administration is unleashing and encouraging the immigration police to go on the offensive and unleash a more far-reaching reign of terror on undocumented immigrants, which will undoubtedly increase and intensify state violence and abuse.

The Arizona-based human rights organization No More Deaths, for instance, produced a comprehensive report that documents thirty thousand incidents where human rights abuses occurred between fall of 2008 and spring of 2011.[4] Since 2010, according to the Southern Border Communities Coalition, forty-six people have been killed on the border.[5] Another study conducted by the Kino Border Initiative, a binational organization promoting humane immigration policies, found that about "40 percent of Mexican migrants deported from the United States said Border Patrol agents violated their human rights, and two-thirds said their families were returned to Mexico separately."[6] These daily abuses were committed during a period when the border police had minimal restrictions on their rules of engagement.

ICE agents operating within the interior are no different, although their patterns of arrest have been more selective and targeted. Even though the claim is to catch and deport "criminals," the initial results show a different reality. Guadalupe Garcia de Rayos, an Arizona-based worker and mother of two, who was detained and deported after an annually required "check-in" with ICE. She had previously been arrested for using false documents to work during a workplace raid in 2008 under the regime of notoriously racist Sheriff Joe Arpaio, charged with "identity theft," and spent one year in prison.[7]

In the era of Trump, this has the potential to be even more political, as illustrated by the fact that another early detainee in the interior of the country was DREAM activist Daniela Vargas. A twenty-two-year-old DACA college student, Vargas was arrested moments after speaking publicly at an immigrant rights rally in Jackson, Mississippi, and transferred to a detention center in Jena, Louisiana.[8] Another DREAM activist, Claudia Rueda, was detained at her Los Angeles home after publicly participating in protests against recently conducted immigration raids that included the arrest of her mother.[9]

Enrique Balcazar, Zully Palacios, and Alex Carillo-Sanchez, community and labor organizers with Migrant Justice, a workers' rights organization in Vermont, were also arrested in late March. Since they had no deportation orders, criminal records, or any other factor that would have brought them to the attention of ICE, this shows that they were surveyed, arrested, and detained by regional agents for no other reason than for their immigrant rights advocacy.[10] Other activists around the country have also been conspicuously targeted.

Not only are the armed enforcers of Trump's immigration orders animated by their new license to target immigrants, but the Far Right is also emboldened. For example, racists in the well-funded, right-wing information production industry are jubilant. The fake think tank Center for Immigration Studies, an overtly anti-immigrant organization that produces bogus research to justify exclusion and receives access to practically every mainstream media outlet, rejoiced at the new rules. Director of the group, Mark Krikorian, claimed that "the message is: The immigration law is back in business."[11] After declining in the first few years of the Obama administration, when it was believed that immigration reform would pass through a Democratic "supermajority" in Congress, the membership levels and total number of anti-immigrant hate groups are once again on the rise.

The political attack on immigrants has also increased the confidence of racist hate groups and individuals to commit acts of violence and terrorism. Encouraged by the rhetoric of Trump and the ratcheting up of state repression, the Far Right has increased its activities. The Southern Poverty Law Center documented 867 incidents of hate crimes in the first ten days of the Trump administration alone, and further attacks have targeted a broad spectrum of people including immigrants, African-Americans, Jewish people, South and Central Asians, and others.[12] For instance, in late February, a racist gunman in Kansas walked into a bar near Kansas City and opened fire on two Indian men killing Srinivas Kuchibhotla while yelling, "Get out of my country!"[13] This is the violence of the anti-immigrant and anti-Muslim policies at the center of U.S. politics in its most unfiltered, toxic form.

Through his attorney general, former Alabama Senator Jeff Sessions, an unreconstructed southern segregationist, Trump is currently tangled up in the courts trying to block federal grant money from going to police in cities where "sanctuary" provisions are on the books. In his current budget proposal, which has stalled in Congress, Trump has allocated $1.6 billion to begin extending the physical wall, currently at around six hundred miles of the two thousand boundary. Amid the tragic flooding of Hurricane Harvey, Trump took the opportunity to publicly threaten a federal budget shut down if the U.S. Congress didn't allocate funding for his wall.[14]

He also used his executive authority to pardon Joe Arpaio, an extremely racist and anti-immigrant sheriff based in the state of Arizona. By pardoning Arpaio, who had been facing prison time related to the unconstitutionality of his heavy-handed tactics of repression within Latino communities, Trump is signaling to his boiled-down, hard-right base and the Nazis who admire him that his tenure in office will be to reestablish racism and xenophobia as part of the mainstream of U.S. politics.

The function of racism as a means to specifically target and repress immigrant workers coincides with the extension of free-market capitalism. As corporations displace workers in their home countries, they become an even more exploitable commodity through their disempowerment as undocumented immigrants, who are purposely denied legal authorization and citizenship rights based on their nationality and social class. Once in the country, state repression keeps them segregated and isolated.

Opening Borders for Capital Accumulation

Commonly referred to as the "neoliberal turn," the last thirty years has witnessed a substantial increase in U.S.-led free trade agreements.[15] From the North American Free Trade Agreement to the Dominican Republic and Central American Free Trade Agreement, to the recently proposed Trans-Pacific Partnership Alliance, bipartisan administrations have made the aggressive push for pro-corporate free trade regimes a centerpiece of the epoch. At the heart of these agreements in relation

to Mexico and Central America has been the dismantling of economic developmentalist policies, the rewriting of trade rules that dismantle
tariffs and favor multinational corporations over smaller producers, the
privatization of state industry, and the requirement of "labor flexibility"
so as to decrease labor costs.[16]

A recent outcome in the ongoing fallout from these policies is the
mass displacement of Haitian workers, thousands of whom began to
leave the country and relocate to Mexico and the United States after the
U.S.-imposed trade policies significantly reduced wages in the country's export sector. There has also been mass out-migration from Puerto
Rico to the United States following the devastation of Hurricane Maria.
The scale of destruction was exacerbated by the country's infrastructur-
al underdevelopment and a deep economic crisis created by a massive
national debt and deep austerity cuts in the social budget tied to neoliberal policies.[17]

The components of trade agreements were perfected by corporations and applied within the United States through successive administrations before being exported to Mexico and Central America under
the aegis of International Monetary Fund debt-restructuring diktats.
This international arrangement has also benefitted capitalists in Mexico, who have become enriched through the plunder of newly privatized
industries or through direct partnership (and corrupt dealings) with
their North American counterparts.[18]

In the U.S., labor flexibility has been a primary strategy employed
by the capitalist class since the 1970s. The overarching goal has been
to increase worker productivity while suppressing working-class living
standards as a means to increase the rate of exploitation of labor.[19] For
workers in the U.S., corporate mobility enabled through free trade policies have been used to close and relocate production across borders
in what are called "runaway shops," or threaten to do so in order to
leverage wages downwards as a condition for staying put. Central to
this strategy is union busting. Employers have relied on a number of
strategies to weaken or break unions as part of this process, and they
have been successful. For instance, the rate of unionization in 2014 sank
to 11.1 percent of the workforce, the lowest it has been in a hundred
years; it plummeted even further to 10.7 percent in 2016.[20] As the need
for capital accumulation moves more aggressively to the forefront of
policy-making priorities, new forms of labor control have evolved and

are being generalized and codified. Another front of this capitalist-class offensive has been the manipulation of immigration policy to fill the ranks of a vast and politically disempowered workforce.

Global economic integration along neoliberal lines, where corporations write the rules of trade, investment, and regulation in their own interest, has destabilized laboring classes internationally. As a predictable result, labor itself has become internationalized. In 2015, an estimated 244 million people were living in a country as migrants, and that number is set to increase.[21] If that were itself the population of a country, it would be the fifth largest in the world, roughly more populous than each of the world's remaining 189 countries. In the United States in 2015, an estimated 26.3 million foreign-born persons were part the U.S. labor force, constituting almost 17 percent of the national workforce.[22]

Displaced workers that cannot be absorbed within their own national economies as a result of corporate-led trade policies have been compelled to cross boundaries into foreign labor markets where they can find work. This has altered workforce demographics internationally, from Qatar to the Dominican Republic to Japan. Exporting free trade policies south has been destructive for Mexico and Central America's laboring classes, dislodging millions of small agricultural producers and urban workers made redundant through skewed competition, privatization of state industry, and the downsizing of the welfare state. Migration has flowed in reverse through these same channels, as workers follow the profit streams that translate into disproportionate job creation north of the border. Once ensconced in U.S. labor markets, undocumented workers are regulated not by a liberal "free market," but by immigration enforcement and employers themselves. In economic terms, the new Brown Scare serves the larger aim of disciplining immigrant workers and providing an updated means for labor control.

Immigration Policy as Labor Control

Free trade–induced destabilization has produced a substantial wave of migration from Mexico and Central America. Upward of ten million people have moved to the United States since 1990, one of the largest population transfers in human history.[23] Since this migration has been composed primarily of working migrants, it has led to a substantial shift in the character of the U.S. workforce. This has been used to the advantage of capital, as Democratic and Republican administrations alike have whittled down the pathways to citizenship for this latest generation of immigrants while simultaneously increasing enforcement penalties.

This has gradually transformed migration from an economic act into a criminal one, at the same time that immigration has increased as a result of U.S.-led policy and as immigrants have been fully integrated into the economy. While their labor is tacitly embraced as both necessary and productive, the criminalization of their presence and denial of citizenship erodes their capacity to participate in activities to improve their wages and working conditions. By keeping a growing segment of the workforce noncitizen and vulnerable to persecution, capitalists can leverage down wages, more easily fire those who attempt to organize or speak out, and foster or exploit racial tensions as a means to divide and segment their workforces to preempt collective bargaining. The use of these tactics can weaken workplace organization as a means to extract higher rates of surplus value from all workers.

This helps explain the exponential rise of the immigration enforcement apparatus and the public spectacle of immigrant repression despite a corresponding *decrease* in crime committed by immigrants.[24] A substantial rise in deportation has not been an episodic or measured response to an existential threat, but a systematic and institutionalized means to police a whole population and fortify the delineation between citizen and noncitizen.

This explains why deportation has become a permanent and normalized feature of the immigration enforcement apparatus, irrespective of other variable factors such as the rate of immigration, crime, or the state of the economy. It also illustrates continuity regardless of which party is in power. During the administration of Ronald Reagan 168,364 people were deported; another 141,326 people were removed under George H. W. Bush. After even harsher restrictions were passed under Democrat Bill Clinton, 869,676 people were deported during his tenure, followed by two million more under George W. Bush.[25] After eight years of the Obama administration, the number of deportations reached over three million, even as the number of attempted crossings declined consistently following the onset of the Great Recession in 2007.[26] Systematized deportation has targeted mostly workers without criminal charges or allegations, a practice continued under Trump, revealing its role as a form of labor policing under capitalism rather than "law enforcement" or the acts of a rogue president playing to a racist constituency.[27]

The most conservative and reactionary elements inside the Republican Party have driven the discourse of immigrant exclusion, including mobilized far-right sectors of the middle class and some sections of the capitalist class.[28] The most vociferous opponents of immigrant integration also profit immensely off the exploitation of immigrants, either individually, or as an industry.[29] At the same time, there has been pushback from other corporate sectors against the more extreme anti-immigrant policy proposals that threaten their access to labor.[30] In general there is substantial political distance on the issue between the far-right wing that has cohered behind Trump and more moderate and liberal elements in both the Republican and Democratic Parties, but despite these differences, the anti-immigrant framework and discourse established by the right wing has led even the most liberal of Democrats to downscale their scope of reform to allow for a threshold that now accepts work authorization over citizenship. For example, the Obama administration's executive order to allow for temporary work permits but not citizenship for undocumented childhood arrivals (via Deferred Action for Childhood Arrivals, or DACA) and the undocumented parents of U.S.-born citizen children (via Deferred Action for Parents of Americans and Lawful Permanent Residents, or DAPA) illustrates the narrowing terrain of discourse among those who once proclaimed in favor of "a path to citizenship."[31]

The precariousness and limited scope of protections for these categories of undocumented workers enacted under Obama were revealed in the way that the right was able to block and dismantle even these threadbare gestures. Opposition to DAPA by twenty-six Republican state administrations prompted a right-wing federal judge in south Texas to issue an injunction against the order, effectively killing it. Furthermore, the Trump administration, represented by the deeply reactionary Attorney General Jeff Sessions, rescinded the executive order that established DACA, moving the status of an estimated eight hundred thousand young workers shielded from removal back into the category of "deportable."[32]

The significant surplus value extracted from an immigrant workforce with limited or no rights and protections has encouraged a gradual evolution in thinking about the value of immigration policy as one of labor procurement and control.[33] The vast majority of super-exploited immigrants work in agriculture, landscaping, housecleaning, as caretakers of children and the elderly, in construction, and in restaurants.

The scope of immigrant labor has also broadened into a variety of other industries and occupations, from meat-processing plants in more rural regions to service and retail workers in urban areas, from teachers and manufacturing workers to tech workers in Silicon Valley. The profitability of immigrant labor has led corporate interest groups as well as philanthropic organizations linked to billionaire investors to close ranks around the issue and form lobbying campaigns to drive policy through the corridors of Washington, D.C.[34]

This has catalyzed the evolution of "immigration reform" from legislation that includes citizenship, such as the 1986 Immigration Reform and Control Act (IRCA), to legislation that is singularly designed to produce captive and more easily controlled labor with only a narrow pathway to citizenship. The most recent "comprehensive immigration reform" proposal, referred to as the Border Security, Economic Opportunity, and Immigration Modernization Act of 2013 (S. 744), requires that prospective citizens work for ten years before they can enter the application process and pay taxes, while they are excluded from government services and could be "disqualified" if they lose their job or slip into poverty—and at the same time it dramatically ramps up spending on stricter punishments and border militarization. This latest manifestation of "reform" reveals how successful corporations have been at redefining discourse and promoting their interests through the Democratic and Republican parties. It also charts the degeneration of discourse as the notion of the criminal immigrant now finds broad acceptance amongst policy-makers and commentators.

The Poverty of Immigration Politics and the Preventable Rise of Trump

While capital and labor have internationalized on starkly unequal terms, immigrant advocates and organized labor have adjusted to the neoliberal capitalist framework that has prioritized enforcement and profitability over citizenship. The coded phrase "comprehensive immigration reform" refers to a perpetual increase in enforcement and restriction and an elusive and highly qualified form of residency that ensures the perpetuation of exploitable noncitizen labor. The complicity of both Republicans and Democrats in enabling this rightward trajectory of corporate leadership on the issue has emboldened the Far Right seeking to appropriate the issue. These factors permitted the rise of Trumpism, which has erased the momentum for immigration reform coming out the mass marches of 2006 and the election of a Democratic majority in 2008, setting it back in reverse. The Obama administration's abandonment of legalization, and the subsequent continuation and expansion of Bush-era repression, shattered the hopes and expectations. The candidacy of Hillary Clinton in 2016, promising a continuation of Obama era "tough on immigration" policy without even a rhetorical commitment to legalization, further demoralized millions of people who voted for Obama in 2008, and who stayed away from the polls on election day. This helped pave the way for Trump.

In the absence of an alternative strategy, organized labor and non-governmental organizations have followed the same path, prioritizing lobbying campaigns to contend with corporations for influence inside the architecture of the Democratic Party. If they can help turn several million undocumented workers into citizens, it is reasoned, they can recruit these workers at the end of the reform pipeline. This has been the strategy since the passage of IRCA in 1986, which created the first model of "comprehensive reform" that traded short-term legalization for long-term militarization of enforcement and the criminalization of today's immigrants. Despite the earlier legalization, the "comprehensive" strategy has failed to produce significant results for a path to citizenship, as corporate entities have consolidated their power and interests within both parties.

Organized labor has proven incapable of leveraging its influence within capitalist political economy by using the same tools and copying the methods of the capitalist class. It cannot exceed or even match corporate funding (in all of its various guises), and it cannot convince corporate-structured and corporate-funded political parties that immigrant legalization and union organization are in their best interests at a time when U.S. capitalism is restructuring for profitability based on squeezing labor at home and abroad. Furthermore, labor unions cannot readily organize millions of workers rendered vulnerable to arrest and deportation, who are subject to the whims of employers empowered to fire them at will or report them to immigration authorities in order to break up organizing drives.

Unions and immigration rights advocates will need to reject the anti-worker logic of border militarization and immigration criminalization, and actively pursue the organization of all workers in the U.S.

regardless of their immigration status if they are to curb the decline of their power and influence, and reposition organized labor for growth in years to come. Extending the fight for citizenship rights across capitalist borders will also strengthen efforts to oppose destructive neoliberal free trade agreements like NAFTA and the pending Trans-Pacific Partnership Alliance.

At the crossroads of the immigrant rights and labor rights struggles, there are two fundamental directions for the future of labor. The continued strategy of aligning with the Democratic Party, which seeks to maintain immigrant labor as a subordinated and segregated segment of the working class, will guarantee another decade of increased state repression and labor degradation and will affirm the further growth and intensified violence of the racist, reactionary, and fascist right. Or, as with the rise of the CIO in 1938, the labor movement could be refounded by uniting with and supporting immigrant workers as part of rebuilding a militant revival capable of overturning the regime of immigrant repression.

The potential for this was shown in the mass strikes, marches, and school walkouts of 2006. In the first few months of the Trump presidency, we also saw the potential for a revival of an immigrant rights movement with large protests at airports across the country against the Muslim travel ban, with participants taking up the slogan "No Ban, No Wall, Sanctuary for All!" from San Diego to New York City. On May Day, 2017, immigrant workers and their union and community supporters once again marched on International Workers' Day, showing the potential to rebuild a working-class resistance to the policies of Trump with immigrants at the forefront.

Now more than ever it has become apparent that the full legalization and integration of the immigrant working class is a precondition for the reversal of the decline of organized labor itself. In the age of Trump, the issue of immigration is also intertwined with all other rights and affects all of us. How broad, interconnected, and resilient we can build social movements, grounded in genuine solidarity with all immigrants and rooted in our workplaces, campuses, and communities, will determine the course of events for all of us in the years to come.

Preface

"You've kicked a sleeping giant." Perhaps no other sign from the million-strong march for immigrant rights that shook Los Angeles on March 25 conveys a more precise summation of events unfolding across the country. Or as an activist speaking at a border rally commented, "they weren't sleeping, they were working!" At the time of this writing, a new civil rights movement for immigrants, involving literally millions of people in cities throughout the United States, is now entering its third month.

With a sudden gale force, the debate over immigration politics, historically the domain of big business and the Far Right, has been blown wide open, its contents scattering into the daily discussions of ordinary people. Largely self-organized and self-mobilized, the new movement has drawn out the most affected communities, who are far ahead of the existing organizations that have historically claimed leadership in the immigrant communities.

This new movement, led by immigrant workers and Latino students, but pushing the whole working class forward, is now beating on the walls of Congress and demanding equality. Homemade signs at protests from San Diego to the Brooklyn Bridge, reading, "We are not criminals" and "*Amnistía sí*" (Amnesty yes), reveal the depths of indignation, the willingness to come out of the shadows, and the desire to be seen and heard. In true mass character, all generations are being hit by the ripple effect of such a large-scale movement. A sixth-grader protesting with one hundred thousand others on April 9 in San Diego expressed the mood succinctly: "At school the rich teach us about their democracy. Here, we show them ours."[1] In a matter of weeks, the movement has shifted from a defensive to an offensive posture, and promises to redefine the landscape of American history, with immigrant workers narrating the story.

The groundswell was brought to the surface in reaction to passage in the House of the draconian HR 4437 (also known as the Sensenbrenner Bill), that, if passed by the Senate, would make felons of immigrants as well as those who help them. This movement has forced the proponents of the bill, who had been able to set the tone for the debate over so-called immigration reform, onto the defensive. It has redrawn the parameters of the debate, which had previously been restricted to criminalization on one side, and partial legalization combined with a guest-worker program on the other. The movement has cast a spotlight on the struggle of ordinary workers and their families to be treated equally, and with dignity as human beings.

Like the great struggles of working people in years past, this movement will face many challenges, twists, turns, defeats, and victories. It contains the seeds that make another world possible: one based on working people gaining control over their daily lives, and giving new definition to the term democracy.

This book will attempt to lay out the historical and contemporary dimensions of the immigrant rights struggle, focusing primarily on the U.S.-Mexico border and the experience of the working people that cross the border (or have been crossed by it). In the section by Mike Davis, the origins and evolution of the anti-immigrant movement are examined, shedding light on its political, racial, and class origins. I then provide a broader look at the formation of immigration policy in the context of the struggle between capital and labor.

Giving a voice to the experience of immigrant workers is greatly aided by the fact that they themselves are making history as of this writing. It is my hope that this book can serve as a resource and help give confidence to the generation of activists taking initiative in the streets, campuses, and workplaces of the new America. I also hope it provokes a wider discussion and debate about what kind of world we want and need as working people, *un pueblo mundial sin fronteras.*

Justin Akers Chacón
San Diego, California
May 15, 2006

Part I

"WHAT IS A VIGILANTE MAN?" WHITE VIOLENCE IN CALIFORNIA HISTORY

Mike Davis

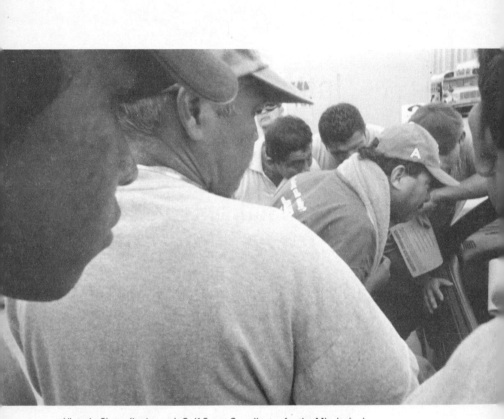

Victoria Cintra (in the car), Gulf Coast Coordinator for the Mississippi
Immigrants Rights Alliance (MIRA), advises undocumented workers
in Hangar 216 of the Naval Construction Battalion Center in Gulfport,
Mississippi. Some of the 270 workers, including 30 women, con-
tracted by a private company accused its owner of imposing subhu-
man working conditions at the New Orleans Naval Base. They lived
in tents with no water or electricity, food was scarce, they were
overworked and underpaid. They were evacuated to Gulfport when
Hurricane Rita struck. September 2005.

Introduction

California's golden fields have too often been irrigated with the blood of its laborers. A notorious case in point was the great strike that spread like wildfire through the San Joaquin Valley in the fall of 1933. Protesting starvation wages that failed to fill their children's empty bellies, twelve thousand defiant, mainly Mexican cotton-pickers walked off the job under the leadership of the leftwing Cannery and Agricultural Workers Industrial Union. Moving between farms in caravans of cars and trucks, mass pickets soon shut down the harvest over a three-hundred-square-mile area. The growers quickly trucked in strikebreakers from Los Angeles, but most of the scabs either deserted to the union or were scared away by the fierce, hunger-driven militancy of the strikers.

The growers, cotton ginners, and chamber of commerce types then resorted to a classic tactic: arming themselves as vigilance groups to impose a reign of terror upon the cotton counties. These Farmers' Protective Leagues broke up the strikers' meetings, drove them out of their encampments and burnt their tents, beat them on the picket lines, stopped and harassed them on the roads, and threatened any merchant who extended credit to the strikers or any small farmer who refused to hire strikebreakers. When strikers complained to authorities, the local sheriffs promptly deputized the vigilantes. "We protect our farmers here in Kern County," explained one deputy sheriff. "They are our best people.... They keep the county going.... But the Mexicans are trash. They have no standard of living. We herd them like pigs."[1]

In spite of beatings, arrests, and evictions, however, the solidarity of the strikers remained unbreakable through early October, with the growers facing the loss of their entire crop. The *San Francisco Examiner* warned that the whole valley was "a smouldering volcano" ready to erupt. Concerned state officials offered a fact-finding commission, which the union readily accepted, but the vigilantes responded with murder. At a rally in Pixley on the tenth of October, union leader Pat Chambers was addressing strikers and their families when ten carloads of shotgun-wielding vigilantes abruptly arrived on the scene. Chambers, a battle-scarred veteran of California's harvest wars, sensed imminent danger and dispersed the rally, urging the strikers to take shelter in the red-brick union headquarters across the highway. Historian Cletus Daniel describes the carnage that followed:

> As the group made its way toward the building one of the growers following it discharged a rifle. When a striker approached the grower and pushed the barrel of his gun downward another armed grower rushed forward and clubbed him to the ground. While he still lay on the ground the grower shot him to death. Immediately the rest of the growers opened fire on the fleeing strikers and their families. Amid the screams of those that lay wounded on the ground, growers continued to fire into the union hall until their ammunition was finally exhausted.[2]

The vigilantes killed two men, one of them the local representative of the Mexican consul-general, and seriously wounded at least eight other strikers, including a fifty-year-old woman. As a San Francisco reporter noted, the wild fusillade also shredded the American flags draped over the union headquarters. Almost simultaneously in Arvin, sixty miles south, another band of farmer-vigilantes opened fire on picketers, killing one and injuring several. Although the workers defiantly returned to their picket lines, the growers threatened to drive their families out of the huge strike camp near Corcoran. Faced with yet more violence of unknown scope, the strikers reluctantly yielded to state and federal pressure and accepted a wage increase in lieu of recognition of their union.

The following year, while public attention was riveted upon the epic San Francisco general strike, vigilante growers and local sheriffs tore up the constitution across rural California, and imposed what New Dealers as well as Communists would denounce as "farm fascism." One of the darkest spots was the Imperial Valley—the West's closest social and racial analogue to Mississippi—where successive lettuce, pea, and melon strikes during the course of 1933–34 were broken by a total terror that included mass arrests, anti-picketing ordinances, evictions, beatings, kidnappings, deportations, and the near lynching of the strikers' lawyers. While urban workers led by the new Congress of Industrial Organizations (CIO) unions were successfully overthrowing the open shop in San Francisco and Los Angeles, California's agricultural workers—whether their names were Maria Morales or Tom Joad—were being terrorized by bigoted deputies and raging mobs. The bitter memory of these brutal events would be woven into John Steinbeck's novels *In Dubious Battle* and *Grapes of Wrath*, as well as recalled in Woody Guthrie's haunting "Vigilante Man":

> Oh, why does a vigilante man
> Why does a vigilante man
> Carry that sawed-off shotgun in his hand?
> Would he shoot his brother and
> Sister down?

But this "vigilante man" was not merely a sinister figure of the Depression decade: as I will argue in this capsule history, he has cast a permanent shadow over California from the 1850s onwards. Indeed, vigilantism—ethno-racial and class violence (or threat of violence) cloaked in a pseudo-populist appeal to higher laws and sovereignties—has played a far larger role in the state's history than is generally recognized. A broad rainbow of minority groups, including Native Americans, Irish, Chinese, Punjabis, Japanese, Filipinos, Okies, African-Americans, and (persistently in each generation) Mexicans, as well as radicals and trade-unionists of various denominations, have been victims of vigilante repression. Organized private violence, usually in tandem with local law enforcement, has shaped the racial-caste system of California agriculture, defeated radical labor movements like the IWW, and kept the New Deal out of the state's farm counties. It has also spurred innumerable reactionary laws and reinforced both legal and de facto segregation. Moreover, the vigilante is no curio of a bad past, but a pathological type currently undergoing dramatic post-millennial revival as many Anglo-Californians panic in the face of demographic decline and the perceived erosion of their racial privileges.

Today's armed and combat-camouflaged "Minutemen" in their various factions, who instigate confrontations on the border, or (in their civilian garb) harass day laborers in front of suburban Home Depots, are the latest incarnations of an old character. Their infantile strutting and posing may contrast rather comically to the authentic fascist menace of the Associated Farmers and other Depression-era groups, but it would be foolish to discount their impact. Just as the grower vigilantes of the 1930s succeeded in militarizing rural California against the labor movement, the Minutemen have helped to radicalize debate about immigration and race within the Republican Party, contributing to the full-fledged nativist backlash against the Bush administration's proposal for a new Bracero Program. Candidates in Republican primaries in Southern California now vie with one another for endorsement by the Minutemen leaders. These armed and media-savvy neo-vigilantes, by threatening to enforce the borders themselves, also spur the increasingly successful campaign to turn local law enforcement into immigration police. And as true dialecticians will concede, what begins as farce sometimes grows into something much uglier and more dangerous.

Chapter One

Pinkertons, Klansmen, and Vigilantes

Americans appear responsible for developing vigilantism, the consummate expression of conservative violence.

—Robert Ingalls[1]

Before looking at the career of vigilantism in California history, it is first useful to map its location within the larger history of American class and racial violence. The eminent labor historian Philip Taft once opined that the United States had the "bloodiest and most violent labor history of any industrial nation in the world." Setting European civil wars and revolutions aside, Taft is probably correct: American workers have faced chronic state and employer violence against which they have frequently responded in kind. Robert Goldstein, in his encyclopedic study of political repression in the United States, estimates that at least seven hundred strikers and demonstrators were killed by police or troops between 1870 and 1937.[2] In contrast to the more politically centralized societies of Western Europe, the worst violence (like the Ludlow and Republic Steel massacres) usually came from local police and militias. But what truly demarcates the United States is not so much the scale or frequency of state repression, but rather the extraordinary centrality of institutionalized private violence in the reproduction of the racial and social order. No European society tolerated such a large, nearly permanent sphere of repressive activity and summary justice by non-state actors.[3] But then again, no European society shared the recent

U.S. experience of genocidal frontier violence—often organized by posses and informal groups—against Native Americans, or the widespread participation of poorer Southern whites in the policing of slavery.

Fig. 1. MODES OF REPRESSION

I. STATE VIOLENCE
    a. *Federal*: regular army
    b. *State*: militias, national guard, state police
    c. *Local*: police, sheriffs, sworn posses
II. PRIVATE OR PERI-STATE VIOLENCE
    a. *Heartland*: corporate police and private detective agencies (*Pinkertons*)
    b. *South*: organized white supremacists (*Klan*)
    c. *West*: vigilantes (*Order of Caucasians*)

In effect, there were three geographically distinct if non-exclusive systems of private repression. First, in the industrial heartland, where local government was occasionally in the hands of Socialists or Democrats sympathetic to the labor movement, the biggest industrial, mining, and railroad corporations, loathe to put their entire trust in the local state, deployed literal armies of armed guards, plant detectives, and company police. There is little equivalent in European history for the formidable repressive role of the Pinkertons, the Sherman Corporation, the Bergoff Agency, the Baldwin Felts Detective Agency, the Pennsylvania Coal and Iron Police, or the Ford Service Department. (The Pinkertons alone reputedly outnumbered the regular U.S. Army in the early 1890s.[4]) Nor is there any counterpart in the experience of European labor to such epic "private" battles as Homestead in 1892, when steelworkers defeated a regiment of Pinkertons, or Blair Mountain in 1921, when ten thousand West Virginia miners battled the Baldwin Felts for more than a week.

Second, throughout the post-Reconstruction South white supremacy was routinely enforced by the noose and pyre in a continuation of the antebellum traditions of seignorial violence against slaves and the conscription of poor whites as slave hunters.

Again, there is no equivalent, except episodically in the imperial Russia of the Black Hundreds, for this sustained terror by false arrest, chain gang, arson, assassination, massacre, and public lynching (thirty-two hundred between 1882 and 1930).[5] When lynching deaths were combined with legal executions, "an African-American was put to death somewhere in the South on the average of every four days."[6] Despite the stereotype of lynch mobs composed of shoeless illiterate whites, the violent overthrow of Reconstruction was led by regional elites, and the planter and business strata continued to condone and orchestrate racial violence whenever it was politically expedient or reinforced their economic dominance. They seldom challenged and often profited from a culture where "community justice included both statutory law and lynch law."[7] Indeed, cotton tenancy and debt peonage, and thus the profits of landowners and merchants, were maintained through chronic racial violence and the extinction of Black civil rights.

Third, vigilantism constituted a distinctive system of locally sanctioned violence throughout the former Western frontier states, but especially in the Southwest where Anglo rule had been imposed by military conquest on Native American, Hispanic, and Mexican populations. In California—the state that was as epicentral to vigilantism as Mississippi was to Klan violence or Pennsylvania was to corporate repression—the domination of a conquered Spanish-speaking population intersected with the social control of immigrants from Asia. Vigilantism—often extolled from the pulpit or editorial page—policed the boundaries of "whiteness" and "Americanism." But vigilantes, sometimes deputized as posses, were also the strikebreakers of last resort, as well as the popular arm of antiradical crusades (such as those from 1917 to 1919 or in the early 1930s).

It should be emphasized, of course, that while these three systems of peri-legal violence had strong geographical foci, there were obviously many overlaps. Blacks, for example, were murdered in the streets of Springfield (1908) and East St. Louis (1917) and lynched in Duluth (1920) as well as in the former Confederacy. Likewise the Pinkertons terrorized the IWW in Montana (the subject of Dashiell Hammett's first novel, *Red Harvest*), and the "second" Klan of the 1920s was probably most powerful in Oregon, Colorado, and Indiana. Middle-class vigilantes often played auxiliary roles in the big showdowns between Midwestern labor and capital, as in Akron in 1913 or Minneapolis in 1934. The best single historical study of antilabor vigilantism, moreover, is Robert Ingalls's book on Tampa, Florida—a New South city—where local business elites terrorized "workers, labor organizers, immigrants, blacks, Socialists, and Communists": a bloody history that culminated in the repression of striking Cuban cigar makers in 1931.[8]

Nor, in the face of the caste-like segmentation of the American working class, is it very profitable to attempt to rigorously distinguish ethno-religious and racial violence from class violence. Thus the 1897 Latimer Massacre, when deputies and vigilantes murdered twenty-one peaceful Slavic miners protesting a newly passed "alien tax," was as much an anti-immigrant pogrom ("We'll give you hell, not water, hunkies!" screamed the deputies) as it was class repression. Likewise many of the Black sharecroppers and independent farmers who were murdered or lynched in the South were singled out because they had defied a boss, competed with whites for land, or achieved unusual prosperity. As Stewart Tolnay and E. Beck have shown in a well-known study, Southern lynchings tended to follow the economic cycle of cotton, with "Blacks safer from mob violence when the profits from cotton were high."[9] Indeed, it is the fusion of racial or ethnic hatred with economic self-interest (real or perceived) that explains much of the extremity as well as the self-righteousness of private violence toward subordinate groups in American history.

Why then even bother to distinguish Western "vigilantism" from Southern mob violence, particularly if vigilantes were usually racists, while Southern terrorists were also apt to strike out at white radicals, Jews, and civil rights supporters? Likewise large-scale agriculture in the Southwest as in the Southeast was capitalized on caste discrimination, disenfranchisement, and employer violence. In *Factories in the Fields* (his non-fiction counterpart to Steinbeck's *Grapes of Wrath*), radical journalist Carey McWilliams was emphatic that California vigilantism, even if "nowadays ... sophisticated by self-conscious artistry," was built on "an antiforeign bias" and infused by "racial feeling."[10] But if any distinction between the West and the South can only be upheld within a more fundamental continuum, California-style vigilantism nonetheless has tended to be more episodic and ad hoc, less firmly anchored in statutory inequality (like Jim Crow laws), more pluralistic in the objects of its intolerance, but less dualistic in its legal and moral legitimation.

The Western vigilante classically claims the right to act because the state is either absent, in the hands of criminals, or in default of its fundamental obligations (for example, to enforce immigration laws or defend private property). Thus the *Brawley News* in 1933 resorted to the following sophistry to justify a particularly brutal vigilante attack on striking Mexican farmworkers: "It was not mob violence, it was a

studied organized movement of citizens seeking the only way out of difficulties threatening the community's peace when the hands of the law
are tied by the law itself."[11] White Southerners, on the other hand, have
always asserted supreme racial prerogatives that override any state or
federal statute and require no convoluted rationalization. The Western-
er defends his actions in the name of unenforced laws and the frontier
principle of *posse comitatus*, while the Southerner appeals to the primal
priority of race and "white honor." If the sadistic frenzy of anti-Black violence in Southern history has found few defenders outside the region,
Western vigilantism—often just as racist and despicable—was praised
by the likes of Hubert Howe Bancroft, Leland Stanford, and Theodore
Roosevelt, and, indeed, is still celebrated today as an essentially "whole-
some tradition of spontaneous communal justice," part of a romantic
heritage of frontier democracy.[12]

What about the social roots of vigilantism? In his study of Tampa, Ingalls finds a fundamental continuity of elite control: "vigilantes
take the law into their own hands to reinforce existing power relationships, not to subvert them.... Whether the particular target was a black
prisoner, a union organizer, a political radical, or a common criminal,
extralegal violence was supposed to preserve the status quo."[13] More
ponderously, Ray Abrahams, who looks at vigilante groups as an international phenomenon, concludes that "vigilantism is rarely simply a
popular response to the failure of due legal process to deal with breaches
of the law. 'The people' and 'the community' are, on inspection, complex concepts, and the populism of much vigilante rhetoric conceals
... a self-satisfied elitism."[14] Richard Brown, in an earlier study of vigilantism on the frontier, argued that "again and again, it was the most
eminent local community leaders who headed vigilante movements ...
[and] the typical vigilante leaders were ambitious young men from the
old settled areas of the East. They wished to establish themselves in the
upper level of the new community, at the status they held or aspired to
in the place of their origin."[15]

In California history, however, there is a striking difference between the class profiles of vigilantism in the nineteenth and twentieth
centuries. Victorian vigilantes (with the notable exceptions of the two
San Francisco vigilance movements of the 1850s) tended to be workers,
petty entrepreneurs, and small farmers fighting in the name of Jacksonian values to preserve a monopoly of "white labor" against what

they construed as elite conspiracies to flood the state with "coolies" and "aliens."[16] From the turn of the century, however, such plebeian nativism, although still present, yielded to anti-Asian and antiradical outbursts now led by wealthier farmers, middle-class professionals, and local business elites, who were as likely to be California Progressives as old-guard Republicans. In the 1930s, vigilantism on an unprecedented scale was franchised as part of the employer counterrevolution led by the fascistic Associated Farmers. Briefly revived by growers during the epic strikes of the United Farm Workers in the late 1960s and early 1970s, the vigilante ethos subsequently migrated from the farm valleys to the conservative suburbs, where the specter of "illegal" immigrants helps fill the aching vacuum in right-wing imagination left by the collapse of the international communist conspiracy.

Chapter Two

White Savages

The vigilantes' first act was to erect a makeshift gallows and hang Joaquin Valenzuela before the entire population of San Luis Obispo. The unfortunate Valenzuela was probably innocent of the most recent murders.

—John Boessenecker[1]

The brief campaigns and little battles in the Los Angeles and San Diego areas that constituted the 1846–47 war of conquest in California were but a prelude to the protracted, incomparably more violent predations of Anglo gangs, filibusters, and vigilantes who expropriated native land and labor during the 1850s. The "border," in the first instance, was not the line drawn by the Army Corps of Topographical Engineers in the aftermath of the Treaty of Guadalupe Hidalgo, but the genocidal violence that Jacksonian democracy unleashed on the Southwest. This ur-violence of the border in the era of what Marx would have called "primitive accumulation" is the subject of Cormac McCarthy's epic *Blood Meridian*—a hallucinatory but historically accurate recounting of the Glanton gang who murdered and scalped their way from Chihuahua to San Diego. For white savages like Glanton, Manifest Destiny was a godlike license—"a personal imperialism"—to kill and plunder as they marauded through Indian camps and adobe villages.[2]

Native Californians were the first victims of the Anglo conquest. The instant society of white males created by the California gold rush had an insatiable hunger for sexual objects and servile domestic labor.

The first legislature accommodated this demand with indenture laws that essentially enslaved Indian women and children to white masters. Bands of "squawmen," led by Glanton counterparts like Robert "Growling" Smith, fanned out through the Napa and Sacramento valleys, kidnapping Indian slaves and killing all who resisted. "You may hear them talk of the operation of cutting to pieces an Indian squaw in their discriminate raids for babies as 'like slicing old cheese,'" wrote the *Sacramento Union* in 1862. "The baby hunters sneak up to a *rancheria*, kill the bucks, pick out the best looking squaws, ravish them, and make off with their young ones."[3]

The abduction or murder of Indians was subsidized by the state government, which issued bonds to pay volunteer companies—shades of Glanton's scalp hunters—to exterminate California's first peoples. Out of an estimated Indian population of 150,000 in 1846 (already reduced by half from pre-Spanish levels), only 30,000 survived by 1870. Bret Harte, together with Mark Twain the premier chronicler of the gold rush era, described an atrocity he encountered in an Indian village attacked by vigilantes along the Redwood Coast in 1860: "The wounded, dead, and dying were found all around, and in every lodge the skulls and frames of women and children cleft with axes and hatchets, and stabbed with knives, and the brains of an infant oozing from its broken head to the ground."[4]

In the gold camps themselves, vigilantes fulfilled their stereotypical role of administrating rough frontier justice from a tree limb to rustlers and dry-gulchers, but they also frequently acted as an ethnic militia to forcibly evict the Spanish-speaking miners who had arrived earliest in the Mother Lode Country. If the goldfields were briefly the closest approximation to the Jacksonian utopia of a "republic of fortune," where independent and formally equal producers dug for gold, it was also a closed, Anglo-Saxon democracy that excluded the "greasers," construed as all "Latin or half-breed races." The punitive foreign miners' license tax passed by the first legislature in 1850 provided a pretext for armed vigilance groups to expel Mexican and Chilean miners from their claims. When Latino miners resisted, they were punctually lynched, as in the case of sixteen *chileanos* in the Calaveras district, or the "beautiful, spirited pregnant Mexican woman by the name of Josefa" in Placer County who had shot an American miner after he called her a "whore."[5]

In the mining region around Sonora, defiant Mexican and Europe-

an miners, led by French and German 1848 revolutionary exiles, resisted Anglo intimidation in a series of confrontations that came close to
full-fledged civil war. "Into the diggings," historian Leonard Pitt relates
of one famous incident,

> marched four hundred Americans—a 'moving engine of terror'—head-
> ing for Columbia Camp, the foreigners' headquarters. They collected
> tax money from a few affluent aliens and chased the rest away, with a
> warning to vacate the mines. One trooper recalls seeing "men, women
> and children—all packed up and moving, bag and baggage. Tents were
> being pulled down, houses and hovels gutted of their contents ... [un-
> til] the posse finally arrested the two 'hot-headed Frenchmen ... of the
> red republican order....' The men liquored up for the road, hoisted the
> Stars and Stripes to the top of a pine tree, fired off a salute, and headed
> for home.[6]

The "red republicans" quickly organized their own column and
stormed the town of Sonora, but ultimately the weight of American
numbers and the presence of the regular army led to a "foreign" exodus
from the gold fields. Many of the Sonorans were then robbed of their
mules and horses by the California militia when they tried to cross the
Colorado River at Yuma on their way home.

Meanwhile, in the southern "cow" counties and along the central
coast, the poorer Mexican and Mission Indian (neophyte) populations
fought a bitter rearguard action against Anglo usurpers. Traditionally
characterized as mere desperados, Tiburcio Vasquez, Pio Linares, Juan
Flores, and the semi-mythic Joaquin Marietta were, in fact, social bandits or even guerrilla chieftains in a grim conflict that pitted vigilante
posses, composed of demobilized soldiers and Indian-killers, against the
dispossessed *gente de razon*. In the south, patrician *Californio* landowners like the Sepulvedas and Picos usually supported the vigilantes, but in
the north some of the great dynasties, like the Berreyesa clan which had
six members murdered, were driven into extinction or exile by chronic
conflict with the Anglos.[7]

One of the biggest vigilance movements—indeed, "one of the
most violent events of the gold rush"—was the campaign organized
in Los Angeles to defeat the so-called "Flores Revolution," led by Juan
Flores and Pancho Daniel. Arrested by Anglos in 1855, Flores soon
escaped from San Quentin to join forces with Daniel, a *compañero* of
Joaquin Murietta, and a dozen other ranch hands and miners. In January 1857, while visiting his young Indian lover, Chola Martina, at San

Juan Capistrano, Flores killed Los Angeles Sheriff Barton and three members of his posse. Vigilantes, including Mexican-hating Texans known as the "El Monte Boys," eventually captured Flores after several battles and escapes; he was lynched before a large crowd at the foot of Fort Hill in today's downtown Los Angeles. Other *Californios* died more anonymously. "Juan Flores was the twelfth man slain by Los Angeles vigilantes," historian John Boessenecker explains. "Ten suspects had been hanged and two shot to death. Of those, only four were definitely connected to the Flores-Daniel band."[8]

Boessenecker sees these incidents as part of a larger race war that raged along the El Camino Real in the mid-1850s, with the San Luis Obispo area as a second epicenter. Here the band of Pio Linares, joined by Joaquin Valenzuela and the Irish horseman Jack Powers, preyed upon Anglo ranchers and travelers, while Anglo vigilantes in turn terrorized the local *Californios*. It was a war without pity on either side. Before the vigilantes were through, they had killed Linares in a famous gun battle and lynched seven of his companions, including Valenzuela (for a murder he most likely didn't commit). Around the same time, two hundred vigilantes broke into the Los Angeles jail, dragged Pancho Daniel, the surviving leader of the Flores band, out of his cell, and strung him up from a nearby gate. The contemporary San Francisco *Bulletin* contrasted the difference in attitudes between the "lower class of Californians, or Sonorans" who vowed to avenge the heroic Daniels, and the "respectable portion" who supported his Anglo executioners.[9]

Although the principal axis of social violence in gold rush California was this conflict between plebeian *Californios* and Indians, on one hand, and the sons of Manifest Destiny on the other, the most famous vigilantes were the San Francisco businessmen and politicians who comprised the two Vigilance Committees of 1851 and 1855. The first committee emerged in public view in June 1851 when, under the histrionic urgings of Sam Brannan—the notorious Mormon filibuster and land speculator who had been the original publicist of the gold discoveries in 1849—an Australian thief named John Jenkins was lynched from the old customs house in Portsmouth Square. When the mayor tried to persuade the vigilantes to leave justice to the courts, Brannan thundered: "To hell with your courts! We are the courts! And the hangman!"[10] Several other "Sidney Ducks"—mainly Irish Australians blamed for arson and crime in San Francisco—quickly followed Jenkins to the noose, while two more were stomped to death in the street. "As foreigners in California," writes Robert Senkewicz in his history of the incident, "the Australians were regarded as poachers in the Garden of Eden." The vigilantes— largely merchants, importers, bankers, and lawyers—closed down shop after most of the Australians fled the city.[11]

They reopened on an expanded scale in 1856 to deal with the challenge of the Tammany Hall–type political machine that the charismatic David Broderick (a former "Locofoco" from New York City) and his largely Irish and Catholic supporters were building in San Francisco. The deaths of two prominent anti-Broderick leaders—William Richardson (a U.S. marshal) and James King (a newspaper editor)—in separate confrontations with erstwhile Broderick supporters Charles Cora (an Italian gambler) and James Casey (a Democratic county supervisor) formed the immediate pretext for the committee's regroupment. But the lynching of Cora and Casey in May 1856 by the Second Vigilance Committee, headed by William Tell Coleman, a pro-slavery Democrat from Kentucky, had less to do with criminal justice than the determination of Protestant merchants, Know-Nothings, and anti-Catholics to check the growth of the Broderick machine.

The vigilantes, in effect, were upper-class insurrectionists bent on a sweeping purge of Irish political power.

> [With] Casey and Cora out of the way," writes Father Senkewica, "the committee swiftly turned to its important task. In short order, a number of Broderick's political operatives found themselves surrounded on the streets by squads of armed vigilantes and hustled to the waiting executive committee. They were tried for a variety of offenses, mostly relating to political fraud and ballot box stuffing. After conviction, which was virtually automatic, they were hurried off for deportation on ships that were already in the process of clearing the harbor.[12]

Democratic elected officials who survived deportation were coerced into resigning; they were replaced in the next election by candidates endorsed by Coleman, the city's temporary dictator, and the vigilantes. The so-called "People's Party" of the Second Vigilance Committee soon merged with the new Republican Party and ruled San Francisco until 1867. The destruction of his urban political machine, however, had the ironic result of refocusing Broderick's ambitions on state politics, where he was quickly elected by the legislature to the U.S. Senate. (Senator Broderick, a Free Soil Democrat, was killed in a famous duel in 1859 with California Supreme Court Chief Justice David Terry, a rabid supporter of slavery.)

One of the contemporary opponents of the vigilantes, William Tecumseh Sherman (then a San Francisco banker), pointed out that "as they controlled the press, they wrote their own history." Indeed, the San Francisco Vigilance Committees later became apotheosized by philosopher Josiah Royce (in his 1886 book, *California)* and historian Humbert Howe Bancroft (in his 1887 book, *Popular Tribunals*) as paragons of liberty and civic virtue. This image of the heroic bourgeois vigilante who episodically buckles on his six-gun to restore law and order to a society overrun by criminal immigrants and their corrupt politicians would be an enduring California myth, inspiring anti-Asian Progressives in the 1910s and 1920s as well as suburban nativists in the beginning of the twenty-first century.

Chapter Three

The Yellow Peril

To an American, death is preferable to life on a par with a Chinaman.

—Dennis Kearney (1877)[1]

The *Times* of London was, of course, the journal of record for the nineteenth century, and the first entry indexed for "Los Angeles" is "Chinese massacre, 24 October 1871." Following the shooting of a sheriff (shades of Juan Flores), a vigilante mob of five hundred Anglos had swept through "Nigger Alley" (near present-day Union Station) slaughtering Chinese boys and men on sight. The official death toll was nineteen (almost 10 percent of the local Chinese population), but contemporary observers thought the actual number was likely much higher. In a modern reflection on the incident, the historian William Locklear argued that two decades of Anglo vigilantism and race hatred in Los Angeles had created "a fertile ground" for the worst pogrom (Indian massacres aside) in California history.[2]

The Chinese (who in 1860 made up about one-fifth of the state's labor force) had often been victimized during the gold rush era—when they were generally allowed to work only abandoned and low-grade claims—but persecution began on a systematic scale during the regional economic downturn of 1869–70. Through the continuing depression of the 1870s, the Chinese became the scapegoats for a disintegrating California dream, as the utopian hopes of the former forty-niners were dashed against the realities of concentrated economic power, the scarcity of homestead land, falling wages, and rampant unemployment. If for a few years in the early 1850s the goldfields had been a producers' democracy, where white men of different class backgrounds toiled side by side, monopoly had become firmly entrenched in land, commerce, and mining by the end of the decade. The rise of the Central Pacific (later Southern Pacific) Railroad and its ruling "Big Four" team of capitalists during the 1860s established semi-feudal baronies upon the ruins of Jacksonian equality; while the long economic crisis of the 1870s ruined thousands of small farmers, self-employed teamsters, ambitious young professionals, and miscellaneous entrepreneurs. Their petty-bourgeois hysteria grew into hallucinatory rage against a fictitious "Yellow Peril," which demagogues like Dennis Kearney (former seaman turned prosperous businessman) then spread throughout the San Francisco and California labor movements, where it metastasized into an incurable obsession for the next fifty years.

In *Indispensable Enemy*, a pathbreaking analysis of working-class "false consciousness," Alexander Saxton explains how an exclusionist, anti-Asian populism, rooted in the contradictions of Jacksonian producerist ideology, preempted the moral universe of California labor. Instead of making common cause with Chinese workers, Kearney's Workingman's Union of San Francisco, and its offshoot, the Workingman's Party of California, screamed "Chinese Must Go!" and demanded the abrogation of the 1868 Burlingame Treaty that had normalized Chinese emigration to the United States. Their huge bonfire processions spilled over into rioting and the destruction of Chinese businesses. The economic crisis was attributed by Kearney and other Workingman leaders to a demonic conspiracy of "coolies" and monopolists, whose ultimate aim was nothing less than the destruction of the American white republic.[3]

Indeed, in his pro-Workingman novel, *The Last Days of the Republic* (1880), the Kearneyite Pierton Dooner described how the desperate efforts of San Francisco's white workers to massacre the Chinese were thwarted by the capitalist militia, leading to the enfranchisement of the Chinese and, ultimately, their conquest of North America. "The Temple of Liberty had crumbled; and above its ruins was reared the colossal fabric of barbaric splendor known as the Western Empire of His August Majesty, the Emperor of China.... The very name of the United States was thus blotted from the record of nations."[4]

Dooner's novel was the ancestor of scores of Yellow Peril and White-Civilization-in-Danger screeds. (Its contemporary descendants

include the immigration apocalypses and "brown perils" retailed in recent books by Victor Davis Hanson, Daniel Sheehy, Tom Tancredo, and
other xenophobes.)[5] His advocacy of preemptive massacre a la Los Angeles also made *The Last Days of the Republic* a kind of *Turner Diaries* for
members of the Workingman's movement and their rural allies. If the
1877 attacks on the Chinese in San Francisco were quelled by bourgeois
vigilantes (a Committee of Public Safety drilled by the venerable William
Tell Coleman) and the timely arrival of U.S. warships, anti-coolie violence became chronic in the California countryside where many Chinese
ex-railroad workers had sought employment as field hands and harvest
workers.

The Order of Caucasians was the rural equivalent to San Francisco's Workingman's anti-coolie clubs, with a rapidly growing membership in the Sacramento Valley. In 1877, at the height of unrest in San
Francisco, unemployed members of the Order attacked Chinese camps
throughout the Valley: burning bunkhouses, beating field hands, and in
March, near Chico, murdering four Chinese workers. That summer the
violence spread to the Great Gospel Swamp near Anaheim in Southern
California, where vigilantes belonging to the Order attacked Chinese
hop-pickers. The following year the powerful state Grange endorsed
Kearney's call for an all-out crusade against the "long-tailed lepers from
Asia," declaring that the Chinese were an "overshadowing curse which
are sapping the foundation of our prosperity, the dignity of labor, and
the glory of the State."[6]

Vigilantism, of course, was also political theater with the chief aim
of scaring politicians into passing vigorous anti-Chinese legislation. In
1879, while tramps continued to assail Chinese immigrants in the rural valleys, a new state constitution was hammered out in Sacramento under the influence of delegates from the Workingman's Party and
the Grange. In anticipation of later Jim Crow constitutions in the Deep
South, it mandated segregated schools for "Mongolians," barred them
from public employment, and allowed incorporated communities to
segregate them in Chinatowns (the artifacts of prejudice rather than
collective choice). Soon afterward, 94 percent of California voters endorsed a referendum to exclude further Chinese immigrants. "California's Karl Marx," the land reformer Henry George, protested that white
hysteria over the Chinese was squandering a historic opportunity for
radical reform of the state's economic system. (George, originally an

anti-Chinese zealot, had distanced himself from the racist demagoguery of the Kearneyites.)[7]

Nor did the "monopolists," allegedly the sponsors of the "coolie menace," defend the Chinese with total ardor. As Richard Street explains in his history of nineteenth-century California farm labor, when Chinese harvest hands in the 1870s and early 1880s began to organize and even strike, many of their employers suddenly lost enthusiasm for the Burlingame Treaty. With white Californians now so powerfully united against Chinese immigration, President Chester Arthur ignored the protests of Beijing and signed the Chinese Exclusion Act in May 1882.[8]

But the termination of immigration only increased pressure to expel the Chinese from the fields. Local Anti-Coolie Leagues and Anti-Chinese Associations organized boycotts of ranchers who employed Chinese labor, and even committed arson and made death threats against the huge Bidwell Ranch. In February 1882, vigilantes drove Chinese workers out of the hop fields north of Sacramento and burned down their bunkhouses near Wheatland. A month later at a huge anti-Chinese convention in Sacramento, lawyer Grover Johnson, the father of future Progressive governor and senator Hiram Johnson, keynoted the call to kick the Chinese out of the state.[9]

The September 1885 massacre of twenty-eight Chinese miners by white members of the Knights of Labor in Rock Springs, Wyoming (which forced President Cleveland to send federal troops to protect the survivors), detonated pogroms across the Far West. As Alexander Saxton put it, "the fund of anger and discontent building up among workingmen [in the bad economy of 1884–86], by a kind of Gresham's law, converted itself into the cheaper currency of anticoolieism." In the first half of 1886, vigilance committees to "abate" and remove the Chinese emerged in thirty-five California towns, including Pasadena, Arroyo Grande, Stockton, Merced, and Truckee. This was ethnic cleansing on an unprecedented scale, and thousands of Chinese were expelled from these smaller cities and towns. Most of them fled to San Francisco's heavily fortified Chinatown, where they were reduced to "fighting in the alleys for garbage and rotten fish," while growers—used to a captive labor supply—complained bitterly about the shortage of cheap farm labor.[10]

For the next few years, anti-Chinese agitation simmered just below the boiling point, until the Depression of 1893 ignited yet another wave of white chauvinism and mob violence. In the Napa Valley, the White Labor Union organized to drive the Chinese from the vineyards, while other vigilantes attacked Chinese immigrants in Selma and murdered two field hands near Kingsburg. Vigilantism also spread to Southern California's orange groves as hundreds of whites drove Chinese immigrants out of the wealthy citrus town of Redlands in "a blaze of gunshots." Thanks to Representative Geary from Sonoma County, Congress had just legislated that Chinese be required to obtain certificates of residence—creating, as Street points out, "America's first internal passport system." The "Redlands Plan," popularized by a local sheriff, used the Geary Act to legalize the expulsion of local Chinese who failed to register. But in many citrus towns—including Anaheim, Compton, and Rivera—unemployed whites didn't bother with legalisms; they simply formed mobs and attacked the Chinese in their camps.[11]

As the depression deepened, vigilantism continued to flare through the winter and into the spring and summer of 1894. Growers gradually conceded to the terror, hiring white tramps and urban unemployed men in the place of a rapidly aging, bachelor Chinese workforce whose ranks were in any event being rapidly depleted by the Exclusion Act and its amendments. For a half century the Chinese had given their sweat and blood to build the state: now they were brutally pushed aside. New generations would have little inkling of the irreplaceable role that Chinese labor had played in constructing the vital infrastructure (roads, railroads, aqueducts, fields, and fruit orchards) of modern California life.[12]

Chapter Four

"Swat a Jap"

Underlying this Japanese problem is the fundamental proposition that this is a white man's country—and will remain so.

—Asiatic Exclusion League (1909)[1]

The first significant stream of Japanese immigrants to California came from Hawaii: plantation laborers escaping the hellish conditions and coolie wages in the cane fields. After the islands' annexation in 1898, migration to the mainland, as well as direct immigration from Japan, became easier. Japanese laborers soon replaced the Chinese in the beet fields and orchards, and immediately inherited their pariah status. As early as 1892, when the state's Japanese population was still negligible, that tireless bigot, Dennis Kearney, was already screaming that the "Japs Must Go!," although, as historian Roger Daniels emphasizes, prejudice toward the Japanese was still "mainly a tail to the anti-Chinese kite." By the eve of the San Francisco Earthquake, however, the Japanese were a significant segment of the agricultural workforce, with a growing reputation for standing up for their rights. Indeed, they were the early twentieth-century pioneers of agricultural unionism and organized an impressive strike with Mexican coworkers in the beet fields of Oxnard as early as 1903. But the powerful San Francisco unions spurned the new immigrants and instead organized the Japanese and Korean Exclusion League in May 1905 (partly, Saxton argues, to distract attention from scandals within the Union-Labor Party).[2] As the geriatric

Chinese population declined, the younger, economically dynamic Japanese became the new incarnation of the Yellow Peril.

In San Francisco, petty violence toward Japanese residents became a chronic problem, with particularly brazen incidents during and after the earthquake in April 1906. "Nineteen cases of assault against Japanese residents ... were reported, despite the fact that the Japanese government had sent funds to aid the stricken city." When the world-renowned Tokyo seismologist Professor Fusakichi Omori arrived with the gift of a new seismograph for the University of California, he and his colleagues were slugged and stoned on Mission Street by a gang of youths and men. The hooligans were later consecrated by the local press as popular heroes.[3]

That fall, moreover, Japanese kids were kicked out of white schools and segregated with the Chinese—an insult that soon became a major diplomatic incident. In contrast to China in the 1870s and 1880s, Japan was an emergent great power that had just achieved a stunning military victory over czarist Russia. Theodore Roosevelt became the first in a series of American presidents reluctantly forced to balance rational foreign policy against the implacable anti-Japanese hysteria on the West Coast. A temporary palliative—which did little to assuage either Japanese or Californian public opinion—was the 1908 Gentleman's Agreement that halted the immigration of laborers, while allowing a trickle of "picture brides."

But by 1908 the social base of anti-Japanese agitation was changing from the urban labor movement to the rural and urban middle classes. Through extraordinary hard work and community solidarity, the Issei (first-generation immigrants) and their children were saving their wages and buying or leasing land. They created dynamic niches in suburban truck farming, berry and flower growing, nurseries, and urban landscaping. California's growers and wealthy orchardists, like the Hawaiian sugar barons before them, were shocked by the gritty determination of the Japanese to become their own masters, "competitors rather than employees." As Carey McWilliams explained, the large shipper-growers opposed Japanese land ownership because "it threatened the continued existence of large units of production and it decreased the supply of farm labor."[4] Likewise, Japanese immigrants encountered the wrath of small farmers who resented the skilled, intensive methods of cultivation favored by Japanese farmers, which tended to raise the value of land and the cost of farm leases.[5] Middle-class Progressives, generally obsessed with social-Darwinist notions of racial competition, embraced the defense of "Anglo-Saxon agriculture" and took up the mantle of "keeping California white." Although labor-supported Democrats as well as the Hearst press continued to fulminate about the dangers of miscegenation and the necessity of school segregation, Progressives emphasized the Japanese as relentless agricultural competitors and sponsored legislation to prevent them from acquiring more farm land. Already ineligible for U.S. citizenship thanks to previous exclusionist laws, the Issei generation would now be forbidden to own land.

The proposed Alien Land Law, however, was immediately and forcibly contested by European rentiers, especially the Dutch and British, who had long owned vast tracts of prime California agricultural land. The Progressive-dominated legislature quickly obliged, with new wording that exempted these powerful interests while focusing the bill even more narrowly on the hardworking Issei.[6] The act's passage in 1913, after a few cosmetic changes to appease alarmed Secretary of State William Jennings Bryan, sparked mass protests in Japan and new demands to send the Imperial Fleet to California. As Kevin Starr explains, California's Progressives irreparably poisoned public opinion in Japan and helped make a Pacific war virtually inevitable.

> During the agitation leading to the Alien Land Law of 1913, a war party, stung by the insult being offered in California, surfaced in the Japanese government, and representatives of this group began to scout the possibilities of a loan to finance a war against the Untied States. Eighteen years before Pearl Harbor, in other words, and well before the seizure of power by the fascist clique in the Japanese cabinet, the Keep California White! Campaign had succeeded in provoking a number of highly placed people in the Japanese government to view war with the United States as the only adequate response to the racial insults that were being offered. It was even suggested at the time that Japan declare war only on California and not the rest of the United States.[7]

The legislation may have inflamed Tokyo, but it did not prevent the Issei from holding land in the name of their U.S.-born children (the Nisei) or leasing more from avaricious white landowners. Further confrontation with white California, however, was temporarily postponed by the soaring wartime demand for agricultural products, which ensured high profits for all farm producers and temporarily abated racial agitation. But demagogic nativism returned with a vengeance during the sharp postwar recession in 1919 and then persisted in various violent and malignant incarnations throughout the 1920s.

This new wave of anti-Japanese activism addressed both the continuing success of Issei as farmers as well as the efforts of their English-speaking, citizen children to integrate themselves into ordinary California life. Under the generalship of two venerable Progressives—U.S. Senator (and former governor) Hiram Johnson and retired *Sacramento Bee* publisher V. S. McClatchy—a broad nativist coalition, including the Native Sons of the Golden West, the American Legion, the State Federation of Labor, the Grange, the Federation of Women's Clubs, and the Loyal Order of Moose, pushed a new, tougher alien land act through the California legislature in 1920, then moved on to Washington, D.C., to lobby for a total ban on Japanese immigration.

While Congress debated the proposed Johnson-Reed (or Quota Immigration) Act, the xenophobic Native Sons pressured colleges to fire their "pro-Japanese" professors and warned parents of the dangerous sexual predilections of the Nisei ("Would you like your daughter to marry a Japanese?"). A common nativist demand (resurrected in 2005 by anti-immigrant Republicans) was an amendment to deny citizenship to children born in the United States of alien parents. Meanwhile, anti-Japanese groups in the Los Angeles area, including the Native Sons and the Ku Klux Klan as well as local homeowner associations, organized a vigilante movement "designed to make life miserable for all Japanese residing there." This 1922–23 "Swat the Jap" campaign involved everything from billboards and boycotts to spitting on Japanese pedestrians to assault and battery, with dark threats of more serious violence if Nisei persisted in moving into "white" neighborhoods and acting like entitled U.S. citizens.

"Swat the Jap," with its emphasis on ritual public humiliation, was an eerie prefiguration of the treatment of Jews in early Nazi Germany; but—as one anti-Japanese leaflet reprinted by Daniels makes clear—it also has considerable resonance with contemporary screeds against Latino immigrants.

> You came to care for lawns,
>   We stood for it
> You came to work in truck gardens,
>   We stood for it
> You moved your children to our public schools
>   We stood for it

....
You proposed to build a church in our neighborhood
   BUT
We DIDN'T and WE WON'T STAND FOR IT
....
WE DON'T WANT YOU WITH US
SO GET BUSY, JAPS, AND
GET OUT OF HOLLYWOOD[8]

Congress, under intense lobbying from Johnson and other Western representatives and senators, passed the Johnson-Reed Bill in 1924 and banned all further immigration from Japan. But alien land laws and immigration bans still failed to evict the Japanese from their farms and businesses. Ultimately, Johnson and his supporters would see their life's work crowned with Executive Order 9102 on March 18, 1942, interning California's Japanese-Americans in desert concentration camps. As Daniels points out, "Mazanar, Gila River, Tule Lake, White Mountain and the other relocation camps are the last monuments to their patriotic zeal."[9]

Chapter Five

The Anti-Filipino Riots

I shall never forget what I have suffered in this country because of racial prejudice.

—Carlos Bulosan (1937)[1]

The victories of the anti-Japanese exclusionists in 1920 and 1924 reinforced an endemic shortage of cheap agricultural labor that the big growers attempted to remedy by importing Mexican and Filipino workers. If California history often seems like a relentless conveyor belt delivering one immigrant group after another to the same cauldron of exploitation and prejudice, the Filipino experience was perhaps the most paradoxical. As citizens of an American colony until 1934, the Filipinos were not technically "aliens" and thus not excluded by the 1924 quota system; but unlike Mexicans or Japanese, they lacked the protection of a sovereign mother country and were more nakedly at the mercy of California's racist legislature and local governments. The Filipino labor migration of the 1920s, moreover, consisted almost entirely of young, single men whose natural gravitation to dance halls and red-light districts provoked racial-sexual hysteria amongst whites of such berserk intensity that it invites comparison with the Faulknerian South.[2]

No one fretted more about the honor of white girls or the dangers of "mongrelization" than Progressive mandarin V. S. McClatchy, who was again seconded in his racial phobias by Senators Hiram Johnson and Samuel Shortridge, ex-Senator James Pheland, and Governor Friend Richardson, as well as by the reactionary "Chandler-Cameron-Knowland" axis of newspaper publishers in Los Angeles, San Francisco, and Oakland. This powerful alliance, whose prejudices continued to be endorsed by right-wing AFL unions, hammered away at the Filipinos as representing (in the words of a Los Angeles Chamber of Commerce official) "the most worthless, unscrupulous, shiftless, diseased, semi-barbarians that ever came to our shores."[3] Filipinos, whose recreational interests were no different from tens of thousands of single, white sailors, day laborers, and hoboes who flocked to Los Angeles's Main Street or San Francisco's Tenderloin, were depicted (again, in images that prefigured Nazi calumnies) as obsessed, serial miscegenators.

Anti-Filipino agitation, however, also had a functional, economic dimension: the ferocity of the appeal to white sexual fear was generally calibrated to labor-market conditions as well as the militancy of Filipinos in defending their rights. By the late 1920s, Carey McWilliams claimed, "the feeling against the Filipino [had] been intensified by reason of the desire of the large growers to get rid of him as a worker." As one contemporary agribusiness leader complained: "It costs $100 per head to bring the Filipino in. And we cannot handle him like we can the Mexican: the Mexican can be deported." Moreover, adds McWilliams, "Filipinos no longer scab on their fellow workers, and they no longer underbid for work.... The Filipino is a real fighter and his strikes have been dangerous."[4] It was precisely this economic "danger" that the class enemies of the Filipinos transmuted into a legend of sexual danger.

Association with white women thus provided the pretext for a small riot in Stockton on New Year's Eve in 1926, and then full-scale vigilantism organized by the American Legion against Filipino farmworkers in the Tulare County town of Dinuba in August 1926 after "the fruit pickers insist[ed] on their rights to attend dances and escort white girls around the city."[5] The onset of the Depression ignited white resentment already made highly inflammable by the ceaseless, lurid innuendo of nativist groups like the Native Sons and the American Legion. "On 24 October 1929, the day of the Wall Street Crash," writes Richard Meynell in his "Little Brown Brothers, Little White Girls," "Filipinos were shot with rubber bands as they escorted white girls at a street carnival in Exeter, southeast of Fresno. A fight broke out, a white man was stabbed, and a riot ensued in which vigilante whites, led by Chief of Police C. E. Joyner, beat and stoned Filipinos in the fields." Three hundred vigilantes burnt down the Filipino labor camp on the nearby Firebaugh Ranch.[6]

Six weeks later, Watsonville police discovered two underage white girls in the room of a twenty-five-year-old Filipino worker; it was soon revealed that the girls' parents were themselves prostituting the older child. White rage crystallized around the lurid accounts of the affair in the local paper, including a provocative photo of the older girl in the embrace of the young worker. Judge D. Rohrback, the shrill voice of race hatred in the Pajaro Valley, warned that "... if the present state of affairs continues ... there will be 40,000 half-breeds in the State of California before ten years have passed." But, as Howard DeWitt has shown in an important study, violent attitudes toward local Filipinos were also shaped by the fact that they worked on large lettuce farms, controlled by out-of-town corporations, that had marginalized local farmers and white workers.[7] In his incessant incitements to vigilantism, Judge Rohrback emphasized a bizarre equation between miscegenation and economic displacement. "He [the Filipino] gives them silk underwear and makes them pregnant and crowds whites out of jobs in the bargain."[8]

The local paper, the *Pajaronian*, which printed Rohrback's fulminations as well as vicious, distorted accounts of relations between Filipinos and white girls, publicized the opening on January 11, 1930, of a taxi dancehall catering to Filipinos in Palm Beach, twenty minutes southwest of Watsonville. It soon became the rallying point for angry white youth and unemployed men, spurred on by the *Pajaronian*'s calls to vigilantism ("State Organizations Will Fight Filipino Influx into Country"). On the weekend of January 18–19, whites made repeated, unsuccessful attempts to disrupt the dances in Palm Beach, followed by rock-throwing in downtown Watsonville. "Whites," writes Meynell, "then formed 'hunting parties' ... after an 'indignation meeting' at a local pool hall." While hundreds of spectators watched from the nearby highway, the mob tried to sack the dancehall but were driven off by buckshot and teargas. The next day vigilantes took their revenge:

> On Wednesday, 22 January, the riot reached its peak with mobs of hundreds dragging Filipinos out of their homes, whipping and beating them, and throwing them off the Pajaro River bridge. The mobs ranged up the San Juan road, attacking Filipinos at the Storm and Detlefsen ranches.... At Riberal's labor camp, 22 Filipinos were dragged out and beaten. This time mob had leaders and organization—it moved 'military-like' and responded to orders to attack or withdraw....
>
> Early the next morning (the 23rd) bullets were fired into a bunkhouse on the Murphy ranch on the San Juan Road. Eleven Filipinos huddled in a closet to escape the fusillade. At dawn they discovered that

a twelfth, Fermin Tobera, had been shot through the heart. [9]

DeWitt explains that the vigilantes who killed twenty-two-year-old Tobera were in fact youths "from well-to-do families," not jobless tramps as later portrayed.[10] Although Watsonville authorities deputized American Legionnaires (some of them probably vigilantes) to restore order, the pogrom in the Pajaro Valley had immediate aftershocks in Stockton, where a Filipino club was dynamited; Gilroy, where Filipinos were driven out of town; and San Jose and San Francisco, where Anglos attacked Filipinos on the street. Filipino bunkhouses were dynamited near Reedley in August and in El Centro in December. In 1933 the legislature bowed to nativist pressure and amended the state's 1901 miscegenation law, which already banned the marriage of whites with "Negroes, Mongolians, or mulattoes"—to include "members of the Malay race" as well.

Meanwhile, as tens of thousands of Mexican residents were being coercively "repatriated" across the border in 1933–34, pressure increased to deport Filipinos as well. As the flood of white Dust Bowl refugees began to arrive in California's valleys, growers had less need of the two groups who had demonstrated such audacity and fortitude in recent agricultural strikes. In August 1934, for example, three thousand striking Filipinos had managed to win a wage increase from Salinas lettuce growers, an almost unprecedented victory in the violent early Depression years. But the following month armed farmer-vigilantes attacked the Filipino camps, nearly beating one worker to death, and forcing eight hundred of the former strikers to flee the county. When the expelled workers tried to find work in the Modesto-Turlock area, they were turned back by other vigilantes. Although transformed into unemployed pariahs, hunted by vigilantes and vilified by the press, California's young Filipinos overwhelmingly rejected the "free boat ride home" offered in repatriation legislation sponsored by exclusionists.[11] Indeed, some would stay in the fields, where thirty years later they would reemerge in struggle as the earliest and most fervent supporters of the National Farm Workers Association union.

Chapter Six

The IWW versus the KKK

During the visit of the Industrial Workers of the World they will be accorded a night and day guard of honor, composed of citizens armed with rifles. The Coroner will be in attendance at his office every day.

—Harrison Gray Otis (1912)[1]

As in other Western states, the Industrial Workers of the World in California were the favorite target of California vigilantes. The Wobblies' original sin, even more than their declared aim of overthrowing the wage system, was their willingness to organize all the pariah laborers—white tramps, Mexicans, Japanese, and Filipinos—whom the conservative AFL unions spurned. Between 1906 and 1921, the radical egalitarianism and rebel spirit of the IWW spread with evangelical velocity through the state's harvest camps, railroad bunkhouses, hobo colonies, and skid rows. The Wobblies championed the cause of oppressed workers regardless of ethnicity, and rejected the wages of whiteness in favor of "solidarity forever." In contrast to some AFL unions that secretly sanctioned dynamite sabotage, the IWW was unwavering in its commitment to non-violent resistance. Yet no other group, not even the Communist Party in the 1930s or 1950s, managed to so enrage employers, or arouse more hysteria amongst the propertied middle classes, than the IWW in its heyday; but, then again, no other group ever fomented such courageous or far-reaching rebellion in the lower depths of California society.

The first large-scale tests of strength between the IWW (organized in 1905) and the vigilantes occurred in Fresno in 1910 and San Diego in 1912. Local 66 in Fresno, like other IWW branches, used downtown street meetings to dramatize its presence and preach the creed of One Big Union to local laborers ("home guards" in Wobbly parlance) as well as the migrant farm and construction workers who constantly streamed through the San Joaquin Valley city. Within a year it had organized the Mexican laborers at a nearby dam and led a group of Santa Fe Railroad workers on strike. Alarmed employers pressured the police chief to re-voke Local 66's speaking permit and jail its organizers. Frank Little, the one-eyed, part-Indian hero of an earlier IWW free-speech battle in Spo-kane, Washington, arrived in Fresno to lead the struggle. Little and the Wobblies defied the ban and packed the local jail with scores of spirited fellow workers. When their landlord evicted them from their skid row headquarters, they erected a large tent on a lot rented from a sympathizer and called for IWWs from all over the West to hop the next freight train to Fresno. Faced with an inundation of his jail by out-of-town radicals, the chief of police, as Philip Foner explains in his history of the IWW, abdicated to vigilantes:

> On December 9, a mob of over 1,000 vigilantes attacked and severely beat a number of IWW men who sought to speak on the streets, then advanced on the IWW tent headquarters, burned the camp and all the supplies, marched to the county jail and threatened to break into the jail and lynch the Wobbly prisoners. The mob had been encouraged by a statement by Police Chief Shaw that "if the citizens wished to act they might and he would not interfere." Shaw's statement followed the discovery that the city of Fresno had no ordinance prohibiting speaking on the streets, and that the actions of the police were entirely without authority.[2]

To the astonishment of the vigilantes and police, the Wobblies, stiffened by the calm courage of Frank Little, refused to abandon the fight. The 150 prisoners in Fresno jail held out for weeks in the face of a sadistic regime of beatings, drenchings with fire hoses, and bread-and-water diets. With "armies" of hundreds of fresh IWW volunteers on their way to join the fight from all corners of California and the Northwest, Fresno authorities reluctantly rescinded the ban and gave the street corners back to free speech.

If Fresno was an inspiring—though hardwon—victory for the IWW, their bitter experience in San Diego in 1912 forewarned of the pitiless repression and vigilante terror that Wobblies and other California radicals would face from 1917 onwards. In San Diego, the courage of the IWW free-speech fighters collided with a granite wall of reaction erected by California's two most uncompromising robber barons: General Harrison Gray Otis, proprietor of the *Los Angeles Times* and chief architect of the open shop, and John D. Spreckels, the publisher of the *San Diego Union* and *Tribune* and owner of almost anything of value in the city of San Diego.

Since the bombing of the *Times* by AFL unionists in 1910, Otis had stumped the Pacific Coast cajoling fellow capitalists to militarize local industrial relations along the lines of Los Angeles's Merchants and Manufacturers' Association (M&M), which he had founded. Otis, one of the most rabid union-haters in American history, advocated an "industrial freedom" (which was the masthead slogan of the *Times*) that left no room for soapboxes, picket lines, or unions. In December 1911, he met confidentially with San Diego business leaders at the U.S. Grant Hotel, urging them to crush the IWW by adopting Los Angeles's draconian bans on street-speaking and picketing. The city's foremost capitalist, John D. Spreckels, needed little convincing. His morning and afternoon papers had been regularly blasting the Wobblies ever since they participated in a brief revolutionary invasion of Baja California in 1911 (supporting the anarchist Liberal Party of Ricardo Flores Magon), and more recently Spreckels had been outraged to discover that the IWW's San Diego Local 13 was trying to organize the employees of his street railroad. Although there was little love lost between the rival publishers, Spreckels supported the extermination of the IWW and soon brought a captive city council and the rest of the business class to the same point of view.

As in Fresno, the Free Speech fight started one-sidedly in February 1912 with a repressive ordinance, mass arrests, fire hoses, and brutal jail conditions, while the Spreckels papers doled out murderous bile that gourmets of innuendo compared to the very best of the *Los Angeles Times*:

> Hanging is too good for them [editorialized the *San Diego Tribune*] and they would be much better dead; for they are absolutely useless in the human economy; they are waste material of creation and should be drained off in the sewer of oblivion there to rot in cold obstruction like any other excrement.[3]

The *Tribune* recommended shooting IWW members in jail, while the more moderate *Union* was content with advocating beatings and deportation. In the meantime, hundreds of Wobblies, with a fearlessness and daring that only further enraged their persecutors, continued to pour into "Spreckelstown" by freight car and shank's mare. This time, however, they discovered that the vigilantes were more than a one-act show. With a *Union* reporter amongst the identified ringleaders, a heavily-armed force of several hundred vigilantes, some of them obviously seconded by their employers, maintained an unprecedented reign of terror for three months. One contingent acted as an ad hoc border patrol, camped at the county line at San Onofre to intercept Wobblies headed south; another gang worked with brutal Police Chief Wilson to terrorize prisoners—often driving them out to the Imperial Desert where they were beaten and abandoned to the cactus and rattlesnakes.[4]

One IWW member, kicked mercilessly in the testicles by his jailers, died of his injuries, and then the mourners in his funeral procession were clubbed. Several other free-speech fighters were maimed and hundreds more were savagely beaten. Al Tucker, a salty member from Victorville, sent IWW National Secretary-Treasurer Vincent St. John an account of the routine treatment dealt out by the vigilante reception committee:

> It was then about 1 o'clock AM. The train slowed down and we were between two lines of something like 400 men armed to the teeth with rifles, pistols and clubs of all kinds. The moon was shining dimly through the clouds and I could see pick handles, axe handles, wagon spokes and every kind of a club imaginable swinging from the wrists of all of them while they also had their rifles leveled at us.... We were ordered to unload and we refused. Then they closed in around the flat car which we were on and began clubbing and knocking and pulling men off by their heels, so inside of a half hour thay had us all off the train and then bruised and bleeding we were lined up and marched into the cattle corral ... now and then picking out a man they thought was a leader and giving him an extra beating. Several men were carried out unconscious and I believe there were some killed, for afterwards there were a lot of our men unaccounted for and never have been heard from since. The vigilantes all wore constable badges and white handkerchiefs around their left arms. They were all drunk and hollering and cursing the rest of the night. In the morning they took us out four or five at a time and marched us up the track to the county line ... where we were forced to kiss the flag and then run a gauntlet of 106 men, every one of which was striking at us as hard as they could with their pick axe handles. They broke one man's leg, and every one was beaten black and blue, and was bleeding from a dozen wounds.[5]

Kevin Starr has written that "the San Diego free speech battles revealed the depths of reaction possible in the threatened middle- and lower-middle classes of California." He argues that vigilantes were recruited from an anxious petty bourgeoisie, "who were uncertain and insecure in what they had gained or thought they had gained by coming to California." As in late Weimar Germany, "the oligarchy, which is to say, the upper-middle and upper classes, loathed and feared the IWW; but oligarchs did not take to the streets as vigilantes. They did, however, encourage the lower-middle classes to do such work."[6]

But according to a key eyewitness, Starr is wrong: the "oligarchy" both instigated and physically participated in San Diego's festival of vigilante violence. Abram Sauer was the editor of a little weekly paper called the *Herald* which alone supported the free speech movement. He was kidnapped, threatened with lynching, and told to leave town (and later his press was damaged). Sauer, however, courageously refused to run away and instead published an article about his kidnapping which identified the vigilantes as prominent bankers and merchants as well as "leading Church members and bartenders, Chamber of Commerce and Real Estate Board ... as well as members of the grand jury."[7] Although Starr's theory of vigilantism may have applied in other historical situations, San Diego's antiradicals (bartenders aside) seemed to have been a cut above the "shopkeepers, the small-scale realtors, the upper-level clerks and first-level supervisors" whom he identifies as the core social stratum.[8] The ordinary middle class, however, was subject to considerable pressure to choose sides.

In an anticipation of witch hunts yet to come, the Spreckels press cajoled San Diegans to monitor each other's "loyalty." So "his neighbors will know just where he stands on a question that just now is of vital important to San Diego," the *Union* advised loyal citizens to wear little American flags on their lapels, with the sinister implication that those who refused to display their patriotism or gave undue consideration to the Bill of Rights might think about relocation.[9]

A famous lynching was narrowly averted in mid-May when America's most celebrated anarchist, Emma Goldman, arrived in San Diego ostensibly to lecture on Ibsen, but obviously to show her defiance of vigilante rule. Goldman's steel nerves were legendary and she didn't flinch in the face of the bloodthirsty mob outside her hotel room chanting: "Give us that anarchist; we will strip her naked; we will tear out her guts." But her lover and manager, Ben Reitman (also a sex education pioneer and author of *Boxcar Bertha*), was kidnapped and then tortured in a manner that betrayed his captors' considerable enjoyment of sexual perversion.

His abductors ("leading Church members and bartenders"?) took him
to a remote mesa, where they urinated on him, stripped him, hit and
kicked him. Then "with a lighted cigar," Reitman later told reporters
in Los Angeles, "they burned the letters IWW in my buttocks ... they
poured a can of tar over my head and, in the absence of feathers, rubbed
sagebrush on my body. One of them attempted to push a cane into my
rectum. Another twisted my testicles. They forced me to kiss the flag and
sing 'The Star Spangled Banner.'"[10]

In the face of such sadism, the Wobblies, incredibly, continued their
fight, supported by Socialists and eventually by outraged AFL unionists
and some Progressives. But the toll of terror was overwhelming. Even
the lawyers who attempted to represent the IWW were jailed, and when
other jurists protested to Governor Hiram Johnson, the champion of
the Progressives, he retorted that "the anarchy of the IWW and their
brutality are worse than the anarchy of the vigilantes." When Goldman
and Reitman tried to return a year later, they were again almost lynched
and had to flee to Los Angeles. Although the City Council eventually
rescinded the anti-open-meeting ordinance and free speech returned to
the street corners of downtown San Diego, it was a strictly pyrrhic victory for the IWW. As Philip Foner points out, some leading IWWs began
to object to the huge human and organizational cost of such ordeals;
while many rank-and-file members heartily agreed with the battered Al
Tucker who swore that if he ever took part in another free speech fight
"it will be with machine guns or aerial bombs."[11]

In the end, however, the IWW continued its defiant but nonviolent campaign to organize harvest tramps, garment workers, construction crews, sailors, and the unemployed. The Wobblies probably posed
the greatest threat in the Central Valley, where each attempt to destroy
their leadership—such as the framing of "Blackie" Ford and Herman
Suhr following the so-called Wheatland Riot in 1914, when deputized
vigilantes fired upon a mass meeting—was countered by the emergence of a new cadre of "camp delegates" and itinerant organizers. Although the IWW failed to build durable locals, its agricultural nucleus
remained intact, threatening to fan any spark of discontent into strike
action. Growers agreed with General Otis and other open-shop leaders:
selective repression of the IWW's leadership was ineffective and the
organization would only be defeated by the application of San Diego–
type methods on a statewide scale.

The First World War conveniently provided the patriotic pretext for such a crusade. Nationally, the American Protective League (APL), which eventually counted 350,000 members, became a "largely out-of-control quasi-governmental, quasi-vigilante agency which established a massive spy network across the land," with the approval of the Department of Justice. In California as elsewhere, the APL focused on "disloyal" Wobblies and Socialists, as did the editorial page of every paper in California. Mobs sacked the IWW offices in Oakland and Los Angeles in August 1917, and in September, the National Guard was sent to crush an IWW-led cannery strike in San Jose. Federal and local officials raided Wobbly offices throughout central California and arrested scores of activists. Forty-six were jailed in Sacramento, where "editorials in the *Sacramento Bee* advocated lynching the prisoners, and rumors of wholesale lynchings filled the air."[12] The IWW was effectively made an illegal organization and assaults on its facilities and members were applauded as admirable patriotism.

The end of the war brought no respite. 1919 was the year of great strikes as well as the Palmer Raids and the mass deportation of "alien radicals." Against the background of a general strike in Seattle, which for the first time allied AFL unionists with the IWW, the California legislature passed a "criminal syndicalism" law. Crafted by the Los Angeles M&M and the San Francisco Chamber of Commerce, it allowed authorities to send dozens of Wobblies to San Quentin simply for their stubborn belief, to quote the preamble to the IWW constitution, that "the working class and the employing class have nothing in common."[13]

A few months later, the *Los Angeles Times*—the Wobblies called it the "Los Angeles Crimes"—published a series urging renewed vigilantism against the IWW. Citrus growers in the San Gabriel and Pomona Valleys had already obliged, by raiding and deporting IWW orchard strikers. Then a mob of soldiers and civilians attacked a Los Angeles IWW meeting in November, wrecking the hall and seriously injuring four people while the police arrested the rest of the victims for "inciting a riot."[14] According to Philip Foner, the American Legion in Los Angeles had organized a paramilitary wing "which specialized in raiding radical bookstores, beating up Wobblies, and harassing the landlord of their meeting hall."[15] IWW meetings of any kind in Los Angeles were then banned for the superbly Kafkaesque reason that public sentiment made it "unsafe for enemies of peace and government to gather in public."[16]

Yet in the very maw of such terror, the Wobblies began to grow again. Labor had lost all the big battles of 1919, leaving many AFL unions broken and the open shop enshrined everywhere on the Pacific Coast, even in San Francisco. The most militant elements of the labor movement blamed this epic defeat on narrow craft unionism and the right-wing AFL leadership. The Wobblies, with their dogged, no-surrender devotion to class struggle and their religious advocacy of industrial unionism, suddenly became an attractive alternative, and the IWW won impressive numbers of new adherents, especially on the strife-torn California waterfronts, where the IWW Marine Transport Workers Industrial Union (MTWIU) led resistance to the open shop. Despite the widespread myth that the Wobblies had died in 1918 when the federal government jailed its national leadership, the actual "final conflict"—at least on the West Coast—was the bold, if quixotic, "general strike to free class war prisoners" that the IWW launched on April 25, 1923.

Although the strike affected both coasts, and indeed was echoed by worldwide solidarity actions from Montevideo to Yokahama, its principal arena was San Pedro. Here MTWIU seamen and longshoremen, supported by sympathetic oil workers, shut down the Los Angeles harbor to the complete surprise of employers and AFL unions alike. While ninety ships lay idle, "a red painted airplane flew over the docks and the oil fields, dropping leaflets, while a red painted automobile, called 'Spark Plug,' drove around the city bringing speakers to address thousands of workers at open air meetings."[17] In Los Angeles, at least, the IWW was suddenly alive and kicking back.

Indeed, the strike turned into an extraordinary and protracted test of strength between opposing class forces. On one side was the harbor area working class, supported by Los Angeles trade unionists and Socialists. On the other side stood the employers (especially the arch-reactionary Hammond Lumber Company), backed by the *Los Angeles Times* (now generaled by Otis's son-in-law, Harry Chandler), the M&M, and the M&M's "military wing," the Los Angeles Police Department (LAPD). The LAPD, proclaiming that strike rallies and meetings had "grown incompatible with public security," arrested so many IWW members and their supporters that the city was forced to construct a special stockade in Griffith Park to handle the overflow. A local sympathizer, Mrs. Minnie Davis, then allowed the Wobblies to meet on a spectacular knoll that she owned, soon christened "Liberty Hill" by the strikers.

Rising two hundred feet above the level of Third Street, Liberty Hill had several flights of stone steps leading up to it. At its top were handmade wooden benches seating about 800 people, a small platform, six by nine feet, and standing room for several thousand. There, on the hill, the IWW held five meetings each week, with the meetings in English usually attended by between 1000-3000 people and those in Spanish by from 500-800.[18]

LAPD chief Louis Oakes responded to Liberty Hill with totally illegal mass arrests, warning that "all idle men at the harbor must explain their loafing and show that they are not IWW's or go to jail." Pasadena's most famous resident, the muckraker and novelist Upton Sinclair, promptly challenged the chief, whom he described as a stooge for the M&M, to a constitutional duel, and was arrested while reading from the U.S. Constitution. But the jailing of Sinclair only enraged a wider radius of progressive opinion and brought five thousand people to Liberty Hill a few days later. At this point, with the police failing to break the strike with arrests alone, vigilantes in white hoods suddenly appeared—the open shop's *deus ex machina*.[19]

In previous postwar confrontations, the American Legion had been the reliable source of antiradical mobs, but by early 1924, the Ku Klux Klan had grown astronomically throughout California and was rumored to control the electoral balance of power in Los Angeles. Exactly how or by whom the Klan was conscripted to fight the harbor workers is unclear, but presumably the motive was nativism as well as antiradicalism, since the IWW had a large Mexican membership in the harbor area, and many waterfront workers spoke with Serbo-Croat, Italian, and Scandinavian accents.

The KKK made its debut in the area in March 1924 when several thousand hooded visitors encircled the IWW hall in San Pedro; two weeks later, police broke into a meeting of the Oil Workers Industrial Union, arrested several leaders, and then evicted the rest of the unionists, while several dozen KKK members set to work completely wrecking the hall.[20] Police cooperation with the hooded terrorists was completely blatant. On June 14, following bogus rumors that IWW members had rejoiced after hearing news of a deadly explosion aboard the USS *Mississippi*, 150 vigilantes, KKK members, and probably off-duty cops as well again attacked the IWW hall at Twelfth and Center Streets.

Three hundred men, women, and children were in the hall attending a benefit for several members who had died in a recent railroad accident. The vigilantes viciously sapped down the surprised men and women, then turned their fury upon the terrified IWW kids, some of them barely more than toddlers.

> They seemed to take a special delight in dipping the children into the urn of boiling coffee. This treatment was given to Lena Milos, age 10, known as the "Wobbly song bird," Lillian Sunsted, age 8, May Sunsted, age 13, John Rodin, age 5, Andrew Kulgis, age 12, and Joyce Rodilda, age 4. Andrew Kulgis received an additional "hot grease" application from one of the sadists in the mob. All the children received beatings as well.[21]

Young Andrew Kulgis was nearly scalded to death, while the other children suffered severe burns. Meanwhile, seven of the men were kidnapped and taken to a remote spot in Santa Ana Canyon, where they were savagely beaten, then tarred and feathered. The vigilantes were never prosecuted (indeed, they were praised by the *Times*), but when several ACLU lawyers attempted to speak at a rally in downtown San Pedro protesting the atrocity, they were punctually jailed. By the end of 1924, the dynamic San Pedro affiliate of the MTWIU was in its death throes, the most dedicated IWW organizers, now convicted of "criminal syndicalism," were leading strikes inside San Quentin, and Harry Chandler's *Los Angeles Times* was declaring victory in the "thirty years' war between labor and capital."[22]

Chapter Seven

In Dubious Battle

"You red son of a bitch," Livingston hollered, "arguing constitutional law. We'll give you a taste of our constitutional law!"

—Vigilante in El Centro (1934)[1]

On the eve of the Great Depression, California might have been a middle-class "paradise to live in or see," as Woody Guthrie put it, but for those without the "do re me"—farm workers and labor radicals, especially—it was a semi-fascist, closed society whose employing classes, especially in the Central Valley and Southern California, were habituated to vigilante violence as a normal mode of industrial relations. The crusade against the IWW had reinforced the already widespread belief that subversives had no consequent civil liberties and that the bourgeois citizenry was perfectly entitled to brandish shotguns, parade in hoods, and smash up union halls.

The great battles of the 1930s, moreover, would leave an ambiguous legacy: the urban labor movement, led by new CIO unions like the ILWU and UAW, would overthrow the open shop and put a union label on wartime mass production; in the valleys, however, the militarized Associated Farmers, together with Sunkist (the citrus growers), would beat down every attempt to establish durable agricultural unionism. In defense of California's system of corporate farming and huge family latifundia, vigilantism would soar to a level not seen since the bloody 1850s.

After the final defeat of the IWW's locals in the Central Valley in

1917–19, growers began to replace white harvest tramps ("bindlestiffs" in IWW parlance) with Mexican family labor. As with ethnic groups like the Chinese and Japanese who had previously occupied the niche of agricultural helots, the Mexicans were first extolled by the growers as paragons of hard work and docility, then excoriated as riff-raff and a racial menace when they began to organize and strike. Despite efforts by local Mexican consuls to promote exclusive ethnic unions (which often, as Gilbert Gonzalez emphasizes, were little more than company unions), the *campesinos* in the fields united with other groups, including whites, African-Americans, and especially the militant Filipinos, to stage some forty-nine different walkouts in 1933–34, involving almost seventy thousand farm and cannery workers.[2]

The most important of these battles—including the epic 1933 cotton strike and the 1933–34 struggles in the Imperial Valley—were fought under the banner of the Cannery and Agricultural Workers Industrial Union (CAWIU), one of the Communist "Third Period" unions established after 1928. To the growers, CAWIU was a tentacle of a vast "red" conspiracy: an ultimate menace to be expunged by any means necessary. In fact, the union was a shoestring operation, financed not by Moscow gold but by members' fifty-cent dues and the extraordinary dedication of a handful of organizers. In contrast to the right-wing myth of a carefully prepared plan of subversion, hammered out by William Z. Foster and his underlings in their Union Square, New York, offices, the CAWIU was a little red fire brigade that responded to spontaneous rebellions in the fields, helping shape them into sustained campaigns and organized strikes. It possessed scant resources—just a few automobiles, mimeograph machines, and *pro bono* left-wing lawyers—but managed to galvanize the struggle of fieldworkers who owned virtually nothing except the tattered clothes on their backs and their children's hunger.

The real threat of the CAWIU, as some growers acknowledged, was that it represented a supercharged version of the IWW, with an urban support base that the Wobblies had lacked. Indeed, the senior organizer, Pat Chambers, was a tough ex-Wobbly, and the CAWIU retained the IWW's participatory organizing model: "each member as he joined became an organizer … with strike leaders and committee chairmen elected by the workers and all major decisions put to a vote. The union carefully limited strike demands to those desired by the workers." Moreover, the CAWIU, in contrast to white supremacist AFL unions, preached a gospel of interethnic solidarity and antidiscrimination, which it backed up with the consistent courage and sacrifice of its organizers.[3] ("Only fanatics," cynically observed an AFL leader, "are willing to live in shacks or tents and get their heads broken in the interests of migratory laborers."[4])

Originally named the Agricultural Workers Industrial League (AFIL), the CAWIU's baptism by fire was the 1930 lettuce strike in the Imperial Valley. The Trade Union Unity League, the parent of the AFIL/ CAWIU, sent some of its most experienced organizers to help build this strike of Mexican and Filipino field hands, but the Communists became targets of criminal syndicalism prosecutions that ultimately sent six of them to San Quentin. A year later, Communists helped lead a big cannery walkout in the Santa Clara Valley that was quickly crushed by the police and deputized American Legionnaires ("vigilantes with badges"), despite supporting protests of the unemployed in San Jose. The first half of 1932 was equally grim. In May, a desperate CAWIU-led uprising of pea-pickers near Half Moon Bay was efficiently broken by the now standard deployment of police and deputized farmers. In June, one of the CAWIU's veteran organizers, Pat Callahan, was almost beaten to death by deputized goons during a hopeless strike of cherry-pickers in the Santa Clara Valley.[5]

The CAWIU regrouped in September around a series of walkouts that followed the grape harvest northward in the San Joaquin Valley. Although a strike in the Fresno area was quickly broken, four thousand grape-pickers in the Lodi vineyards showed impressive grit in the face of the usual wave of arrests and beatings. The growers, in turn, mobilized their own army. "Scores of growers, local businessmen, and American Legionnaires," writes Cletus Daniel, "were deputized as soon as the strike call was issued, and placed under the command of Colonel Walter E. Garrison, a leading farm employer and retired military man. Once this special strikebreaking force was formed, duly constituted law enforcement officials in the region faded into the background." Garrison's vigilantes went after the strike leadership, jailing thirty CAWIU organizers and picket captains. They also forced relief agencies to cut off aid to the strikers' families and blocked every attempt to hold strike meetings or rallies. But the CAWIU responded inventively with guerrilla tactics, using "hit and run" pickets that stymied the introduction of scabs and forced several growers to accede to strike demands. The growers, in turn, appealed to mob violence.

On the evening of October 2, approximately 1500 vineyardists, businessmen, American Legionnaires, and other Lodi residents met in a local theater to perfect plans to end the strike without further delay. After much debate, a "Committee of 1500" was established to drive strikers out of the area on the following morning....

At six o'clock the following morning several hundred vigilantes armed with a variety of clubs and firearms gathered in the center of Lodi to carry out their plan. When a group of about 100 strikers assembled in front of the CAWIU headquarters to plan the day's picketing activities the storm broke. Abandoning their pledge of nonviolence, vigilantes led by a small group of local cowboys charged into the strikers' midst with clubs and fists flailing. As vigilantes drove the frightened and battered strikers toward the edge of town, strikers offered no resistance. However, when a few strikers sought to defend themselves against their attackers, the police intervened to arrest them for "resisting an officer" or "rioting." Assaults continued throughout the morning as vigilantes cruised the area in automobiles routing strikers from their camps. Later in the day when strikers attempted to regroup they were attacked by vigilantes and local authorities using fire hoses and tear gas bombs.[6]

The defeat of the grape strike fed an already intense debate amongst Communists about the need to prioritize organizing targets rather than just chasing spontaneous strikes around the state. In November, after careful preparation, the CAWIU dug in its heels in Vacaville where four hundred fruit-pickers—Mexican, Filipino, Japanese, and Anglo—walked out in a pre-arranged protest against wage cuts. The response was predictably brutal and followed the same tactics used by San Diego vigilantes a generation earlier. "In the first week of December," wrote Orrick Johns, "when the strike was a few weeks old, a masked mob of forty men in a score of cars, took six strike leaders out of the Vacaville Jail, drove them twenty miles from town, flogged them with tug straps, clipped their heads with sheep clippers, and poured red enamel over them." Yet the striking orchard workers held out for two months against overwhelming odds, even defying AFL officials who came to Vacaville to denounce them. In the end, the "pinch of hunger," and death threats against Filipinos in particular, forced a return to work, but CAWIU organizers were encouraged by the strikers' solidarity and heroic stamina. Many were buoyed by the possibility that farm fascism might be defeated after all, if such fearlessness could be alloyed with efficient organization and—most importantly—sympathetic publicity about the strikers' conditions and grievances.

As it turned out, the great agricultural strike wave of 1933, in the very nadir of the Depression, caught growers and trade unionists alike by surprise. Agribusiness, according to Donald Fearis, believed that Spanish-speaking farm workers were too terrified by the mass deportations of Mexican nationals (and their citizen children) then taking place in Los Angeles and other areas to stick their necks out in a strike.[7] But in the event, *la raza* was enraged, not intimidated. The cotton walkout was the largest agricultural strike in American history, and was, as we saw earlier, a partial success: failing to win union recognition but overcoming the growers' vow never to yield to strikers' wage demands.

The fighting spirit of the field workers of all races was magnificent, but it was virtually impossible to defeat the growers as long as local courts and sheriffs were firmly aligned with the vigilantes, and the state and federal governments stood on the sidelines. Despite innumerable protests to Governor Rolph about the terror in the cotton counties, he refused to order California's state police, the Highway Patrol, to protect strikers' civil liberties and lives. Both Sacramento and Washington, to be sure, sent fact-finders and official emissaries to the agricultural battlefields, most of whom corroborated the grievances of workers struggling to survive in the face of vicious wage cuts while growers were being bailed out by new federal agricultural subsidies. But fact-finding alone could not remove the iron heel from the neck of farm labor.

Moreover, the growers were not tempered by the unexpected tempest in the fields. In the Imperial Valley, where the CAWIU rallied in fall 1933 to support a new struggle of the lettuce workers, farm fascism assumed its definitive form. Whereas in previous struggles, the vigilantes tended to group themselves in posses of 40 to 150 men—usually farmers, ranch foremen, and local businessmen with personal stakes in the strike—the big grower-shippers in El Centro sought complete militarization of the Valley's middle and skilled working classes. The Imperial Valley Anti-Communist Association, formed in March 1934, refused to tolerate neutrality in the class struggle: "Operating on the coercive principle that anyone not willing to join the association was almost by definition a Communist or communist sympathizer, the group's leaders reported that within a little more than a week of its founding the association had between 7,000 and 10,000 members in the Imperial Valley."[8] Newspaper reporters were soon calling the Valley "California's Harlan County" in reference to the notorious Kentucky mining county where free speech had been extinguished by company gunmen.[9]

Indeed, the CAWIU soon lost any vestige of protected legal or public space in which to operate. "Officials announced that no meetings of any kind, anywhere, would be allowed in the Valley," A. L. Wirin, the chief counsel of the Southern California ACLU, told his members. "Meetings on a private lot, or in a private meeting hall have come under the ban. Half a dozen Mexican workers chatting on a street are a 'public meeting' and dispersed by the police."[10] When attorney Grover Johnson arrived in El Centro to file a writ of habeas corpus on behalf of jailed strike leaders, he and his wife were attacked and beaten in the street by anticommunists and then nearly lynched after seeking refuge in the jail. Public beatings were also administered to two other out-of-town lawyers, and Wirin, one of the most prominent civil libertarians in the state, was kidnapped by vigilantes ("one of whom he later claimed was a state highway patrolman in full uniform"), roughed up, robbed, threatened with death, and abandoned barefoot in the desert. Even Pelham Glassford, an anticommunist retired general who was the personal representative of Secretary of Labor Frances Perkins, was received with hostility and treated to anonymous death threats. As a Highway Patrol captain told two agents of the state labor commissioner after they had been detained and interrogated by vigilantes, "You men get out of here. You are hurting our work. We don't want conciliation. We know how to handle these people and where we find troublemakers we will drive them out if we have to 'sap' them."[11]

Chapter Eight

Thank the Vigilantes

The California farm workers emerged from the 1930s as political "for-gotten men." They could not count on any of the protections afforded their industrial co-workers, neither the assurance of minimal economic security nor the guaranteed right to help themselves through collective action.

—Donald Fearis[1]

In the summer of 1934, the San Francisco Embarcadero was the scene of the most important labor struggle in California history. It took the form of a three-act drama, beginning with a longshoremen's revolt that quickly grew into a maritime strike that closed every port on the Pacific Coast, then finally became a San Francisco general strike that lasted three days. A fourth, Armageddon-like act was only narrowly avoided. With employers screaming that a "red insurrection" was in progress, Governor Frank Merriam sent forty-five hundred heavily armed National Guard troops to San Francisco under the command of "outspokenly anticommunist" Major General David Barrows, whose military curriculum vitae, as Kevin Starr points out, included "the American Expeditionary Force sent to assist the White Russians in their counter-revolution against the Bolsheviks."[2]

The entire country watched in anxious suspense to see if General Barrows, as many conservatives hoped, would order his machine-gunners to massacre the local "Bolsheviks" on the waterfront. In the event, the maritime strikers, backed by a general strike representing the entire family of San Francisco labor, calmly crossed their arms and refused to back down, even after a major raid on the headquarters of the Marine Workers Industrial Union. But if a bloody showdown between the troops and strikers was averted, the Industrial Association, representing the city's largest employers, used the military occupation to unleash goon squads masquerading as "irate citizen vigilantes" upon the local Communist Party and other progressive groups, including Upton Sinclair's Epic (End Poverty in California) movement, whom it blamed for instigating and supporting the strike. In *The Big Strike*, radical journalist Mike Quinn recalled the notorious, week-long "anti-red" raids that began on July 17:

> The plan of attack was identical in every instance. A caravan of automobiles containing a gang of men in leather jackets, whom newspapers referred to as "citizen vigilantes," would draw up to the curb in front of the building. They would let fly a hail of bricks, smashing all windows, and then crash into the place, beating up anyone they found, wrecking all furniture, hacking pianos to pieces with axes, throwing typewriters out of windows, and leaving the place a shambles.
>
> Then they would get back into their cars and drive off. The police would arrive immediately, arrest the men who had been beaten up, and take command of the situation.[3]

With the complicity or participation of the San Francisco police, the vigilantes smashed up the offices of the *Western Worker*, beat three men senseless at the Workers' Open Forum, wrecked the Mission Workers' Neighborhood House, and were in the process of demolishing the interior of the Workers' School when they unexpectedly encountered Homeric resistance.

> Here [at the Workers' School] the vigilantes wrought havoc on the first floor, but when they attempted to mount the narrow staircase leading to the upper stories they were confronted by the huge bulk of David Merihew, an ex-serviceman who worked as a caretaker in the building. Merihew brandished an old cavalry saber in one hand and a bayonet in the other. Flourishing his weapons he beckoned to them to come ahead. They took a few steps forward and he slashed out with his saber, taking a huge chip out of the banister. The raiders discreetly retired and left the field to the police, to whom Merihew surrendered after striking a bargain with them not to turn him over to the vigilantes if he yielded his weapons.[4]

While Captain Joseph O'Meara of the San Francisco Red Squad was boasting that "the Communist Party is through in San Francisco—the organization can't face such adverse public sentiment," other communities were panicking at the specter of further general strikes and "Communist invasions" as luridly predicted by the press.[5] Employer groups in the East Bay and other areas sponsored "Leagues Against Communism" and debated how to best combat the "Red Menace":

> Vehement demands were made that public libraries be "purged" of all allegedly Red books. Other patriots wanted to reorganize the public school system on a basis of rigid censorship to make certain that no Red ideas were lurking in the primers. Some urged the institution of concentration camps, either in Alaska or on the peninsula of Lower California, to which all communists would be exiled.[6]

For veteran labor activists, of course, the return to vigilantism was déjà vu, recalling the free speech fights of 1910–12, the patriotic pogroms in fall 1917, and the attacks on the IWW in 1919 and 1924. But the outcome, this time around, was radically different: despite the threat of injunctions, machine guns, and vigilantes, the maritime core of the upheaval remained impregnable in the face of repression. To the surprise and consternation of employers across the country, the rank-and-file longshoremen led by Australian immigrant Harry Bridges won a spectacular victory over the shipping magnates and opened the door to new industrial unions. Within the next five years, this urban labor insurgency would sweep away most of the repressive apparatus of the open shop, including the shadowy urban vigilantes, the unconstitutional anti-picketing laws, even the "red" squads and labor spies.

But rural California was a different story. Here, to borrow an expression of Regis Debray's from the context of Latin America in the 1960s, the "revolution revolutionized the counterrevolution." What was universally perceived by agricultural elites as the "Communist victory" in San Francisco massively reinforced their determination not to yield an inch even to moderate unionism. Private violence, always in tandem with repression by local sheriffs, became better organized and more centralized than ever before in California history.

Camouflaged by the hysteria surrounding the general strike, Sacramento police—advised by William Hynes, former chief of the LAPD's infamous Red Squad—raided the state headquarters of the CAWIU, arresting veteran leader Pat Chambers, twenty-one-year-old Caroline Decker ("La Passionara of the cotton strike" according to Kevin Starr), and more than a dozen others. Eventually eighteen organizers would be indicted under the Criminal Syndicalism Act and eight convicted and imprisoned after the longest trial in state history. The CAWIU was forced to divert its resources from organizing in the fields to a desperate defense of its key personnel. Later their sentences would be reversed on appeal, but this "anti-red carnival," as McWilliams called it, "crippled and destroyed the Cannery and Agricultural Workers' Industrial Union. With their leadership in prison, the workers were momentarily demoralized, and the great wave of strikes subsided."[7]

Meanwhile a sinister new organization had emerged to regionally coordinate the struggle against striking farm workers and their embryonic unions. After defeating the CAWIU's last stand in the melon fields in spring 1933, the Imperial Valley growers decided to franchise their strikebreaking methods and militant antiradicalism to farmers in the rest of the state. The Associated Farmers of California—also inspired by Los Angeles's Merchants' and Manufacturers' Association and its statewide offspring, the Industrial Association—were "pledged to help one another in case of emergency. They agreed to cooperate to harvest crops in case of strikes and to offer their services to the local sheriff immediately as special deputies in the event of disorders arising out of picketing and sabotage."[8]

Although the roots of the organization were in the American Legion halls of El Centro and Brawley, the Associated Farmers—as Carey McWilliams emphasized—only became a statewide power because California's largest corporations (as well as reactionary newspapers like the *Los Angeles Times*) favored the institutionalization of the vigilante movement:

> The initial funds were, in fact, raised by Mr. Earl Fisher, of the Pacific Gas and Electric Company, and Mr. Leonard Wood, of the California Packing Company. At this meeting [the Associated Farmers' founding convention in May 1934], it was decided that farmers should "front" the organization, although the utility companies and banks would exercise ultimate control.... When one realizes that approximately 50 percent of the farm lands in Central and Northern California are controlled by one institution—the Bank of America—the irony of these "embittered" farmers defending their "homes" against strikers becomes apparent.[9]

The Associated Farmers provided a Pinkerton-like infrastructure of industrial espionage and employee blacklists to local growers, and acted as a powerful legislative lobby in all matters concerning farm labor. The organization opposed not only radical unionism, but collective bargaining and industrial mediation per se. It also agitated against urban workers and their new unions. The Associated Farmers stood, in short, for the untrammeled despotism of agribusiness over its workforce. With the Bank of America, Calpack, and the Southern Pacific Railroad as its ultimate ventriloquists, the organization asserted the hegemony of larger, labor-hating growers over the smaller farmers, Grangers, and businessmen who might incline toward negotiation or settlement with the unions. Philip Bancroft, the folksy grower son of the famous nineteenth-century historian who had mythologized the original vigilance committees, impersonated the "voice of the small farmer" when circumstances demanded nostalgic appeals to agrarian mythology, but the real decisions were made in bank chambers and corporate boardrooms.

One of the Associated Farmers' first projects was hiring LAPD Red Squad veteran William Hynes and Imperial County District Attorney Elmer Heald to assist Sacramento authorities in the aggressive prosecution of the CAWIU defendants. Indeed, the extensive application of the Criminal Syndicalism Act to destroy the left wing of the labor movement was one of the Associated Farmers' principal aims, and the group pledged each member as a special deputy to help quell organizing campaigns and strikes.[10] More ambitiously, it urged the mobilization of antilabor "citizen armies" along the lines of the Imperial Valley's Anti-Communist League. Across the state, these so-called California Cavaliers or Crusaders (with the American Legion halls as their recruiting depots) began to arm and drill. Meanwhile, with the Associated Farmers warning that the "Reds would be back," county supervisors passed anti-picketing ordinances; spies infiltrated harvest crews; ranchers strung barbed wire and even dug moats; and local sheriffs stocked tear gas and built stockades for the expected overflow of prisoners.

But the militarized Associated Farmers did not wait for strikes to come to them; they proposed to preempt through "systematic terrorization of workers in the rural areas" the very capacity for sustained class struggle. "We aren't going to stand for any more of these organizers from now on," boasted one grower. "Anyone who peeps about higher wages will wish he hadn't." Another leader of the Associated Farmers returned from Germany full of praise for Adolf Hitler (who "ha[d] done more for democracy than any man before him") and the admirable Nazi definition of citizenship: "you simply say that anybody who agrees with you is a citizen of the first class and anybody who does not agree with you is a non-voting citizen."[11] Fascism had become the explicit model for agricultural labor relations in California, and as the

1935 summer harvest season began, crosses burned on hillsides across the state, warning field hands that vigilantes were nearby and watching.

In Orange County, several hundred Mexican citrus strikers were rounded up by a small army of what McWilliams described as "special armed guards, under the command of former 'football heroes' of the University of Southern California masquerading as amateur storm troopers." Growers' sons were cheerfully advised by the Orange County sheriff to "shoot to kill" if necessary, and strikers' camps and meetings were teargassed. A few months later, a mob of Cavaliers in Santa Rosa seized five pro-labor "radicals," whom they paraded through the streets and then forced to kneel and kiss the American flag on the courthouse steps. When two refused to agree to leave town, they were beaten, tarred, and feathered, all to the editorial delight of the Hearst papers in San Francisco and Los Angeles.[12]

By 1936 the Associated Farmers exercised an extraordinary surveillance over every aspect of life in rural California. "There is no parallel," McWilliams wrote, "in any state for this interlocking network of farm employer organizations which represents a most unique combination of social, economic and political power."[13] Moreover, the organization was flush with cash from "a list of major backers reading like a Who's Who of California enterprise," while the arrival of a huge labor surplus of desperate Dust Bowl refugees made it easier than ever to find replacements for striking field hands or cannery workers.[14]

1936's most dramatic, if completely one-sided, battle took place in the lettuce-growing Salinas Valley, classic Steinbeck country. Here the Vegetable Packers Association—which followed its seasonal workforce from the Imperial Valley to the Salinas Valley and back each year—was the only agricultural union still active in the state. A whites-only affiliate of the AFL, it represented the largely Texan and Okie workforce in the packing sheds. (The field hands, ineligible to join the Association, were largely Mexican and Filipino.) The Associated Farmers of Monterey County, operating through a well-financed front group, the Citizens Association of the Salinas Valley, decided to lock out and destroy the union, replacing its core membership and "trouble raisers" with more docile workers.

The murder of the Vegetable Packers Association was planned with such meticulous precision, and involved such overwhelming superiority in firepower and legal resources, that it recalls the monstrous massacre of poor immigrants by millionaire ranchers chronicled in Michael Cimino's epic 1980 film, *Heaven's Gate* (a loose retelling of Wyoming's Johnson County Land War). To assure complete coordination between growers, police agencies, and citizen vigilantes, the Associated Farmers persuaded state officials to let Colonel Henry Sanborn, a notorious anticommunist who had trained vigilantes (called the "Nationals") during the 1934 San Francisco general strike, go to Salinas as generalissimo of all the antiunion forces. In that role, he stockpiled tear gas, installed machine guns in packing plants, and coordinated a "regular army" of local sheriffs and Highway Patrol officers whom Sacramento officials had placed at his disposal.

Sanborn also conscripted a vigilante militia, Imperial Valley–style. "On September 19 [1936]," writes Carey McWilliams, "the Sheriff emerged from his temporary retirement, and ordered a general mobilization of all male residents of Salinas between the ages of 18 and 45, and threatened to arrest any resident who failed to respond. In this manner the celebrated 'Citizens' Army' of Salinas was recruited."[15] In Sanborn's view, no one was too young to help defend white civilization in Salinas: the Boy Scouts were drafted as auxiliaries while the woodshop students in Salinas High School manufactured heavy clubs for bashing strikers. At one point, the town was barricaded and all highway movement was subjected to a strict dragnet: pedestrians and motorists wearing Roosevelt campaign buttons (it was an election year) had them ripped from their lapels.[16]

Not surprisingly, the lettuce lockout unfolded as a hyperbolic show of force tending toward atrocity. Chemical warfare was the order of the day and no privilege was attached to the workers' white skins. Police used copious quantities of tear gas and vomiting gas to disperse picket lines, then chased unionists down and savagely beat them. When eight hundred frightened people took refuge in the Salinas Labor Temple, "the police, deputies and highway patrolmen bombarded the Temple with tear gas, then, under protection of this barrage, moved in closer to toss tear and nausea gas and sulphur into the union headquarters. Hundreds of strikers fled the building, only to be met by police with even more tear gas bombs or deputized vigilantes wielding axe handles and clubs."[17]

The editor of the *San Francisco Chronicle*, Paul Smith, visited Salinas after two of his reporters had been seriously injured and threatened with lynching by vigilantes. He was incredulous to discover that the governor and attorney general of California, along with local officials, had willingly ceded the state's monopoly of legitimate violence to the fanatic Colonel Sanborn and the Associated Farmers. "For a full fortnight," he wrote, "the 'constituted authorities' of Salinas have been but the helpless pawns of sinister fascist forces which have operated from a barricaded hotel floor in the center of town."[18]

For the Okies, meanwhile, the lockout was a brutal mirror that reflected back not their traditional self-image as rugged white pioneer folk, but the growers' contempt for them as a "white trash" caste. They discovered that there were no exemptions, even for ancient Anglo-Saxons, from the racialized stereotypes structurally associated with farm labor in California. "I can remember," recalled one organizer, "the biggest impression I had of those days was watching those white people coming in from Oklahoma and Arkansas and Texas, coming in with their ingrown prejudices and hatred, and learning in the course of the strike that they had more in common with that worker with the brown skin and black skin than they had with the vigilantes with the white skin who were beating everybody up."[19]

The Salinas lockout, whether it was a preemptive strike against the AFL's involvement in agricultural unionism or a dead-serious rehearsal for American fascism, was a decisive victory for the Associated Farmers. It inspired the blitzkrieg tactics used the following year when another AFL affiliate, the Cannery Workers Union, attempted to strike the Stockton Food Products Company. "Instantly the call went forth for the usual 'citizens' army,'" writes McWilliams, and fifteen hundred loyal burghers, armed with shotguns and axe handles, punctually responded. Colonel Garrison, the hero of the El Centro vigilantes, was now president of the Associated Farmers, and he personally led the attack on the picket lines on April 24, 1937. "For over an hour, 300 pickets continued to fight 'coughing and choking,' as 'vigilantes' and 'special deputies' poured round after round of tear-gas bombs at them." When tear gas proved ineffective, Garrison's troops used buckshot, seriously injuring fifty workers.[20]

Kevin Starr observes that when some Stockton businessmen, supported by the local district attorney, realized that they lived in an occupied city subject to the whim of the Associated Farmers, they protested to Sacramento, asking that the National Guard be sent to restore order. "As in the case of Salinas, [Governor] Merriam refused; and Colonel Garrison and his army remained the preeminent force in the area." The governor, in other words, ratified the vigilantes as a legitimate authority: a dangerous recipe, complete with shades of shirts brown and black, for ceding all power to the growers and cannery owners.[21]

But it was hard to argue with success: in California's cities, as in the rest of the country, 1938 was a legendary year of sit-down strikes, mass pickets, and CIO fever. Yet the fields and packing sheds were eerily quiet, with no more than a dozen small strikes that involved less than five thousand workers, a bare fraction of the 1933–34 turnout. Nor did New Deal victories in Washington and Sacramento translate into any fundamental amelioration for farm laborers, who were excluded from the coverage of both the Wagner Act (NLRA) and the Social Security Act. The election of Democrat Culbert Olson as governor in 1938 may have been a victory for city unions (his first act in office was to pardon radical trade unionist Tom Mooney, who had been wrongfully imprisoned for twenty-two years). But legislative initiatives to help farm labor—even measures as seemingly non-controversial as forbidding the Highway Patrol from taking sides in labor disputes or assuring that relief was provided "solely on the basis of need"—were easily scuttled by a coalition of rural Democrats and Republicans.[22]

Although two union movements—the AFL's "federal" locals and the CIO-chartered United Cannery, Agricultural, Packing, and Allied Workers of America (UCAPAWA)—were now active in California agriculture, they shied away from apocalyptic confrontations in the fields. They focused their efforts instead on the organization (successful in Northern California) of town-based food-processing workers whose bargaining rights were protected by the NLRA and whose strike power was leveraged by the clout of powerful allies like the Teamsters or the Longshoremen.

If there was any doubt about the fundamental role played by private and state repression in turning field workers into the New Deal's pariahs—without a home in either its social programs or within the organized labor movement—it should have been dispelled by the fate of the strikes in the Marysville area, north of Sacramento. The first strikes took place during the spring and summer of 1939, followed by a large cotton strike in the fall in the San Joaquin Valley. The last great farm strikes of the 1930s, these were also the crowning victories of the Associated Farmers.

In Marysville, the fruit workers who lived in "Okieville" faced off against Earl Fruit, a subsidiary of the giant DiGiorgio empire—the General Motors of California agriculture. Only a minority of the members of the Associated Farmers in the area were actually farmers; the rest were realtors, publishers, mayors, and cops, including the Marysville police chief and the local Highway Patrol commander. Earl Fruit's bullying owner, Joseph DiGiorgio, could count on a vigilant, fully mobilized local ruling class to back up his ranch foremen and armed guards.

The first dispute broke out in the spring when, according to historian Donald Fearis, a popular foreman quit in protest over the company spies (a major Associated Farmers' initiative) who now infested every level of agricultural production. Earl lured striking crews back to work with the promise of higher wages and no sanction against strike leaders; when retaliatory layoffs quickly followed, angry workers called in the CIO, and by the beginning of the pear harvest in early July, Local 197 of UCAPAWA had put up picket lines around the orchards. The Sutter-Yuba Counties Associated Farmers immediately responded with the usual arrests, beatings, and death threats; the growers had earlier weighed the idea of a "citizens' army," but preferred the selective deputization of foremen and ranchers. They were temporarily foiled, however, when Okie women began to replace their arrested fathers and husbands on the picket lines. "The tenacity of the women and the supplying of food by friendly farmers and state agencies," writes Fearis, "momentarily kept the strike alive." But a raid on the union headquarters soon lopped the head off the strike and forced the workers either to return to work or leave the area.[23]

The fall UCAPAWA strike, detonated as in 1934 by wage-slashing, spread from an initial uprising at Madera across the entire San Joaquin cotton belt. Despite the passionate response from the largely Okie workforce, the union was unable to withstand the Associated Farmers' patent recipe of mass arrests, evictions, and vigilante terror. The fatal blow was delivered in the form of a furious attack on a strike rally in Madera in late October by three hundred growers armed "with clubs, tire chains, fan belts, and pick handles while the local sheriff stood by."[24]

The 1939 cotton strike was a last gasp: UCAPAWA soon abdicated field organizing to concentrate on processing and canning workers protected by the NLRA, while the Okies eventually found their way into supervisory jobs or moved to the cities to work in war plants.[25] Their place was taken from 1942 onwards by Mexican braceros as the racial caste system in California agriculture was restored under the aegis of an international treaty to address the wartime labor shortage.

Vigilantism, raised to the level of a science by the Associated Farmers, had inflicted a historic defeat not just on the super-exploited field workforce, but upon the entire project of progressive labor and New Deal reform in California. A U.S. Senate committee chaired by Robert LaFollette of Wisconsin, which investigated labor relations in California agriculture in 1939–40, would later conclude that the Associated Farmers had organized a conspiracy "designed to prevent the exercise of their civil liberties by oppressed wage laborers in agriculture, [which] was executed ruthlessly with every device of repression that antiunionism could muster." Moreover, when the employers' "complete monopoly in controlling labor relations"—a euphemism for a monopoly of violence—was combined with the workers' equally complete lack of political clout or legal status, "local fascism was the result."[26]

Road from Altar to Sasabe. A fee of $3.00 is charged to all using the unpaved road. It is the path going north for vans packed with immigrants and sometimes for trucks loaded with marijuana.

Chapter Nine

The Zoot Suit Wars

Let's get 'em! Let's get the chili-eating bastards!

—Anglo mob (Santa Monica, 1943)

Pearl Harbor gave California's anti-Japanese forces the license to execute the ethnic cleansing that had been their chief goal for more than a generation. No one argued more fiercely for the removal of the Nisei and their parents than the attorney general of California, Earl Warren, a longtime member of the Native Sons of the Golden West and political protégé of chief "Jap-swatter" V. S. McClatchy. Describing Japanese-Californians as a "fifth column" and an "Achilles heel," Warren convened a conference of state law enforcement officers in early February 1942 to demand relocation and internment of the Japanese. When it was pointed out that not a single instance of treason or sabotage had been attributed to the group, Warren responded that this was simply "ominous" proof of the Japanese refusal to report disloyalty.[1]

Meanwhile self-appointed vigilantes were throwing rocks through the windows of Japanese-owned stores and attacking Nisei teenagers in the streets, with warnings of greater violence to come. The campaign of intimidation was most serious in rural counties, as indicated in a memo sent to Sacramento in early January 1942 by state Department of Agriculture field staff: "They [Japanese-Americans] do not leave their homes at night.... The police authorities are probably not sympathetic to the Japanese and are giving them only the minimum protection. Investigations of actual attacks on Japanese have been merely perfunctory and no prosecutions have been initiated."[2]

In testimony before Congress, Earl Warren invoked these attacks as an argument for internment, warning that widespread and uncontrollable vigilantism would be inevitable unless President Roosevelt signed an executive order to deport the Japanese from the coastal area. California's chief law enforcement officer made it clear that he was completely sympathetic to the vigilante instinct: "My own belief concerning vigilantism is that the people do not engage in vigilante activities so long as they believe that their Government through its agencies is taking care of their most serious problems."[3]

German- and Italian-Americans, of course, were not interned on the West Coast, nor did Westerners seem to find anything unusual in the spectacle, common by late 1943, of Italian and German prisoners of war picking fruit and working on local farms. The real menace of the Nisei had been their economic success, and their internment forced a fire sale of their hard-earned assets, including farmland situated in areas already targeted for postwar residential development, like West Los Angeles. In the name of patriotism, their enemies were able to cherry-pick the fruits of two generations of diligent labor. Although some Nisei would return to farming after the war, they would never regain the influential position in California agriculture they had occupied in 1941.[4]

Despite the internment of the Japanese, bigotry took no rest. But the once despised Okies were now white citizens again, usefully toiling in aircraft plants or fighting with the U.S. Marines at Guadalcanal, and the "heroic'" Chinese and Filipinos were temporarily exempted from the Yellow Peril while it suited wartime propaganda purposes. Instead, the brunt of wartime racial prejudice and mob or vigilante violence, especially in the Los Angeles area, was directed against Chicano and African-American youth. The vigilante movement—deliberately instigated by the Los Angeles press—that is customarily recalled as the "zoot suit riots," was, of course, only the local franchise of a nationwide outburst of white violence during 1943's "summer of hate." In this larger context, two distinct species of white grievances—one rooted in workplace white privilege, the other in the social imaginary—were alloyed in different proportions in different cities.

First was the backlash of rank-and-file white war workers against the Fair Employment Practices Commission that Roosevelt had established in the face of threats by Black leaders to lead a march on Washington in 1941. By 1943, some real progress was finally being achieved in integrating shipyards, aircraft plants, and urban transit despite protests by segregated AFL locals and local demagogues. In defense boomtowns on the West Coast or in the Midwest, incoming streams of white and Black labor migrants from the Mason-Dixon states were competing over housing and services as well as seniority and skills. As a *Life* magazine article warned in a 1942 headline, "Detroit is Dynamite. It can either blow up Hitler or blow up the U.S."[5] Oakland and Los Angeles (where ten thousand Black in-migrants from Oklahoma and Texas arrived every month during 1943) were almost as volatile.[6]

Urban public space was the other arena where racist agitation sowed seeds of violence in different North American cities. Thanks in large part to reactionary newspaper campaigns, the "swing kid" subculture of the early 1940s, with its jive talk and "zoot suit" attire, had been conflated with a racialized and almost entirely imaginary menace of teenage gangsters and draft dodgers. Unlike the anti-Black backlash in the war plants, hysteria about "zooters" targeted different ethnic groups. In New York, despite hordes of similarly attired white youth, the problem zooters were largely identified as Black delinquents, and in Los Angeles, Blacks and especially Chicanos were singled out. In wartime Montreal, which had its own "zoot suit riot" in June 1944, the English-language press incited soldiers to violence against supposedly "anti-patriotic" Francophone youth who hung out (and competed for the attention of young females) in the same clubs and dancehalls as the military.[7]

The roots of the wartime zoot suit obsession go back to the national economic recovery in 1940–41, when newspaper editors, police chiefs, and ministers across the country began to complain about the rise of a flamboyant, antiauthoritarian youth culture based on the fashions of big-band swing and showing its most dangerous inclinations among minority youth. The chief complaint was that a new racial pride and generational insolence no longer acknowledged traditional color lines or segregated ethnic boundaries in public spaces like amusement parks, theaters, and transportation. (We have already seen, of course, a preview of this in the case of the proud and unsubmissive young Filipinos who collided with white supremacy in rural California dancehalls and honky-tonks in the late 1920s.) As Spike Lee portrays in the vivid, opening scenes of his film *Malcolm X*, the uninhibited exuberance of the zooters represented both embryonic cultural nationalism as well as the stirrings of an interracial youth culture. In response, a truly extraordinary amount of newsprint was expended in stern laments about declining social control of youth and wrathful tirades against the "new delinquency." In the opinion of local authorities, the children of color were out of control.[8]

The death of a Chicano teenager under confused circumstances near a ranch pond called Sleepy Lagoon in August 1942 provided the pretext for a sustained campaign by the Los Angeles daily press—especially the Hearst papers and the *Los Angeles Times*—against Chicano gangsters, *pachucos,* and zooters. Although the alleged crime wave was largely an editorial fabrication, it provided a lurid core for the coalescence of all kinds of wild allegations, including claims that Eastside youth were being groomed into a fifth column by the shadowy Sinarquista movement (a Mexican fascist group with only a handful of actual members in Southern California) and that "the Japanese, upon being evacuated, had incited the Mexican population of Los Angeles to violence." Such calumnies, of course, were nonsense—obscene, even—in the face of the number of posthumous Congressional Medals of Honor and Navy Crosses being awarded to Chicano youth in the Pacific. But as Carey McWilliams, who became the chair of the Sleepy Lagoon Defense Committee, emphasized, the Mexican-American contribution to the war effort was obscured by the incessant front page equation of Mexicans with crime. "Every Mexican youngster arrested, no matter how trivial the offense and regardless of his ultimate guilt or innocence, was photographed with some such caption as 'Pachuco Gangster' or 'Zoot-suit Hoodlum.'"[9]

By the spring of 1943, Los Angeles public opinion had been persuaded that gang violence was raging almost uncontrolled in the "disloyal" neighborhoods around the downtown area and east of the river. At the same time, Black-white workplace tensions were peaking over the impending federal integration of Los Angeles street car crews: a conflict that would eventually require army intervention to prevent mob violence. Added to this fraught mix was the chronic and unavoidable friction between different groups of young men—sailors, marines, war workers, neighborhood youth—as they competed for fun and female attention in crowded entertainment districts downtown, in Hollywood, and at the beach. What might have been, at most, minor scuffles or small riots between white sailors and Chicano and Black youth were magnified by newspaper hysteria with police complicity into a large-scale, if short-lived, vigilante campaign against Los Angeles's youth of color.

The foreshock was a riot at Venice Pier in mid-May. According to historian Eduardo Pagan, a false rumor that Chicanos had stabbed a sailor incited a mob hunt for revenge at the Aragon ballroom:

> As one eyewitness later said, "They didn't care whether the Mexican kids wore zoot suits or not, and for that matter most of the kids dancing were not in drapes—they just wanted Mexicans." When the dance ended and the Mexican-American teenagers started to leave the ballroom, a crowd of about five hundred sailors and civilians began to chase them down the boardwalk. "Let's get 'em," the mob shouted as they ran past the bingo parlors and concession stands. "Let's get the chili-eating bastards!"[10]

Several weeks later, following further small-scale confrontations between sailors and Chicano youth, a group of sailors returning to the Naval Armory in Elysian Park claimed they were attacked by zoot-suited youth from a nearby slum neighborhood. When the assault was reported to the LAPD, the cops formed a "Vengeance Squad," as they called it, but were unable to find the supposed assailants. As McWilliams points out, "the raid accomplished nothing except to get the names of the raiding officers in the newspapers and to whip up the anger of the community against the Mexican population, which may, perhaps, have been the reason for the raid." The next night, several hundred sailors in a fleet of twenty taxicabs cruised around the downtown and Eastside areas, beating up any zoot-suited Mexican youth they encountered; a ritual that was repeated for the next two nights without interference from the police, who, instead, "mopped up" after the military vigilantes by arresting any zooters or neighborhood youths they encountered.[11]

Egged on by papers like the *Los Angeles Daily News*, which warned "Zoot Suit Chiefs Girding for War on Navy," thousands of white servicemen and civilian youth, unimpeded by the police, gathered downtown on Monday, June 7, for a culminating night of infamy. Any young Chicano was fair game.

> Pushing its way into the important motion picture theaters, the mob ordered the management to turn on the house lights and then ranged up and down the aisles dragging Mexicans out of their seats. Street cars were halted while Mexicans, and some Filipinos and Negroes, were jerked out of their seats, pushed into the streets, and beaten with sadistic frenzy. If the victims wore zoot suits, they were stripped of their clothing and left naked or half-naked on the streets, bleeding and bruised. Proceeding down Main Street from First to Twelfth, the mob stopped

on the edge of the Negro district. Learning that the Negroes planned a warm reception for them, the mobsters turned back and marched through the Mexican east side spreading panic and terror.[12]

Although the servicemen wisely decided not to attack the Central Avenue ghetto, a Black war worker was pulled off a street car and one of his eyes gouged out. Carey McWilliams, a lawyer and civil-rights activist as well as a journalist, took affidavits from many of the victims, not more than half of whom were actually wearing zoot suits. Like the outbreak of a disease that spreads and becomes a national epidemic, the Los Angeles violence was immediately followed by other race riots and attacks on people of color across the country, finally culminating in the terrifying Detroit events of June 20–21, which took the lives of twenty-nine people. McWilliams, whose contemporary articles were unsurpassed in their honesty and passion, claimed that the riots had exposed "the rotten foundations upon which the City of Los Angeles had built a papier-mâché facade of 'Inter-American Good Will.'"[13]

Chapter Ten

Beating the UFW

It was like being in a war. They arrested farmworkers; they hit them with sticks. Everywhere you looked there were Teamsters. If the truckers saw that you had eagles on your car, they would stop you and break your windshield.

—UFW supporter (1973)[1]

As the war ended, sporadic racist attacks continued—terrorism against returning Nisei, arson against Blacks attempting to buy homes in white neighborhoods, and so on—but vigilantism appeared to have been put in mothballs. Its major constituency, the corporate farmers, no longer had to mobilize shotgun-wielding "citizen armies" when they could manipulate the Bracero Program to import strike-breaking labor and then, if the braceros themselves organized, call upon the Border Patrol to deport them. Indeed, the Border Patrol now became integral to the repressive relations of production in California agriculture: vigilante violence seemed less necessary when deportation could so easily dispose of impudent strikers.

Postwar attempts to organize farm labor, like the October 1947 strike against giant DiGiorgio in Kern County, were thus efficiently repelled by the use of imported strike-breakers, mass arrests, selective deportations, evictions of strikers' families, red-baiting by the California House Committee on Un-American Activities, and employer terrorism (one strike leader was shot in the head). The Associated Farmers also organized a

Citizens' Committee in support of DiGiorgio, but felt no need to arm its members with axe handles or send them out to storm workers' camps. After the defeat of the DiGiorgio strikers and a massive purge of the pro-union labor force in the Imperial Valley, any further attempt to bring collective bargaining to California agriculture seemed fruitless.

But the end of the Bracero Program in 1964 and the reemergence of a settled, family workforce made possible the new revolt in the fields led by the National Farm Workers Association (NFWA). The great Del-ano grape strike that began in 1965 was as unexpected as the 1933 cotton uprising and mobilized equal passion and commitment from an exploited workforce. The extraordinary endurance of the strikers and the charisma of the new union, with its appeal to both class and ethnic pride, shook the growers' belief in their own omnipotence. The strike faced the classical repertoire of intimidation by ranch foremen and se-curity guards, who turned dogs on them, ran them down in their pickup trucks, shoved shotguns in their bellies, and beat them with near impu-nity; yet such tactics only seemed to infuse *la huelga* with more ener-gy. Eventually, agribusiness with the biggest corporations, like United Fruit and DiGiorgio, in the fore decided to resurrect the Depression-era "armies of the night." The vigilantes this time around, however, weren't growers' sons or American Legionnaires, but highly paid members of the Teamsters' Union, imported by the hundreds to intimidate, beat, and drive away NFWA strikers.

By 1967, major employers had decided to sign sweetheart contracts with the Teamsters in order to preclude and sabotage organization by the farmworkers. Because farmworkers were not protected by the Na-tional Labor Relations Act, "there were no unionization elections or even attempts to ascertain the preferences of field workers covered by the [Teamster] contracts. Nor were the workers given an opportunity to ratify the contracts, although they were required to join the Teamsters and have weekly union dues deducted from their paychecks."[2] More-over, the Teamsters made little effort to conceal their disdain for their new, involuntarily conscripted members: "I am not sure," said Einar Mohn, head of the powerful Western Conference of Teamsters, "how effective a union can be when it is composed of Mexican-Americans and Mexican nationals with temporary visas."[3]

The Teamsters immediately enforced their scab agreements with such pervasive strong-arm tactics that farmworker leader César Chávez had great difficulty preventing his own outraged members from retaliating in kind. Confrontations in 1970 between the Salinas-area Grower-Shipper Association and the Teamsters, on one side, and the United Farm Workers Organizing Committee (UFWOC, formed when the NFWA merged with the Agricultural Workers Organizing Committee), on the other, evoked the worst memories of the 1936 lockout.

> Growers hired guards armed with shotguns to patrol their proper-ty, and Teamsters sent in thugs wielding baseball bats to frighten off the Chavistas. One of the most infamous of these goons ... was Ted "Speedy" Gonsalves, who wore black-and-white pinstriped suits and drove an armored limousine.... The imported thugs menaced pickets, pounded on the walls of rooms where UFWOC negotiators were meet-ing, and knocked over coffee cups and cursed at UFWOC members whom they encountered in restaurants.[4]

The terror was meant to remind farmworkers that growers and their vigilante henchmen were still the kings of the valley. The UFWOC's at-torney, for instance, was hospitalized after being beaten unconscious by Teamster goons; meanwhile, a foreman ran his tractor into pickets and the UFWOC (soon to be the United Farm Workers, or UFW) of-fice in Hollister was dynamited. César Chávez was jailed for refusing to comply with a one-sided court injunction to stop the boycott of scab lettuce. When Ethel Kennedy (Robert F. Kennedy's widow) came to vis-it Chávez in the Salinas jail, she was mobbed and physically threatened by several hundred opponents of the strike, including a large contingent from the local John Birch Society.

The growers' deployment of Teamsters as vigilantes and goons came to a climax during the brutal spring and summer of 1973, when UFW strikers attempted to picket the grape harvest as it moved from the Coachella Valley near Palm Springs to the San Joaquin Valley. Under the "mobbed-up" leadership of Frank Fitzsimmons, the Teamsters had become major supporters of Richard Nixon, supplying massive dona-tions and even physical muscle to his notorious reelection campaign in 1972. Now the Nixon White House, via Chief Counsel Charles Colson (later to be hired by the Teamsters), ordered the Justice Department and the National Labor Relations Board to side with Fitzsimmons and the growers against César Chávez's strikers.

The Pentagon first tried to break the UFW boycott by forcing Amer-ican troops to consume huge quantities of scab grapes: "the quantity of grapes shipped to U.S. forces in Vietnam increased from 555,000 to

2,167,000 pounds from 1968–69."[5] Then the Justice Department looked the other way as hundreds of Teamster goons, paid seventy dollars per day and wielding tire irons, terrorized the picket lines, beating up scores of strikers and their sympathizers, including a Catholic priest. When FBI agents learned from one of their informants that the Teamster leadership had ordered their beer-bellied thugs to "escalate the violence" by singling out strike leaders and picket captains for vicious hit-and-run attacks, the Justice Department did nothing to warn or protect the victims.

In Coachella, at least, the Riverside County sheriffs maintained neutrality and occasionally came to the aid of the UFW, but when the picket lines moved north to the San Joaquin, the strikers faced local sheriffs—shades of 1933, 1939, and 1947—who sided shamelessly with the growers and Teamster goons. Almost thirty-five hundred strikers were arrested and two were murdered. Twenty-four-year-old Nagi Dai-fullah, a Yemeni immigrant and UFW picket captain, was clubbed to death by a Fresno County deputy in August, and soon afterwards Juan de la Cruz was shot to death on a picket line near Arvin, not far from where one of the cotton strikers had been killed in 1933.

But 1973 was not 1933, and the UFW rank and file were eager to move toward a more active self-defense. In contrast to the situation forty years before, there was now a militant Chicano power movement in the cities that was ready to aid, and if necessary to raise hell on behalf of, the struggle in the fields. Precisely because he feared such counter-violence and likely radicalization, César Chávez made a fateful decision to shift the union's scarce resources away from the primary strike and toward intensification of the grape boycott. The union's sympathizers across the world, rather than its own rank and file in the fields, became the key actors in a struggle that was increasingly centralized and led by a small clique around Chávez. Although this strategy preserved nonviolence and generated huge public sympathy—some which helped win passage of the Agricultural Labor Relations Act of 1976 that finally provided farm labor with a modicum of rights—the growth of the boycott was matched by the atrophy of membership activism at the base. Despite an eventual peace treaty with the Teamsters (who promptly lost interest in agricul-tural labor), the union was unable to consolidate its gains or hold the ground it had won by heroic mass struggle.

Chávez had become an American saint by the time he died in 1993, and the UFW had become a beloved liberal cause. Yet paradoxically, most farmworkers remained unorganized, desperately poor, and largely invisible. In those heartlands of traditional farm fascism—the Salinas, San Joaquin, and Coachella-Imperial Valleys—indigenous immigrants from Mexico, Mixtecs especially, continue to labor in the early twenty-first century under conditions little different from those that the IWW protested in 1914 or against which the CAWIU rebelled in 1933. Indeed, looking back on the 1970s, it is hard not to conclude that once again, vigilantism and private violence, allied with local law enforcement and a tolerant federal government, had defeated an epic uprising of farm labor.

A group of twenty-seven people leave Sasabe, Mexico. Women and children are among them. The U.S. side of the border and the Buenos Aires National Wildlife Refugee and Arivaca are in the background. Daytime temperatures in the area reach 115 degrees. June 2004.

Chapter Eleven

The Last Vigilantes?

Americans Doing the Job Government Won't Do.

—Slogan of the Minuteman Project

There is extraordinary consistency in white prejudice over the last 150 years of California history. The wrath of nativists and vigilantes has always been focused on the poorest, most powerless, and hardest-working segment of the population: recent arrivals from Donegal, Guangdong, Hokkaido, Luzon, Oklahoma, and now Oaxaca. And the rant, as broadcast daily on dozens of AM hate radio programs in California and the Southwest, remains virtually the same as described by Steinbeck in 1939: "Men who had never been hungry saw the eyes of the hungry.... They said, 'These goddamned Okies are dirty and ignorant. They're degenerate, sexual maniacs. These goddamned Okies are thieves. They'll steal anything. They've got no sense of property rights.'"[1]

The most publicized of today's neo-vigilantes are the so-called Minutemen (actually a fissiparous miscellany of grouplets and leaders) who began their armed patrol of the Arizona-Mexico border, appropriately, on April Fools' Day 2005. The media-oriented, Tombstone, Arizona–based movement is the latest incarnation of anti-immigrant patrols that have plagued the borderlands for more than a decade. Vowing to defend national sovereignty against the "Brown Peril," a series of shadowy paramilitary groups, led by racist ranchers and self-declared "Aryan warriors"— and egged on by right-wing radio jocks—have harassed, illegally detained, beaten, and probably murdered immigrants crossing through the boiling cauldrons of the Arizona and California desert.

The Minuteman Project was a theater of the absurd as well as a canny attempt to move vigilantism back into the mainstream of conservative politics. The Tombstone organizers—a retired accountant and a former kindergarten teacher, both from Southern California —mesmerized the press with their promise of one thousand heavily armed super-patriots bravely confronting the Mexican hordes along the international border in Cochise County. In the event, they turned out 150 sorry-ass gun freaks and sociopaths who spent a few days in lawn chairs cleaning their weapons, jabbering to the press, and peering through military binoculars at the Saguaro-covered mountains where several hundred immigrants perish each year from heatstroke and thirst. "Armageddon on the border" that April was never very likely, if only because undocumented immigrants read or hear the news like everyone else. Confronted with the Minutemen and the hundreds of extra Border Patrol agents sent to keep them out of trouble, *campesinos* simply waited patiently on the Sonora side for the vigilantes to get sunburned and bored, and go home.

Yet it would be a mistake to underestimate the impact of the fanatics in camouflage suits: their successive farces in the desert (different Minutemen factions repeated their border patrols near San Diego in 2005 and 2006) have had an electrifying impact on the conservative grassroots. For the first time, the Bush administration has felt seriously embattled—not by Democrats (they would never be so impolite)—but by the anti-immigrant rebellion on its own flanks. In the fervid world of suburban Republican politics, the Minutemen have become superheroes fighting a criminal conspiracy (shades of the original "Yellow Peril") to flood the country with brown-skinned welfare cheats and future street gang members. The contradiction between shabby demagogues passing as vigilante warriors and their larger-than-life image in right-wing rhetoric, of course, is no greater than the contradiction between the Republican *herrenvolk*'s abhorrence of illegal immigration and their personal dependence upon Spanish-speaking slaves to blow-dry their lawns and wipe their babies' behinds.

The roots of this neo-vigilantism go back to 1996 and California's polarizing debate about Proposition 187, which proposed to deny public education and health services to undocumented people. The anti-Latino backlash which that evil sorcerer, former California governor Pete Wilson, helped summon to life, has failed to quietly die away as Karl Rove and other White House electoral strategists might have wished. Over the last decade, instead, the campaigns that originated in California—against immigrant social rights and the use of Spanish in the schools—have been exported to Arizona, Colorado, and several southern states with growing Latin American populations. Like earlier antiabortions protests (which culminated in right-wing terrorism), the vigilante movement offers a dramatic tactic for capturing press attention, galvanizing opposition to immigration, and shifting the balance of power within the Republican Party.

Moreover, to the discomfort of the White House, the Minutemen found a gushing (if inarticulate) admirer in California governor Arnold Schwarzenegger: "I think they've done a terrific job. They've cut down the crossing of illegal immigrants a huge percentage. So it just shows that it works when you go and make an effort and when you work hard. It's a do-able thing." Later, after furious Latino leaders accused him of "scapegoating and immigrant bashing," and even after President Bush had characterized the group as "vigilantes," Schwarzenegger defiantly reiterated that he would welcome the help of the Minutemen on the California border. (As he so often does, the "Governator" followed this with the non sequitur reassurance that he was a "champion of immigrants."[2])

Veteran political observers who thought this was all just a tempest in a teapot were subsequently stunned in November 2005 when one of the founders of the Minuteman Project, Jim Gilchrist, running as a third-party candidate with the endorsement of the Border Patrol union, won almost as many votes as the Democratic nominee in an Orange County congressional race. In subsequent Southern California races, like the 2006 special election for a successor to that disgraced crook, Congressperson "Duke" Cunningham, Republicans have competed for endorsements from prominent vigilantes and Brown Peril demagogues. Meanwhile Gilchrist and his supporters have made Costa Mesa, an Orange County town with a large Latino minority, into a showpiece for their policies—especially the deployment of local police to check immigration status. In their Manichaean worldview, there are no neutrals: you're either part of the border patrol or a felonious alien.

Such bigotry in a state with a rapidly emerging Latino majority might seem like the last gasp of a dying culture, and indeed it probably is. But for the moment, at least, the neo-vigilantes are high in the saddle, their eyes firmly turned backward to that glorious California past exemplified by the Glanton gang, the Order of Caucasians, the Native Sons of the Golden West, the American Protective League, the Ku Klux Klan, and the Associated Farmers.

Part II

MEXICO: CAUGHT IN THE WEB OF U.S. EMPIRE

Justin Akers Chacón

Fourteen-year-old Sixto Mendez Goyazo, from Chiapas, has never attended school. He is illiterate. He does not know the United States and does not know where he is going to be taken to work after crossing the border at Sasabe. Sixto travels with his thirty-two-year-old uncle Felipe Coyazo, a peasant who has no job in Chiapas because imports of subsidized American corn have driven the price so low that local farmers can't make a living. Sixto wants to work in the U.S. to support his parents.

Introduction

Humans have always been on the move, and mass migrations punctuate the great epochs of human history. Early anthropologists believe that "Lucy," the first archeological humanoid, died while migrating.[1] Most people extricate themselves from familiar environs only when their survival and well-being are in jeopardy. As of 2004, roughly one in every thirty-five people was an international migrant.[2] If they all lived in the same place, they would constitute the world's fifth-largest country. Modern immigration is motivated by the same human desires for sustenance, exacerbated by the destabilizing effects of global capitalism, although the debate is often "nationalized" by immigration opponents to deprive it of this essential context. Corporate capitalism, also called *neoliberalism* by its detractors, dictates that state policy decisions favor profitability over social sustainability—the interests of corporations and investors over those of workers, indigenous peoples, the world's poor, and the environment.

Corporate capitalism has also dictated a single development strategy for poor nations, a market-driven, private sector–led, export-based strategy that opens them up to foreign capital and foreign investment.[3] What's more, the practical application of neoliberalism has redefined the role of the state in relation to its people on the one hand and the imperatives of the global capitalist system on the other.[4] Consequently, wealthy nations are able to reassert control over developing nations, creating a situation reminiscent of the colonial period that divided nations into rich and poor in the first place. Government-directed redistributive processes that fund social welfare, investments in infrastructure, housing, health care, job creation, and education have been dramatically reduced or dismantled. Instead, government intervention is focused on creating a pro-business climate. Regulations and restrictions on the movement of corporations and concentration of capital have been dismantled, allowing them to exert nearly omnipotent influence over all aspects of daily life.[5]

Exported from the world's most powerful nations (particularly the United States), and enforced through the policies of global financial institutions such as the International Monetary Fund (IMF), the World Bank, and the World Trade Organization (WTO), neoliberal policy has assimilated governments and capitalist classes across the globe. Over the last few decades, radical, internal economic reorganizations have displaced millions of workers, primarily in less developed countries, sending them on a desperate odyssey to find work elsewhere, and triggering mass out-migration from poorer countries to wealthier ones. Most immigrants choose their destinations on the basis of proximity, job availability, and the hope of attaining some degree of social security—or in some cases where an existing economic interrelationship facilitates easier movement.[6] For instance, it is estimated that up to 180 million people worldwide now live outside the countries where they were born, with 40 percent moving into more developed nations, which tend to have the most stable economies and encourage immigrant labor as a means of depressing wages.[7] Immigrants are also recruited to fill labor shortages in particular industries periodically, which is why immigrants in Spain, Italy, and France often do many of the same jobs that Mexicans do in the United States.

"Neoliberal immigration"—in other words, displacement accompanied by disenfranchisement and often internal segregation in host countries—has been implemented on an international scale with the GATS (General Agreement on Trade in Services) Mode 4 stipulation within the World Trade Organization, which deals with the migration of "natural persons." Mode 4 codifies the legality of guest-worker programs, or the relocation of the displaced as temporary workers in foreign countries. GATS 4 legitimizes the denial of citizenship rights for guest workers, and binds them to individual employers. This is allowed on the basis that migrants are "service providers" rather than workers, and their movement across borders is "trade" rather than migration. Thus they are not entitled to protection under the minimal standards established by the International Labor Organization or the laws of whichever host country they work in. The language of Mode 4 only guarantees migrant workers the protections afforded them in their home countries.

According to Basav Sen, immigrant rights activist and journalist,

> In practice, [GATS 4 is] meaningless—being in a foreign country, they will lack physical access to labor unions, legal services, human rights organizations, and courts in their own country. Even in the extremely unlikely event that they were to surmount these barriers and attempt to file legal proceedings in their home country against their employer, the jurisdiction of these courts in most cases will not apply because the abuse will have occurred outside the territory of the worker's home country. [With multinational corporations,] it's also quite likely that the employer will be based in a third country.[8]

The global relocation of peoples happens regardless of where political borders are located, since the migration of peoples—much like the migration of corporations—is the result of global economic transactions. As Nestor Rodriguez explains, "The crisis of the border is not that 'illegal aliens' are swarming across the U.S.-Mexico Border, but that global capitalist growth is overwhelming nation-states as units of socio-economic development."[9] In other words, while global immigration is instigated by an increasingly internationalized economy, the reaction to it has been the retrenchment of national borders and the resurgence of the politics of exclusion. The Far Right blames social and economic problems on foreign-born workers, a refrain that has gained currency in an environment where war, poverty, and class conflict prevail.

In the United States, this attack on immigrants comes on the heels of one of the greatest transfers of wealth from the poor to the rich in the nation's history. According to the Center on Budget and Policy Priorities, the total cost of the Bush administration's tax cuts will equal $3.9 trillion, reducing revenue by $297 billion in 2004 and reaching a whopping $600 billion in the year 2014, and will primarily benefit the mega-rich.

> The tax cuts have conferred the most benefits, by far, on the highest-income households—those least in need of additional resources—at a time when income already is exceptionally concentrated at the top of the income spectrum.... The top 1 percent of households will receive tax cuts averaging almost $35,000—or 54 times as much as that received on average by those in the middle of the income spectrum....The tax cuts will confer more than $30 billion on the nation's 257,000 millionaires in 2004 alone.[10]

Another form of economic class war is taking place through the coordinated suppression of the minimum wage. According to a study conducted by the Economic Policy Institute,

> The inflation-adjusted value of the minimum wage is 26% lower in 2004 than it was in 1979. In addition, comparing the wages of minimum wage workers to average hourly wages, we find that the wages of minimum wage workers have not kept up with the wages of other workers. The minimum wage is 33% of the average hourly wage of American workers, the lowest level since 1949.
>
> Congress has not increased the minimum wage in seven years—the second-longest stretch of government inaction since the minimum wage was enacted in 1938. When Congress does not increase the minimum wage, the minimum wage continues to lose value.[11]

Another revealing study by the Economic Policy Institute shows that the recovery after the economic downturn of 2001 has not been equitable:

> Corporate profits have risen 62.2% since the peak, compared to average growth of 13.9% at the same point in the last eight recoveries that have lasted as long as the current one. This is the fastest rate of profit growth in a recovery since World War II. Total labor compensation has also turned in a historic performance: growing only 2.8%, the slowest growth in any recovery since World War II and well under the historical average of 9.9%. Most of this growth in total labor compensation has been accounted for by rising non-wage payments, like health care and pension benefits. Rapidly rising health care costs and pension funding requirements imply that these higher benefit payments are not translating into *increased living standards* for workers, but are rather just covering the higher costs of health care and pension funding. Growth in total *wage and salary income*, the primary source of take-home pay for workers, has actually been negative for private-sector workers: -0.6%, versus the 7.2% gain that is the average increase in private wage and salary income at this point in a recovery.[12]

Pundits on immigration are far too willing to edit corporate America out of the script in their blame game. By consciously ignoring the roles of big business and the government in driving down wages for American workers, they instead point the finger at immigrants, whose culpability becomes "conventional wisdom," repeated ad nauseum by the corporate media. Wealthy interests in the United States have been able to blend into the background on the national political stage, an artful feat considering that they are the ones to blame for declining working conditions and living standards, not immigrants.

Lastly, the national debate over immigration takes place against the backdrop of massive spending on the war in Iraq. According to a January 2006 study conducted by Columbia University economist Joseph E. Stiglitz and Harvard lecturer Linda Bilmes, the total costs of the war could *top the $2 trillion mark* should the U.S. remain in Iraq through 2010. As of January 2006, according to a Marine Corps spokesperson, this works out to about *$4.5 billion a month* in military "operating costs" alone (to say nothing of the costs of the procurement of new weapons and equipment).[13]

Overall military spending in 2005 was a whopping $419.3 billion, 41 percent more than in 2001. Meanwhile, the Bush administration unveiled a massive round of spending cuts in 150 areas of the federal budget in 2005, "eliminating dozens of politically sensitive domestic programs, including funding for education, environmental protection and business development, while proposing significant increases for the military and international spending."[14] It is amidst this monumental transfer of wealth from the working class to the U.S. war machine and corporations that immigrants now find themselves in the crosshairs of the U.S. Congress, a compliant media, and a host of well-funded and well-placed anti-immigrant apparatchiks.

While this book will focus primarily on the phenomenon of immigration across the U.S.-Mexico border, an awareness of the international context is necessary to fully appreciate its significance. Far-right racist movements like the Minutemen have their precursors both in other countries and in the U.S. For instance, western European countries have seen the rise of substantial anti-immigrant political movements, coinciding with economic restructuring programs designed to reduce spending in the public sector. In France, the National Front, an overtly fascist organization that promotes opposition to immigrants as its central crusade, has witnessed an alarming degree of success in elections like those held for the presidency in 2002. The growth of the Far Right has been aided by the government of Jacques Chirac, eager to blame social woes on immigrants.

In late 2005, the senseless deaths of two immigrant youths—racially profiled by police and chased to their deaths by electrocution while hiding behind a power transformer—sparked mass protests in the working-class, North African suburbs outside of Paris. The protests spread across the neglected, immigrant districts in at least nine surrounding towns, reflecting the growing disaffection of the predominantly Muslim communities. A third of an estimated six million citizens of North African descent in France live in suburban ghettos. Unemployment among Algerians and Moroccans, the largest immigrant groups, hovers above 30 percent, compared with a nationwide rate of 9.6 percent. Christophe Bertossi, an immigration specialist at the French Institute of International Relations in Paris, points to the real source of the conflict. "Behind [the] veil of equality, discrimination flourishes, feeding longstanding racial divisions and depriving immigrants of wealth and opportunity."[15]

The response of French Interior Minister Nicolas Sarkozy was to call the protesters "scum," vowing to "clean" the suburbs of their "riff-raff" and fight a "war without mercy." In early 2006, he introduced new exclusionary legislation that promised to restrict mostly Arab and Muslim working-class immigrants from entry (as well as introduce a guest-worker program), declaring, "we no longer want an inflicted immigration, we want a chosen immigration."[16]

It is also important to recognize that the criminalization of migration is also playing itself out within "worker-exporting" nations. For the five hundred thousand Guatemalan migrants in Mexico, for example, racial profiling and violence at the hands of corrupt law enforcement agents are common features of daily life. According to José Luis Soberanes, president of the Mexican National Human Rights Commission, "One of the saddest national failings on immigration issues is the contradiction in demanding that the North respect migrants' rights, which we are not capable of guaranteeing in the South."[17]

Like their counterparts in the United States, business interests in Mexico see the value of employing vulnerable Guatemalans in order to drive down wages overall. Since current law in Mexico designates undocumented migration a felony (much like what the notorious Sensenbrenner Bill seeks), and since parts of southern Mexico suffer from chronic labor shortages due to out-migration to the north, Guatemalan workers are another addition to the internationally dispossessed working class. Their migration, segregation, impoverishment, and victimization make for "good business."

This pattern of exploitation, violence, and attacks on immigrants is playing itself out in country after country. The scenario of orchestrated campaigns targeting immigrant communities (particularly those of color) is playing itself out with Moroccan immigrants in Spain, eastern

Europeans in England, Turkish migrants in Germany, and Koreans in Japan. In the United States, a similar process has been underway since September 11, with the detention, deportation, and racial profiling of Arabs and Muslims providing a precedent for racially and politically motivated attacks on Mexican migrant workers. The attack on Mexican workers is also bound up with a long and ugly history of victimization based on their segregated status within the United States.

Parts one and two of this book will highlight the historical inter-relations between the United States and Mexico, especially U.S. expansionism and the nexus between Mexican workers and the U.S. economy. My premise is that Mexican workers are an integral and inseparable part of the U.S. working class, despite the presence of border walls. Mexican workers, since the early twentieth century, have provided necessary labor for U.S.-based capitalist enterprises, both within the United States (as conquered labor, migrant labor, and "guest-workers") and in Mexico proper (laborers in maquiladoras and multinational corporations).

While supporters pay homage to the borderless world of the "free market" (i.e., corporate hegemony and the absolute freedom of movement for capital and the wealthy), they complain bitterly about the transnational migration of displaced workers. Increased immigration has become a stalking horse issue for politicians seeking to build their careers and augment the power of capital over labor through the criminalization of trans-border movement. In other words, concomitant with the "denationalization" of the global economy is the "renationalization" of politics in the form of an intensive, state-directed orientation on border enforcement and immigration restriction.[18] While global transportation networks have made it easier for goods to traverse the world in short order, newly reinforced borders are designed to obstruct, control, and regulate the movement of workers.

Part three explains why the contours of the capitalist system require these obstacles as a means to foster divisions in the working class. Within the context of the class system, the power of workers to negotiate a larger share of the wealth they produce—in the form of wage increases, social welfare, and democratic rights—is in direct proportion to their ability to engage in collective struggle: unionization, strikes, social protest, and other forms of organized resistance. The less unified workers are (because of borders, restrictions on political participation, and the perception of cultural difference), the more power capital has to impose its conditions on individual workers.

By exercising a monopoly over the granting of citizenship, the capitalist class (via its political representatives in the state) is able to create tiers of integration/segregation within the working class, and thus reinforce the physical, cultural, and political isolation of its various sections. These chapters will chronicle the genesis and evolution of immigration policy as a means to weaken the labor movement and prevent its cohesion, institutionalize racial, national, and political discrimination, and fragment working-class consciousness.

Furthermore, I will show how immigration is politicized in times of economic stagnation or downturn and during periods of social polarization. Often, perceptions of immigration are projected through the lens of foreign policy objectives, as a means to rally domestic support from the working majority for the external aims of the state, which represents the goals of the most preponderant sections of capital.

For example, chapter 25 examines the changing dimensions of immigration discourse since September 11, and how the U.S.-Mexico border has been ramped up in the public consciousness as a major battleground in the "War on Terrorism." All immigrants and border crossers now carry the stigma of "potential terrorists" and bear the burden of racial profiling, increased harassment, and outright violence. Later chapters will illustrate how the lack of a cohesive political opposition and the complicity of the Democratic Party in the calls for "immigration crackdowns" allow the Far Right to capture the political high ground on the issue and advance their extremist agenda into the mainstream.

Anti-immigrant movements and politicians have inflated the issue into a "national crisis." They appeal to racism and xenophobia to shape the national discourse, and are the primary sources for a host of dubious (yet almost universally accepted) assumptions about the negative consequences of immigration.

These groups seek to cultivate a following among disaffected native-born workers, especially in times of economic uncertainty. Shrouding themselves in populist language as "defenders" of the interests of citizens, they seek to promote the idea that migrant workers are a source of competition for finite resources as well as social and cultural "degeneration." Immigration opponents also attempt to leverage their activism against corporations, since big business is eager to maintain access to low-wage, disenfranchised labor and the dollars it generates.

When racial animosity seeps into mainstream debate, as chapters 27 and 28 will argue, extreme-right formations are legitimized and reactivated, and their conclusions about the need for racial violence are allowed to gain a wider hearing. And whatever the schisms between business interests and the Far Right, the debate is carried out from a common starting point: that immigrant workers should not have access to the basic human and democratic rights of the native-born. That is why part four will focus on the need to rethink our understanding of immigration in the context of a general struggle for social justice, and what it will take to build a movement for immigrant rights that advances collective opposition to borders and immigration restrictions while supporting fundamental and absolute equality for all working people.

Chapter Twelve

Conquest Sets the Stage

It is common among many in the anti-immigrant camp to ask why Mexicans don't just "go back to their own country." What most fail to realize (intentionally or not) is that many of the states that make up the United States used to form the northern portion of Mexico. This territory only became part of the United States after the Mexican-American War of 1846–48. The war proved to be a decisive turning point in relations between the United States and Mexico and capped a period of aggressive Anglo-American conquest and expansion across the North American land mass. Underwritten by southern slave and northern industrial interests, expansionists found northern Mexican territories ripe for the taking. Mexico was especially vulnerable because it was in the throes of civil strife, and successive governments were incapable of committing sufficient resources to settle the far north. The expropriation and annexation of northern Mexico was conducted under a direct military occupation by U.S. forces. It was legally enshrined by the imposition of the Treaty of Guadalupe Hidalgo in 1848, whose ratification by the Mexican government was a precondition for troop withdrawal. The treaty ceded California, Arizona, New Mexico, Nevada, Utah, Colorado, and parts of Wyoming and Oklahoma. It also forced Mexico to drop any further claim to Texas. As a form of conscience-cleansing, the U.S. government gave Mexico the symbolic payment of $15 million for what amounted to nearly half of Mexico's land and three-fourths of her natural resources.

The conquest of Mexico by the United States demonstrated the global-historic process by which wealthier, industrializing nations forcibly subdue less developed nations for the purpose of economic exploitation. One offspring of such conquest is racist ideology, generated and perpetuated by the intellectuals and politicians on the payroll of the dominant economic interests. The conquest of northern Mexico found upwards of 125,000 Mexicans crossed by a new border, one that defined them as foreigners in their own ancestral lands. The doctrine of Manifest Destiny defined the relations between incoming Anglo migrants and the Mexicano population in the unequal terms of conquerors and the conquered.[1] According to historian Reginald Horsman, the notion of Manifest Destiny encapsulated a host of fabricated theories that sought to justify the nullification of Mexican and Indian sovereignty and territorial integrity in tandem with westward expansion.

> By 1850, the emphasis was on the American "Anglo-Saxon" as a separate, innately superior people who were destined to bring good government, commercial prosperity, and Christianity to the American Continents and to the world. This was a superior race, and inferior races were doomed to subordinate status or extinction.[2]

The birthing cry of American imperial ascendancy, Manifest Destiny was a crude materialistic philosophy that proclaimed the economic and political superiority of U.S. institutions, and declared that capitalism and the plantation system had the right to transcend borders and expropriate the territories of others if they were not able to properly defend them. As early as 1801, Thomas Jefferson stated:

> However our present interests may restrain us within our limits, it is impossible not to look forward to distant times, when our rapid multiplication will expand beyond those limits, and cover the whole northern if not the southern continent.[3]

In order to condition the American laboring classes to support the project of expansion, the doctrine promoted the superiority of European Americans while promising that the newly acquired lands would be available to the poor workers and farmers who did the fighting.[4]

Meanwhile, Mexicans residing in the newly acquired portions of the United States were reduced to second-class citizenship. While the Treaty of Guadalupe Hidalgo contained a set of guarantees protecting the land and voting rights of Mexicans, "American local, state, and national courts later ruled that the provisions of the treaty could be superseded by local laws."[5] Anglo economic interests used the federal government, in the form of the Federal Land Act of 1851, to deprive Mexicans of their land, and state and local governments to implement a Jim Crow–like social structure across the Southwest.[6] Most Mexican land-holdings were nullified in the decades following the war, reducing the majority to the ranks of the working class.

In the years preceding the conquest of Mexico, an ideological ferment took place that conditioned the process of expansion. The idea of a distinct "Anglo-Saxon" race, superior in composition to the other inhabitants of North America, permeated national discourse leading up to the conflict. According to this view, Mexican peoples were inherently inferior to Anglos, on the grounds that they were "mongrelized" by the fusion of Indian and African blood with that of the European Spaniard. American intellectuals and political leaders with ties to expansionist interests gave vocal and written expression to the self-serving idea that Mexicans comprised a "sub-species," a fact that nullified any claims to sovereignty. Richard Henry Dana, a famous nineteenth-century congressman and advocate of northern commercial expansion into Mexican territory, described Mexicans as an "idle, shiftless people" and proclaimed "[I]n the hands of an enterprising people, what a country this might be!"[7] Waddy Thompson, a southern diplomat and career politician from South Carolina who became a national figure through his advocacy of U.S. territorial expansion into Texas, shared these views. In his famous autobiography, *Recollections*, published on the eve of the Mexican American War, he concluded:

> That the Indian Race of Mexico must recede before us ... is quite as certain as that is the destiny of our own Indians ... [and that Blacks in Mexico are] the same lazy, filthy and vicious creatures that they inevitably become where they are not held in bondage. [Overall, Mexicans are] lazy, ignorant, and of course, vicious and dishonest.[8]

This unabashed racial disgust provided ideological cover for the land-grab of U.S. expansionism, a process well under way by the time the ideologues of race had begun to promote their theories. Westward expansion began as an outlet for the pressures of class inequality, with poor farmers and laborers migrating into the western territories (Indian and Mexican lands) to seek opportunities denied them in the established states, where land was concentrated in the hands of the privileged few. Out-migration was encouraged by elites as a means to diffuse class consciousness, and to turn European workers against native peoples and Mexicans, for whom they now competed for territory. Ultimately, these "pioneers" paved the way for later land consolidation in the hands of the railroads, mining, and agricultural interests.

Between the years 1820 and 1924, 36 million global workers entered the United States, and between 1820 and 1850, over 4 million people moved to the West.[9] Many of the early German and Irish immigrants, persecuted as "invading hordes," poured out into the frontier with the hope of acquiring land. Immigrants were derided from the highest levels of society. For instance, Ben Franklin openly queried,

> Why should the Palatine boors be suffered to swarm into our settlements, and by herding together establish their Language and Manners to the Exclusion of ours? Why should Pennsylvania, founded by the English, become a Colony of *Aliens*, who will shortly be so numerous as to Germanize us instead of us Anglifying them, and will never adopt our Language or Customs, any more than they can acquire our complexion.[10]

Though targets of bigotry themselves, these migrants often adopted the racist ideology directed at them by the expansionists, and became the bulwarks of territorial conquest. As labor historian Sharon Smith explains, the European-American working class supported the project of westward expansion because of the way in which class consciousness developed among American workers: First, the lack of a feudal tradition in the United States meant that pre-industrial workers did not have the experience of forming organizations in the struggle for democratic rights that workers in countries like England and France experienced. Class consciousness was therefore coopted by bourgeois parties that incorporated populist platforms. Second, rapid industrialization in the United States enabled a large number of workers to become high-level managers and/or explore their own entrepreneurial pursuits. Third, the workforce of the United States was stratified and segregated, and legally subdivided by a constellation of laws underpinned by a "divide and conquer" strategy by the American ruling class. Women, African-Americans, and various groups of immigrant and native-born workers were consistently pitted against each other by unscrupulous employers, who were backed up by their allies in Congress and the White House. These factors inhibited the formation of independent working-class consciousness—thereby facilitating racial and national divisions within the class—and also allowed for the penetration of the ruling-class ideas of the day: racism, expansion, and conquest.[11]

Believing themselves entitled to the lands, European-American migrants moved westward in increasing numbers, expecting their passage to be sanctioned and ultimately protected by the U.S. government. The "Indian Wars," which stretched across the nineteenth century in tandem with forays of expansion, reflected the increasing willingness of the federal government to intervene to protect the land claims of migrants.[12]

Thus, from the very beginning, racism defined relations between the incoming Anglo settlers and the Mexican population, as well as between the two nations subsequently. The process of expansion ultimately opened up Indian (and later Mexican) territories for the proliferation of the plantation system and industries such as the railroads.[13] The acquisition of the Mexican north proved a boon for the U.S. economy, as this region contained 75 percent of Mexico's natural resources. The new border, open for all intents and purposes until the advent of a need for "managed" immigration in the twentieth century, served as the means through which the United States asserted its claims on the newly acquired territory. Nevertheless, U.S. economic interests "continued to consider the land below the border as a storehouse of treasure and opportunity."[14] In other words, in the minds of the expansionists, the border served primarily as the next jumping-off point for further U.S. penetration into Mexican territory.

While some in Washington clamored for the acquisition of *all* Mexican territory, corporate interests turned to foreign investment as a means of extracting profit without having to provide for the maintenance of a colonial regime. Enabled by the compliant dictatorship of Porfirio Diaz (1876–1911), U.S. capital flooded into the veins of the Mexican economy.

Mexico's own economic development had been deformed and stunted through the last two centuries by the suffocating bequest of Spanish colonialism: a decrepit, semi-feudal agricultural system retained by an entrenched oligarchy and an authoritarian church. Successive civil wars and the incessant circling of foreign invaders (Mexico suffered an average of one invasion every ten years between the years of 1821 and 1920[15]) encouraged U.S. administrations to periodically intervene in the affairs of Mexico to ensure pro-U.S., pro-business conditions.

These interventions were increasingly imperative, as Mexico became an important repository of U.S. capital investment in the period after the war. When strong-arm diplomacy didn't work, the U.S. relied on the military. During the Mexican Revolution, for instance, U.S. troops invaded Mexican soil on at least two occasions in order to tilt power away from leaders deemed a "threat" to Yankee business interests.[16]

Mexico was not the only victim of U.S. meddling. By the late nineteenth century, American finance capital began to assert itself across the globe. V.I. Lenin described this process of "imperialism" in the following way:

> Monopolist capitalist combines—cartels, syndicates, trusts—divide among themselves, first of all, the whole internal market of a country, and impose their control, more or less completely, upon the industry of that country. But under capitalism the home market is inevitably bound up with the foreign market. Capitalism long ago created a world market. As the export of capital increased, and as the foreign and colonial relations and the "spheres of influence" of the big monopolist combines expanded, things "naturally" gravitated toward an international agreement among these combines, and toward the formation of international cartels.[17]

By the turn of the twentieth century, U.S. capital extended far beyond the Mexican border, controlling important sectors of the Mexican economy, such as oil, railroads, mining, and other capital-intensive industries. As journalist-historian John Ross explains:

> Famous American fortunes were made in Porfirian Mexico. Rockefeller's Standard Oil bought in on the ground floor of development. The refined, art-loving Guggenheims befouled the air of El Paso-Juarez with their ASARCO refinery for a century. J. P. Morgan established banks and annexed great swatches of the Mexican countryside with greenbacks. Railroad tycoon Jay Gould hooked up with Ulysses Grant, but went broke on the Mexican Southern Railroad to Diaz's home in Oaxaca. The Hearsts claimed enormous tracts of Mexican forest lands in the Chimilapas on the Oaxacan Isthmus and the Tarahumara Sierra of Chihuahua. The volume of U.S. business ... jumped 14 times during Diaz's immense tenure.... The U.S. dominated commercial trade, with 51 percent of the market ... [and] had a total $646 million USD investment in the continuing stability of the Mexican economy.[18]

By the 1920s, U.S. interests controlled 80 percent of Mexican railroads, 81 percent of the mining industry's total capital, and 61 percent of total investment in the oil fields.[19] The railroads, which linked U.S. "company towns" in Mexico to markets across the border, also allowed for the northward movement of Mexican workers. One of Mexico's most significant rail lines linked its second largest city, Guadalajara, to Nogales,

Arizona, ensuring that Mexican workers followed the flow of Mexico's wealth as it was extracted and exported to U.S. markets and banks.

The economic changes wrought by this massive influx of foreign capital resulted in the mass dislocation of Mexican workers. Mexican capitalists, particularly those tied to foreign capital, encouraged the state-sponsored disintegration of communal landholdings (*ejidos*) in order to encourage large-scale production for the market in the interests of Mexican landlords and foreign investors. In the urban regions, markets were opened to foreign companies, overwhelming small producers and squeezing the weaker sections of Mexican capital.

Using the Mexican federal troops and armies of rural enforcers (*rurales*), large haciendas and foreign interests displaced millions of small farmers, pushing them into the agricultural proletariat or the stream of migrant labor. By 1910, 96 percent of Mexican families were landless, while the influx of cheaper manufactured goods from abroad displaced the traditional artisan class in the cities.[20]

The Mexican Revolution was a popular response to the seismic economic disruption of the masses and the radically unequal society that emerged. The masses were joined by sections of the Mexican capitalist class that had been subordinated to foreign capital and neglected by the Diaz regime. The revolution killed nearly one in ten Mexicans and pushed another 1.5 million across the border as they attempted to escape the violence.

While the revolution succeeding in toppling the Diaz regime and destroying the last vestiges of feudal power, it did not result in a long-term, radical restructuring of the economy in favor of Mexico's vast population of impoverished workers and subsistence farmers. Nevertheless, the social character of the revolution produced a constitution that attempted both to prevent any form of neo-colonization by foreign economic powers and to guard against the return of a pliant regime that would do the bidding of foreign governments. For example, it designated "the people" as the owners of the soil, and forbade majority ownership of a Mexican enterprise by any foreign company.

Furthermore, it contained clauses that affirmed the Mexican government as guarantor of the rights of workers and the poor, and included a progressive labor code as well as the famous Article 27, which obligated the government to distribute land to the peasants, as well as protect and support smaller farmers. Despite the radical character of the constitution, the enforcement of such a visionary government would have required a workers' and peasants' revolution, a stage the revolution was not able to reach.[21] In the end, the revolution signified the ascension of the Mexican capitalist class, though it had to negotiate with militant and powerful organizations of workers and campesinos for decades to follow, a fact which contributed to the rise of populist president Lázaro Cárdenas.[22]

During his presidency (1934–40), Cárdenas nationalized major portions of the economy, including the lucrative oil industry. He redistributed land to the poor, and also helped institutionalize a form of populism called corporatism, which brought the leadership of popular movements into the government. By granting concessions and even personal favors to the leaders of trade union and campesino organizations, Cárdenas was able to tamp down independent working-class activity. Incorporating the movements and buying off their leaders effectively demobilized workers and peasants, and rendered them unprepared for the rightward, pro-capitalist shift that succeeding presidents after World War II would carry out.

The laboring classes would bear the brunt of this shift, especially in the countryside, where the concentration of land in the hands of the few displaced millions of small farmers in the decades following the revolution. Despite the ongoing use of revolutionary rhetoric that held out the promise of reform, the Mexican government instituted a qualitative shift toward large-scale capitalist agriculture after 1940. For example, an estimated 90 percent of its social sector investment was directed to large-scale farms producing for the market, while smaller-scale and communally held landholdings were neglected.[23] Furthermore, many peasants displaced during the revolution never acquired land and entered the growing stream of landless agricultural workers. As Tom Barry explains:

> The land distribution that did occur in this period was not aimed so much to increase economic progress or better the lot of the poor campesinos but as an instrument to pacify rebellious peasants and to create communities of cheap workers near commercial farm operations.[24]

Although mass struggle in the 1930s had encouraged populist president Lázaro Cárdenas to institute some significant reforms,[25] the opening shots of World War II changed the trajectory of the Mexican economy. The war produced a new opening for Mexican exports on the world market as the United States and its allies retooled production for the war effort and encouraged a substantial acceleration of Mexican government investment in the export-oriented sector of agriculture. At the same time, the government successfully coopted the main organizations of the popular classes, through a combination of force, corruption, and patronage. This dual process—directing resources toward large-scale, export-oriented production while containing workers' and peasants' ability to organize—continued over the next several decades, and reached its climax with the advent of neoliberalism. As historian Judith Hellman observed,

> Each new [Mexican] administration continued to repeat the rhetoric of the past ... [yet at the same time] each of these administrations pursued specific policies which ... reflected the interests of the dominant bourgeoisie. Taken as a whole, these policies undercut peasant gains of the past, and slowed the process of land reform until the trend culminated in the 1980s, under president Jose Lopez Portillo, with a virtual abandonment of the [agrarian] commitment of the revolution.[26]

Altar, Sonora, is a major hub for immigrants from Mexico and Central America. The highway, which connects the town to Southern states and runs all the way north to Mexicali and Tijuana, is Altar's main (and only) avenue.

Chapter Thirteen

Neoliberalism Consumes the "Mexican Miracle"

The shift to export production reflected the desire of the Mexican capitalist class to institute a state-directed development program as a means to increase its share of the world market in agriculture (and later oil) and fund the modernization of Mexico. This, coupled with protectionism, fostered development in the urban centers. Between 1940 and 1970, government efforts focused on raising agricultural productivity, and investment poured into large-scale, export-oriented agricultural operations, a process that came to be known as the "Green Revolution." As a result, the economy expanded at the rate of 6 percent per year (such that Mexico was heralded as a "miracle"), but the interests and well-being of Mexico's large class of small and subsistence farmers were factored out of the equation.

These smaller farmers were unable to compete with the large capitalist farmers. The majority, producing corn and beans for domestic consumption, lost ground to a tiny minority of capitalists producing coffee, tomatoes, and strawberries for the U.S. market. As Mexican production increased overall, the distribution of the gains of modernization flowed away from the laboring classes toward capitalists on both sides of the border. Despite pet projects to try to sustain peasant agriculture, the gradual deterioration of conditions for the rural poor pushed them into the cities,[1] where they filled the ranks of an expanding industrial workforce and state bureaucracy, or forced them to look for work in El Norte, a hemorrhaging that continues to this day.

While the agricultural population steadily declined as a percentage of total population, the absolute number of people throughout Mexico increased from 14 million in 1940 to an estimated 28 million in 1980.[2] Over that same period of time, land ownership stayed virtually constant, with 20 percent of all arable land concentrated in the hands of only 2 percent of the biggest capitalist farmers, and the rest distributed over a spectrum of medium, small, and subsistence farmers.[3] Since then, the balance has continued to shift toward further land concentration on the one hand, and increased proletarianization on the other. Census studies show that by 1970, 1.2 million Mexicans in the countryside were landless workers.[4] As a percentage of the total rural population, the number of agricultural proletarians has skyrocketed, reaching 46.2 percent in 1990, and increasing to a massive 55.6 percent in 1995 following the passage of NAFTA, as well as the final dismantling of state-sponsored agrarian support for small farmers.[5]

One major factor that helped to sustain the "Mexican miracle" of agricultural expansion was an increasing dependency on U.S. loans to underwrite the project. For instance, between the years 1952 and 1958, the foreign debt increased by 500 percent, to over half a billion dollars, primarily in debt to the United States. These loans carried Trojan horse clauses that gave U.S. capitalism a means by which to increasingly assert its influence over the Mexican economy. According to John Ross, "One such loan that helped bind Mexico to Washington's mandate [the adoption of neoliberalism] followed the February 1982 devaluation of the peso—the $75 million jolt pried loose from the U.S. Federal Reserve carried a laundry list of anti-protectionist suggestions, reveal U.S. State Department documents."[6]

It is in the context of this roughshod capitalist development of Mexican agriculture and its integration into the world market—primarily through its orientation toward the United States—that we must understand the establishment of patterns of cross-border migration. The subordination of Mexican capitalism to U.S. imperialism and the global institutions of neoliberalism set the stage for further economic convulsions. Out-migration served as a release valve for the socially dislocated.[7] This by-product was welcomed by a U.S. market eager to absorb not only Mexican imports, but also its reserve armies of labor, since migrants could be paid less and leveraged against unionized workers.

In order to take full advantage of the opportunities presented by a virtually limitless supply of highly vulnerable workers, the government, at the behest of big business, has periodically sponsored "guest worker" programs, through which migrant workers can be imported and exported like commodities on a contractual basis. These programs have instituted a caste system of labor, by depriving their "guests" of the fundamental rights purportedly accorded to workers in a democratic society, and creating a segregated class of workers whose participation in society—beyond contributing the products of their arms, legs, and sweat—is proscribed by law.

The most significant guest-worker scheme to date, the Bracero Program (1942–1964) gave official sanction to the use of migration to satisfy the needs of the United States and Mexico (this program will be discussed in detail in chapter 17). It also established channels for unofficial migration, since it endorsed the mass northward movement of Mexicans for over two decades, establishing patterns of migration that would continue even though the laws eventually changed. Thus, Mexican immigration became an "officially unofficial" institution that continues to this day.

By the 1970s, Mexico's attempt at state-sponsored national development began to falter, and Mexican workers once again faced a series of economic crises that pushed them to migrate.[8] The gradual opening of the Mexican market to foreign investment by transnational corporations, ostensibly a means by which to speed the process of industrialization, led instead to the domination of the industrial sector by foreign capital, accomplished with the complicity of the Mexican government.[9] By 1970, for example, 70 percent of the income from capital goods production went to foreign corporations (mainly American) with only 20 percent going to the state and 10 percent to private Mexican firms.[10]

The massive export of wealth from Mexico to the United States has been exacerbated by massive borrowing on the part of successive Mexican governments. Beginning during the presidency of Adolfo Ruiz Cortines (1952–1958), loans from the United States flowed into the Mexican treasury, inflating the national debt to $500 million. With the discovery of new oil deposits in Mexico and the boom in oil prices after the 1973 OPEC oil embargo, Mexican presidents began to borrow even more heavily to finance the development and maintenance of the domestic economy.[11] The influx of "petro-dollars," as they were called, gave the impression of a booming economy. Meanwhile, Mexico became increasingly dependent on such loans, with few other means of generating currency to finance the growing debt than selling oil. During the presidency of Luis Echeverría, heavy borrowing was undertaken to purchase and nationalize numerous state industries. The intention was to use oil to develop the economy. But by the late 1970s, the oil boom had transformed Mexico into a single commodity exporter, undermining the development of other sectors of the economy.

By the presidency of José López Portillo (1976–1982), Mexico's national debt had mushroomed to $80 billion, primarily owed to U.S. banks and negotiated through the International Monetary Fund, which traded hard cash for neoliberal restructuring.[12] By 1994, Mexican debt reached $130 billion. By 1982, interest payments on debt amounted to half of the total value of Mexico's exports (now predominantly oil), moving north into the United States. In exchange for the loans that contributed to this accumulating debt, the Mexican government signed eight "letters of intention," agreeing to further open Mexico's economy to foreign corporations, downsize the state and public spending, and reorient production toward export. For instance, a 1984 letter of intention committed Mexico to divest itself of twelve hundred state enterprises and reduce public spending (as a percentage of the GNP) from 18 to 8 percent.[13]

Mexico found itself in even more trouble when the price of oil plummeted in the mid-1980s, creating the need for more loans in exchange for more "structural adjustments," in what became known as *la crisis*. And Mexico was not alone; between the years 1968 and 1980, Third World debt increased from $47 billion to a whopping $560 billion. By 2003, total debt accumulated by developing countries reached $2.3 trillion.[14] The mounting interest on these loans and the restructuring of the rules of production and trade in favor of foreign corporations comprised one of the most massive transfers of wealth from poor to rich nations in world history.

While some Mexican capitalists were able to profit, Mexican workers made the ultimate sacrifice. For instance, by 1996, twenty-four Mexican families had joined the ranks of the world's one hundred wealthiest families, buying up a lion's share of the privatized industries responsible for creating 14 percent of Mexico's GDP.[15] At the same time, the standard of living for Mexico's workers and poor had reached the level of catastrophe.

According to a study produced by the International Labor Organization (ILO), the wages of the Mexican working class fell faster than in any other nation in Latin America over the last few decades. Peso devaluations, implemented to counteract inflation, have largely pushed the social costs of neoliberal restructuring and economic failure onto the workers, campesinos, and poor of Mexico. There have been four devaluations of the peso (1976, 1982, 1986, and 1994) that have decimated the value of workers' wages and savings, as well as the landholdings of small farmers, rendering them cheap, potentially migrant labor almost overnight.[16]

Prior to the neoliberal era, the average wage for Mexican workers was about one-third of the average for a U.S. worker. The average now is less than one-eighth and as low as one-fifteenth in some industries.[17] Overall, the poverty rate in Mexico encompasses more than 50 percent of the population,[18] though a study by the Colegio de México estimates that almost 80 percent of Mexicans live in poverty.[19] Consequently, millions of Mexicans depend on the remittances of their loved ones working over the border.

Not surprisingly, the international and national capitalist restructuring of the Mexican economy has decimated Mexico's unions. While three-quarters of the workforce in Mexico belonged to unions three decades ago, less than 30 percent do so today.[20] This has occurred primarily through privatization, mass firings, migration, and overtly antiunion intervention by state forces to ensure a "pro-business" climate.

Mexico's troubled history began with the long struggle to shed the remnants of Spanish feudalism, segued into an era marked by American imperial ascendancy, the loss of half its territory, and its economic subordination to the United States. Despite the heroic struggles of Mexican workers and peasants, the consolidation of Mexican capitalism and its integration into the world system, vis-à-vis increasing dependency on U.S. loans and neoliberal restructuring, led to the overthrow of the nationalist legacy of the Mexican Revolution. This propelled a new cabal of "technocratic" leaders into power, who set out to restructure the Mexican economy according to the dictates of Washington, for the benefit of small cliques of Mexican capitalists and international investors, and at the expense of the vast majority of Mexicans.

Chapter Fourteen

From the Maquiladoras to NAFTA: Profiting from Borders

n line with neoliberalism's emphasis on export-driven development and encouraged by the rapid growth of transnational corporations seeking to invest in overseas markets, the Border Industrialization Program (BIP), initiated in 1965, redirected national efforts at industrialization away from the state and toward foreign capital. The BIP signified the first foray of the Mexican state away from "Import Substitution Industrialization" and toward the emerging neoliberal orthodoxy of industrialization through foreign direct investment (FDI). It resulted in the creation of maquiladoras, foreign-owned assembly plants situated in "free trade zones" along Mexico's northern border.

> U.S. manufacturers were invited to move their factories south across the 2,000-mile-long border between the United States and Mexico to take advantage of much lower wage rates. Mexican federal subsidies encouraged the rapid growth of industrial parks, and new regulations allowed manufacturers to import duty-free machinery, parts and raw materials. The program has been a highly successful accumulation strategy; in its short life span of thirty years, it has been revamped and expanded several times.[1]

The Border Industrialization Program was initially justified as a means to absorb displaced agricultural workers after the end of the Bracero Program of the same year, but has since become a lucrative institution along the U.S.-Mexico border. The maquiladora program primarily seeks to take advantage of large, concentrated populations of

Mexican workers living in border cities, many of which are now "sisters" to major U.S. border cities. Fourteen large metropolitan centers, such as Tijuana-San Diego and Ciudad Juarez-El Paso, contain 90 percent of the nearly 12 million people that live in the border region.[2] While topographically contiguous, these mega-cities are artificially divided by walls, degrading both groups of workers' rights in the process.

Aside from the benefit of major tax breaks, the BIP allows for the hyper-exploitation of Mexican workers, who are paid a fraction of the wages earned by workers north of the border. According to Maquiladora Management Services, a San Diego–based marketing firm that promotes the industry and bills itself as "your connection to Mexico's low-cost labor force," companies that relocate across the border are assured that labor costs will be cut by 75 percent.[3]

According to the *Twin Plant News*, a trade magazine that promotes the maquiladora industry, it is the virtual total control a prospective owner can wield over Mexican workers that makes them so attractive:

> The primary advantage for a U.S. company to operate a maquila is the lower cost of labor in Mexico. Labor typically costs about $21 an hour in the United States, compared to about $5 an hour in Mexico. Other advantages include more favorable labor law in Mexico and fewer union-driven work rules. In other instances, maquilas fill jobs that U.S. workers are no longer willing to work. Assembly line operations that require nothing more than simple hand work for eight hours a day frequently go unfilled in the United States.[4]

What's more, maquiladora owners can count on low wages staying low, as workers in free trade zones have no recourse to real trade union organizing. Instead, membership in so-called "white unions" is mandatory in many places. These "unions" collude with the companies and the local, state, and federal government to prohibit any productive union organizing among ordinary workers.[5] In addition to busting unions, the Mexican government subsidizes the maquiladoras with money "redistributed" from Mexican taxpayers—all in the name of keeping Mexico attractive to foreign investment. For example, U.S.-based Electrolux was given tax breaks totaling five hundred thousand dollars by the Chihuahua state government to open a plant in Ciudad Juarez.[6] In other words, not only are there no obstacles to exploiting cheaper Mexican labor, but Mexican workers *themselves* pay (through their tax dollars) for these foreign businesses to profit from their labor.

The profitability of moving assembly plants to Mexico proved irresistible to U.S. companies. "By 1972, nearly a third of the value for all U.S. components sent abroad went to Mexico, and by 1977 more than $1 billion worth of maquiladora-assembled products was being returned to the United States every year." The program reached its zenith in the year 2000, with over four thousand maquiladoras operating across the country, employing over 1.6 million workers[7] and eclipsing the efforts of state-directed industrialization. The sector has become a critical source of profits for American corporations, who own about 90 percent of all maquiladoras.[8] By the year 2005, maquiladoras had produced $113 billion worth of goods—90 percent of which went to U.S. markets[9]—and a profit windfall for U.S.-backed corporations such as GM, Dupont, and Dow Chemical.

The shift to free trade production has caused an erosion of the traditional state-sponsored industrial core through underfunding, privatization, and the gradual abandonment of "non-profitable" industrial sites. For instance, after the debt crisis of 1982 and the implementation of IMF "structural adjustment programs," the six years of the presidency of Miguel de la Madrid witnessed the fire sale of nine hundred firms to private interests.[10] Despite a flurry of strikes by workers to protect their historic gains, this process further reduced union centers, and once again unemployed workers were pushed into other regions to find work. In other words, one major reason for migration north, especially from the interior regions of Mexico, has to do with the process of deindustrialization brought about by the "maquiladoraization" of the economy.

The shift toward market-oriented policies has also had a long-term deleterious effect on overall wages. Real wages, which had already declined 20 percent between the years 1977 and 1982, plummeted an additional 66 percent between 1980 and 1990.[11] Today, the largely American-owned factories of the maquiladora sector employ about 1.2 million people. Maquiladora workers—unlike the American-born middle managers who flock south across the border to take up lucrative positions in the maquiladora plants—live in squalor and are paid a pittance. Wages hover slightly above the minimum of four dollars a day, though no one can survive on this amount. The poverty facing maquiladora workers is astounding. In Baja California, during strawberry season, whole families often work together—children alongside their parents—in agricultural maquiladoras because adult pay amounts to only about six dollars a day, three dollars a day for children. As one worker said, "We can't live if we all don't work."[12] As veteran border rights activist Enrique Davalos explains,

> Maquiladoras combine traditional ways of exploitation (cheap labor, low wages, poor health and safety regulations) with new, intensive ways of exploitation based on high-speed productivity. Working in a maquiladora means [living] in poverty with no hopes of getting better wages, any promotion, seniority, or labor security. Average daily wages in Tijuana maquiladoras are about six to seven dollars for ten working hours. This is enough to pay only 25 percent of the very basic expenses, without including rent and education. So maquiladora workers are condemned to live in shantytowns without piped water, power, sewage or trash collection. Temperatures in Tijuana fluctuate from 30 to 110 degrees Fahrenheit, but 66 percent of the houses don't have piped water.
>
> The maquiladoras are risky and unhealthy labor places. Most of the companies force the workers to deal with dangerous chemicals with no training and no appropriate protection. As a result, labor diseases and accidents are common in Tijuana. Workers ruin their eyes, lungs, hands, backs, and nervous systems after a few years of work in a maquiladora. In addition, workers without fingers and hands are not rare, but workers' negligence is always used to explain recurrent "accidents." In fact, maquiladoras not only deteriorate workers' lives, they also pollute their families and communities. Ejido Chilpancingo is a neighborhood located near to Otay, one of the most expensive industrial parks in Tijuana. Because of maquiladora pollution, residents of Ejido Chilpancingo are exposed to lead at levels three thousand times higher than U.S. standards.[13]

Since communities along the border have become economically integrated, the daily cost of living on either side has reached parity in many goods and services. The super-exploitative conditions in the maquiladoras are made even clearer when one considers that a gallon of milk costs about three dollars, half the daily wage of a typical worker.[14] The conditions are so profitable for capital (and so egregious for workers), that most U.S. manufacturers favor the Mexican maquiladora sector as one of their top two global sites for cheap labor, second only to the virtual slave-labor conditions of China. In recent years, however, Chinese investors have been expressing interest in the Mexican border region, as a way of getting around U.S. trade restrictions and utilizing the North American Free Trade Agreement to their advantage.[15]

Despite the interest in the maquiladora project, the global corporate race to the bottom is pushing the bar even lower for Mexican and migrant Central American workers. Competition from super-exploited workers in Asia and other parts of Latin America is being used as a justification for wage reductions and further crackdowns against unions.

Low pay has contributed to a gendered division of labor by encouraging most male migrants from the interior to bypass the maquiladora zone in favor of more substantial wages across the border. This results in a concentration of women in the maquiladoras, an arrangement embraced by maquiladora operators since women tend to have fewer social and political rights, and therefore less bargaining power. Nevertheless, women workers do resist, and owners find ways to discipline them. For example, according to a study by Human Rights Watch, women workers are "routine[ly] required to undergo pregnancy testing as a condition for employment." These tests are often conducted monthly, and those who become pregnant are fired, thus creating a high turnover rate and a constant downward pressure on wages.[16]

Cross-border commerce is mega-business. While the border restricts the movement of labor, no such obstacles exist for capital. There are about 250 million crossings per year, with only about 1 percent unauthorized.[17] The border is open for business. About $733 million are exchanged *each day* along the U.S.-Mexico border.[18] Seventy thousand people cross the border each day to work and shop, pumping $3.3 billion each year into the San Diego economy alone.[19] And it is not uncommon for businesses to relocate or create "subsidiaries" just south of the border to cut labor costs, while Mexican workers—the 1 percent that attracts such fury and derision—must risk life and limb crossing to the north.

The maquiladora industry serves as a monument to U.S. imperialism's power to make rules solely for the benefit of corporations. The border is used to keep wages at a minimum for workers on both sides, while it artificially divides them to prevent a collective response. Nevertheless, its impact is becoming increasingly apparent to those seeing their wages and jobs evaporate. As Dave Johnson, international representative for the United Electrical Workers (UE), explains,

> Because of regional economic integration and developments like NAFTA ... the wages and conditions of Mexican workers are the new floor of our economy. To put it a little more simplistically, either our wages and conditions are going to go down to the level of Mexico's, or we're going to figure out ways to help Mexicans raise their wages and conditions up to our levels.[20]

The passage of the North American Free Trade Agreement (NAFTA) in 1994 officially formalized neoliberal policies that had been implemented piecemeal in previous years, especially regarding agriculture. For example, Article 27 of the Mexican Constitution (which protected small Mexican farmers from unequal competition with U.S. agribusiness) was abolished in 1992. NAFTA opened the Mexican grain market to U.S. imports in exchange for the opening of the U.S. market to Mexican fruits and vegetables.

NAFTA also guaranteed that the Mexican government would not interfere with the operations of foreign corporations, favor domestic over foreign capital, or require "technology transfers" that would force corporations to share technology with local hosts. In other words, it created a virtual state within a state, where corporations could function for the most part independently of government oversight or regulation. As a result, little investment has been put into industries producing for local markets. Instead, businesses focus on using cheaper Mexican labor to produce for export.

NAFTA contained no binding protections for unions, wages, or displaced workers. As a result, all three member nations (the U.S., Mexico, and Canada) experienced a decline in wages for the majority of their workforces while corporate profits skyrocketed. But Mexico was hit the hardest. From 1993 through 1994, about 40 percent of Mexico's clothing manufacturers went out of business as U.S. retail stores moved to Mexico and started importing cheaper fabrics from Asia. This phenomenon also affected a host of other industries, such as toys, leather, and footwear.[21] The Mexican government estimates that in the year that followed NAFTA's ratification, the Mexican economy shed about one million jobs.[22]

Agriculture also took a mortal blow. In 1993, Mexico, a civilization born and built on corn, began to import more ears of corn from the United States than it produced domestically, adding to the havoc being wreaked on small and subsistence farmers dependent on government subsidies and price controls. With the passage of NAFTA, these protections were abandoned, completing the "ascendance of neoliberalism":

> In the agricultural sector, the internationalization of capital had been gradually reorganizing local, regional, and national systems of production and trade.... In Mexico, this was seen with the expansion of the feedgrain industry, the greater integration of agriculture and food processing, the expanding role of the TNCs [transnational corporations], and increasing government attention to the most technologically advanced and profitable farm sectors.[23]

With NAFTA, Mexico has become almost entirely dependent on the United States for trade. A reorientation toward an export-driven economy has bound Mexico to the U.S. market. For instance, the United States absorbs 88 percent of Mexican exports, which account for about 25 percent of the country's GDP.[24] In exchange, Mexico has opened its borders to U.S. corporations. According to the Office of the United States Trade Representative, the stock of U.S. foreign direct investment in Mexico reached $61.5 billion in 2003, the majority in manufacturing (maquiladoras) and banking (see later discussion on remittances).[25] Mexico also opened up its markets to U.S. agriculture.

Opening Mexico to U.S. corn, for instance, has devastated local producers. According to the U.S. Department of Agriculture, exports to Mexico have doubled since the passage of NAFTA, reaching $7.9 billion by 2003. Corn alone accounted for $653 million in 2002. This has made Mexico the third-largest recipient of U.S. agricultural exports.[26] The United States government, now haranguing migrant Mexican workers, facilitated their dislocation in the first place, both through NAFTA and through direct incentives for U.S. corporations in Mexico. According to the U.S. State Department,

> In 2005, the USDA provided $10 million for 71 U.S. agricultural trade projects in Mexico, Brazil, Venezuela, Central America and elsewhere under what is called the "Emerging Markets Program." The program supports the promotion and distribution of U.S. agricultural products, trade missions, research on new markets, and activities that encourage free-trade policies.[27]

Over 1.3 million small farmers in Mexico were pushed into bankruptcy by cheap American grain imports between 1994 and 2004.[28] Luis Tellez, former undersecretary for planning in Mexico's Ministry of Agriculture and Hydraulic Resources, estimates that as many as 15 million peasants will leave agriculture in the next few decades, many seeing migration north as the only option.[29] This dynamic was cited by the Zapatista rebels in southern Mexico as one of the main reasons for their uprising.

Meanwhile, the deindustrialization of Mexico continues unabated. Mexico lost an unprecedented 515,000 jobs in the first three months of 2005 alone.[30] Mexico has continued to deindustrialize since the passage of NAFTA, so that manufacturing now accounts for 16 percent of GDP, decreasing each year between 2000 and 2005.[31] This helps explain why an increasing number of migrant border crossers—nearly 50 percent—come from urban areas in Mexico.[32]

By absorbing an ever-increasing number of U.S. exports, Mexico has become the United States' second largest trading partner, devastating its industrial and agricultural bases in the process. The hemorrhaging continues in the form of displaced workers, not only in Mexico, but in the United States as well. U.S. NAFTA, the consortium of industrial corporations that lobbied for the passage of the agreement, alleged that passage of the treaty would create one hundred thousand jobs in the export sector of the U.S. economy. While this goal was achieved over a period of four years, 151,256 jobs were lost in the manufacturing sector over the same period.[33] According to David Bacon, U.S. job losses amount to nearly three-quarters of a million, while Canada has lost 18 percent of its manufacturing jobs since 1995.[34] Though workers have lost out with NAFTA, the corporations that lobbied for its passage have made out like bandits. About half of the initial lobbyist consortium pushing for NAFTA sent jobs to Mexico and increased their profits by 300 percent by 1997.[35]

Despite the correlation between "free trade" policies and worker displacement, neoliberal politicians march onward, decrying "illegal immigration" as they go. Without an ounce of irony, Arizona Congressman Jim Kolbe (R-AZ) celebrated the 2005 passage of CAFTA (Central American Free Trade Agreement) by the U.S. Congress by proclaiming, "Increased integration can only add jobs and help alleviate poverty, reduce the flow of migration northward and make the region more competitive in world markets."

Part III

MEXICAN WORKERS: THE "OTHER" AMERICAN WORKING CLASS

Hurricane Katrina cleanup and reconstruction. Immediatelly upon arriving at the Mississippi Gulf Coast from Beaumont, Texas, thirteen roofing workers were employed to fix an apartment complex at W. Pine and Hill in Gulfport. There is one Honduran in the group. The rest are from San Luis Potosi, in Central Mexico.

Chapter Fifteen

Mexican Workers to the Rescue

In the late nineteenth century, Mexican workers began to move into the United States to work in agriculture and industry. Enticed by the promise of jobs and recruited by both private economic interests and the U.S. government, Mexican workers helped forge the modern United States through their labor, culture, and political participation. In doing so, they joined the first *Americans* in the Southwest: the Mexicans and indigenous peoples who had watched traditional borders migrate south or evaporate with U.S. conquest of their lands. Finding them insufficient as a labor pool for westward-expanding industry, early capitalists and their allies looked to other nations to address the labor deficit.

The absence of a large, stationary proletariat in the Southwest forced the industrial and agricultural capitalists to rely on large populations of immigrants. For this reason, the U.S. had *open borders* for nearly half of its history, permitting the formation of an international proletariat within the territorial boundaries of the United States as a necessary stage in the consolidation of capitalism. Once in the country, immigrants filled the ranks of the new "American working class," which was, and continues to be, a multiethnic amalgamation of the native- and foreign-born.

Close proximity, economic interrelation, and a shared history made migration to the United States a natural choice for Mexico's displaced workers. In the initial stage, Mexican workers entered American factories and fields like other migrating workers from across the globe. After immigration restrictions closed the door to most immigrants in the 1920s, Mexican workers continued to join the ranks of the American working class. In fact, Mexican workers came to be preferred by some policy-makers. As Democratic president Woodrow Wilson stated in 1916, "personally, I believe that Mexican laborers are the solution to our common labor problem, this was once part of their country, they can and they will do the work."[1]

When the federal government introduced the first comprehensive immigration restrictions in 1917, Mexicans were excluded because many western and southwestern legislators "insisted that their regions needed Mexican agricultural labor."[2] Initially, Mexican workers were favored due to the temporary nature of their migration. Many workers followed the seasonal harvest and returned to Mexico in the off-season. This relieved the growers of the need to pay wages to sustain workers year round. At the end of the harvest, most workers would simply move on to other farms or return to their homes.

Since the cyclical routine of farm labor migration was established before the advent of immigration restrictions, it continued during and after the gradual erosion of the status of the Mexican worker. From the Central Valley of California to the Mississippi Delta, growers also began to appreciate the value of using "non-citizen" workers. Immigrant workers had fewer political rights, they could not vote, and they could be isolated from other workers, which made it more difficult for them to form unions.

Government agents, private contractors, and a motley assortment of other middlemen in the service of big agriculture saturated Mexican villages and towns with advertisements for jobs in El Norte. Beet sugar growers published alluring ads and distributed bilingual posters and fliers, coaxing Mexicans to the "land of plenty." A Texas newspaper reveals why bosses looked south:

> Not for a number of years has there been such a demand for cotton pickers in southwest Texas. Almost every neighborhood is calling for help to take care of the crop. To meet the demands agents have been sent across the border into Mexico to secure help…. Many of those [recruited Mexican workers] going into the cotton fields of Texas are accompanied by their families. This is to the liking of the planters, for it is maintained that children as a rule will pick as much cotton as the grown-ups.[3]

Heavy industry, such as the railroads, also appealed to Mexican workers for help. Often, the preference for immigrant workers was based on a stereotypical portrayal of Mexicans as less likely to protest bad working conditions and more tolerant of exhausting labor. In 1909, western railroads employed about six thousand workers, 98 percent of which were Mexican migrants. Explaining the increasing reliance on migrant labor, the commissioner-general of immigration casually remarked that Mexicans

> met an economic condition demanding laborers who could stand the heat and discomforts of that particular section. The Peon makes a satisfactory track hand, for the reason that he is docile, ignorant, and non clannish to an extent which makes it possible that one or more men shall quit or be discharged and others remain at work; moreover, he is willing to work for a low wage.[4]

While it is without doubt that Mexican workers were willing to work for lower wages upon arrival (wages that were, nonetheless, substantially higher than the highest wages at that time in Mexico), the stereotype of the "malleable peon" was dispelled after Mexicans engaged in the first strikes for union recognition in the early twentieth century. After purposefully enticing Mexican labor into their regions to flood local markets, potato growers in Colorado found that, "first they [Mexicans] worked by the sack. Then they wanted a contract by the acre…. [Then] the rascals struck for their own rates…." Farmers complained that "they will all sit down in the field, and not work if they hear somebody is paying a couple cents more."[5]

The defiance of Mexican workers both demolished the myth of their alleged passivity and precipitated combination and collusion among growers eager to pacify them. As workers struggled to form unions, their "willingness" to work for low wages had to be enforced by several layers of repression, from the local sheriff to the border patrol. For example, the Cotton Growers' Association was able to reap huge profits from migrant labor by colluding to keep wages fixed at the lowest rate and agreeing not to break ranks in the advent of labor action. An Arizona representative boasted, "If the Association had not protected the [Salt River] Valley in the matter of picking price … each farmer would have been bidding against his neighbor and the price would have jumped and jumped."[6] The encouragement of Mexican migration continued, but it now occurred in tandem with efforts to restrict migrants' rights—including their right to form unions—through legal means or otherwise.

By the 1920s, migrant workers were commonplace in many industries. A Labor Department official reported in 1925 that "every major corporation in California and Nevada that employed unskilled labor maintained a recruiter in Los Angeles who secured workers from the numerous agencies specializing in Mexican labor."[7] Owners also encouraged recruitment through family and kinship networks, which was seen as both effective and economical. Migration and settlement created binational familial networks, with established families allowing for the migration of additional family members, who then moved into other industries. In 1928, it was estimated by the Texas commissioner of labor that 75 percent of construction work in the state was carried out by Mexicans. In the same year, an industrial survey of 695 factories in California revealed that Mexican labor comprised 10.8 percent of the workforce.[8]

Northern and Midwestern employers also tapped into the Southwestern labor stream. As immigration restrictions squelched the cross-Atlantic labor flow after 1924, Mexican workers were enticed to make further peregrinations northward, a prospect embraced by workers eager to escape the harsh hand of Jim Crow segregation in the Southwest. Workers moved onto the sugar beet farms of Michigan, worked the rail lines eastward from Chicago, and ultimately reached the Midwestern steel mills, meat-packing plants, and auto factories that defined industrial America. By 1927, the Mexican population in the Midwest hit eighty thousand, expanding the grooves of passage that would allow successive waves of migrants to define the American economy and the working class that shouldered its weight.[9]

By 1912, Mexicans became the majority in rail gangs working west of Kansas City and helped build rail lines stretching from Tijuana to Chicago. In order to exploit the racial diversity of work crews, railroad officials set up pay scales based on ethnicity, with Mexican workers often assigned the lowest wages.[10] Despite this, by 1929, 59 percent of railroad workers in the Pacific Northwest had come from Mexico.[11]

Women also entered the workforce in substantial numbers. According to Chicana historian Vicki Ruiz, the proportion of Mexican and Mexican-American women in sales and clerical positions increased from 10.1 percent in 1930 to 23.9 percent in 1950. By 1930, approximately 25 percent of Mexicana and Mexican-American women wage-earners were industrial workers, many working in California canning factories.[12] When upwards of 250,000 to 500,000 Mexican and Mexican-American men entered the ranks of the military during World War II, substantial numbers of Latinas worked in heavy industry, from the railroads to aircraft manufacturing. One worker at Douglas Aircraft in Burbank, California, recalled that her coworkers were "Native Americans, Mexican girls, Blacks, and Anglos." In the war years, women made up 42 percent of the workforce in the largest defense-related manufacturing plants, and in areas like Los Angeles, Latinas made up a substantial portion of that percentage.[13]

Chapter Sixteen

Segregated Workers:
Class Struggle in the Fields

Mexicans were not the only workers encouraged to find work in the United States. Land consolidation and the increasingly intensive nature of farm work led to ongoing labor shortages. By the 1920s, agriculture was shifting from small-farm local production to large-scale production for the world market. Mega-farms began to dot the landscape of the Southwest. By 1929, "California, Arizona, and Texas accounted for 47 percent of the nation's large-scale cotton farms, and California alone contained 37 percent of all the large-scale farms in the United States."[1] To deal with the consequent labor shortages, western growers devised systems to import workers from the eastern states as well as from overseas. They subsidized discounted rates for railroad travel from eastern states, and hired labor contractors and smugglers to transport workers from China and Japan.

The rapid development of the Southwest and the consolidation of power by railroad and agricultural interests was astounding. A prescient observer of the rise of capitalism, Karl Marx, remarked that "California is very important for me because nowhere else has the upheaval most shamelessly caused by capitalist centralization occurred with such speed."[2] Capitalists in California had consolidated their grip over the state. Land was distributed en masse to railroad magnates and agricultural entrepreneurs. By 1871, railroad bosses controlled 20 million acres, while 516 wealthy agricultural capitalists controlled another 8 million acres of prime farmland.[3] While California set the standard, a similar process of land concentration occurred across the Southwest.

By the 1930s, the biggest agricultural interests had coalesced into the "Associated Growers," a cartel that came to dominate California agriculture. The association merged its large holdings with those of the Chamber of Commerce, Bank of America, Pacific Gas and Electric, and the California Packing Company, creating a financial juggernaut that came to dominate California government and exert great influence within the federal government as well.[4] Similar combinations came to dominate other state agricultural systems, all poised to create agro-industrial empires.

With the state apparatus firmly on the side of the growers, an agricultural labor force was consciously constructed so as to ensure its complete subordination to the dictatorship of farm capital. Eager to turn a hefty profit, growers tended to over-recruit, creating a vast "reserve army" of unemployed workers. This large, transient, and impoverished population was left to its own devices in the off-season, a trend favored by growers as a cost-saving device.[5]

The conditions of super-exploitation that resulted from the growers' desire to squeeze maximum profits out of the workers reduced the agricultural workforce to a state of powerless dependency reminiscent of earlier forms of medieval servitude. According to a report from the State Fruit-Grower's Association in 1902, "We [the growers] have so degraded a certain class of labor, that there is not a man that lives in any agricultural locality who wants to get in and do this work."[6] At the time of the formation of the agricultural-industrial working class, class-conscious capitalists were able to set and control the parameters of labor, leaving few options for workers but to flee the fields. This led to the isolation of agricultural workers from their urban counterparts, increased difficulties for union organizing, and the bosses' ability to use disempowered immigrant labor as a means to separate the kindling from the flame.

As many white and native-born workers moved into other industries to escape the hardship of agricultural life, migrant and immigrant workers were imported to fill the gap. Having a culturally and ethnically diverse workforce allowed growers to segregate groups around each stage of production, keeping them isolated from each other as much as possible. This worked against the forging of unity around common demands to improve working conditions, and enabled growers to isolate and crush strike or union movements in one section without disrupting production as a whole. As one grower in Hawaii recommended to others, "Keep a variety of laborers, that is different nationalities, and thus prevent any concerted action in the case of strikes, for there are few, if any, cases of Japs, Chinese, and Portuguese entering into a strike as a unit."[7]

By the turn of the twentieth century, strike prevention was already a primary concern, as union agitation began to spread across the Southwest. Growers transformed the labor force to defuse its gathering power. Not only were immigrant groups used to displace or replace native-born workers, but different ethnic groups were set against each other, a strategy aided by federal and state immigration agencies that worked hand in glove with growers to secure cheap labor. Variegated immigration policies favored Chinese, Japanese, Filipino, Indian, and Mexican workers at different periods. As California historian Carey McWilliams observed,

> From the grower's point of view, the Hindus fitted nicely into the pattern of farm labor in California. Not only were they good workers, but they could be used as one additional racial group in competition with other racial groups, and thereby wages would be lowered. A notable fact about farm labor in California is the practice of employers to pay wage scales on the basis of race, i.e. to establish different wage rates for each racial group, thus fostering racial antagonism and, incidentally, keeping wages at the lowest possible point.[8]

Despite the barrier this created for unions, workers fought back throughout the twentieth century. Beginning in 1903, attempts at unionization sent shockwaves across the industry, leading a growers' magazine to call for "a general law prescribing a closed season for strikers during the gathering and movement of staple crops."[9] Since most native-born workers (with the exception of Blacks) could walk away from the hyper-exploitation of the fields and had access to the basic rights of citizenship, sustaining an accessible population of workers to toil within the egregious conditions of agriculture proved difficult without relying on the importation of foreign laborers.[10]

The artful molding of immigration law allowed workforces to be imported from impoverished nations under conditions favorable to the growers. For instance, the first comprehensive immigration policy, the Immigration Act of 1917, excluded "political radicals" (union organizing was considered a radical idea at the time) and created the first guest-worker programs in which workers were denied citizenship and the right to form unions. Workers were required to return home after the harvests, which undermined organizing efforts and reduced costs for the growers. Legislative policies regulating immigration, many of which contained language that had been written and submitted by grower combinations, gave agricultural bosses powerful leverage against their workers.[11]

Growers could also count on the fact that unwanted immigrants can be deported. Beginning with the Chinese Exclusion Act of 1882 and the subsequent Geary Act of 1892, select immigrant workers (in this case Chinese workers) were targeted for forced removal.[12] This benefited the growers in multiple ways. First, it allowed agricultural interests to dangle citizenship as a carrot for immigrants to work in substandard conditions. When jobs were cut, or the economy was in shambles, this distinction encouraged "citizen workers" to direct their disaffection toward "non-citizen workers."

Second, the threat of deportation could be used to discourage labor agitation. Deportation was used to break strikes and deflect periodic capitalist crisis away from the system and toward particular ethnic groups. The consolidation of the Immigration and Naturalization Service (INS) and the creation of the Border Patrol in 1924 amounted to a labor policy bonanza for the growers. Rather than getting rid of undocumented workers, the INS served as a wedge between them and the native-born. As one agent in Salinas, California, pointed out, they were not staffed for large-scale removal but rather "to keep a presence" in the fields.[13]

The political segregation of workers based on citizenship gradually isolated all immigrant workers from the rest of the working class. Many native-born workers and their unions became convinced that there was something to be gained by excluding immigrants, even though in practice it led to the decline of the conditions of labor for all workers, as demonstrated by the overall degeneration of the conditions of farm labor, and the mass exodus of native-born workers from the fields. Nevertheless, the main trade union federation, the American Federation of Labor, and its successor, the AFL-CIO, opposed immigration and immigrant rights over much of the twentieth century.

Lastly, increasing segregation between "legal" and "illegal" produced a growing underclass of workers and a rigidly defined dichotomy of labor. "Legal" immigrants, often wealthier, whiter, and more highly skilled, decreased as a percentage of overall immigrants as it became virtually impossible for newer immigrants to afford the process of becoming documented workers. The process of applying for citizenship, as it came to be defined after the 1920s, required paying for lawyers, taxes, and application fees, as well as taking civics classes and filing legal documents.

Meanwhile, corporations and growers came to prefer disenfranchised, undocumented workers for manual labor. Denied citizenship and union protection, these workers became a large part of the labor force and are used by bosses to depress wages and conditions in several sectors to this day.

Although a multiethnic labor force provided the greatest opportunities for sowing divisions among workers, and was thus preferred by many growers, the two-thousand-mile Mexico-U.S. border ensured that Mexican workers would make up the largest section of undocumented labor, especially since geographical and physical barriers to movement were largely non-existent for most of the history of the two countries. By 1917, growers had begun to favor Mexican workers. The proximity of the border created a natural route for seasonal migration. Deportation provided a feasible and relatively inexpensive solution to the problem of union agitation or strike activity. Sheriffs and vigilantes simply rounded up Mexican workers and dumped them off across the border, often breaking whole strikes in the process.[14]

Despite their isolation from the rest of the working class, immigrant workers benefited from the rise of mass labor militancy that grew out of the era of the Great Depression. The costs of the meltdown of the capitalist system were pushed onto the working class in the form of mass unemployment, wage cuts, and the often violent restriction of union organization. Despite the tumult and instability, workers seized the opportunity to organize and resist on the most massive scale in U.S. history. Between the years 1936 and 1945, there was a colossal number of strikes—35,519 in all—involving 15,856,000 workers.[15]

The strike movement galvanized and gave coherence to an emerging industrial working class, which not only muscled back the general assault on working conditions, but shifted the balance of class forces in the United States. The general crisis, coupled with a mobilized and vigilant working class, allowed Franklin Delano Roosevelt to split the myopic capitalist class and implement comprehensive reforms that not only led to democratization, but also introduced the working class as a decisive force in U.S. politics.[16]

In the fields, economic crisis and class struggle raged as well. As one farmworker put it during the Vacaville strike of 1932, "We would have to starve working, so we decided to starve striking."[17] Between 1930 and 1932, there were ten major agricultural strikes in California, involving thousands of workers. The wave of agricultural strikes peaked in 1933, when there were over sixty strikes involving sixty thousand workers in seventeen states.[18]

Unfortunately, the power of the growers also reached its zenith in the 1930s. Despite the mass radicalization among workers and a flurry of industrial union drives, growers were able to isolate immigrant and native farm labor and prevent them from reaping the kinds of gains won by the urban industrial working class.

The dominant unions lent them a hand by refusing to support the struggles of immigrant workers, as did Southern segregationist "Dixiecrats" in Congress, who opposed the expansion of unions and other democratic rights into the Jim Crow South. As if that were not enough, the defeat of the farmworkers' strikes was further ensured by a bevy of legal and extra-legal measures employed by state and local governments. When those failed, hired thugs were employed to terrorize the workers to such an extent that some historians consider their actions to be the closest thing to a substantial fascist movement the United States has ever seen. Describing the prolific rise of grower-funded vigilante squads, labor historian Jim Miller notes:

> These organizations were filled with officials from county government and were integrated into the highest levels of the county commissioners, the Highway Patrol, the Police, and the courts. Some of the nastiest work was done by deputized vigilantes that were drawn from the American Legion, Ku Klux Klan, and the Silver Shirts, a fascist group modeled after the German SS.[19]

The balance of forces aligned against agricultural workers kept the agricultural sector of the U.S. economy in a backward and semi-feudal state. Even the National Labor Relations Act of 1935—a turning point for the industrial labor movement that guaranteed the right of workers to organize unions without fear of reprisal—excluded farmworkers from all of its provisions. According to Greg Schell,

> Virtually every labor protective standard passed on both a federal and state level prior to 1960 excluded agricultural workers. As the lot of industrial workers consistently improved, the earnings of agricultural workers lagged further and further behind. By the end of World War II, a marked gap existed between the protections enjoyed by industrial workers and the nineteenth century conditions endured by farmworkers.[20]

In the aftermath of World War II, immigration patterns were altered by the Bracero Program, which initiated the formal participation of the U.S. government in recruiting Mexican workers on behalf of agriculture, and the institutionalization of the "legal vs. illegal" mode of border crossing. Begun in 1942, the Bracero Program brought nearly 5 million "guest workers" into the country over a twenty-year period. For every bracero recruited, several workers were denied entry. Many crossed over anyway, encouraged by growers eager to increase the pool of undocumented workers.

A group of immigrants detained along Highway 92 between
Bisbee and Sierra Vista, Arizona.

Chapter Seventeen

The Bracero Program: A Twentieth-Century Caste System

Although American labor made its greatest gains in the 1930s and 1940s, there were significant segments of the economy where a union-free environment prevailed. The defeat of the farmworkers' movement preserved the South and Southwest as anti-union strongholds—especially in agriculture—for years to come. The creation of a differentiated urban-rural workforce represented a significant hurdle for American labor, since it resulted in a virtual union-free zone in one of the most significant sectors of the U.S. economy. It enabled growers to craft legislative policy that took advantage of the tractability of agricultural labor, consolidating and institutionalizing the previous victories of the growers. It created a throw-away workforce that denied guest workers the right to move freely from job to job, to form unions, and to stay in the country when their contracts ended. It was, in form, a throwback to a bonded labor system that, according to the Presidential Commission on Migratory Labor, supplied growers with

> a labor supply which, on one hand, is ready and willing to meet the short term work requirements and which, on the other hand, will not impose social and economic problems on them or on their community when the work is finished.... The demand for migratory workers is thus essentially two-fold: to be ready to go to work when needed; to be gone when not needed.[1]

While introduced as a "wartime expediency" plan to ease a labor shortage in agriculture, the guest-worker initiative was in fact a concerted effort by agribusiness to further restructure the social relations of agricultural capitalism. The defeat of the labor movement in the fields in the late thirties encouraged growers to continue to use immigrant labor as a retaining wall against further union incursions.

As white, native-born workers fled the low wages, grueling conditions, and totalitarian structure of work in the fields in favor of urban union jobs, a shortage of "exploitable" labor did truly arise, from the vantage point of the growers. Full employment and the growth of unions increased the negotiating power of domestic agricultural workers, a phenomenon that was transformed into a "labor shortage" by the political spokesmen of capital. As veteran labor organizer Ernesto Galarza put it:

> [The demand for labor] was to be understood to mean sufficient numbers [of braceros] to take the place of the thousands of domestics who were seeking higher wages in wartime industries throughout the Southwest—and sufficient also to displace them permanently when the pressure of war would disappear and the labor force would be thrown into another of those massive reversals that Congress seemed never to foresee.[2]

The Bracero Program, referring literally to "one who works with their arms," set up a labor contracting system by which the U.S. government negotiated the temporary importation of 4.8 million Mexican workers to be used primarily in agriculture between the years 1942 and 1964.[3] Under the contract, Mexican workers were transported to the farms to manage the harvests. They were guaranteed work, a minimum wage, transportation, and housing, while they covered their own food, health services, and other expenses through payroll deductions.[4]

The contract bound the "guest worker" to perform consistent labor, and then return to Mexico at the end of the harvest. Any "breach" of the contract by the individual, such as stopping work, leaving, or otherwise "willfully refusing" to carry out the agreement, resulted in deportation. By individualizing the contract, collective bargaining was precluded. This secured a way to detach bracero lbor from the rest of the working class and legally redefine temporary workers as the virtual property of the growers.

While the Bracero Program granted the formal right for temporary workers to join American unions, the process was sabotaged by multiple layers of obstruction. First, unions put very few resources into organizing braceros. When braceros did speak out, or when unionization attempts did take place, efforts were undermined by an alliance of government forces and growers. According to Ernesto Galarza,

When the National Farm Labor Union ... began admitting the Mexicans in 1950, employer opposition quickly appeared. Consultation of local farm labor unions by the Department of Labor was quashed. An ambiguous provision was written into the 1951 agreement. This provision, Article 21, purported to recognize organizational prerogatives and collective action by the contract workers through their elected representatives. The text of this important article was drafted by employer attorneys in consultation with the United States negotiators of the Department of Labor. It limited the bargaining rights of the braceros to "maintaining the work contract." Since no procedures were indicated for the election of worker representatives, and since the Department of Labor systematically refused to meet with American union officials to contract grievances presented by Mexicans who had joined the union, Article 21 was stillborn. It remained embalmed in the meaningless language of the international agreement.

He concludes,

These difficulties aside, the organization of braceros as union members in any case would have been difficult. Their camps were isolated. They were totally lacking, as a group, in trade union experience. Gangs were dispersed overnight and men transferred to other camps continuously. Leadership was completely absent; its infrequent manifestations only led to sharp reprisal.[5]

The temporary character of the workforce had other embedded benefits. As the American Farm Bureau Federation put it, "Mexican workers [braceros] unaccompanied by wives and families ... can fill our seasonal peaks and return home ... without creating difficult social problems."[6] The phrase "difficult social problems" was code for growers being forced to take responsibility for the schooling, housing, and health care of farmworkers that was necessary to produce and maintain a stable workforce on a year-round basis. In other words, Mexican tax-payers and Mexican workers themselves paid the initial costs of socializing, training, educating, and sustaining Mexican labor that was then inserted into the U.S. economy. U.S. growers were absolved of this "reproduction of labor" and reaped the short-term benefits during harvest season. As Chicano historian Erasmo Gamboa concluded, "[the braceros'] work, in rich agricultural states like California, Arizona, and Texas, subsidized the nation's food consumption through low prices during an extraordinary period of postwar economic prosperity."[7] Furthermore, since the U.S. government paid the costs of distributing workers to worksites, it meant that, through their tax dollars, other workers in the United States footed the bill for this as well.

To add insult to injury, braceros could be moved by their employers or the government, but could not leave a worksite independently. An attorney speaking on behalf of the agricultural industry blithely told a state legislative committee that, therefore, the Bracero Program "completely removes the possibility" of these workers ever becoming part of the American labor movement. The California Farm Bureau also chimed in, contrasting the value of braceros to the "domestics" that were able to move elsewhere if dissatisfied with conditions.[8]

Initially, the program was jointly administered by both the U.S. and Mexican governments, with stipulations that allowed the Mexican government to monitor the treatment of its workers in the United States. By 1951, the U.S. government had completely taken over the management of the Bracero Program with the passage of "Public Law 78." This legislation empowered the Department of Labor to be the official contractor for corporate agriculture. The U.S. government had subsidized the program to the tune of $55 million in previous years; now it was the primary procurer and guarantor of cheap labor for big business. As Assistant Secretary of Agriculture Mervin L. McClain described it, the Bracero Program redefined the "role of government as the hired hand on the farm."[9]

As the government increased its role as provider of labor, it commensurately decreased its role as enforcer of contractual agreements. During his tenure as deputy director of farm placement in the early period of the Bracero Program, Don Larin became the champion of agribusiness. Larin allowed for the priority placement of braceros, thus enabling farmers to use them as a "negotiating chip" against the current workforce, and gave virtual carte blanche to the growers to police themselves when it came to holding up their end of the contract.[10] Since the federal government was responsible for certifying wage levels, this "laissez-faire" approach allowed growers to drive wages even lower—with government sanction.

As time went on, growers found it increasingly easy to avoid their obligations and defraud the braceros on a regular basis. The gradual abandonment of enforcement ensured that these practices remained largely unchecked. For example, in 1959, 182,000 braceros were brought into California and Arizona alone, but only 22 field agents were made available to address grievances.[11] This sort of government neglect helped to set the "bracero benchmark"—the use of braceros to lower wage standards throughout the industry. As a result, during the 1950s, all agricultural wages stagnated or dropped below World War II–era levels.[12] The urban-rural proletarian wage gap yawned even wider. Farm wages dropped to 36.1 percent of manufacturing wages, down from 47.9 percent in 1946.[13] While working conditions were gradually improving in other sectors, labor relations in the fields were being thrown back to the nineteenth century.

The Bracero Program thus became a tool for the complete transformation of agriculture, directly under the aegis of the U.S. government. As the President's Commission on Migratory Labor concluded, "Following the war, we virtually abandoned effective scrutiny and enforcement of the Individual Work Contracts to which employers and individual Mexican aliens were the parties." [14]

It soon became apparent that the protection of workers was never a primary concern for the state. As Galarza explains, "From its highest to its lowest levels, the Department of Labor was less an advocate of workers than a sensitive barometer of the powerful forces that focus in the national capital."[15]

The more profitable the program proved, the more it moved away from being a temporary arrangement. As soldiers returned to the ranks of workers, many avoided the fields in favor of the urban-industrial centers. Soon braceros and other migrant workers became the majority of the rural workforce, buttressing both the program and the widely held belief that only immigrants will do the back-breaking labor that "Americans don't want to do."[16]

Although the program was becoming permanent, individual workers' stays in the U.S. were not. In order to ensure that Mexican workers returned to their country of origin, a number of safeguards were built into the system. First, the wives and families of the braceros were not allowed into the country, which motivated braceros to return home at the conclusion of their contracts. Second, the U.S. government retained up to 10 percent of bracero wages until the end of the contract. Ostensibly designed to set up a pension fund, this was to ensure that braceros returned to Mexico, where they could obtain the remainder of their pay.[17] As a representative of the Agricultural Land Bureau of the San Joaquin Valley put it, "We are asking for labor only at certain times of the year— at the peak of our harvest—and the kind of labor we want is the kind we can send home when we get through with them."[18]

The state apparatus regulated the ebb and flow of labor through the auspices of the Border Patrol. Created to police labor, border agents served as "foremen," enforcing segregation in public places and disciplining "agitators" and malcontents. For example:

> A senior immigrant agent told a State Department official in 1944, according to a memorandum of their telephone conversation, that "the immigration service was concentrating on those who were not engaged in the preparation and harvesting of perishable crops." In 1949, the Immigration Commissioner explained to Congress that the "Border Patrol would not go on the farms in search of 'wetbacks,' but rather confine their activities to the highways and places of social activities. Immigration commissioner Watson Miller told the House committee on agriculture … that it was the "duty" of the agency "to protect valuable and necessary crops." [19]

By 1954, the last pretenses of a binational program were abandoned. The Mexican government conceded its right to intervene on behalf of its nationals. This forfeiture happened for a few significant reasons. According to Bracero historian Mae Ngai, the U.S. government, which became the official arbiter between braceros and agricultural employers, increasingly bypassed the Mexican government through a process notoriously referred to as "drying out the wetbacks." Braceros were encouraged to return several feet into Mexico and then return as "illegals," who would then be legalized and administered accordingly. This process negated contractual obligations, thus negating Mexican oversight, primarily as a means for the U.S. government to demonstrate to the Mexican government its monopoly over labor relations.

The retreat of the Mexican state could also be explained as the result of an ideological shift in Mexico away from the nationalist paradigm that called for the preservation of the traditional agricultural sector. Capitalization of agriculture and the shift to an export-based economy were seen as the means to help subsidize industrialization in the urban sector.

The United States also began to advocate for increased economic integration between the two countries, as a means to penetrate the growing Mexican market as well as increase its influence in Mexican politics. The dramatic expansion of the U.S. economy after World War II was enough to convince many within the Mexican ruling class that growth through economic subordination to the United States would prove more profitable than the nationalistic development envisioned by the revolution.

Despite ceding control, the Mexican government continued to reap subsidiary benefits from the Bracero Program. The trajectory of Mexican urban industrialization, coupled with a massive increase of agricultural output, catalyzed mass dislocation of small and subsistence farmers and fueled the growth of the Mexican agricultural proletariat, which couldn't be absorbed into the cities and so flocked to the north. Exporting this "surplus population" both ameliorated intensifying social conditions and proved lucrative for the Mexican government. During the 1950s, braceros sent home about $30 million a year in remittances, making the Bracero Program the third-largest "industry" in Mexico.[20] Out-migration remains an essential social outlet to this day, albeit now as a consequence of deindustrialization in the cities as well as further land concentration in the countryside. Closing the border would be detrimental to both nations and have long-term repercussions, a fact that is often concealed behind nationalist and xenophobic rhetoric.

As Mexican workers streamed into the fields of U.S. agriculture, they became a part of the U.S. working class, though they remained segregated, like a separate caste inside the political boundaries of the country. Those who migrated north often returned to Mexico in the off-season, where their political identity remained intact. Unions and Mexican-American civil rights organizations tended to see braceros as rivals and objects of indignation, further reinforcing their exclusion from the polity. This stifled the development of class consciousness and redirected expressions of class anger against the braceros themselves, or into arenas where working-class power is weakest, such as political lobbying.

Growers did what they could to widen this divide by using the subjugated bracero workforce to help police the rest of the working class. More than a million workers went on strike in the volatile years of 1945–1946, and according to labor historian James Cockroft, "many of these braceros proved useful for 'scabbing' in many of these post-war strikes."[21]

The "success" and continuation of the program also created an unforeseen tier of opportunity. Though it provoked mass migration from poor villages to recruitment centers along the border, the program's stringent requirements excluded most that made the journey. For every bracero selected, another five to seven were not. Many were encouraged to cross without papers, and found work in the fields and rail lines alongside the braceros. According to a study conducted in 1951, some

60 percent of the workforce picking the tomato harvest that season were undocumented workers.[22] As one immigration historian concluded,

> It is entirely implausible to regard the United States's role in undocumented entry as unintentional, naïve, or innocent. Policymakers in the United States must have been aware that recruitment activities designed to promote the Bracero Program would encourage poor Mexicans to believe the United States was a land of opportunity, encouraging those who would not be admitted legally to enter without inspection.[23]

These undocumented workers provided all of the "benefits" of braceros, but with less bureaucracy. Undocumented workers were still powerless to protest conditions or form unions, but now growers were not responsible for providing even the most basic necessities required for braceros. And the growers could reap other benefits. For example, growers didn't have to pay the twenty-five dollar bond required for each bracero, nor the fifteen-dollar contracting fee imposed by the U.S. government, and they could evade the minimum employment period, fixed wages, and other safeguards built into the official Bracero Program.[24] Undocumented workers were able to move like free labor, but their indentured status (the inability to attain basic democratic rights) followed them wherever they went. Growers began to entice workers to cross the border without papers, which was initially allowed by the U.S. government. As a result, the undocumented flow of labor soon eclipsed the stream of binationally negotiated braceros. Between 1947 and 1949, 74,600 braceros entered the fields, while the number of unauthorized crossers registered through the U.S. government upon arrival ballooned to 142,200.[25]

These undocumented braceros began to move out of the fields and into other sectors of the economy, where they were welcomed by the heads of other industries.

> Changes in the structure of the American economy after World War II opened up large numbers of relatively low paying service and light manufacturing jobs in American cities.... New York's and Los Angeles' garment factories, and restaurants, laundries, hotels, and hospitals nearly everywhere willingly employed persons without proper papers.[26]

By 1960, about three quarters of the agricultural workforce in Texas and California consisted of "mixed crews" of braceros and undocumented workers.[27] The threat of a crackdown by immigration authorities, or *la migra*, still looms over workers who step out of line or whose services are no longer required. While the Bracero Program ended in 1964, the grooves of agricultural capitalism had been established and growing sections of the Mexican working class became integrated into the U.S. economy as subjugated noncitizens.

"Illegalized" migration, facilitated by and operating in tandem with the Bracero Program, proceeded in full force after 1964. "Illegalized" Mexican labor migration became the preference of U.S. capital, which ultimately dismantled the last vestiges of "legal" migration. Undocumented workers were now responsible for providing their own transportation, housing, and food while still working for subsistence wages, relieving the U.S. government of the last of its responsibilities.

Unauthorized migration into the fields became regularized thereafter through the informal networks that link farmlands across the country to cities, villages, and towns across the Mexican landscape. The absolutism of agricultural capital, the degradation of farm work, and the formalization of the caste system is the legacy of the Bracero Program, structures now maintained by "illegality" and the socially powerless workforce it provides.

Chapter Eighteen

Poverty in the Fields: Legacy of the Bracero Program

S haking off the early morning chill, Algimiro Morales and the other farmworkers get ready for another long day in the vegetable fields outside of the coastal city of Oceanside, California. Like the others, Morales migrated from a Mixtec Indian village in southern Mexico. Kept out of the city by high rents and the omnipresent threat of *la migra*, Morales and the rest established their homes in the secluded outlying areas beyond the farmlands. They did this by digging six-by-six foot holes in the ground and covering them with salvaged planks or by moving into small caves at the base of the surrounding hillsides.[1] There are now over one hundred thousand Mixtec immigrants from Mexico living and working in California. Most make no more that four thousand dollars a year, kept poor by a combination of low wages and the denial of basic human rights.[2]

Impoverished farmworkers like Morales go to work for the most sophisticated and profitable enterprises in California. From computer-controlled irrigation systems to laser-leveled fields, the $28 billion-a-year California fruit and vegetable industry churns out half of the yearly harvests that stock the produce sections of the neighborhood supermarkets across the country.[3] Behind the roadside farms and among the distant, ordered rows of ripening vegetation lies the hidden world of modern agribusiness, a combination of twenty-first century industrial technology and nineteenth-century labor relations. This dichotomy is the result of a century of class war in the fields, one that continues to this day.

As of 1997, there were about 1.92 million farms in the United States, employing about 2 percent of the population. About 8 percent of these farms accounted for 72 percent of agricultural sales and employed 77 percent of farmworkers. Close to 163,000 large, corporate-sized farms coexisted with 575,000 medium-sized family farms, while around 1.3 million qualified as low-production farms (small residential or hobby farms).[4] The giant industrial farms—many of which are owned by behemoth corporate enterprises such as Monsanto, Archer Daniels Midland, and Cargill—are bolstered and subsidized by large government handouts. The average size of today's farm is 588 acres; small farms comprise almost 80 percent of total farms, but less than 25 percent of agricultural production.[5] Trends show that small and medium-size farms are losing out to the corporate giants, and farming itself constitutes the fastest declining occupation in the United States.[6]

According to Bill Christison of the National Farm Family Coalition, the decline of family farms has its roots in corporate globalization:

> U.S. corporate agribusiness has been imposing their agenda through international trade agreements for the past two decades. U.S. farm policy has been tinkered with for many years with ConAgra and Cargill and other transnational corporations often directly influencing the legislative process as well as the regulatory process through their influential role within the U.S. Department of Agriculture.[7]

An example of such "tinkering" was the passage of the Federal Agriculture Implementation and Reform (FAIR) Act in 1996, legislation firmly in line with mandates dictated by the World Trade Organization (WTO). Using the rhetoric of free trade, then president Bill Clinton signed the bill, effectively ending the New Deal–era practice of guaranteed minimum loans and subsidies to help insulate small farmers from market volatility. The act eliminated the use of "deficiency payments" and replaced them with "Production Flexibility Contracts" that fixed payments according to past levels rather than the ups and downs of market prices. The Act further redirected a higher percentage of government loans and subsidies toward high-volume, export-oriented agricultural production in order to increase market share and profitability and decrease government subsidies over time.[8]

The FAIR Act and subsequent legislation have thus made smaller farmers more vulnerable to market fluctuations and unable to compete with the corporate giants. The upward flow of subsidies to the large producers has not only helped insure insulation from erratic market fluctuations but has allowed them to reap behemoth profits, a process which continues at full speed under George Bush.

Despite his partiality for the rhetoric of free trade, Bush's 2002 comprehensive Farm Security and Rural Investment Act allocates $248.6 billion toward agricultural programs, loans, and subsidies. The dispersal of funds is based on "profitability," which ensures that most of the money will flow into the pockets of agribusiness and large growers. According to the organization Food First:

> The 2002 farm bill can be best described as agribusiness welfare. The federal crop subsidies will go not to farmers who resemble John Steinbeck's Joad family, but to rich recipients, such as the fourteen members of Congress that crafted the law; wealthy American corporations like Westvaco (a paper products conglomerate), Chevron, and the John Hancock Insurance Company; and top Time-Warner entertainment executive Ted Turner, ABC correspondent San Donaldson, and billionaire David Rockefeller of Chase Manhattan Bank. Most family farms will get nothing but a tax bill. The farm bill only further tilts the playing field against them.[9]

Corporate agribusiness, kept fat and flush with government handouts, stands in stark contrast to the super-exploited workers who perform the labor.

According to the United States Department of Agriculture, there are between 3 and 5 million farmworkers in the United States who pick the seasonal fruit, nut, and vegetable harvests.[10] Of this number, 1.3 million are migrant workers, including four hundred thousand children.[11] Of farmworkers, 77 percent were born in Mexico, and federal estimates indicate that over half of all farmworkers are undocumented, 24 percent have work visas, and 22 percent are citizens.[12]

Whatever their legal status, what defines the farmworker is universal poverty. Overall, three-fifths of all farmworkers are poor, with 75 percent of farmworkers earning less than ten thousand dollars annually. The average wage of farmworkers was $5.94 in 1998, with purchasing power declining steadily each year since 1989. What's most startling is that each income statistic is halved when applied to undocumented workers.[13]

This abject poverty is compounded by a host of associated consequences. Health risks are pervasive in the fields. Farm work is one of the most deadly occupations in the U.S. Aside from the strain of labor, accidents, and exposure to toxic chemicals, workers also face unsafe housing, physical isolation, and lack of access to health care. In essence, the costs of the reproduction of labor are pushed onto the farmworkers themselves. As Daniel Rothenberg states:

> When farmworkers find jobs far from home they cover their own travel expenses, including transportation, lodging and food. Once they arrive at a particular site, they often have to wait days or even weeks for work to begin, and again they are responsible for all the related costs. Even after a job begins, full-time employment is often not available immediately. The inherent unpredictability of agriculture—the freezes, droughts, heat waves, crop diseases and market-price fluctuations—only heightens the general uncertainty of farm labor. Farmworkers are almost never given extra compensation to cover the constant displacement and downtime that marks their lives.[14]

Most farmworker families have no health coverage and instead rely on a patchwork of charitable institutions to provide basic services. In some areas, fewer than 20 percent of farmworkers have access to any health coverage at all.[15] As a consequence of this neglect, the disability rate is about three times the rate for the general U.S. population. Child workers are the most vulnerable to the precarious conditions. According to Human Rights Watch, as many as one hundred thousand children suffer from agriculture-related injuries each year.[16] These same conditions produce an average of three hundred child deaths in the fields annually.[17]

Far from being the "harbingers of disease" that anti-immigrant demagogues decry, Mexican migrant workers are largely the victims of ailments and disease that they contract *while working in the United States*. For instance, according to a study conducted by the California Department of Health, 49 percent of blood tests reporting unhealthy concentrations of lead were from Latinos, and this lead was not shipped up from Mexico but absorbed by workers in the fields. Furthermore, the forty-five thousand different pesticides used in agriculture have been linked to

> Leukemia, lymph node cancer, multiple myeloma (bone cancer) in adults, leukemia and brain cancer in children; birth defects, spontaneous abortion, sterility, and menstruation dysfunction; liver and kidney dysfunction, nervous system disorders such as poor motor coordination and thought processes, anxiety and depression; and immunological abnormalities.[18]

This problem is exacerbated by the fact that many states do not provide workers' compensation for migrants and most agricultural states make exceptions for child labor in agriculture. According to federal law, children as young as nine years old can pick berries in Oregon, ten-year-olds can work on any farm in Illinois, and twelve-year-olds are commonly seen working alongside their parents on the agricultural horizons of California.[19]

But farmworkers continue to struggle against great odds. The Coalition of Immokalee Workers (CIW), for example, gained national attention in 2001 when they took Taco Bell to task through a national boycott. The coalition is a community-run organization of Latino, Haitian, and Mayan immigrant farmworkers based in Florida, and it has successfully focused national attention on the falling wages of farmworkers. Their campaign, called the "Taco Bell Truth Tour," pointed to the fact that the hourly wage for some farmworkers had fallen by more than 50 percent (adjusted for inflation) between 1980 and 2005.[20] Prior to the launch of the tour, farmworkers in Florida were earning about forty cents for each thirty-two-pound bucket of tomatoes they picked—a rate that had remained constant for the last thirty years. The average farmworker had to pick two tons of tomatoes just to earn around fifty dollars.[21] Since some of the biggest fast food chains depend on Florida tomatoes, the CIW made Yum Brands, which owns Taco Bell, Pizza Hut, and KFC, the target of their boycott. After four years of struggle, through solidarity campaigns, pickets, marches, and other tactics organized across the country, the coalition was able to force Yum Brands to increase their pay per pound of tomatoes. For its part, Taco Bell announced that it will "ensure that none of its tomato suppliers employ indentured servants," a demand raised by the Immokalee workers as well.[22] The coalition has now set its sights on the McDonald's chain of restaurants, because the farmworkers who pick tomatoes bought by McDonald's also face incredible exploitation.

Due to horrific conditions in the agriculture industry, it is not surprising that an estimated 40 percent of undocumented agricultural workers have already migrated to the construction industry, creating the "artificial shortage" that growers are trumpeting as a means to demand a new guest-worker program. Facing a $1 billion loss of their winter crop in early 2006, Arizona growers channeled their efforts into lobbying for a twenty-first-century Bracero Program, rather than raising wages to attract labor. Such a program is preferred over "illegality," since even undocumented workers can negotiate higher wages during labor shortages. A new guest-worker program would once again place *absolute control* over the workers back in the hands of the agricultural bosses.

Chapter Nineteen

Immigrant Workers Continue to Build America

Today, the annual incorporation of undocumented workers from Mexico into the U.S. economy continues the tradition of working-class formation through immigrant infusion. At the same time, it aids capitalist attempts to reorganize the labor market. Corporate "globalization" allows the free movement of capital, shifting some centers of production beyond borders and away from the physical loci of union power. Intensification of the concentration of capital has militated against a concomitant mobility for labor. In fact, border enforcement and immigration restrictions as attributes of labor control have increased commensurately with corporate power. But even with these greater restrictions, out-migration has been accelerated, pushing migrant workers to risk life and limb to find work or sanctuary away from home, particularly in the United States.

> Two factors of the late twentieth century were especially important in creating this scenario. First, as many observers have noted, globalization has promoted higher rates of immigration. The expansion of U.S. private investment and trade; the opening of U.S. multinational assembly plants (employing mostly women) along the U.S.-Mexico border and in the Caribbean and Central American nations, facilitated by government legislative efforts such as the Border Industrialization Program, the North American Free Trade Agreement, and the Caribbean Basin Initiative; the spreading influence of U.S. mass media; and U.S. military aid in Central America have all helped rearrange local economies and stimulate U.S. bound migration from the Caribbean, Mexico and Central America.[1]

Neoliberal immigration policy involves the planned influx and absorption of immigrants, though they have been stigmatized, denaturalized, and disempowered by the legislative process of "illegalization." According to immigration specialist Saskia Sassen,

> Measures commonly thought to deter immigration—foreign investment, or the promotion of export-oriented agriculture and manufacturing in poor countries—have had precisely the opposite effect. Such investment contributes to massive displacement of small-scale agricultural and manufacturing enterprises, while simultaneously deepening the economic, cultural, and ideological ties between the recipient countries and the United States.[2]

Capital, with the help of the state, has been able to not only depopulate union strongholds through capital mobility, but also "deunionize" (through "illegalization") the new labor populations that are moving into the low-wage sectors of the economy. Today, undocumented migration has once again surpassed "legal" migration as a result of these trends. According to a Pew Hispanic Center Poll, of the 35.2 million foreign-born people in the U.S.:

> [T]he number of persons living in families in which the head of the household or the spouse is an unauthorized migrant [was] 13.9 million as of March 2004, including 4.7 million children. Of those individuals, some 3.2 million are U.S. citizens by birth but are living in "mixed status" families in which some members are unauthorized, usually a parent, while others, usually children, are Americans by birthright.[3]

While as many as one-third of the undocumented are "overstays"— those who come on visas primarily from wealthier countries and remain after their expiration—virtually all negative attention is focused on migrant Mexican workers, who comprise about 56 percent of the total undocumented population.[4] This racialization of immigration enforcement, the "brown divide" within the immigrant community, becomes apparent when one drives through the northern and eastern corridors of San Diego County, California. Border checkpoints stop the vehicles of those who fit the "profile" of an undocumented worker. The transaction takes place with a fleeting glimpse. If you are white you are waved through, but if you are brown, you are suspect. Monuments to institutional racism like these border checkpoints are kept in place solely to reinforce the physical barriers between Mexican migrants and the rest of the working class.

These workers comprise the vast connective tissue that allows the American economy to function. The bifurcation of this workforce along national lines channels the invisible "illegal" workforce into the tributaries of nonunion or "deunionized" industries and regions of the economy. Ruminating on the economy of Southern California, one sociologist observed,

> Think about it. The janitors, cooks, busboys, painters, carpet cleaners, and landscape workers who keep the office buildings, restaurants, and malls running are likely to be Mexican or Central American immigrants, as are many of those who work behind the scenes in dry cleaners, convalescent homes, hospitals, resorts, and apartment complexes…. The Los Angeles economy, landscape, and lifestyle have been transformed in ways that rely on low-wage, Latino immigrant labor.[5]

Overall, undocumented workers make up about 5 percent of the total national workforce (in some states, such as California and Texas, the percentage is much higher), and in recent years, migrant workers have become concentrated in key industries scattered across the country. According to a 2005 Labor Department survey, they're a quarter of workers in the meat and poultry industry, 24 percent of dishwashers, and 27 percent of drywall and ceiling tile installers. It is also believed that undocumented workers comprise up to 25 percent of the construction workforce, and about a third of garment workers.[6] In agriculture, about 24 percent of all farming jobs are held by the undocumented, 17 percent of cleaning jobs, 12 percent of food preparation, and about 31 percent of overall work in the service industry.[7] Studies conducted in 2005 also show a substantial population of day laborers, informal workers regularly hired by building contractors and homeowners. It is estimated that there are over 117,000 itinerant day laborers, although that number is probably low since it is difficult to measure such a transient population.[8] In select "growth counties" across the South, Latinos comprise upwards of 57 percent of manufacturing workers. In 2004, more than 1 million of the nation's 2.5 million new jobs went to migrant workers.[9]

Women make up a significant percentage of these migrants. This is demonstrated by the fact that foreign-born Latinas make up about 68 percent of nannies, housekeepers, and house-cleaners in major population centers.[10] Women have comprised about 35 percent of migrants apprehended and deported from the United States every year since 2002.[11] Figures from Mexico's National Women's Institute report that about half of the six hundred thousand Mexicans who emigrate each year are women.[12] Tragically, it is estimated that women made up about 25 percent of the four thousand deaths that have occurred along the border between 1994 and 2005. What's more,

> According to Laura Velasco Ortiz, a researcher with Tijuana's Colegio de la Frontera Norte, more than 60 percent of the estimated $20 billion in remittances received by Mexico are now sent by women as opposed to about 39 percent sent by men.[13]

According to the U.S. Department of Labor, the number of jobs in America increased by 15 million between 1990 and 2003, and it is projected that more than 33 million new job openings will be created between 2000 and 2010. Largely low-skilled jobs that will likely be filled by immigrant workers, they represent 58 percent of all new job openings.[14]

Why does immigration continue? As previously mentioned, cheap labor is profitable and neoliberalism causes displacement, but there is another reason: the native-born working population is shrinking. According to Lewis W. Goodman, an American University expert on U.S.-Latin American relations, "If we didn't have those elements [immigrant workers], we would be moving into a situation like Japan and Europe ... where the populations are graying in a way that is very alarming and endangering their productivity and endangering even their social security systems."[15] In many first world countries, the very *stability* of the economy depends on the absorption of immigrant workers.

This phenomenon is most clearly demonstrated in California, where immigration is the cornerstone of the nation's largest economy. According to a September 2005 study by the California Budget Project, the fastest growing segment of the population is the over sixty-five set. While the African-American population is expected to remain constant, the Anglo population is decreasing overall (expected to fall by 1 million by 2020); another one in four will be sixty-five by the year 2020. Across the United States, the number of workers aged fifty-five to sixty-four will have increased by more than half in this decade, at the same time as thirty-five- to forty-four-year-olds will have declined by 10 percent.[16]

Meanwhile, Latinos are filling the void, adding youthful vibrancy to an ossifying society. By 2014, for instance, half of all schoolchildren in California will be Latino, and the population will emerge as the majority by 2020.[17] This growth in the Latino population is not limited to California. For instance, the migrant Latino population has grown precipitously throughout the South: North Carolina (394 percent), Arkansas (337 percent), Georgia (300 percent), Tennessee (278 percent),

South Carolina (211 percent), and Alabama (208 percent) registered the highest rates of increase in the Hispanic population of any states in the United States between 1990 and 2000, with the exception of Nevada (217 percent).[18]

Though you'd never know it by listening to the hyperbolic cries of the Far Right (given ample coverage by virtually every mainstream news outlet in the country), the majority of population growth will come from citizens, not the undocumented. In fact, while birthrates among undocumented workers are increasing overall, their pace is slowing.

A 2005 study determined that, "while immigration to California will continue, the share of the state's population accounted for by recent immigrants will continue to decline. The share of recent immigrants is projected to fall to 7.5 percent by 2020 and 7.0 percent by 2030."[19] In fact, according to the *Globalist,* the addition of undocumented workers to overall population growth is negligible. In 2005, undocumented migrants contributed to population growth at the rate of about 3.3 for every 1,000 people.[20]

About 12 percent of the population is foreign-born, and of those, 71 percent are "legal permanent residents" and about 29 percent are residents without papers.[21] Trends also show that as many as 30 percent of undocumented crossers return to their country of origin. Immigration continues to provide the "necessary labor," just as it has throughout the history of the country.

Behind the political smokescreen, those that recognize the danger to their own interests are beginning to feel squeezed by tighter immigration restrictions. According to the *Washington Post:*

> Yuma [Arizona] Mayor Larry Nelson, a Republican, said he once believed the border should be closed entirely. Responsibility for his community's economic health has changed his mind, he said. "We have more jobs in America than we have workers," he said. "If you took every illegal out of the United States right now, you would shut down the food industry, the vast majority of the hotels and all the service industries. If you stop [immigration], this nation will come to a screeching halt."[22]

A report released by the American Farm Bureau Federation claims that if migrant labor is cut off by acts of Congress, $5 to $9 billion of agricultural revenue would disappear, along with up to one-third of farm producers.[23] Worker shortages are occurring throughout western agriculture, bringing $300 million in losses to raisin growers in California's San Joaquin Valley in September 2005 alone.[24]

Immigrant workers come to the U.S. to work. According to a June 2005 study by the Pew Hispanic Center, 92 percent of undocumented males are gainfully employed, higher than any other sector of the population. Immigrant workers are also taking on more diverse jobs within the economy, as one-quarter of them have at least some college education and another quarter has finished high school.[25] Migrant labor actually creates *more jobs* than it occupies. The U.S. economy is expanding by a long-term average rate of 3.5 percent per year. More than one percentage point of this increase can be attributed to the increase in population through immigration.[26]

Not only do immigrants come to work, they come *for* work that they know is available. Anti-immigrant pundits ignore their own "golden rule" when it comes to supply and demand. Undocumented workers, like all workers, follow real, available jobs, not the perception of social welfare. According to a report of the California Regional Economies Project,

> California's population growth rate is also dependent on the amount of job growth. Between 1992 and 1996, for example, during the economic recession in California, domestic migration out of California equaled 1.4 million residents. This out-migration was greater than the amount of foreign immigration into the state.[27]

Despite the mischaracterization of immigration as an infinite and inexorable torrent, the actual rate is generally proportionate to the requirements of different economic periods. According to immigration specialists Jeffery Passell and Roberto Suro,

> the United States experienced a sharp spike in immigration flows over the past decade that had a distinct beginning, middle and end. From the early 1990s through the middle of the decade, slightly more than 1.1 million migrants came to the United States every year on average. In the peak years of 1999 and 2000, the annual inflow was about 35 percent higher, topping 1.5 million. By 2002 and 2003, the number coming to the country was back around the 1.1 million mark. This basic pattern of increase, peak and decline is evident for the foreign-born from every region of the world and for both legal and unauthorized migrants.[28]

Furthermore, because immigrants *create* jobs and thus wealth, their presence could actually help raise wages or hold them constant. This is evidenced by what is happening in California, which contains the highest percentage of undocumented immigrants in the country. According to a 2005 study,

In 1990, average wages in California were 10.9 percent above the national average. In 2004, despite the loss of aerospace and high tech jobs and despite continuing high levels of immigration, wage levels in California had climbed to 13.4 percent above the national average.... California [also] continues to outpace the rest of the nation in job growth.... If anything, California's large immigration flows should have raised job levels and provided support for construction markets.[29]

In a study published in *USA Today*, job growth in ten U.S. inner cities with high immigrant populations outpaced job growth in their broader metropolitan statistical areas. The study found that the average inner city wage grew 1.8 percent, to $39,300, between 1995 and 2003, outpacing an average wage growth of 1.7 percent in metropolitan statistical areas.[30] While this data demolishes the idea that immigrant workers steal jobs from other workers, their segregation within the labor market has led the Pew Hispanic Center Study to conclude that, though Latino immigrants and native-born workers appear to be on "different paths," "[immigrants'] growing supply and concentration in certain occupations suggests that the newest arrivals are competing with each other in the labor market to their own detriment."[31]

It has become the rallying cry of the anti-immigrant movement to accuse these workers of subverting the economy. Nothing could be further from the truth. According to San Jose State University economist Benjamin Powell:

Basic economic reasoning shows that when you increase the supply of any good, holding other things constant, its price should go down. However, immigration brings many secondary effects that offset the increased supply. Most immediately, when immigrants earn money, they demand goods and services. This increases the demand for labor, which in turn creates more jobs and pushes wages back up.[32]

A study conducted in late 2005 by the Kenan Institute of Private Enterprise at the University of North Carolina at Chapel Hill concluded that Latinos pumped $9 billion into the state economy in 2004. The study estimated that 45 percent of the state's approximately six hundred thousand Latinos in the state are undocumented workers, who contribute a sizeable proportion of that gargantuan sum through their labor.[33]

A Thunderbird study found that "the buying power, or after-tax income, of undocumented immigrants also is important in Arizona. Mexican immigrants, legal and undocumented, accounted for 3.1 percent, or nearly $4.2 billion, of the purchasing power of all consumers in the state in 2002."[34] In San Diego, "the [C]hamber [of Commerce] estimates that as much as 8 percent of the retail transactions in San Diego come from cross-border buyers. With sales reaching $40.8 billion in 2003, that means Mexicans and other border crossers contribute about $3.3 billion."[35] While immigrant workers send a significant portion of their income to their home countries in the form of remittances, a study cited in *Time* magazine concluded that 80 percent of their earnings is reinvested in their local economies.[36]

Far from bringing economic hardship, immigrants revitalize communities. In many cases, inner-city decay has been countered by what has been called the "sweat equity" of Latino migrants. For example, "75,000 or so Mexican and Salvadoran homeowners [have] become an unexcelled constructive force (the opposite of white flight) working to restore debilitated neighborhoods to trim respectability."[37] This phenomenon has been reinforced by housing data collected in 2005 and 2006 from across the nation.

A Harvard University study found that between 1998 and 2001, immigrant homebuyers purchased 8 percent of new homes and 11 percent of existing homes sold, making up 12 percent of first-time homebuyers in 2001. The study concludes that immigration is an important driver of demand in this vital sector of the economy.[38] This was echoed in a *USA Today* article that reported, "almost a third of California homebuyers had Hispanic surnames in June 2004.... That's up from less than a fifth in 2002. The top surnames of buyers: Garcia, Hernandez, Lopez and Rodriguez."[39]

According to the National Association of Hispanic Real Estate Professionals, over 216,000 *more* undocumented immigrants would buy homes if they had better access to the market. According to Mary Mancera, spokeswoman for the association, "There are quite a few who have been working and saving money and raising kids and going about their lives and want to achieve that next step, but haven't been able to because of the barriers."[40]

A December 2005 article in the *Los Angeles Times* showed that the stagnant housing market in Watts has rebounded, with resale home values increasing by more than 40 percent in 2004, and the countywide median rising by 24.8 percent. This turnaround has been fueled by demands from prospective Latino homeowners, many of whom are undocumented, prompting a growing number of real estate agents to begin running bilingual ads.[41] Other studies have demonstrated similar effects caused by Latino immigration in stagnating cities and towns across the country, all the way into the farthest corners of the Northeast.[42] Aside from purchasing homes, migrant workers are also bolstering the booming real estate market through their labor. Substantial numbers of migrants are leaving agriculture to build homes, high-rises, and condos, helping to produce numerous multi-millionaires.

The increasing purchasing power of undocumented workers is attracting the attention of big business. Referring to undocumented immigrants as an "untapped engine of growth," *BusinessWeek* commented,

> In the past several years, big U.S. consumer companies—banks, insurers, mortgage lenders, credit-card outfits, phone carriers, and others—have decided that a market of 11 million or so potential customers is simply too big to ignore. It may be against the law for the Valenzuelas to be in the U.S. or for an employer to hire them, but there's nothing illegal about selling to them.... What's more, 84 percent of illegals are 18-to-44-year-olds, in their prime spending years, vs. 60 percent of legal residents. Corporate sales and profits will get a shot in the arm if more of them move out of the cash economy, put their money in banks, and take out credit cards, car loans, and home mortgages. U.S. gross national product could get a boost, too, since consumers with credit can spend more than those limited to cash.[43]

Immigrant workers are becoming an increasingly important component of the international economy, not only because they sustain shrinking labor forces in developed countries, but also because they send home remittances, hard currency to family members that adds up to over $167 billion per year.[44] Remittances from migrant workers to developing nations have actually surpassed direct aid from wealthier countries and institutions.[45] In Mexico, about $20 billion in remittances are sent back each year—constituting Mexico's second-largest source of legal foreign exchange, topped only by petroleum exports.[46] More than 60 percent of this total comes from Mexican women living in the United States.[47] The four Central American nations of El Salvador, Guatemala, Honduras, and Nicaragua received a combined $7 billion from migrant workers in 2004 alone.[48]

Remittances are also a substantial source of profit for banks in the host countries. For the $72 billion sent to developing nations in 2001, the workers had to pay multinational banks the hefty fee of $12 billion, and U.S.-based banks were no exception:

U.S. banks make huge profits on *remesas*, the remittances sent home by Latin American immigrants. In 2001, $28.4 billion were sent to the developing countries from the United States. Nearly a third of this went to Mexico, procuring about $1.5 million for U.S. banks.

Recent projections from the Bank of Mexico estimate that dollar remittances for 2005 will reach at least $20 billion, an amount double the earnings from the vegetable export sector of the economy promoted under the North American Free Trade Agreement.[49]

And, as usual, U.S. capital finds a way to profit on *both* sides of the border:

> The largest and fastest-growing business opportunities associated with workers' remittances have attracted at least two major FDI [foreign direct investment] deals in Mexico recently. Valued at $12.5 billion, the Citigroup-Banamex deal in 2001 is the single biggest investment south of the border for any U.S. company.... In December 2002, Bank of America paid Santander [Bank] $1.6 billion for part of Serfin.[50]

The profitability of money transfers is encouraging U.S.-based corporations and politicians to find more ways to cash in. A growing number of banks is offering services for migrants. An article in *La Jornada* reported that

> According to the Bank of Mexico, 51 million money transfer operations from the United States to Mexico are realized each year, with each transaction averaging $326. The business has been very profitable for U.S. banks and other firms which charge fees for the money transfers. A report by the Washington-based National Council of La Raza estimated that from mid 2002 to early 2004, about 400,000 new bank accounts were opened in the United States at branches which offer remittance services.
>
> Ultimately, many of the remittance dollars are recycled in border cities like El Paso and Laredo by Mexican shoppers who prefer buying on the U.S. side.[51]

The hypocrisy of persecuting immigrants while profiting from them reached new heights in Arizona in early 2006. The Arizona House Appropriations Committee approved a resolution that would attach an 8 percent state tax on electronic money transfers to Mexico. The tax, which will generate $80 million every year, will be used to pay for a double and triple-walled border fence between Arizona and Mexico.[52] This carries the same colonialist logic that politicians have used in Iraq; first destroy a region, then make the inhabitants pay for its reconstruction.

Immigrant workers also pay taxes. According to a 1997 study, immigrant households paid an estimated $133 billion in direct taxes to federal, state, and local governments. Another study by the National Academy of Sciences found that immigrants benefit the U.S. economy overall, have little negative effect on the income and job opportunities of most native-born Americans, and may add as much as $10 billion to the economy each year. Overall, according to the study, further analysis would likely show "that 49 of the 50 states come out ahead fiscally from immigration."[53] While migrants may draw resources from local governments, a 1997 National Academy of Sciences study found that they contribute on average a net of eighteen hundred dollars more per person than they use, which amounts to a net contribution of eighty thousand dollars more than what their descendants receive in local, state, and federal benefits.[54] Even former Federal Reserve chair Alan Greenspan has quietly credited undocumented workers with an important role in keeping down the inflation rate. In fact, even the nation's preeminent business mouthpiece, the *Wall Street Journal*, concluded that immigration is more of a boon than a bane. A survey of the nation's leading economists conducted by the paper found that 59 percent believe the effect of illegal immigration on the wages of low-income workers is slight, while 22 percent believe immigrants have no effect whatsoever. Moreover, "nearly all of the economists—44 of the 46 who answered the question—believe that illegal immigration has been beneficial to the economy."[55]

According to the *New York Times*, since the Immigration Reform and Control Act of 1986 set penalties for employers who knowingly hire undocumented immigrants, most have been forced to buy fake Social Security cards to obtain work. Though most undocumented workers (estimated at about 75 percent[56]) pay into Social Security and Medicare through payroll deductions, they are denied remuneration in the form of benefits.

Since the 1980s, the Social Security Administration has seen a steady increase of W-2 earnings reports with phony Social Security numbers that cannot be matched to their undocumented earners. Stashed into what is called the "Earnings Suspense File," since there are no accurate records of who paid the taxes, the fund has mushroomed to a whopping $189 billion in wage receipts, generating $6 to $7 billion in Social Security tax revenue and about $1.5 billion in Medicare taxes, none of which can be claimed by the people who worked for it.[57] This puts many migrant workers in the same boat as "Miguel": "I've worked here fifteen years and have never gotten anything back at the end of the year.... Without papers, you get nothing back. The government has gathered up that retirement and medical money. I don't know what they do with it."[58] A *Time* magazine article estimates that through 2002, undocumented migrants have contributed up to $463 billion to Social Security.[59]

As part of its effort to track down the unassigned wages, the Social Security Administration sends about 130,000 letters a year to employers with large numbers of mismatched pay statements. A consequence of these so-called "no-match letters" is the firing of undocumented workers, or their voluntary exodus, provoked by fear of apprehension. Nevertheless, an analysis of Social Security Administration data by the National Foundation for American Policy (a nonpartisan policy organization) finds that at current immigration levels, new immigrants entering the United States will provide a net benefit of $407 billion to the Social Security system over the next fifty years.[60]

Anti-immigrant politicians, eager to get their hands on other people's money, are scurrying to block any attempt to match these funds to their rightful owners. A bill passed in Congress in June 2005 by Representative J. D. Hayworth (R-AZ) prohibits distribution of Social Security funds to the undocumented. Gushing after his victory, he declared, "I am proud that a unified House stood with me to declare our determination that illegal aliens will not plunder Social Security funds that are intended solely for retired and disabled Americans."[61] In other words, the wages earned by migrant workers are being stolen and will be used to subsidize an aging population of U.S. citizens through Social Security payments.

In addition, undocumented workers pay other taxes, such as property taxes. Nearly a decade ago, the IRS began giving out "Individual Taxpayer Identification Numbers" (ITINs) so that people without legitimate Social Security numbers could pay income taxes and purchase homes.[62] Many choose to pay income taxes to show a willingness to contribute to society and comply with the law, in the hope of one day obtaining citizenship. Ironically, the IRS creates its own separate laws in order to get its hands on the money of undocumented people, while other institutions of the same federal government persecute the same people. The IRS has issued more than 9.2 million ITINs since 1996, with 1.2 million issued in 2005 alone. As IRS Commissioner Mark W. Everson explained, "Our job is to make sure that everyone who earns income within our borders pays the proper amount of taxes, even if they may not be working here legally."[63] And, of course, undocumented immigrants pay local and state sales taxes every time they make purchases.

Anti-immigrant pundits like to point to the "costs of illegal immigration" by selective use of isolated, regional statistics in education and health care, while consciously circumventing a macro-analysis of economic contributions overall. By repeating ad nauseum the bald-faced lie that undocumented immigrants are a "drain on resources," they ignore or hide the fact that social spending *for all workers* has been drastically cut or reduced in the last decades, creating an unnatural scarcity. For example, about 46 million working people do not have access to health care, a statistic that cuts across the whole working class. More than half of all bankruptcies are the result of health care bills, and eighteen thousand people die per year as a result of insufficient access to medical services. This happens despite the fact that the United States spends more on health care than any other nation.[64]

In fact, the crises in health care and education are national ones that affect all workers. The implementation of a universal health care system, which would redirect more of the wealth workers produce *themselves* into meeting the health care needs of all (instead of the corporate profits of the few) would eliminate scarcity instantly. Increasing funding for schools instead of slashing education budgets would eliminate problems associated with overcrowding that affects working-class people across the country.

The pundits also conveniently leave out the fact that many of the children born in the U.S. to undocumented parents are *citizens*. And even though a slight majority of the undocumented are uninsured, it is not because they don't work. According to journalist Hilary Abramson, "nearly two-thirds of the state's uninsured children have parents with full-time jobs. But many employers have passed on the escalating costs by cutting benefits for spouses and children. Those seeking private health insurance may find lower premiums, but usually have higher deductibles and … 'skimpy' coverage." Abramson quotes E. Richard Brown, director of UCLA's Center for the Study of Latino Health, who argues, "I think that the trends we're seeing are a clear indication that we are all headed over the cliff in not being able to afford health insurance coverage for ourselves and our families."[65]

Furthermore, current laws give undocumented persons access only to emergency services, as they are excluded from receiving other health programs available to citizens. Figures from a March 2006 study published in the *Los Angeles Times* show that only 15 percent of those who end up in California emergency rooms are uninsured.[66]

In addition, according to a study conducted jointly by the University of California and the Mexican government's National Population Council: "most Mexican immigrants arrive in the United States *in better health* than the white American population, but their health deteriorates the longer they stay, due partly to lack of insurance and the change in lifestyle."[67] The escalation of anti-immigrant hysteria has worked to discourage undocumented workers from seeking medical care. According to Tanya Broder, a public benefits lawyer for the National Immigration Law Center, "We've seen a real rise in anti-immigration measures ... and it's engendered confusion and fear that prevent immigrant families from getting the care they need."[68]

For example, in 2004, the Centers for Medicare and Medicaid Services proposed that hospitals report the immigration status of emergency room patients in exchange for more federal money. As one undocumented worker named Alejandra explained, "I heard that if you go to the emergency room or go to the doctor, they were going to deport you ... so then my four children are going to be without me because I don't have documents here."[69] These policies, which increase the poverty and underdevelopment of immigrant communities, occur due to discriminatory practices associated with their civic exclusion, despite the fact that their labor *subsidizes* the rest of U.S. society.

Political scientist Rodolfo O. de la Garza attributes the confinement of the majority of Mexican workers to the lower echelons of the working class to their relative segregation. The racial divide ensures that even fourth-generation Mexican-Americans lag behind other Americans in education, home ownership, and income.[70]

Though "illegalization," and the racism that comes with it, drags down all wages, the undocumented are the hardest hit. The average family income in 2003 for undocumented migrants in the country for less than ten years was $25,700, while average family incomes were considerably higher for both legal immigrants ($47,800) and the native-born ($47,700).[71] What's more, poverty rates are astronomical for immigrant children. According to an article in the *Los Angeles Times*, in California, "18.6 percent—or more than 1.7 million children—lived in poverty last year, up from 18.2 percent in 2002. Three-fourths of the state's poor children are from immigrant families."[72]

Perhaps there is no greater irony than the fact that the anti-immigrant movement supports the segregation of undocumented workers, while claiming that *they* refuse to assimilate. For instance, Colorado Congressman Tancredo can hardly conceal his contempt for Latinos in this regard:

> In a 2003 floor speech, he noted "previous generations of immigrants expected that their children would learn English," adding that "only in the recent past have we seen a political movement that seeks to perpetuate a parallel culture that does not speak English and thus cannot participate fully in the mainstream of American life."[73]

The shop-worn myth that Mexican immigrants are "unwilling to assimilate" and that they "degrade work, shun education, and are prone to crime" is still on the tongues of racists like Tancredo today. Such myths continue to substitute for rational discourse and fuel the actions of modern-day nativists, despite a contrary reality. In fact, Mexicans have a better assimilation record than earlier immigrants:

> An 1892 annual report of the U.S. superintendent of immigration referred to "an enormous influx of foreigners unacquainted with our language and customs." It noted that "the majority of these unfortunates came here without money and without skill as workmen," and warned that they were turning into a "new undesirable class."

However,

> Those groups long ago entered the American mainstream, and there's reason to believe that the advancement of Mexicans has been as fast or faster. James Smith of Rand Corp., a think tank in Santa Monica, Calif., found that educational progress across three generations of Mexicans—immigrants, their children and their grandchildren—is the same or greater than the progress of Europeans who arrived in the late 1800s and early 1900s.[74]

Claims that the undocumented "refuse" to assimilate are patently false. According to a 2005 study of English language usage among immigrants, "Language dominance changes dramatically between generations of Latino immigrants and their children. More than 70 percent of the first generation are Spanish dominant, but that amount falls to 4 percent in the second generation and 0 percent in the third generation."[75]

Despite their demonization, immigrants in general and Latino immigrants in particular are always welcome in the U.S. military. According to a *New York Times* article, "As of January, about 41,000 permanent resident aliens were in the U.S. armed forces in Iraq, 3,639 of them from Mexico. The Mexicans are the largest group among the 63 immigrants who have been killed in action in Iraq, the Pentagon says."[76] As the government throws up walls against Mexican workers trying to enter the United States, it throws open the door to the military and war. As a special incentive, Congress created a one-year fast track to citizenship in November 2003 for immigrants serving in the military.[77] For immigrants, this may not seem like the most dangerous option, since about one migrant worker dies each day trying to cross into the United States to work.

If it is confusing that the worshippers of "supply and demand" reject their own "iron laws" when it comes to the distribution of labor, that they erect borders and conceal the indispensable contribution of immigration to their own well-being, the economic dimensions are more easily decipherable when examined through a political lens. The anti-immigrant choir is a reflection of conflicts taking place within the U.S. economy. On the one hand, immigrants provide an easy target for politicians seeking to deflect attention from the systemic deficiencies of capitalism; on the other hand, their legal integration into the working class creates the conditions for participation in unions and the political process, and is thus a threat to the mega-profits of corporate America.

Part IV

THE WAR ON IMMIGRANTS

Six Guatemalan and two Honduran women are arrested at a checkpoint in Hermosillo; three of them are pregnant. The group consisted of sixteen people from both countries who planned to reach the U.S.– Mexico border via Altar.

Chapter Twenty

Immigration Policy as a Means to Control Labor

The American educational system still teaches children to believe that the United States is a land of immigrants, despite the fact that the philosophy behind that claim is now buried under an avalanche of restrictions. In fact, the official response to immigration has always been schizophrenic, embracing immigrants at some moments and decrying them at others. It has always included prophets of doom, convinced that immigration will destroy the nation, yet both immigration and the nation continue. At a certain point, the majority of "immigrants" became "Americans" while others were excluded from that right. At each stage of immigration, the path to citizenship has been contested. Why is this issue so fraught with conflict? Because the very foundation of American capitalism rests upon its manipulation.

Throughout the early history of the United States, the peopling of North America was considered a precondition for the success of American capitalism. The first "immigration policy," The Naturalization Act of 1790 (which would stay on the books for about the next one hundred years), "opened the borders" to (most of) the workers of the world, and allowed for an immediate path to citizenship, declaring that, "Any alien, being a free white person, who shall have resided within the limits and under the jurisdiction of the United States for the term of two years, may be admitted to become a citizen ... and the children of such persons ... shall also be considered as citizens of the United States."[1]

Because of the need for labor, there were no barriers to the worlds' workers— so long as they were not African or Indian, the two groups excluded from freedom and citizenship from the very beginning. To justify expulsion and genocide, Indians were denied membership—ideologically speaking—in the human race. Africans were similarly dehumanized, in order to justify their enslavement. Slavery was the first mass-controlled labor system in United States history. When slavery was abolished, the ruling class continued to use racism to divide and control the working class, and it is through a combination of racism and exclusivity over the rights of citizenship that American capital maintains degraded, segregated Mexican labor.

The development of American capitalism has been predicated on institutions of control over the working class, depriving different sections of the working class citizenship, freedom of movement, and political participation at successive stages of history (and up to the present day). The most effective means of control, aside from physical subjugation, has been the institutionalization of racism. Immigration laws have historically honed the sharpest edges of racial prejudice favored by the ruling class as a means to divide their workers.

In a capitalist economy, the most wealthy and powerful interests exert the most influence and control over the official institutions of the state, and can therefore use the state as a labor supplier and regulator. Since the primary desire of capitalists is to make *maximum* profit, they seek the cheapest and most controllable human material to do their labor. Immigration laws are, therefore, necessarily contradictory. Initially, immigration proposals derive from economic imperative: that is, the ratio of existing workers to expected job growth determines whether there will be a walls-up or doors-open policy. They take further political shape on the basis of *how* imported labor can be separated, controlled, or used as a wedge against existing labor organization. Once basic core elements are established and codified, secondary issues are negotiated with the representatives of civil society, which creates the illusion of a pluralistic approach, as does the fact that capitalists work through interest groups and political representatives to meet their labor needs and ensure labor passivity.

A united multiracial, multinational working class is the greatest threat to the hegemony of capital, since workers realize their greatest power to combat exploitation through collective organization rooted in the workplace and in the community. Immigration policy has served to atomize the working class along racial and national lines and to encourage separate planes of consciousness, such as being "American," "white," or a "citizen" versus being "Mexican," an "immigrant," or an "illegal." These designations artificially relocate the divisions in society *within* the working class, rather than along the actually existing fault lines between capital and labor. At the heart of immigration restriction is competition, the fact that, under capitalism, different workers must compete over scarce resources, as allocated by a supposedly neutral state. As Karl Marx explained,

> Competition separates individuals from one another, not only the bourgeois but still more the workers, in spite of the fact that it brings them together. Hence, it is a long time before these individuals can unite.... Hence every organized power standing over and against these isolated individuals ... can only be overcome after long struggles. [2]

Immigration policy has also served to filter out and exclude immigrants with sympathies for unions or class-conscious politics, providing a means by which to isolate, punish, and deport those who participate in class-conscious activity while working inside the United States.

At times, different sections of capital may conflict over more inclusive or exclusive legislative proposals, but the universally beneficial clauses of "labor control" are rarely contested. In the final analysis, immigration legislation has come to reflect the means by which the capitalist class sustains a fragmented working class and ideological hegemony.

By the turn of the twentieth century, the United States was unparalleled in industrial production, with the value of manufactured products rising from $1,885,862,000 in 1860 to $11,406,927,000 by 1900.[3] The transition to an industrial economy, the incorporation of vast resource-rich territories through conquest, and the maintenance of an increasing share of the world market were complicated by an insufficient labor pool. To facilitate the formation of an industrial proletariat, successive administrations adopted the conscious policy of open borders. As labor historian Kitty Calavita points out:

> By 1880, more than 70 percent of the populations in each of America's largest cities were immigrants or children of immigrants.... The foreign born increasingly made up the bulk of the industrial labor force ... [so much so that] Samuel Lane Loomis noted that "Not every foreigner is a working man, but in the cities, at least, it may almost be said that every working man is a foreigner."[4]

In the formative years of industrial expansion, immigrant workers were mass-recruited, naturalized upon entry, and fed into the mills, factories, and fields. During peaks of capital investment and high rates of return, immigration and unfettered access to a lucrative "stream" of foreign labor became hailed as a sacrament by business interests.

During times of labor shortage or economic expansion, the archetype of the sturdy, earnest, and malleable immigrant—yearning for opportunity—serves to facilitate more porous borders. During times of capitalist contraction, such as recession or depression, or other threats to the stability of profits, admiration for the immigrant gives way to disdain. During these volatile periods, the immigrant is portrayed as a malicious force in society, responsible for a constellation of social ills that threaten the nation.

Unions and left-wing organizations that seek to strengthen the collective power of workers define the left edge of public consciousness, while nativism, a populist political current that seeks to divide native- and foreign-born workers along national lines, represents the right edge. While both currents exist within the popular consciousness of the working class, they are conflicting ideologies, with nativism serving the interests of capital, and internationalism serving those of the working class. At times, unions have been on the wrong side. For instance, the American Federation of Labor and its successor, the AFL-CIO, have supported restrictions on immigrant workers' rights in times of crisis.

While the downward swings of the economy do not automatically determine immigration policy, they can contribute to the conditions in which political forces can manipulate feelings of insecurity and isolation. It is within the uncertain folds of the business cycle that nativist organizations grow, contract, and reemerge. More commonly, ruling capitalist cliques determine immigration discourse themselves either through competing legislative proposals or political parties, or at other junctures, with a unified voice.

In the post-Civil War years, the trajectory of industrial growth made capital open to the mass importation of immigrant workers. The jubilant optimism begat by economic growth was reflected by the *Chicago Tribune*'s characterization of the role of immigration: "Europe will open her gates like a conquered city. Her people will come forth to us subdued by admiration of our glory and envy of our perfect peace. On to the Rocky Mountains and still over to the Pacific our mighty populations will spread ... [until] our thirty million will triple in thirty years."[5]

A leading business journal also promoted the "essential immigrant" in 1882, stating, "Every immigrant that lands on our shores adds to the wealth producing capacity of the nation. More than that, he infuses a new life and energy into every branch of business, trade and industry. Both consumption and production are increased by his presence."[6]

The particular history of the United States as a nation consciously populated with foreign labor has meant that, at any given point, foreign-born workers can comprise between 8 percent and 20 percent of the population, while another significant portion is made up of the children of immigrants.

In the formative years of the modern American economy, foreign-born workers were not only required for growth but were also useful in policing class consciousness among assimilated American workers. Immigrants were consciously imported to replace strikers or were selected for employment on the basis of their marginality and exclusion while within the United States. "Wage reductions were frequently achieved through the use of newly arrived immigrants as strike breakers. Strike after strike among machinists in Pittsburgh in the 1840s was broken by imported immigrants. Weavers' strikes in Kensington were repeatedly defeated by the recruitment of scab labor among recent immigrants."[7] Consequently, capitalists had a stake in keeping immigrants manipulated, intimidated, and vulnerable.

The exclusionary practices of most early unions contributed to the alienation of impoverished immigrants or migrants from other regions who could be enticed to cross picket lines. While immigrants have historically accommodated to lower wages (since even low wages in the United States tend to be higher than those in their home country), once integrated into the working class—that is, once able to acquire citizenship and union rights—they rapidly acclimate to higher standards of living and should be seen as excellent targets for union organization.[8]

Unfortunately, labor leadership has not always appreciated this fact. The isolation of immigrants led to a general acceptance of the idea of "immigrant work," those categories of jobs that "Americans won't do." In reality, the super-exploitation of immigrants is merely a monument to the degradation of the conditions of labor in a particular sector, leading an observer to comment, "Working conditions and pay scales then reflect this ability to treat labor individually rather than collectively: 'immigrant workers do not exist because there are "arduous and badly paid" jobs to be done, but, rather, arduous and badly paid jobs exist because immigrant workers are present and can be sent for.'"[9]

Consequently, it is mainly through participation in strikes, protests, and other arenas of class struggle that immigrants achieve real sociopolitical integration and become "Americanized" in the sense that they are accepted into class-based, collective formations that afford them protections and advancement previously denied. Kitty Calavita explains this process as it pertains to earlier immigrant groups:

> ... [T]he same immigrant groups, the Irish and Germans, which had provided capitalists with a cheap and compliant workforce, now are the very ones who, like a Trojan Horse welcomed into their midst, comprise the backbone of the class struggle via strikes and union activity. This necessitates the continued immigration of cheap labor, a condition that contributes to the class-conflict nature of the situation as this tactic is protested. This irony, that the same national groups that now advance the class struggle had been elements of its resolution ... underlines the fact that the dialectical process is not propelled by personal attributes of individuals or individual ethnic groups, but is structurally driven.[10]

It is for this reason that capitalists remain hostile to unionization and seek to deprive succeeding generations of immigrant labor of membership rights, utilizing the state directly when necessary to prevent access to unions.

By the late nineteenth century, capitalists invested more time and energy into the arena of immigration politics, creating, funding, or allying themselves with ideological movements that sought to develop restrictive legislation. Policy proposals moved toward restricted citizenship, not as a means to stop immigration, but as a means to expand the ranks of non-citizen labor. In times of class struggle or economic decline, capitalists were also willing to form temporary alliances with groups espousing exclusion based on cultural, racial, or economic grounds.

As capital is not monolithic, competing sections push up against each other over the question of short-term needs versus long-term interests. Even during periods of stagnation or downturn, immigrant-dependent industries advocate for continued access to cheap labor, while less dependent sections of the ruling class bemoan the costs of the maintenance and reproduction of surplus labor in the form of welfare, schooling, imprisonment, and health care costs. Both see the political value of shifting the costs of systemic failure onto the workers themselves. These sorts of schisms often produce multiple legislative proposals reflecting sectional interests. But it is important to remember that all sections of capital are interested in maintaining the maximum tractability of the workforce as a whole, and can therefore unify around anti-immigrant sentiment in the form of political restrictions on immigrants once they are in the United States, while still allowing for the entry of more migrant workers.

To fully open or close the borders would have a deleterious effect on profits, since the former would enable equalization of rights for workers and the latter would restrict business's access to both *necessary* labor and *necessarily cheap* labor. The result is that immigration policy contains mechanisms for both labor importation and deportation. Meanwhile, the social construct of the border combined with the actual physical barriers that mark it serve to remind members of the working class of their status: either "legal" or "illegal," and, in either case, in a tenuous position.

To sum up, class-conscious capitalists realized the need to disrupt and retard the process of class integration and class solidarity that ultimately enables immigrant labor to increase its negotiating power. Policy-makers, acting in the interest of capital, developed a dual strategy for labor control, externally in the form of immigration "filtration," and internally in the form of legally sanctioned segregation through the practice of selective citizenship. This process gradually transformed the state apparatus into a mechanism through which labor would be provided and policed, according to the dictates of immigration policy and with the aid of its ancillary enforcement agencies.

Chapter Twenty-One

The Race and Class Construction of Immigration Restrictions

T he Industrial Revolution in the United States created massive changes in the production of goods and the nature of work. The rise of an industrial proletariat—grouped in increasingly larger factories, super-exploited, and often made up of immigrant workers— signaled the decline of the "traditional laboring classes." Artisans, craft workers, farmers, and small business proprietors were displaced by factory production and the industrialization of agriculture. While new immigrants became the backbone, flesh, and muscle of the industrial labor movement, many of those displaced filled the ranks of nativist movements. Meanwhile, in response to the growing industrial labor movement and instability brought on by the business cycle, capitalists actively supported immigration restrictions.

As the workers' movement struggled to overcome barriers to organization and unionization (since these were not legally protected activities until the 1930s), nativist organizations and bourgeois thinkers launched a major ideological offensive. Aiming to split the working class along ethnic and national lines, these groups attacked the non-Western roots of many immigrant workers, attributed poverty and radicalism to their "foreign origins," and inspired the acquiescent legislative and executive branches to sculpt legislative policy restricting immigration on the basis of race and nationality.

The racial construction of identity in the United States predates the nation's founding. The bloody birth of slavery in the colonial period required a conscious racial division between rebellious European and

African indentured servants. The "founding fathers" linked citizenship with race when they bestowed "naturalized citizenship" on "free white persons" in 1790.[1] Following their lead, nineteenth- and twentieth-century capitalists manipulated the newly formed and racially diverse industrial proletariat to their advantage. Disparate ethnic groups were segregated in living quarters and remained in cultural and linguistic isolation within the workplace, often by design. As a union organizer with the American Federation of Labor wrote in 1911:

> We found that the Americans in the textile mills of New England are gradually being displaced by Poles, Italians and Greeks, and this has created very grave difficulties in establishing unionism in these mills. The employers have two, if not more, nationalities employed, and generally manage to engender more or less national dislike between them.[2]

In the early stages, conflict between different ethnic groups was promoted by capitalists based on cultural differences like language and religion. Irish workers, often at the frontlines of class struggle in the mid-nineteenth century, were derided by nativist organizations as "savages" and "agitators," said to be "prone to violence," and chastised for their Catholic roots. In fact, the first national anti-immigrant movement, the Know-Nothing Party, was born out of opposition to the presence of Irish and German immigrant workers in the 1850s.[3]

Anti-Irish sentiment grew in part out of the residual disdain that many English immigrants felt toward "their" Irish colonial subjects, combined with a class-based distaste for the Irish as workers, since they were often unskilled, produced some of the first unions, and were a steady source of labor militancy.[4] The Know-Nothings blamed Irish immigrants for the displacement experienced by skilled Anglo workers. "Our native-born citizens hate to work by the side of an Irishman … and [feel] dishonored by the contact.… It is the same feeling which makes it impossible for a respectable white man to labor by the side of slaves in the south."[5]

Not satisfied with simple bigotry, the nativists developed pseudo-scientific theories to support their exclusionary efforts. In doing so, they entered on a project first devised by the supporters of slavery. As early as the 1840s, scientists in the pay of the plantation owners were constructing theories to help save the embattled slave system. One of these scientists, Dr. Samuel Cartwright, theorized

> that the black skin of African-Americans in conjunction with a deficiency of red blood cells led to smaller brain sizes in blacks, which resulted in both less intelligence and less morals. This theory led Cartwright to postu-

late that slavery was a cure for the physiological illnesses of blacks, because it "makes the lungs perform the duty of vitalizing the blood more perfectly than is done when they are left free to indulge in idleness." [6]

The impact of this "divide and rule" strategy faded when workers overcame their linguistic divisions to unite, join unions, and strike, which they did increasingly as the century wore on. First- and second-generation Irish and eastern European workers spoke perfect English and were indiscernible from western Europeans. As the descendants of European immigrants melted into the Anglo-American pot, immigration restrictionists set their sights on biology and race, a shift that coincided with an increase of non-European immigrants.

The advocates of immigration restriction built on earlier racial theories that had aimed to justify slavery—promoting intrinsic, biological differences as a justification for the exclusion of immigrants. Different ethnic groups were assigned biological or cultural traits that impeded their "assimilation" into American society or imparted them with a greater propensity for "antisocial" behavior. The first target was Chinese workers.

Since these reactionary organizations attacked the most vulnerable sections of the immigrant working class in times of social crisis, they won the support of capitalist interests seeking both to mitigate the scope of class struggle and redirect class anger away from the point of production. This became most urgent when white workers engaged in class struggle and directly challenged capital. For instance, in the aftermath of the Great Railroad Strikes of 1877, nativists argued that the presence of Chinese workers was to blame for the turmoil, especially since it was Chinese workers that had organized a railway strike ten years prior. As one group, the "Asiatic Exclusion League" argued:

> Conflict is inherent in the situation whenever and wherever two races so diverse that they do not readily amalgamate dwell in large numbers in the same community, for history proves that the invariable result is closely drawn social and other lines of distinction attended with jealousy and discord culminating in a contest for race supremacy.... Don't be deceived by any delusive hope that the yellow race can possibly become amalgamated ... through intermarriage. The very thought is preposterous and revolting in view of their physical, mental, and moral differences.... [7]

The Chinese Exclusion Act of 1882, barring most Chinese immigration on spurious racial grounds, created the first comprehensive exclusion of an ethnic group on the basis of "inherent qualities." Subsequent migration from China was now "illegal" and the Chinese were criminalized. Similar patterns of racial segregation of the immigrant working class would follow suit, providing the ruling class with a means of constructing scapegoats and deflecting class anger. As historian Ronald Takaki explains, "The Chinese Exclusion Act was in actuality symptomatic of a larger conflict between white labor and white capital: exclusion of the Chinese was designed not only to diffuse an issue agitating white workers but also to alleviate class tensions within white society."[8]

Somehow, separating out workers according to their "irreconcilability" with Anglo-centric notions of American identity (after all, the capitalists, the politicians, and the intelligentsia were "Anglo"), created the impression that wages would increase and more state resources would be directed toward white workers if the Chinese were removed, a result that never materialized. At the same time, immigration was posited as the reason for poor economic conditions, rather than the failures and inequities of the system itself.

"Asian exclusion" was broadened to include the Japanese not long after. Japanese laborers had succeeded both at coalescing into collective bargaining units and at acquiring land in California. Large California growers, the Goliaths of state politics, orchestrated the legal dismantling of Japanese citizenship through their agents in government, in part due to the success Japanese farmers enjoyed in their competition with Anglo growers. As the governor of California, William Dennison Stephens, lamented in 1920,

> The Japanese in our midst have indicated a strong trend to land ownership and land control ... and by standards and methods that are widely separated from our occidental standards ... have gradually developed to a control of many of our important agricultural industries.... So that it is apparent without much more effective restrictions that in a very short time, historically speaking, the Japanese population within our midst will represent a considerable portion of our entire population, and the Japanese control over certain essential food products will be an absolute one....[9]

The developing radicalism of "white" workers (both native- and foreign-born) caused the paradigm of white supremacy to be overhauled. According to the nativists and their capitalist backers, even some white "foreigners" were now inherently threatening. The nativists subsequently developed "genetics theories" that catalogued all peoples into a genetic hierarchy and served to justify exclusion and the explosion of racist movements. As historian Matthew Frye Jacobson explains,

[T]he political history of whiteness and its vicissitudes between the 1840s and the 1920s represents a shift from one brand of bedrock racism to another—from the unquestioned hegemony of a unified race of "white persons" to a contest over political "fitness" among a now fragmented hierarchically arranged series of distinct white races.[10]

The participation of immigrants in strikes and social movements encouraged the inclusion of "radicals" as an unsavory category of immigrant. Since many industrial workers—and consequently trade unionists and strike leaders—at the turn of the century were foreign-born, capital was able to represent labor militancy as a foreign import. According to a declaration by the National Association of Wool Manufacturers, decrying the strike activity of the militant Industrial Workers of the World (IWW), "This baleful organization of European origin" was created by a foreign invasion of anarchists and socialists, criminals and outcasts from other nations. The American Protective Tariff League rationalized the Lawrence Textile strike of 1912 by claiming that all those involved were "Italians and other foreign born operatives."[11]

The growing clamor to crack down on labor militancy reached the highest echelons. In 1915, speaking on behalf of big business, Theodore Roosevelt called for a crackdown on foreign workers.

We cannot afford to leave American mines, munitions plants, and general resources in the hands of alien workmen, alien to America and even likely to be made hostile to America by machinations.... We cannot afford to run the risk of having in time of war men working on our railroads or in our munitions plants who would in the name of duty to their own foreign countries bring destruction to us.[12]

The waning years of World War I saw a confluence of factors that precipitated the advent of comprehensive "racialized" immigration restrictions. Explosive strikes swept through the country: during the war years between 1914 and 1917, the number of strikes (and lockouts) skyrocketed from 1,204 to 4,450. In the tumultuous year of 1919, over 4 million workers struck or were locked out.[13] Labor militancy in the United States coincided with a triumphant workers' revolution in Russia, which altered the international political landscape, forcing capitalists around the world to watch in horror as workers took over the reigns of Russian government.

This period of worker militancy coincided with a gradual shift in immigration patterns, as western and northern European immigration gave way first to immigration from southern and eastern Europe and

Asia, and then to mass Mexican migration. The resulting massive, diverse industrial workforce, with a taste for unions and a desire to eradicate the squalor and violence of nineteenth-century labor conditions, presented a major threat to the hegemony of corporate capital.

When the U.S. economy sank into recession in 1919, growing concentrations of unemployed and impoverished immigrant workers become increasingly visible in the "land of opportunity." It was under these conditions that new nativist movements emerged and gained a hearing in the corridors of power. Their anti-immigrant activities ran up against the growing radicalism of the immigrant working class. In 1919, the Federal Immigration Bureau began to round up foreign-born workers associated with IWW members—the "Wobblies"—for the crime of labor militancy. President Woodrow Wilson's attorney general, A. Mitchell Palmer, eager to squash the burgeoning workers' movement, appealed to Congress for a "special appropriation" to deport radicals, promising the legislators that the "Reds" were planning to "rise up and destroy the government in one fell swoop." [14]

On January 2, 1920, after receiving the green light, Palmer led various police agencies, the Bureau of Immigration, and the Justice Department in conducting raids across thirty-three cities, rounding up immigrant workers suspected of radical sympathies. About three thousand people were incarcerated and/or deported. Since most were alleged members of radical parties (such as the IWW and Communist Labor Party), it was decided their presence violated previous legislative exclusions of "anarchists and other subversives." With the consent of Wilson, warrants were issued post-hoc that retroactively legalized the martial incarcerations. [15] The deportations played a significant role in weakening the postwar labor movement, and served as a stark warning to immigrants who wanted both to improve their working conditions and stay in the country. The raids also served as the catalyst for the career of J. Edgar Hoover—Palmer's lieutenant—and the rise of the Federal Bureau of Investigation (FBI), the shadowy agency that went on to serve as the nation's political police force.

The mass poverty of the industrial working class eventually became a point of concern for managing the image of capitalism. Leading twentieth-century industrialists like Henry Ford worried that the widening crevasse of inequality would serve as a systemic indictment of capitalism. To counter allegations of structural inequality, he, like many capitalists of his day, embraced Social Darwinism, the creed that poverty was a consequence of maladjusted "inferior breeds" unable or unwilling to emulate the "enterprising spirit" deemed genetic in "good Americans." This philosophy continues to this day in the axiom that poor people are poor because they lack ambition or intelligence, or come from a culture that does not promote success. It is also embedded in the commonly expressed view that immigrants "live off the welfare system," since this (incorrect) assumption associates poverty with immigrant status, rather than low wages, poor working conditions, and racism.

Immigrant workers were imported to work and were then made cyclically idle and indigent by an erratic economy, not by culture or character. Being impoverished then forced them into lives of crime, disease, and general squalor. But it is more convenient (and cheaper) to blame the victims than change the system. In 1903, the U.S. Congress mulled over a bill that would exclude poor immigrants from entering the country, and thus reduce "the financial burden" on the state. Their considerations reflected, but did not seem to recognize, the relationship between poverty and the needs of industry:

> The statistics of the various states present some startling revelations concerning the great burden placed by immigrants upon the penal and charity institutions of the country ... [nevertheless] it is evident ... that legislation must be carefully considered ... [and we] must avoid measures so drastic as to cripple American industry, agriculture, and the great shipping and transportation interests.[16]

That is, they needed to be sure to import just the right amount of poor people, and be able to move them out when they were no longer needed. By shifting the blame for poverty onto impoverished workers, capital absolved itself of the need to maintain a large surplus population of workers during times of downturn. Such legislation also expanded the ideological wedge between native and immigrant workers, permitting social problems and competition for scarce resources, themselves derivatives of the vagaries of the boom and bust cycle of capitalism, to be attributed to biological and cultural defects distinct to "foreigners."

For capitalists such as Andrew Carnegie and Leland Stanford, the burgeoning "eugenics" movement offered a "scientific" method to rationalize their vast riches and the stark inequality of industrial society. It lent legitimacy to the apocryphal notions of Social Darwinism, which explained social classes as a natural and inexorable by-product of "natural selection."[17]

Eugenicists argued that abilities, behaviors, and traits are all pre-
determined by race. Using counterfeit data, they plotted races on a grid
of superiority that placed northern Europeans at the pinnacle and various persons of color on the lowest rungs. Furthermore, they attributed
crime, deviance, poverty, and other malevolent social phenomena to
race. They sought to counter a systemic critique of social conflict, and
therefore won the hearts and minds of those seeking to preserve their
wealth and power. As historian Edwin Black notes, "America was ready
for Eugenics ... because the most established echelons of American society were frightened by the demographic chaos sweeping the nation."[18]
In other words, they hoped to discipline an immigrant working class
getting "out of control."

Promoting a white, "Anglo-Saxon" American identity served as a
bulwark against a multi-ethnic working class seeking a larger share of
the national wealth. "Scientifically detached" racism began to flourish
at the highest levels and influenced academia, the three branches of
government, and a bevy of wealthy supporters in big business. It pene-
trated the consciousness of the native-born white working class in the
form of the dubious notion of "privilege through membership," which
the white ruling class advocated in order to divide, differentiate, and
thus weaken working-class collective consciousness.

The eugenics movement did more than just "identify" racial "difference." It advocated the sterilization of "inferior peoples," criminals,
the mentally ill, and others who threatened to "degrade" the "American
stock." Well-funded foundations emerged to promote eugenic "science"
and facilitate its absorption into academia. By 1914, some forty-four institutions of higher education offered eugenic instruction, and by the
1920s that number grew to hundreds, reaching some twenty thousand
students annually.[19] The academic super-strata of the ruling class became
the theory's chief proponents; rectors and directors of the major univer-
sities, psychologists and sociologists in prestigious positions, and even
high-ranking politicians joined in the chorus of praise for eugenics, until

> Eventually, the Eugenics movement and its supporters began to speak
> a common language that crept into the general mindset of many of
> America's most influential thinkers. On January 3, 1913, former Pres-
> ident Theodore Roosevelt wrote [Charles] Davenport [one of the
> founders of the American eugenics movement], "I agree with you ...
> that society has no business to permit degenerates to reproduce their
> kind ... some day we will realize that the prime duty, the inescapable

duty, of the good citizen of the right type, is to leave his or her blood behind him in the world; and that we have no business to permit the perpetuation of citizens of the wrong type. [20]

Several states passed varying degrees of eugenicist legislation, with Indiana allowing forced sterilization of "degenerates." They also advocated the closure of the borders to "inferior immigrants," a practice that dovetailed with the desires of both nativists and sections of capital.

The 1924 Immigration Act "set up strict quotas limiting immigrants from countries believed by eugenicists to have 'inferior' stock, particularly southern Europe and Asia." President Calvin Coolidge, who signed the bill into law, had said when vice president that, "America should be kept American…. Biological laws show that Nordics deteriorate when mixed with other races."[21] The Act established a quota grid based on the 1890 census, which registered the highest percentage of "preferred racial stock." These quotas preserved an imbalance in immigration that favored northern and western Europeans, who received 85 percent of the quota allowances until 1965.

Central Americans detained in a checkpoint by Mexican federal officers are jailed in Hermosillo, Sonora, before deportation.

Chapter Twenty-Two

Constructing the "Illegal" Mexican Worker: Racism and Mexican Labor

For Mexican workers, the history of separation and segregation began with the Mexican-American War (discussed in chapter 12), a war of conquest by which the United States acquired half of Mexico's territory. Since the war, Mexico has continuously subsidized the growth of the U.S. economy by exporting whole generations of workers to the north, providing much of the labor that built the industrial and agricultural infrastructure of the nation, as well as much of its cultural foundation.[1] Nevertheless, the legacy of the Mexican contribution is both ignored and distorted in order to deny Mexicans immigrants' historic connection to the land and their right to legitimately participate in the U.S. political system as citizens.

Although favored as laborers, Mexicans have never been fully welcomed as citizens or good candidates for social integration. For instance, California's first constitution restricted the right to vote to "every white male citizen of the United States and every white male citizen of Mexico."[2] The exclusion of "non-white Mexicans" ensured that Jim Crow–like segregation was sanctioned for the majority. Similar segregation statutes were codified in Texas and throughout the Southwest, laying the basis for a sweeping set of exclusionary laws that made Mexican natives into "foreigners" in one generation's time.[3] Mexican immigration, encouraged because of the explosive growth of U.S. industrial capacity, was funneled into the chiseled confines of a racially segregated society.

Laws that excluded most immigration after 1924 exempted "those from the western hemisphere" so that Mexican migration could continue unabated, as Mexican laborers were considered the optimal workforce by Southwestern capital. Despite the historic bigotry against them, they were largely isolated from the anti-immigrant hysteria directed at Asians, as well as eastern and southern Europeans. They were also isolated from large population centers, congregating predominantly in agricultural regions.

However, this period of relative grace was short-lived. In 1928, both the House and Senate conducted hearings on Mexican immigration in which an assembly of restrictionists held court. The opponents of Mexican immigration—from Texas congressman John C. Box and the Carnegie Institution's Eugenics Office to various "Patriotic Societies" and "Restriction Leagues"—cawed in unison for the Hoover administration to exclude Mexicans from the U.S. because their "inferior racial biology" outweighed the temporary benefits of cheap labor. The chairman of the House Immigration and Naturalization Committee, Albert Johnson, sanctified the chorus and concluded, "the task of our committee is to prepare proposed statutes that will develop the American people along the racial and institutional lines laid down by the founders of the country, so far as the control of immigration can do it."[4]

Ultimately, Mexicans were drawn into the eugenicists' crosshairs, creating a "Brown Scare" among those obsessed with racial purity. Aside from advocating closure of the border, eugenicists argued that Mexican migrants in the United States should undergo sterilization, be excluded from public services, and ultimately, be subjected to forced deportation. Shortly thereafter, Mexicans (and Mexican-Americans) fell victim to the country's first mass deportation campaign. Subsequent immigration was criminalized, segregated, and dehumanized through the emergent status of the "illegal."

At the House Committee on Immigration and Naturalization hearings in 1930, a narrow debate pitted agricultural interests against angst-ridden nativists over the question of the Mexican population within the United States. Testifying on behalf of agricultural interests for the toleration of Mexican immigrants, a doctor reassured the congressmen: "The Mexican is a quiet, inoffensive necessity in that he performs the big majority of our rough work, agriculture, building and street labor. They have no effect on the American standard of living because they are not much more than a group of fairly intelligent collie dogs."[5]

Calls for exclusion and deportation, drawing on the language of the new "racial science," became a cacophony with the outbreak of the Great Depression. Speaking from the floor of the House of Representatives, Texas congressman John Box introduced legislation to deport the Mexican population, arguing that "every reason which calls for the exclusion of the most wretched, ignorant, dirty, diseased, and degraded people of Europe or Asia demands that the illiterate, unclean, peonized masses moving this way from Mexico be stopped at the border...."[6]

After this sentiment was roundly approved by Congress, Mexicans (and Mexican-Americans) across the country were rounded up and deported, or left voluntarily out of fear. Between 1929 and 1935, it is estimated that more than half a million people returned or were returned to Mexico. If one considers that the children of the deportees were likely U.S.-born, and therefore U.S. citizens, it is easy to conclude that over half of those deported were citizens.[7]

It is also easy to see how the social instability and working-class militancy precipitated by the Great Depression contributed to the about-face in attitudes toward Mexican labor. Amid the economic meltdown of the late twenties, the capitalist class and their spokespeople in the Hoover administration grasped for the buoy of racial scapegoating to keep afloat. By attacking the growing population of Mexican workers (the 1930 census counted over 1.4 million Mexicans residing in the United States.[8]) the country's elite hoped to direct the anger of the white working class away from itself.

Deportation, the state-orchestrated export of undesired workers, affords the capitalist class complete control over worker mobility. By singling out and ejecting a section of the working class, the ruling class also saves itself the trouble of having to ameliorate unemployment, impoverishment, and other consequences of economic contraction by creating social welfare programs. Deportation, because it is carried out by the state, even pushes the cost of removal onto other sections of the working class. When capitalism stabilizes, the state can move to reimport workers (through guest-worker programs or liberal immigration policy), once again passing the costs along by using taxpayer money to implement its policies.

Deportation can be used selectively to police the behavior of undocumented workers and other immigrants in the United States. According to immigration historians Francisco E. Balderrama and Raymond

Rodriguez, selective deportation has been used historically by "unscrupulous employers" in league with local immigration agents:

> [Immigration and deportation] was done in order to serve the needs
> of influential growers and industrialists. Regulations were loosely en-
> forced when Mexican workers were needed to harvest crops or increase
> production in the mines or on the assembly lines. Conversely, the strict
> letter of the law was applied when Mexican labor exceeded the seasonal
> demand. Then deportation raids at the work sites, usually before pay-
> day, became common occurrences. The raids were sometimes conduct-
> ed at the request of unscrupulous employers.[9]

A closed border and selective deportation also serve foreign policy
objectives during times of war by acting as devices to fan the politically useful flames of fear and anxiety. In 1952, during the ascension of
McCarthyism, a reactionary backlash was directed toward immigrants
in the form of the Walter-McCarran Act. The act reinforced a racist
national quota system, and was aimed at countering what conservatives called a lax attitude by the government toward "illegal immigration" and the threat of "Communist infiltration" of the borders. The
Walter-McCarran Act made it a felony to import or harbor—but not
to employ—an undocumented worker. The right to employ without
punishment, a brazen concession to growers, shifted the locus of persecution to low-level contractors, smugglers, and workers themselves. It
also forbade the admission or presence of "Communist" or other "sub-
versive" immigrants. This became a handy tool in the hands of growers
and immigration officials, who could simply apply the label of communist to intransigent labor organizers and have them removed.

The confluence of racism, McCarthyism (amplified by the United
States invasion of Korea), and the economic recession of 1953 influenced the mass paramilitary round-up and deportation conducted as
part of Operation Wetback in 1954: "INS officials, the Border Patrol,
the FBI, other federal agents, the army, the navy, and local sheriffs and
police swung into action in a veritable militarized dragnet operation
that sent 1 to 2 million Mexicans to the nearest jailhouse, detention
center, or border crossing."[10]

Deportation proved an effective tool for preventing the formation
of unions among Mexican workers. In 1936, miner and union organizer
Jesus Pallares was deported as an "undesirable alien" despite the fact
that he had lived in the United States for twenty-three years. New Mexico mine operators and local sheriffs petitioned immigration officials to

bring Jesús in on charges that he was a "troublemaker" and sympathizer with "communistic organizations." As the local sheriff put it, "[We're] having trouble with Jesus Pallares on strike in this county.... He is an alien from Old Mexico. We must act at once to save trouble and maybe lives in this county."[11]

During the agricultural organizing campaigns of the 1960s and 1970s, the Border Patrol was frequently called in to break strikes. As one striker explained, "as long as we were quiet and worked for nothing, the Border Patrol did nothing. Now that we are on strike they show up at picket lines and threaten us...."[12]

More than sixty-four years after Jesus Pallares was kicked out of the United States, deporting immigrant workers to prevent unionization has become routine. For instance, in 2000, the manager of a Minneapolis Holiday Inn reported eight of his own undocumented employees to the INS while they were involved in a union drive. All eight maids were members of the union negotiating team, and they were arrested four days after a majority of workers voted to join the union. Six of the eight were jailed and all were brought up on deportation charges.[13]

Immigration policy, influenced by issues of race, class, and proximity to Mexico, ultimately reflects a two-track system by which Mexican workers become segregated and separated from the rest of the working class through the designation of some Mexicans as "illegal." This pejorative is loaded with the anti-Mexican bias of the past, now encoded in "acceptable" discourse. Couched in the language of legality, it remains a means of division and exclusion to better sustain the hegemony of capital over labor.

Immigration Double Standards

While some immigrants were excluded on the basis of race, politics, and nationality, the U.S. Congress made special arrangements for more "savory" immigrants, that is, those politically aligned with the foreign policy of the United States. Starting with the Eisenhower administration, the doors were opened by executive decree to blocs of immigrants fighting or fleeing the "enemies" of the United States. Referred to as "parole power" and originally designed for individuals, it was expanded to include large groups of anticommunist Hungarians, Cubans, Chinese, and Vietnamese.[1]

These immigrant blocs tended to be replete with exiled capitalists, military personnel, and members of outlawed political parties. In the United States, they regrouped as highly organized, well-funded, and politically connected communities that aligned themselves with the most aggressive imperialist objectives of their adopted country. In doing so, they not only improved their economic status in the United States, but also curried support for an eventual U.S.-supported "return" to power in their homelands. It is worth noting that refugees from countries not "at odds" with the United States, although they were just as likely to fall victim to despotic regimes, were not afforded the same treatment. Salvadorans fleeing civil war in the 1980s were often repatriated, many to face certain persecution. In Haiti, people who fled the country after the military coup in 1991 were incarcerated in concentration camps before being repatriated to face death squads.

Other "exemptions" include selective visas for those with special-ized skills, and citizenship for those willing to risk their lives in the ser-vice of U.S. imperialism. For instance, while their brethren were cat-egorically excluded from entering the country, Filipino soldiers who joined the U.S. military during World War II were granted citizenship. Since September 11, the Pentagon and recruiters have taken advantage of the difficulties immigrants face obtaining citizenship. "Green Card Soldiers," as they are cynically called, commit to active duty in exchange for a faster track to citizenship. Most of these immigrant soldiers are Mexican, encouraged to fight for the ideals of the nation while their brothers and sisters face racism and exclusion back at home. According to David Reimers, favorable immigration policy has also served as an international bargaining chip, used to placate "America's overseas al-lies, or to win the favor of neutral powers."[2]

For those immigrants who bring big bucks with them, the U.S. rolls out the red carpet, another way that the global wealthy enjoy freedom of movement. The 1990 Immigration Act, for instance, shifted the class re-lations of immigration by giving those with enough money to invest in the U.S. easier access to citizenship. The act included provsions for ten thousand immigrants annually who invest one million dollars or more in American businesses, or five hundred thousand dollars in econom-ically depressed industries. Howard Ezell, former director of the INS and a proponent of giving free access to rich migrants, took advantage of this provision and began "selling car washes and Wienerschnitzel hot dog franchises to the soon-to-be-arriving 'yacht people' of the world." He then went on to co-author California's notoriously anti-immigrant Proposition 187.[3]

National quotas based on "preferred racial stock" were finally dis-mantled in the context of the civil rights movement and its demolition of overtly racist American laws. Instead, "universal" quotas were estab-lished, including what amounted to a cap on Mexican immigration for the first time: lawmakers limited "Western hemispheric" immigration to 120,000 per year. Legal immigration from Mexico was further re-duced to twenty thousand per year in 1977. Fully aware that nearly half a million undocumented workers were deported each year, Congress consecrated the process of illegalization, ensuring that after 1965, the inexorable influx of Mexican labor would be relegated to the under-world of the labor-caste system.[4]

The two main legal ways to enter the country are through family or work-based channels. Most new legal immigrants come through as infant children, spouses, or parents of American citizens. Another 226,000 slots are set aside for other family members, with about 27,000 slots for each country. For countries where there is a high number of petitions, the process is backlogged. The current wait time for a citizen to bring in a spouse or young child is seven years, while bringing in a sibling or adult child means, on average, a twenty-two-year wait.[5] For Irene Velazquez, the agony of waiting more than five years for a visa to visit her husband—who was a mushroom picker in Pennsylvania—pushed her to make a desperate attempt to cross the border through the Arizona desert. She perished in the sweltering heat and was recovered only after her distraught husband left his job to frantically search for her body in a remote mountainous region.[6]

The second legal channel, the work visa, allows only 140,000 applicants per year, and only 10,000 slots are set aside for low-skilled labor. The process requires that the employer first prove that he couldn't find an American to take the job, which can take up to two years. After that, the wait can be up to four years for the worker trying to obtain the visa.

When one considers that there are 10.3 million gainfully employed undocumented workers in the U.S., it becomes obvious that the legal channels are designed to fail. As one immigrant declared, "We have played by the rules and gotten nowhere. I'm better off telling my son to come here illegally."[7] Meanwhile, businesses continue to profit from a highly exploitable situation. Having access to a large pool of very vulnerable workers who have been forced to enter the country without any rights allows bosses almost total latitude in establishing working conditions and wages.

Immigration law and deportation have been crafted and implemented over the years not to streamline citizenship or stop immigration but to permanently fragment the working class. The comprehensive appropriation of the state apparatus of immigration control by capital has created the "illegal" worker, an entirely artificial construction whose sole purpose is to deprive the international "American" working class of its democratic rights.

At the border fence between Agua Prieta and Douglas, people watch as a man is injured after jumping to the U.S. side.

Chapter Twenty-Four

Militarizing the Border: Death Warrant for Migrant Workers

T he advent of borders signified the increasing domination of an "owning class" over the market, resources, and labor of a particular region, and defined the territorial limitations of rival owning classes. Over generations, borders have been reified as natural extensions of "nationality" even though they have existed for perhaps 1 percent of the history of humankind.[1] For most of U.S. history, there was no border with Mexico, either real or imagined. It wasn't until after 1917 that regulated crossing points were established to monitor Mexican migration, and unobstructed movement across the border was possible until World War II. Although the main points of entry were gradually militarized after 1954, the idea of the border as a means to prevent movement has been neither the intention nor the reality. Only since the 1970s has the idea of a border been transformed from a political partition between two countries to that of a "fortress barrier," the last line of defense of the "homeland."

Even today, the border is largely an act of political theater. While walls have been present in certain regions since 1994, they are really only there to create an image of control. The border does more to determine the status of immigrants within the United States than it does to "keep out the invader." Nevertheless, it has been politically cultivated as the "last line of defense" for the American people, their culture, and their economy, designed and redesigned to fit the foreign policy objectives of successive U.S. administrations. Over the course of the twentieth century, the border has provided a means to exploit the fears of and garner support from the broader public. The militarization of the border—which includes increasing personnel, joint patrols with the armed forces, the infusion of military technology, and the construction of a border wall (originally a by-product of the Cold War)—began in earnest in the 1970s under the Ford and Carter administrations.

In 1976, then INS commissioner Leonard Chapman railed against "a vast and silent invasion of illegal aliens."[2] William Colby, former CIA director, made similar remarks. "The most obvious threat is the fact that there are going to be 120 million Mexicans by the turn of the century," Colby said. "[The Border Patrol] will not have enough bullets to stop them."[3]

A surge in migration in the 1970s and the emergence of Central American revolutionary movements opposed to U.S.-supported and -funded dictatorships further intensified the focus on the border. Presidents Carter and Reagan both used the issue of an imminent immigrant invasion as a justification to increase funds for border militarization. Under the Carter administration, the budget for the Border Patrol rose by 24 percent while the number of personnel went up 8.7 percent.[4] The force also experienced a significant upgrade in equipment, "ranging from the increased construction of fences to the deployment of helicopters and improved ground sensors."[5]

The alarmism of the Carter administration paved the way for a further lurch rightward by the Reagan administration. Reagan radically altered public perceptions of the border by portraying it as a doorway for the three greatest "threats" to the United States: hordes of poor migrants, Central American subversives, and narco-traffickers. Acting to prevent a "tidal wave of refugees" and to deter "terrorists and subversives [who] are just two days' driving time from Harlingen, Texas," Reagan paved the way for a new era of border policing. Funding skyrocketed, the involvement of military personnel in training border agents to use military hardware was authorized, and all was justified by a new national security doctrine:

> Pressures on our borders from the Caribbean and Central America—particularly Mexico—make it certain that in the foreseeable future, as never in the past, the United States is going to have to maintain a foreign policy, including preemptive and prophylactic measures, which has as one of its objectives the protection of our frontiers against excessive illegal immigration.[6]

During the Reagan years, funding for the Border Patrol increased 130 percent, the majority of the funds going toward enforcement. Detention centers were expanded, checkpoints set up, and the number of agents increased by 82 percent.[7] Immigration hysteria culminated with the passage of the Immigration Reform and Control Act of 1986, which cross-designated Border Patrol members as drug enforcement agents.

But the gravest consequences of border militarization have occurred since former president Bill Clinton launched Operation Gatekeeper in 1994. "We must not tolerate illegal immigration," he wrote in 1996, boasting that "since 1992, we have increased our Border Patrol by over 35 percent; deployed underground sensors, infrared night scopes, and encrypted radios; built miles of new fences; and installed massive amounts of new lighting."[8]

Clinton set a new standard for border militarization, and the current Bush administration has pushed the process even further. "Our goal is clear: to return every single illegal entrant, with no exceptions," Bush assured senior congressmen and intelligence officers in the White House[9] in December 2005. This was after he signed a $32 billion Homeland Security bill for 2006 that contained large increases for border enforcement, including a thousand additional Border Patrol agents.[10]

Current legislative proposals, whether sponsored by Republicans or Democrats (or both), contain both the language and means to intensify the war on immigrants. Under HR 4437 (the Sensenbrenner-King Bill), the nation would have to spend more than $2.2 billion to build five border fences in California and Arizona that would add up to a length of 698 miles—at the astronomical cost of $3.2 million per mile. It would not only make undocumented migration a felony, it would criminalize the very act of *associating* with undocumented immigrants. Though massive pro-immigrant protests have rendered HR 4437 a non-starter, other, more "centrist" "compromise" bills also represent threats to immigrants' rights and lives. The bipartisan Kennedy-McCain Bill, also called the "Secure America and Orderly Immigration Act," seeks to support Bush's call for a guest-worker program, while "cracking down" on unauthorized crossings. As Republican co-sponsor John McCain explains,

> Homeland security is our nation's number one priority, this legislation includes a number of provisions that together will make our nation more secure. For far too long, our nation's broken immigration laws have gone unreformed—leaving Americans vulnerable. We can no longer afford to delay reform. I am proud to join my colleagues today as an original Sponsor of this legislation.[11]

The proposal requires the nation to "increase border security enforcement with new technology, information sharing, and other initiatives." In other words, it would continue *and expand* the current death-warrant policy of border militarization, and set the stage for a new round of punitive measures against migrant workers.

In 1999, Alejandro Kassorla, a twenty-three-year-old cane cutter, decided to try to cross the border into the United States because he was having trouble supporting his family in Mexico. When he had traveled to the United States six years before, he had come home with enough money to build a small home for his wife and two children. He got together with his friend Samuel and a married couple, Javier and Elvia, who also wanted to cross. The smugglers they paid to guide them said it would be a short trip through the rugged mountains near San Diego, but in fact the trip normally took three days. After temperatures dropped below freezing on the third day, the smugglers abandoned Alejandro and his group. When Javier and Samuel began to suffer from hypothermia, Alejandro and Elvia went for help. After Alejandro collapsed from hypothermia, Elvia went on. When she finally returned with help, the other three had already frozen to death.[12]

This story captures the impact of border militarization as embodied in the four-part federal project begun in 1993 to "take control" of the U.S.-Mexico border. Operation Gatekeeper in California, Operation Safeguard in Arizona, and Operations Hold the Line and Rio Grande in Texas employ similar strategies to seal off popular border-crossing points using a combination of new border fences, increased border personnel, and the latest military hardware and training, all with the participation of various military agencies.

Operation Gatekeeper, for instance, began by spanning sixty-six miles from the Pacific Ocean through San Diego and into the mountains, and has been expanded into Yuma, Arizona. It includes a seventy-three-mile-long, ten-foot-high steel wall. Secondary fences span fifty-two of those miles, and a triple fence spans fourteen miles, from the Pacific Ocean to the Otay Mountains. The border wall is comprised of welded sections of recycled Gulf War landing strips, and incorporates the latest cutting-edge military hardware as part of its enforcement strategy. This includes the use of Black Hawk helicopters, heat sensors, night-vision telescopes, electronic vision detection devices, and computerized fingerprinting equipment, which have been integrated into routine border operations. Recent years have also seen a dramatic increase in agents. The Border Patrol is now the largest federal law enforcement body, with over twelve thousand agents in the field.[13] This amounts to a 51 percent increase since 1999. Furthermore, the 2004 Intelligence Reform and Terrorism Prevention Act calls for adding two thousand agents in each of the next five years, subject to funding. Even if staffing remains the same, the agency must replace the 5 percent of agents it loses every year to retirement and other jobs.[14]

The implementation of neoliberal policies in Mexico and Central America and border militarization in the U.S. have combined in the last two decades to force displaced migrants to cross the U.S.-Mexico border in more remote areas, where they are subject to extreme exposure and a host of other geographical dangers. While Immigration and Customs Enforcement (ICE)—formerly known as the INS—promotes this program as a policy of "prevention through deterrence," it is, in reality, a death sentence for many immigrants crossing the border. Since it is not intended to halt the flow of migration so much as rechannel it through less visible routes, the results have been horrific. Over four thousand migrants—men, women, and children—have perished crossing the border since the inception of border militarization in 1994.[15] The death toll continues at an increasing rate. Over the last fiscal year, 460 people are known to have died on the border. That far exceeds the previous record of 383 in fiscal 2000.[16] This does not include the unknown number of missing or those injured while crossing.

Dying at the rate of four people every three days, casualties on the border have surpassed the number of people who perished in the World Trade Center attacks, and constitute ten times the number of people who died attempting to climb over the Berlin Wall during the Cold War. Border militarization has not stopped migration; it has only imposed deadly rules upon it. Despite the tragic human loss, it is a *success* from the point of view of policy-makers. It has strengthened the control of business over immigrant labor, provided political capital in the "War on Terror," and is, in itself, a profitable institution, as defense contractors compete to corner the emerging market of border enforcement.

Border militarization has failed to stem migration because it ignores the structural processes that push people to make desperate sojourns looking for work. But as Peter Andreas argues, this failure is also its greatest success.[17] While shifting the flow of unauthorized crossings to barren deserts and mountainous regions, border fortification has amplified anti-immigrant sentiment and pushed migrants further into the shadows, setting the stage for further crackdowns. It has helped to create the sensationalist spectacle of the modern conquest of an illusory "no-man's land," while establishing new markets for the defense industry and convincing low-paid workers across the United States that "the thin green line" of the Border Patrol is keeping their jobs safe.

In California, militarization has forced migrants to cross the Otay Mountains, whose peaks reach as high as six thousand feet. Temperatures in the mountains remain below freezing for at least six months out of the year. In the scorching Arizona deserts, temperatures climb as high as 120 degrees, with sand dunes that reach three hundred feet. It is in these dead zones that the most egregious effects of border militarization take their human toll.

According to Doris Meisner, former chief of the INS who oversaw the initial implementation of border militarization policy, "We did believe geography would be an ally."[18] Deaths have increased so rapidly in Arizona that the Pima County coroner's office, which handles cases from the Border Patrol's Tucson sector, was forced to rent a refrigerated truck to store bodies that could not be accommodated inside its facility.[19] The fear of apprehension has also caused migrants to pay exorbitant fees to be smuggled in the cargo holds of trucks, often with little or no precautionary measures taken by their traffickers. In May of 2003, nineteen people perished in the furnace-like heat of a truck trailer crossing through a Texas point of entry.[20]

According to a human rights investigation conducted by the American Civil Liberties Union, most of the deaths can be attributed to exposure to freezing temperatures in the mountains during the winter or to the heat of the desert in the summer.[21] In May 2000, fourteen migrants were found dead after attempting to cross miles of desert in 115-degree heat at a place Border Patrol agents call "The Devil's Path" near Yuma, Arizona. "Nobody should be surprised by these deaths," said Claudia Smith, a lawyer for the California Rural Legal Assistance Foundation. "They are an entirely foreseeable consequence of moving the migrant traffic out of the urban areas and into the most remote and dangerous areas."[22]

Another significant portion of the deaths can be attributed to drowning, as migrants attempt to escape the heat and *la migra* by crossing through the All-American Canal and other border canals and rivers. The New River, one such crossing point, is one of the most polluted rivers in the border region. It is a favored crossing point because the Border Patrol agents avoid its toxic shores.

The political smokescreen that is "border control" and the fundamental disregard for human lives that it represents is made shockingly clear once the text of the policy is scrutinized. Operation Gatekeeper's architects assumed that "most of the 'influx' would not be deterred by the 'mortal dangers' which came with the new routes."[23] As one INS supervisor explained in the San Diego Union-Tribune in 1996, "Eventually, we'd like to see them all out in the desert."[24] It was understood and expected that migrant workers would continue to trek north and that some would perish in the process. Ironically, stricter border enforcement is encouraging more migrants to take up permanent residence in the United States. A study conducted in 1997 showed that half of all Mexican immigrants returned to Mexico within two years. Now, an increasing number prefer to avoid the uncertainty of multiple crossings.[25]

While the death toll rises, other forms of terror and abuse can also be attributed to the Border Patrol and other U.S. agencies. According to a report by Amnesty International that condemns Operation Gatekeeper:

> The allegations of ill-treatment Amnesty International collected include people struck with batons, fists and feet, often as punishment for attempting to run away from Border Patrol agents; denial of food, water and blankets for many hours while detained in Border Patrol stations and at Ports of Entry for INS processing; sexual abuse of men and women; denial of medical attention, and abusive, racially derogatory and unprofessional conduct toward the public sometimes resulting in the wrongful deportation of U.S. citizens to Mexico. People who reported that they had been ill-treated included men, women and children, almost exclusively of Latin American descent. They included citizens and legal permanent residents of the USA, and members of Native American First Nations whose tribal lands span the U.S.-Mexico border.[26]

The behavior displayed by the Border Patrol and the social and political isolation of those stigmatized as "illegal" creates an environment that gives racists and vigilantes the confidence to carry out acts of terrorism and brutality against real or perceived undocumented immigrants. Ranchers in Arizona and Texas have gone so far as to "hunt" for immigrants. One south Texas landowner was offended when a migrant asked him for water after walking through the brush for days to avoid the Border Patrol. According to subsequent charges, the landowner fired on the man and calmly watched him die. Elsewhere in Texas, numerous other shootings by ranchers have occurred.

In another situation, a rancher from Arizona set up hunting expeditions for migrants with his brother, as punishment for drinking the rancher's water and leaving trash on his land. When asked about this, and the fact that the brothers were inviting tourists to join in the hunts, a Border Patrol officer remarked to the press that they "appreciated the help."[27] Along with violent ranchers, other vigilante groups have set up patrols along the border, including right-wing "citizen" groups, the Ku Klux Klan, and the skinhead group White Aryan Resistance.[28] Just north of San Diego, migrant workers were attacked in a rural camp they inhabited by several teenagers with pellet guns who had spray-painted "go home" and racist slogans around the area.

Joint operations with military personnel have also proven deadly for many people in the border region. For example, Joint Task Force 6 (JTF-6) grew out of George Bush Sr.'s National Drug Control Strategy and is used under the Texas militarization policy, Operation Alliance. In one operation, the marines cooperated with the Border Patrol in anti-drug missions on the Texas border. In 1997, an eighteen-year-old U.S. citizen, Ezekiel Hernandez, was shot and killed by marines under suspicious circumstances. Hernandez was riding his horse with his hunting rifle—something he did routinely—when he was shot. No charges were brought against the marines, who claimed they fired in self-defense.

In July 2004, the *San Diego Union-Tribune* heralded the "success" of Operation Gatekeeper in a spread celebrating the program's ten-year anniversary. Conjuring up the racist imagery of the "invading hordes," the paper praises the way the absence of Mexican immigrants will make a coastal suburb more attractive for investors and real estate speculators. Since the introduction of Gatekeeper, the *Union-Tribune* notes, "The city that was often crowded with desperate illegal immigrants running from armed Border Patrol agents and thumping helicopters is now a quiet, cleaned-up beach town with increasing property values and plans for more than $20 million in redevelopment."[29] The paper then trumpets the dramatic drop in arrests in the San Diego metropolitan area as a success for the program, while completely ignoring the consequences of pushing migration into the deserts and mountains to the east: a 500 percent increase in border-crossing deaths since the inception of the program.[30]

According to Wayne Cornelius, director of the Center for Comparative Immigration Studies at the University of California, San Diego, Operation Gatekeeper, despite the $10 to $15 billion spent for the operation over the last decade, is "a failed policy."[31] While proponents of the policy point to the decline in arrests as a result of "deterrence," they fail to mention that detentions have increased many-fold east of San Diego, which is also where most of the deaths occur.

Roberto Martinez, of the American Friends Service Committee, agrees that tightening controls at certain parts of the border simply means that people try to cross in different places:

> Operation Gatekeeper is not only causing one of the worst human rights tragedies in border history, but it's totally ineffective in stopping the flow of people in crossing the border. All they are doing is moving them from San Ysidro and Otay to East County and Imperial Valley and into Arizona where the number of apprehensions has quadrupled. The same number of people are crossing—just in another area. They are touting the success of Operation Gatekeeper because they've reduced the number of apprehensions in this area, but it's very deceptive. It's a bubble effect, you squeeze here and they pop up over there.[32]

Plus border crossers are often able to stay one step ahead of the high-priced technology and manpower that have been poured into border enforcement. Chicano journalist Ruben Martinez highlights the creative abilities of common people in outwitting refined military hardware in a discussion he reports on with a coyote named Marcos:

> But for every high-tech weapon the *migra* employ, Marcos says, there's a guerrilla-like response from the [migrants] and the coyotes. Take the laser traps, for example, grids of beams that, when breached, immediately alert the *migra* to movement. One [migrant] crew Marcos crossed with was equipped with spray cans. You sprayed ahead of you in an area already known to be a problem from previous busts. The beams glittered in the mist, and you make your way around the grid. The coyotes claim that the Border Patrol constantly relocates its tracking equipment. But each group of migrants that gets caught actually helps new migrants cross. Each bust is valuable intelligence gathered.[33]

While it is impossible to know exactly how many migrant workers cross the border in a given year, many statistics indicate that militarization of the border has not cut down on border crossings. INS officials claim a 30 percent apprehension rate of migrants along the border, with a record 1,643,679 apprehensions in the year 2000.[34] While apprehensions in San Diego have declined from 450,152 in 1994 to 151,681 in

2000, the number of apprehensions east of San Diego has increased 761 percent in El Centro, 351 percent in Arizona, and 55 percent in Texas.[35]

In 2004, the Border Patrol apprehended 1.1 million migrant crossers and, in 2005, 1.2 million.[36] In other words, migration has remained fairly steady. Rather than curtailing the number of immigrants who enter the country, border militarization has only increased the hazards of crossing, and is really aimed more at creating the illusion of government "controlling an invasion." Immigration expert Douglas Massey argues:

> Unlike the old crossing sites, these new locations were sparsely settled, so the sudden appearance of thousands of Mexicans attracted considerable attention and understandably generated much agitation locally. Perceptions of a breakdown at the border were heightened by news reports of rising deaths among migrants; by redirecting flows into harsh, remote terrain the United States tripled the death rate during border crossing.
>
> Less well known is that American policies also reduced the rate of apprehension, because those remote sectors of the border had fewer Border Patrol officers. My research found that during the 1980's, the probability that an undocumented migrant would be apprehended while crossing stood at around 33 percent; by 2000 it was at 10 percent, despite increases in federal spending on border enforcement.
>
> Naturally, public perceptions of chaos on the border prompted more calls for enforcement and the hardening strategy was extended to other sectors. The number of Border Patrol officers increased from around 2,500 in the early 1980's to around 12,000 today, and the agency's annual budget rose to $1.6 billion from $200 million. The boundary between Mexico and the United States has become perhaps the most militarized frontier between two nations at peace anywhere in the world.
>
> Although border militarization had little effect on the probability of Mexicans migrating illegally, it did reduce the likelihood that they would return to their homeland. America's tougher line roughly tripled the average cost of getting across the border illegally; thus Mexicans who had run the gantlet at the border were more likely to hunker down and stay in the United States. My study has shown that in the early 1980's, about half of all undocumented Mexicans returned home within 12 months of entry, but by 2000 the rate of return migration stood at just 25 percent.[37]

Debbie Nathan argued in a 2000 North America Congress on Latin America report that there are comparisons to be drawn between U.S. paramilitaries on the border and the U.S.-supported right-wing paramilitaries in Colombia. Both are fighting a war against civilian populations. And both are designed to fail. In Colombia, the war will do nothing to curtail the drug trade, nor is it designed to; instead, it sows terror to prevent support for a popular guerrilla movement and to keep profits flowing for oil and weapons manufacturers.[38] On the border, Operation Gatekeeper will do nothing to stop immigration, but it will sow terror in the hearts of immigrant workers by keeping them divided from other workers, without rights or recourse against their abuse and exploitation.

"Illegalization" is profitable, and business interests have successfully shifted the burden of enforcement to taxpayers and to the migrants themselves. Sanctions against employers of the undocumented—while on the books—are largely ignored. From 1993 to 2003, the number of arrests at worksites nationwide went from 7,630 to 445. The number of fines dropped from 944 in 1993 to 124 in 2003.[39] By 2004, immigration authorities issued only three citations to companies.[40] Agents routinely arrest workers, not employers. Little concern for punishment allows companies to "self-police" their workers. It is not uncommon for employers to call ICE agents on their own workers if they try to organize unions. As journalist Eduardo Porter explained in the *New York Times*,

> That may explain why fines for hiring illegal immigrants can be as low as $275 a worker, and immigration officials acknowledge that businesses often negotiate fines downward. And why, after the I.N.S. raided onion fields in Georgia during the 1998 harvest, a senator and four members of the House of Representatives from the state sharply criticized the agency for hurting Georgia farmers.[41]

As economist Gordon H. Hanson concluded, "Employers feel very strongly about maintaining access to immigrant workers, and exert political pressure to prevent enforcement from being effective."[42]

Since September 11, border militarization has meshed with Bush's so-called "War on Terrorism." The concept of "permanent war" against an invisible and internal enemy has dovetailed with the interests of the well-funded anti-immigrant movement that has been striving to keep immigrant workers disenfranchised. The minimal rights of undocumented immigrants are now refracted through the lens of terrorism. For example, California Governor Arnold Schwarzenegger (himself an immigrant) balked at a bill to allow undocumented workers the right to have a driver's license, saying "It would make it too easy for terrorists to use the documents to create new identities."[43]

In the lead-up to the 2006 congressional elections, Republican hopeful Alan Uke ran his campaign on the platform of "closing the border." Claiming that "drug-traffickers and terrorists can now walk across the border," Uke promised to "protect Americans" by building a new border wall. Such promises create the image of a fantastic forti-fied boundary in the mind of the public and are used by politicians to stoke fear and generate support. It is this "image" of the border that has been deemed successful, more than any attempt to stem immigration. Through the manipulation of this image, drug traffickers and workers become one and the same, attempting to cross through the "unguard-ed wastelands" failed by fortress America. In fact, according to a Drug Enforcement Agency (DEA) report in the aftermath of NAFTA and the further opening of the borders to cargo traffic, it is estimated that the majority of cocaine smuggled into the United States enters through of-ficial ports of entry, occasionally with the collusion of corrupt customs agents.[44] According to Jose Luis Santiago Vasconcelos, head of Mexico's Deputy Attorney General's Office for Special Investigation into Orga-nized Crime (SIEDO), the Mexican government is currently investi-gating possible links between state police in Baja California and U.S. Border Patrol agents in drug trafficking.[45] Image and reality conflict in the drug war, and migrants are the victims.

It is estimated that 90 percent of the 1–2 million annual unautho-rized border crossings now rely on the use of smugglers. Estimated to be an $8-billion-a-year industry, human smuggling relies on a vast net-work that operates on both sides of the border to circumvent the immi-gration authorities.[46] The smuggling industry, while the only means for most immigrants to cross the border, also sets up a secondary level of exploitation, as many border crossers are forced to pay exorbitant fees and are robbed, abandoned, beaten, or raped by unscrupulous coyotes. But the coyote that collects the biggest payoff is big business, by not paying a dime to acquire a cheap, exploitable workforce that pays for its own passage.

Furthermore, Border Patrol agents often participate in the lucrative human and drug smuggling racket. According to Roberto Martinez of the American Friends Service Committee, "Over the last twenty years, hundreds of customs and border patrol agents have been indicted for taking bribes to allow smugglers to bring over not only people but also drugs, cocaine."[47] One immigration inspector, Jose Olvera, was caught accepting bribes of between two thousand and four thousand dollars to allow the passage of drugs and undocumented migrants.[48] From April 2004 to March 2005 alone, over twenty border agents were arrested, indicted, or convicted of crimes.[49]

Whether an undocumented workforce remains in the shadows, or a steady stream of temporary, non-citizen labor flows across the border under the auspices of guest-worker programs, business is provided access to disenfranchised labor. That is because the costs of producing and reproducing a growing percentage of Mexican labor *in the U.S.* is pushed onto the Mexican government and the Mexican workers themselves, since the Mexican worker will derive most of his or her social benefits and sustenance south of the border.

Meanwhile, the Far Right has been given legitimacy and a platform by the mainstream media to howl for further restrictions. The moral and ethical contradictions of deporting and importing workers simultaneously—along with the daily human rights violations against undocumented immigrants—are ignored by the media, who dutifully avoid even the most glaring failures of current border policies, while laying the ideological groundwork for the next stage of border militarization. Tragically, in May 2006, President Bush took the unprecedented step of announcing the deployment of National Guard troops to the border to assist in keeping undocumented crossers out of the United States. This will likely increase the death toll, as people seek even more remote and deadly crossing points. At a time when borders and walls are becoming increasingly obsolete for workers—and even for the functioning of capitalism—big business, politicians from both parties, and restrictionist organizations are working in feverish conceit to construct a new Berlin Wall on the backs of the very people who feed them, clothe them, and provide the roof over their heads. Like all imperial walls—forged in violence, racism, blinding arrogance, and a sense of superiority—it is built on an unsustainable foundation. The push that will cause the fall of the "American Wall" will come from the same calloused, brown hands that provided the wealth to build it.

Chapter Twenty-Five

Inventing an Invisible Enemy: September 11 and the War on Immigrants

B y the turn of the second millennium, the gale force of the global justice movement had elevated the language of workers' rights to an international level. The AFL-CIO—reflecting its own decline in traditional sectors, and growth in the immigrant-heavy service sector—reversed its history of restrictionism, offered its support for a general amnesty, and endorsed the right of the undocumented to join unions.

As the most vibrant section of the union movement in the nineties, immigrant workers pushed their union leadership to open up a political front in the simmering debate on immigration. The AFL-CIO thereby put the potentially massive power of the U.S. labor movement on record in favor of the most traditionally neglected section of its own ranks. Just as a new generation of immigrant worker-leaders, the global justice movement, and the unions began to move into political alignment, the United States was rocked by the September 11 attacks.

In a micro-flash, the tragedy of September 11 allowed right-wing forces to regain the initiative against an advancing immigrant rights agenda. The policy of immigrant containment dovetailed with the domestic component of the protean "War on Terrorism," which has unabashedly singled out, restricted, and/or criminalized the presence of Arabs, Arab-Americans, Muslims, and others profiled as "potential terrorists."[1] The omnipresent phantom of domestic terrorism, refracted through the border-phobic imagery of "invading hordes," created an opportunistic wedding between pro-war hawks and anti-immigrant restrictionists. The rightward shift has been aided by key Democrats, whose dogged devotion to the "War on Terrorism" helped shift the focus to the U.S.-Mexico border.

The "War on Terrorism" led to the passage of the PATRIOT Act, extra-legal detention of Arabs and Muslims, and the restructuring of the INS into the ICE and Customs and Border Protection (CBP), both of which were incorporated into the Department of Homeland Security (DHS). Since then, an alliance of well-funded political action groups, reactionary "think tanks"—such as the Federation for American Immigration Reform (FAIR) and the Center for Immigration Studies (CIS)—federal and state legislators, and a host of far-right activist organizations have coalesced into a national anti-immigrant front.[2]

The translation of immigration into a national security issue has allowed anti-immigrant forces, particularly in the Republican Party, to tighten control over all aspects of immigration policy, especially those regulating the role of Mexican labor. The domestic "War on Terrorism" erased any discussion of amnesty and effectively supplanted the concept of human rights with the "terrorist" profiling of undocumented workers.

Although mass demonstrations in the spring of 2006 have completely changed the national debate, the years 2001–2005 saw a one-sided immigration chorus successfully pushing the image of a border "out of control." To maintain a climate of uncertainty and a fear of immigrants, the border region is portrayed as "ground zero" for instability and vulnerability. While the influx of migrant workers is nothing new, the threatening imagery is a more recent phenomenon. According to Peter Andreas,

> Public perception is powerfully shaped by the images of the border which politicians, law enforcement agencies and the media project. Alarming images of a border out of control can fuel public anxiety; reassuring images of a border can reduce such anxiety … [therefore], successful border management depends on successful image management and this does not necessarily correspond to levels of actual deterrence.[3]

This "image management" is used in the current context to criminalize migration while moving the focus away from the real issues. While no "terrorists" have been caught crossing through the Arizona desert, politicians cultivate a permanent fear that terrorists are across the border, blending into the stream of migrant workers coming into the country.

In fact, a study published in the *New York Times* in September 2005 exposed the increasingly political nature of immigration prosecution.

While undocumented immigration actually declined between the years 2000 and 2003 (from an average of 1.5 million/year to 1.1 million/year), immigration prosecutions against undocumented workers increased from 16,300 to 38,000 during the same time frame.[4] According to David Burnham, codirector of the research group at Syracuse University that conducted the survey, "This is a substantial shift any way you measure it.... We're seeing choices being made by United States attorneys and by the president about what's important and what's not, and clearly, the administration has changed the priorities of the federal law enforcement machine." Another study by the same group revealed that

> the Justice Department was now bringing many criminal charges in immigration cases that once would probably have been handled as administrative matters. This was particularly true in South Texas, where prosecutors went into "super drive" on immigration crimes last year and spurred a 345 percent increase in recommendations for criminal prosecutions, rising in a single year to 18,092 from 4,062.[5]

An example of these sorts of prosecutions occurred in early 2003 when "terrorism" charges were filed against twenty-eight Latinos accused of possessing false Social Security cards in order to work at Austin Airport.[6] Such campaigns work to restrain and reverse the momentum toward the naturalization of undocumented workers. One disillusioned FBI agent publicly criticized the agency's methods:

> The vast majority of the one thousand persons "detained" in the wake of 9-11 did not turn out to be terrorists. They were mostly illegal aliens. We have every right, of course, to deport those identified as illegal aliens during the course of any investigation. But after 9/11, headquarters encouraged more and more detentions for what seemed to be essentially [public relations] purposes. Field offices were required to report daily the number of detentions in order to supply grist for statements on our progress in fighting terrorism.... [F]rom what I have observed, particular vigilance may be required to head off undue pressure (including subtle encouragement) to detain or "round up" suspects, particularly those of Arabic origin.[7]

Thus, September 11 has facilitated the confluence of economic and political interests around an ideological framework designed to further isolate the immigrant section of the U.S. working class. By promoting the illusion of "out of control borders" and "invading hordes," the right wing seeks to inflate the issue and deflect attention away from its failures and unpopular policies—like the war in Iraq. According to the *Los Angeles Times*, "Some Republican strategists contend that the immigration issue offers an opportunity for the GOP to revive its flagging fortunes at a time when Bush and the party have been hobbled by public discontent over the war in Iraq, the response to Hurricane Katrina and ethics scandals."[8]

The brazen opportunism of the Bush administration, now committed to making this "their issue," shone through in a tour of the border region in late November 2005. Flanked by two black surveillance helicopters, a hand-picked crew of stone-faced agents, and large Orwellian signs that read, "Protecting America's Borders," Bush vowed to drive out the undocumented, declaring, "We want to make clear that when people violate our immigration laws, they are going to be sent home—and they need to stay at home."[9]

The Bush administration has also used the post-9/11 climate of paranoia to terrorize immigrants in the workplace. One particularly nefarious practice was for Homeland Security agents to set up fake Occupational Safety and Health Administration (OSHA) meetings and promote them at worksites as a means for migrants to "know their rights." Agents would then detain and deport those who showed up. The practice only stopped when unions intervened. Jill Cashen, spokeswoman for the United Food and Commercial Workers union, condemned the actions, declaring that OSHA "is the agency charged with keeping people safe on the job.... To use it as a trap is outrageous and undermines safety on the job."[10]

Ramping up hysteria around immigration politics allows the Far Right to position themselves as power-brokers in the political arena. Reactionaries like Angela "Bay" Buchanan and her arch-conservative brother Pat have formed the Team America Political Action Committee, which is dedicated to raising money for anti-immigrant candidates in the 2006 mid-term elections. The fact that mainstream politicians are using immigration for their own gain allows those most dedicated to the issue to push the terms of the discussion even further to the right. For instance, one anti-immigrant group SOS ("Save Our State") described the motive of their "street actions": "There is currently a mayoral race in the city of San Bernardino and we are hoping to fan the anti-illegal immigration flames and force each candidate to make clear their position on illegal immigration and enforcement at the local level."[11] Others, like Minuteman Project founder James Gilchrist, have sought to further polarize the issue by shifting from armed "migrant hunts" to the electoral arena. In his failed campaign for a congressional seat in

Orange County, California, Gilchrist sought to make immigration the central feature of the contest, issuing leaflets that claimed "a vote for John Campbell is a vote for more illegal aliens."[12]

A significant test case for using the "immigration wedge" took place in the Virginia gubernatorial campaign of 2005. Republican Jerry Kilgore made immigration the defining issue of his campaign, calling "illegal immigration a public-safety emergency," while trumpeting his opposition to allowing in-state tuition for children of undocumented immigrants. He promised to give local police the authority to enforce federal and civil immigration laws, and even invoked the hackneyed anti-immigration sound bite, "what part of illegal don't you understand?" in his commercials.[13] Ultimately, this strategy backfired, as he was handily defeated by his Democratic rival Timothy Kaine. But his campaign demonstrated how the Right is attempting to use immigration as one of its main rallying points.

By presenting Arabs, Muslims, and Latino migrants as a foreign threat, anti-immigration forces also attempt to revive support for unpopular imperialist war objectives abroad. Thus, a crackdown on immigrants facilitates cheaper labor, since those in fear will be less likely to speak out and join unions, and ratchets up nationalism, binding native-born workers to the ideological and economic interests of the owning class. At the same time, it does nothing to change the systemic factors that encourage migration in the first place.

Essentially, a two-front war has been opened. From above, sweeping anti-immigrant legislation is being cycled through the federal and state governments, while from below, reactionary nativist groups are mustering the troops and the confidence to take their message to the streets. In the first six months of 2005, states considered more than three hundred immigration-related bills and passed thirty-six of them, according to the National Conference of State Legislatures. The new legislation generally falls into one of three categories: denying benefits, allowing local police to arrest people for being in the country without authorization, and increasing fines on employers who hire undocumented workers.[14]

With little discussion in the media, Congress passed the Real ID Act in 2005. Under the pretext of isolating domestic terrorists, the act enables the Department of Homeland Security to establish standards for a national identification system by 2008 through centralizing all state drivers' license information into a federal database. Furthermore, it restricts the amnesty process, and gives the Department of Homeland Security free rein over further construction of the U.S.-Mexico border wall.[15] The ID card will effectively eliminate the last vestiges of mobility for the undocumented within the United States. Without IDs, they cannot legally drive, fly, take trains, or enter any government building. It will also override the twelve states that currently don't require proof of citizenship or legal status to get a driver's license.[16]

In late June of 2005, Georgia Congressman Charlie Norwood (R-GA) and Senator Jeff Sessions (R-AL) introduced the CLEAR Act (Clear Law Enforcement for criminal Alien Removal) into both houses of Congress. If passed, the CLEAR Act will allow the nation's 660,000 law enforcement agents to arrest and detain suspected undocumented immigrants, elevate unauthorized immigration from a civil to a criminal offense (punishable by jail terms and fines), crack down on locales that provide sanctuary, and fund the construction of twenty new immigrant detention centers.

Plunging into the rightward-moving currents of immigration politics, state lawmakers across the country are also working feverishly to roll back rights for immigrants. Maryland legislation passed in 2005 cuts off the thousands of children of legal as well as undocumented immigrants from health care benefits, and denies state-funded health care to immigrant pregnant women. Virginia has passed a measure denying the undocumented public benefits, including access to Medicaid, welfare, and local health care services.[17] Arizona set a new standard for the disregard of basic human rights in November 2005 with the passage of the notorious Proposition 200. The law denies undocumented immigrants access to all state and local benefits, including public housing, food assistance, college tuition, and employment benefits. The proposition, modeled on California's failed Proposition 187, ups the ante by requiring all state and local officials to report any undocumented immigrants who request services. It also makes Arizona the first state in the country to require proof of citizenship to vote.

What makes propositions like 187 and 200 so insidious is that they are largely directed at children, those most likely to use or need public services and education. Already, about half of all foreign-born Latinos drop out of school because of economic and political difficulties.[18] And the further restriction of health care will be devastating. For example, according to Human Rights Watch, as many as one hundred thousand children suffer from injuries each year in agriculture alone, along with about three hundred deaths.[19] This problem is exacerbated by the fact that many states do not provide workers' compensation for migrants. Include the random mishaps, illnesses, and scores of other health problems migrant children face, and these propositions add up to disaster.

Open season on immigrants has also filtered down into the lower echelons of the state apparatus, provoking novel interpretations of the meaning of law enforcement. In 2005, a police chief in Hudson, New Hampshire, took it upon himself to "do his part" by arresting Jorge Mora Ramirez on suspicion of being in the country without papers. The police chief, W. Garret Chamberlain, arrested Mora by charging him with criminal trespassing laws since he was "trespassing" on U.S. soil as an undocumented migrant. Justifying this controversial act, the county prosecutor Nicole Morse compared migrant workers to rapists and pedophiles. "Just as with a sex offender," Ms. Morse said, "the hope is that they will go and register with the state. And if they don't, then they are violating the law."[20] In response to a lawsuit that blocked the continuation of this practice, Republican legislators are pushing a bill that would enable the state to invoke trespassing laws against illegal immigrants, and states such as South Carolina have inquired about the approach. Florida, taking it one step further, has "authorized" all of its state law enforcement officials to arrest and detain "suspected" undocumented workers, creating a new standard for racial profiling.[21]

In early 2005, the Border Patrol staged "roving raids," sweeping suspected undocumented workers from the street, out of markets, and off of public transportation. In San Diego County, officials rescinded a long-standing order that kept the Border Patrol from harassing "suspected undocumented immigrants" in their own communities.[22] The raids function as a form of low-intensity warfare, instilling fear in the targeted population.

In border towns, a hyper-empowered Border Patrol runs roughshod over local populations. For instance in Douglas, Arizona, where 93 percent of the population is Latino, border agents have begun to operate like a force of occupation, making frequent raids on local stores and markets, trespassing in residential areas, and engaging in frequent, reckless car chases and other instances of endangerment. In the case of Blanca Mendoza, this "surveillance" cost her her freedom and almost cost her her life. While walking out of her relative's one day with a glass of water in her hands, she was surprised by a border agent pointing an automatic rifle at her head. Although she screamed, "I'm a citizen! I'm a citizen!" the agent refused to lower his weapon, later justifying his actions by stating that he believed the glass of water was in fact a dangerous weapon. To this day, Blanca Mendoza will not leave her house at night.[23]

By engineering a siege atmosphere, in which immigrants are demonized in the media and openly derided by a chorus of government officials, the anti-immigration movement has provided an ideological defibrillator for politicians seeking to resuscitate moribund political careers. California's governor, Arnold Schwarzenegger—himself an undocumented immigrant at one point—announced his support for "closing the border" and cracking down on immigrants. "Close the borders. Close the borders in California, and all across Mexico and the United States," he said to the Newspaper Association of America Convention in April 2005.[24] Further arousing the animosity of many Californians, he went on to praise the actions of the Minutemen, claiming "they've done a terrific job."[25] These statements came at a time when his popularity had plummeted to an all-time low of 37 percent, forcing him to go to great lengths to reinvent his image.[26]

Given the actions of politicians like Schwarzenegger, it is not surprising that border vigilantes have confidently begun armed patrols along the California border and are now gaining more prominence within the mainstream. Anti-immigrant hysteria, produced and packaged by bipartisan forces in Washington, D.C., and Sacramento—both for the sake of big business and to prolong their own political careers—opens the floodgates not only for the foot-soldiers of bigotry, but also for racial profiling and the oppression of whole communities now identified as the "enemy" other. In addition to being a cornerstone of labor control and a means of projecting fear in the "War on Terror," border enforcement has become a profitable enterprise. "According to an MPI study of appropriations from 1985–2002, funds for border control jumped from $700 million to $2.8 billion per year; funds for detention and removal skyrocketed from $192 million to $1.6 billion, while funds for interior investigations rose from $109 million to over $458 million."[27] The ICE and the CBP have also had their budgets expanded (proposed budgets for fiscal year 2006: CBP $6.7 billion, ICE $4.3 billion[28]) and their range of powers and jurisdiction increased. This unprecedented investment in border enforcement has spawned the term "border-industrial complex" to denote the changing nature of immigration enforcement.

Joseph Nevins cites Christian Parenti, who associates border militarization with "a much larger nationwide law-and-order crackdown that one sees in the boom of the U.S. prison population, the growth of militarized policing, and the federalization of the 'war on drugs.'"[29] Like the prison industry, the management of "illegal immigrants" has become a privatized and profitable concern. Today, the ICE holds about twenty-three thousand people in detention on a given day, and about two hundred thousand overall each year, in over nine hundred facilities across the country.[30] The construction of detention centers and the outsourcing of incarceration to corporations or other public facilities have proven very lucrative. For instance, in 2003, 60 percent of ICE detainees were held in local prisons and by private corporations such as the Corrections Corporation of America (which got its start housing undocumented workers in Texas) and the Wackenhut Corrections Corporation (which has similar origins in Colorado).

> Days after the [Nebraska] Hasting Correctional Center closed as a state prison, it reopened as an [immigration] detention center.... "It's a win-win," says [HCC employee] Jim Morgan. "The [ICE] is desperate for more beds for its ever expanding detainee population.... And the state of Nebraska, collecting $65 per detainee per day from the [federal government], rakes in more than $1 million a year over and above the cost of running the place.... [S]everal county sheriffs and wardens have described such detainees as a 'cash crop.'"[31]

The boon of immigration detention has spread from state to state. Local prison officials across the country have been eager to get their hands on detainees. The federal government paid York County, Pennsylvania, to house detainees for two years, allowing them to rake in a $1.5 million profit. An official from the neighboring county complained, "We tried like the dickens to get some of the [detainees] ... but it didn't pan out.... If no immigrants are secured, some layoffs may be inevitable." Meanwhile, a Miami immigration official confirmed that administrators of a Florida jail were calling repeatedly, requesting "more business" in the form of detainees.[32] The handling of immigrant detainees has become so arbitrary that "Richard A. Posner, a prominent and relatively conservative federal appeals court judge in Chicago, concluded that 'the adjudication of these cases at the administrative level has fallen below the minimum standards of legal justice.'"[33]

After September 11, private prison profiteers were ecstatic. The head of Houston-based Cornell Companies told investors,

> It can only be good ... with the focus on people that are illegal and also from Middle-Eastern descent.... [I]n the United States there are over 900,000 undocumented individuals from Middle-Eastern descent.... That's half of our entire prison population.... The federal business is the best business for us ... and the events of September 11th are increasing that business for us.

He was not alone; the head of the Wackenhut Corporation also saw the potential surge in profits and gushed, "As a result of the terrorist attacks in the United States in September we can expect federal agencies to have urgent needs to increase offender capacity if certain antiterrorism and homeland security legislation is passed."[34]

In late December 2005, the Corrections Corporation of America (CCA) gleefully announced a new federal contract to house six hundred detainees at a jail it operates in Taylor, Texas. Upon the announcement, CCA stocks rose 3 percent on the New York Stock Exchange.[35] According to the *Village Voice*, the boom in immigrant detentions is helping to revitalize the flagging operations of these corporations, which had been losing profits prior to September 11. Halliburton subsidiary Kellogg, Brown and Root, notorious for its profiteering off the war in Iraq, obtained a $385 million contract in early 2006 to construct temporary detention centers capable of incarcerating up to five thousand immigrant detainees.[36]

Immigration enforcement is also profitable as a staging ground for the defense industry, eager to showcase its latest wares. The U.S. Marines Web site boasts,

> Working under the tactical control of Joint Task Force North, the U.S. Northern Command unit that manages and coordinates military homeland security support to federal agencies, the marines of HMLA-267 deployed their FLIR[Forward-Looking Infrared Radar]-equipped AH-1W Super Cobra and UH-1N Huey helicopters to the border city of El Paso, Texas. Serving as "the eyes in the sky" for the agents on the ground, the marines used their FLIR systems to identify and report suspected illegal activities.[37]

Before "debuting" in the air-to-ground missile assassinations of alleged "terrorist targets" in Yemen, Palestine, and Pakistan, UAVs (Unmanned Aerial Vehicles) have been employed by the U.S. Customs and Border Patrol under the Arizona Border Control (ABC) Initiative as a means of remotely monitoring, patrolling, gathering intelligence on, and tracking activity along the U.S.-Mexico border.[38] Meanwhile, Arizona Republican Russell Pearce has proposed installing, at state expense, a $50 million radar system along his state's border with Mexico to identify immigrants crossing the desert into the United States.[39]

To sum up, the target of the "War on Terror" has been expanded to include *all* immigrant workers, in addition to the Arab, Muslim, and "Middle Eastern–looking" people originally victimized. This expansion in turn facilitated the transformation of border enforcement into a growth industry, and an easy means of stockpiling political capital while serving the interests of big business both at home and abroad.

Three mothers and their children make a stop before crossing the desert. Daytime temperatures in the area can reach 115 degrees.

Chapter Twenty-Six

The Bipartisan
Segregationists of Labor

As both the Democratic and Republican Parties are dependent on corporate capitalism, neither can deviate from serving its demands. Like celestial bodies, the closer politicians are to the centers of power within the two parties, the more irresistibly they are pulled into the orbit of big business. What results is a very slim separation between competing policy proposals, "bipartisan" efforts, and the intermarriage of economic and political objectives. In other words, both parties are committed to supplying cheap labor to corporate America and maintaining the "War on Terror."

At the center of the current legislative proposals for immigration "reform" are the demands of corporate America for a new guest-worker program. According to journalist David Bacon, "These proposals incorporate demands by the Essential Worker Immigration Coalition—36 of the U.S.'s largest trade and manufacturers' associations, headed by the U.S. Chamber of Commerce." He concludes that, "[d]espite their claims, there is no great shortage of workers in the U.S. There is a shortage of workers at the low wages industry would like to pay." [1]

The Essential Worker Immigration Coalition is organizing to push through its agenda. Membership in the new coalition costs between $50,000 and $250,000, with the funds being channeled into a political campaign that will combine demands for a guest-worker program *and* tighter border controls. [2]

"The economy needs them," says John Gay, cochair of the Essential

Worker Immigration Coalition, an alliance of service-industry employers. The number of American-born, low-skilled workers fell by 1.8 million between 1996 and 2000, meaning there is a dwindling supply to staff the booming construction, health-care, and hospitality industries.[3]

The Bush administration, representing the most unadulterated aspirations of corporate capital, is pushing for a guest-worker program that entails the unprecedented entry of braceros into *all sectors* of production, not just agriculture. Additional overt support for a guest-worker program is split between two main corporate factions. The previously mentioned Essential Worker Immigration Coalition is the more "liberal" of the two, and unites major health care, hotel, restaurant, construction, retail, wholesale, and other service industries and trade organizations eager for unfettered access to migrants. It supports longer-term access for employers to low-wage, undocumented labor, and therefore supports a proposal sponsored by Ted Kennedy and John McCain. According to EWIC's Web site:

> Hats off to the brave legislators in both the House and Senate for addressing the issues of comprehensive immigration reform through the introduction of The Secure America and Orderly Immigration Act. The Essential Worker Immigration Coalition (EWIC) hails the introduction of both a bicameral and bipartisan bill and commends Senators John McCain (R-AZ) and Ted Kennedy (D-MA) and Representatives Jim Kolbe (R-AZ), Jeff Flake (R-AZ) and Luis Gutierrez (D-IL). They have taken the baton from the White House on immigration reform and produced a bill that addresses head-on the serious issues of immigration reform—security, safety and lawful immigrant worker programs. This legislation will shore-up momentum and may provide the architecture for the development of a truly secure and orderly immigration system.[4]

The other, more conservative political vehicle promoting the guest-worker agenda, Americans for Border and Economic Security (ABES), is a bipartisan coterie of politicians and "insiders" including former GOP Chairman Ed Gillespie, retired congressmen Dick Armey (R-TX), and former Democratic Representative Cal Dooley (of the largely agricultural California District 20), as well as representatives of Wal-Mart and Tyson Foods. ABES was ostensibly formed to promote the White House's vision of an immigration policy that combines increased border enforcement along with a new bracero-style program. This combination seeks to appease sections of capital, namely the defense industries, who are not as dependent on immigrant workers as they are on the lucrative perpetuation of the "War on Terror." Bush's

Homeland Security chief, Michael Chertoff, expressed how the two seemingly opposite processes of taking workers in and keeping workers out could be combined, saying, "We must gain full control of our borders to prevent illegal immigration and security breaches." He added, "control of the border will also require reducing the demand for illegal border migration by channeling needed workers through a new [guest-worker program]."[5]

Also infused in the debate are sections of capital (allied with nativists) trying to push national security objectives, achieve major cut-backs in the welfare apparatus, continue pro-corporate restructuring of the tax system, and release built-up pressure in flagging industries. The competing demands of different sectors of capital have created fractures within the Republican Party, as disagreement over emphasis (guest-worker program versus "enforcement") leads to competing legislative proposals. For instance, while Colorado Congressman Tom Tancredo calls immigrants a "scourge that threatens the very future of our nation," Senator Mel Martinez (R-FL) has retorted, "Republicans have made significant gains [among Latinos] … and we're risking all of that by allowing ourselves to be positioned as anti-immigrant…. We are at great peril."[6]

According to the *Wall Street Journal*, "Immigration divides Democrats as well, which is one reason why the subject has languished in Congress for several years."[7] As Ron Harris wrote in the *St. Louis Post-Dispatch*,

> "There's no party divide on the issue, which is really interesting at a time when almost every issue is so partisan," said Michael Dimock, associate director of the Pew Research Center for the People and the Press. "The balance of opinion is split in each party. For instance, on the question of guest workers, business-oriented Republicans like guest workers, but socially conservative Republicans or more blue-collar Republicans don't like it. They see immigrants as a burden on the country."[8]

As a party dedicated to keeping capitalism alive and well, the Democrats cannot operate outside of the paradigm that social well-being derives from the maintenance and promotion of corporate interests. Like the Republicans, the Democrats conform to the guidelines of "electability" by formulating their political programs in a way that reflects the hopes and desires of the business class, and their socially conservative boosters in the middle class.

Unlike the Republicans, the Democrats must also present themselves as a popular "opposition," since their secondary constituents are unions, communities of color, and social movements. Nevertheless, without the visible, organized pressure of mass movements—which enable the liberal wing of the Democrats to push the rest of the party into the reluctant role of arbiter of class struggle—the party program is confined to a competition with the Republicans for the hearts and minds of the corporate elite. In other words, it is only when class struggle breaks out into the open—in the form of strikes or sizeable protest movements that threaten to expand beyond the control of established leaders—that power shifts within the party from the inner echelons (those tied directly to big capital) to the outer (those with closer links to unions and liberal, mass constituency organizations). In these periods, liberal politicians and trade union leaders are able to negotiate concessions and reforms for working people in exchange for curtailing social movements, preserving the legitimacy of capitalism, and redirecting the energy of grassroots activists into electoral support for Democratic candidates. Without struggle as a countervailing force, the pull of capital shifts the power back toward the corporate core of the party.[9] As former right-wing pundit Kevin Phillips explains,

> Part of the reason the U.S. "survival of the fittest" periods of economic restructuring are so relentless rests on the performance of the Democrats as history's second most enthusiastic capitalist party. They do not interfere much with capitalism's momentum, but wait for the excesses and the inevitable populist reaction.[10]

It is for this reason that the Democratic Party is incapable of presenting a coherent, progressive alternative to the Republicans on the issue of immigration. Instead, the Democratic Party is pulled in different directions, often reflecting the same schisms within the business class that afflict the Republicans. In fact, they were often the champions of immigration control over the course of the twentieth century, and have helped set the pace of immigration restriction in this century. As a party, the Democrats appear on both sides of the controlled labor/border enforcement debate. In some cases they lead, and in others they follow.

Some of the icons of the Democratic Party have also been the staunchest anti-immigrant proponents and advocates for big business interests of their day. The notorious Palmer Raids, which inaugurated the first orchestrated mass deportation of immigrants, were the brainchild of the Wilson administration. Franklin Delano Roosevelt continued the racial quota system and deportation regime initiated by his Republican predecessor, Herbert Hoover. According to immigration historian Roger

Daniels, "The administrative restrictions adopted by Herbert Hoover's regime were simply continued by Franklin Roosevelt's. There was nothing even resembling a New Deal for immigration.... Even before the Depression the Democratic Party's position on immigration was hardly distinguishable from the Republican's."[11] Daniels goes on to point out that on the other side of the immigrant divide was Lyndon B. Johnson. A fierce advocate for growers as a Texas congressman and Senate Majority Leader, he "thwarted efforts to put effective legal measures in place to halt and/or reverse the flow of migrants."[12]

Many rightfully attribute the origins of the current anti-immigrant movement in California to Proposition 187—which aimed to bar undocumented workers and their children from social services and required public employees to report undocumented children to the INS or face punishment—and Republican Pete Wilson, who was governor at the time. Wilson described California as undergoing an "invasion" by the undocumented, and charged the government with not doing enough to curb migration.[13] Despite the deep ignominy of Wilson, it was the Clinton administration that led the charge from Washington. As previously discussed, Clinton's Operation Gatekeeper was the most formidable anti-immigrant undertaking ever by the federal government, and is directly responsible for the deaths of over four thousand migrant workers in the last eleven years. Clinton also presided over the passage of the 1996 Antiterrorism and Effective Death Penalty Act and the Illegal Immigration Reform and Immigrant Responsibility Act, which

> expanded the scope of crimes considered deportable offenses, made detention mandatory for almost all people facing deportation, and increased the number of Border Patrol officers apprehending illegal entrants, especially in the Southwest. Meanwhile, changes in federal sentencing law increased the length of prison sentences for immigration offenses. Between 1986 and 2000, that average increased from 3.6 months to roughly 21 months.[14]

Clinton's "get tough on immigrants" effort coincided with his campaign to "eliminate welfare as we know it," the Personal Responsibility and Work Opportunity Reconciliation Act of 1996, which

> reinforced the derogatory view that immigrants are motivated by welfare rather than work. The law took away a wide range of federal benefits and services from both the undocumented and legal immigrants (e.g., food stamps and Supplemental Security Income [SSI]) and initiated new requirements for sponsors of alien relatives for immigration.[15]

Other core Democrats have tried to outflank the Republicans to the right on the issue by appearing more willing to "crack down" on undocumented workers. California Senator Dianne Feinstein has championed strict border controls for most of her career.[16] A stalwart in the putative "wars" on drugs and terror, Feinstein has positioned herself as an immigration "hawk."

> U.S. Senator Dianne Feinstein (D-CA) reintroduced legislation to require counterfeit-proof worker ID cards for all workers and to cut some welfare benefits now available to immigrants. Feinstein's bill also proposes stiffer penalties for alien smuggling, streamlines mechanisms for deporting criminal illegal aliens, and establishes a $1.00 border-crossing fee to help pay for beefed-up enforcement.[17]

Hillary Clinton, the party's hopeful for the presidency in 2008, has moved so far to the right on immigration that the conservative *Washington Times* accused her of "staking out a position on illegal immigration that is more conservative than President Bush, a strategy that supporters and detractors alike see as a way for the New York Democrat to shake the 'liberal' label and appeal to traditionally Republican states."[18] In an interview on WABC radio, she said, "I am, you know, adamantly against illegal immigrants," and in an interview on Fox News she accused Bush of not doing enough to "protect our borders and ports."[19] Even amid the mass immigrant rights protests that swelled nationally in April 2006, she lurched further to the right. After seeming to shift on the question, decrying the Sensenbrenner Bill as one that would "literally criminalize the Good Samaritan—and probably even Jesus himself," she backtracked, telling the *New York Daily News* that "she wants U.S. borders secured with a wall or fence, possibly surveillance drones and infrared cameras."[20] Her vacillation and right-wing posturing reveals the commitment of the Democratic Party to the "War on Terrorism," another name for the militarization of U.S. society and an extremely aggressive foreign policy. By focusing on the border, the Democrats hope to outflank the Bush administration on the issue, showing their commitment to continuing Bush's policies and the "War on Terror," while attacking him for failing in the endeavor. In fact, the Democratic Party has not only made "winning the war on terrorism" its clarion call, but it is also responsible for helping to shift the debate to the border.

Stopping "terrorism" has justified a wide range of government actions, from domestic wire taps and increased detentions and deportations to the *further* militarization and criminalization of immigration.

During the 2004 presidential elections, the Kerry-Edwards campaign sought to present itself as the champion on the issue. In the presidential debates, for example, Kerry claimed that a Democratic administration could "do a better job of homeland security. I can do a better job of waging a smarter, more effective war on terror and guarantee that we will go after the terrorists.... I will hunt them down, and we'll kill them, we'll capture them. We'll do whatever is necessary to be safe." In the same debate he concluded, "The fact is that we now have people from the Middle East, allegedly, coming across the border.... Here's what I'll do: Number one, the borders are more leaking today than they were before September 11. The fact is, we haven't done what we need to do to toughen up our borders, and I will."[21]

In other cases, Democrats offer only "softer versions" of Republican proposals. In Oklahoma, Republican legislators want to bar undocumented immigrants from receiving state benefits or medical care. While Tom Adelson, Democratic chairman of the state Senate's health care committee, has vowed to fight this effort, he is promoting his own proposal to fine employers of undocumented workers and revoke their state charter, which would take away their right to defend themselves in court.[22]

After telling Bush to "stand up to the right wing of his own party," Senate Minority Leader Harry Reid (D-NV) went on to promote both the right wing's deceptive characterization of the border and the need for a guest-worker program. "Unless we address the gap between our immigration laws and reality, illegal immigration will not stop, and the situation on the border will continue to be chaotic," Reid said.[23]

Liberal Democrat Ted Kennedy has teamed up with conservative Republican John McCain to offer crucial "bipartisan" support to the Bush administration's call for a new guest-worker program by promoting the Secure America and Orderly Immigration Act of 2005. Designed to bridge the divide between competing sections of capital, the bill claims to address America's "economic, social, and security interests."

The bill, a major concession to the "border alarmists," allows the Department of Homeland Security to close down additional border areas and "establish and carry out demonstration programs to strengthen communication, information sharing, technology, security, intelligence benefits, and enforcement activities that will protect the border without diminishing trade and commerce." It further provides for four hundred thousand guest workers (one hundred thousand more than the Bush proposal).[24] While Kennedy sells it as a liberal alternative to the Right's proposals, McCain pitches it to his conservative base, describing it as a means to protect "Americans" from immigrants. According to a press release on Ted Kennedy's Web site:

> This is a comprehensive bill that doesn't try to solve the hemorrhaging immigration problem with a band-aid—this bill is major surgery. The majority of the illegal immigration is happening in Arizona, and I will not stand by and let southern Arizona be the doormat for this country's failed immigration policy. They are illegal immigrants—they have broken the law and must be punished. That is why this legislation includes strict fines and penalties for those already in this country illegally and tough punishments for employers who hire illegal immigrants.[25]

Other liberals and Latino politicians within the party—those who are perhaps more in tune with the party's liberal base—are nevertheless unwilling to break ranks and go against the party's overall direction. Antonio Villaraigosa, the mayor of Los Angeles, avoided any discussion of immigration during his campaign. While claiming support for immigrant rights (he himself is the son of undocumented workers), he also admonished continued unauthorized immigration, stating, "[W]e have every right to enforce our [immigration] laws.... I believe in a great America we should always enforce them, while observing the civil rights of people."[26]

In mid-August, New Mexico's Democratic governor, Bill Richardson, who takes pride in being the nation's only Hispanic governor, declared the border region to be in a "state of emergency." In a statement defending his actions, he declared, "Recent developments have convinced me this action is necessary—including violence directed at law enforcement, damage to property and livestock, increased evidence of drug smuggling, and an increase in the number of undocumented immigrants."[27]

Other Democrats have followed suit. Governor Janet Napolitano declared a "state of emergency" in Arizona and "unveiled a $100-million proposal that includes posting National Guard troops along the border, toughening penalties for fraudulent identification papers and punishing businesses that employ illegal immigrants."[28] California Assembly Speaker Fabian Nuñez also called for a "state of emergency" to "make sure California is getting its fair share of funds" for imprisoning undocumented immigrants and other costs.[29] This put Nuñez to the right of Arnold Schwarzenegger on the question, since the governor has opposed calling for a state of emergency as "going too far." Similarly, Alabama

State Representative Randy Hinshaw, a Democrat, introduced legislation that would limit state services to undocumented immigrants. Reveling in the fact that he beat his Republican rivals to the punch, he said: "I think we caught them off guard; that rarely happens."[30]

Even progressives and activist organizations have fallen in line behind the Democrats. For instance, United for Peace and Justice (UFPJ) has officially endorsed the Kennedy-McCain guest-worker bill, which is virtually identical to Bush's proposal. Even when progressive liberals have a genuine critique of the anti-immigrant movement, they fall short of a solution. For instance, in an article in early 2006, Katrina vanden Heuvel of the *Nation* rightfully criticized the anti-immigrant onslaught, claiming "that it is not undocumented immigrants' presence in the U.S. labor market that harms American workers, but rather it is the immigrants' disempowerment in the workplace, stemming from employers' ability to threaten deportation, that is a danger to U.S. workers." Nevertheless, she went on to offer back-door support for the guest-worker bill, stating that, although it lacks a truly "enlightened" character, "McCain/Kennedy is the best of the pack."[31]

Perhaps most shamefully, some self-described liberals have even called for unity with the anti-immigrant right, under the faulty logic of "protecting American jobs." Thom Hartmann, Air America host and frequent contributor to the Common Dreams Web site, asked in early 2006, "How can progressives join with the few remaining populist Republicans (like Lou Dobbs and Patrick Buchanan) to forge an alliance to make [opposing illegal immigration] an all-American effort?"[32]

Since the Democratic Party is a creature of the American capitalist system, it can't stray too far from its master's side. In this case, supplying cheap labor to big business and projecting U.S. military power abroad fall firmly within the objectives of the party. Such objectives seemingly conflict with the Democrats' image as the "opposition" when social movements erupt, producing a schism that leads the party's "left wing" to try and coopt grassroots activism.

As the new immigrant civil rights movement spilled into the streets in mass protest in the spring of 2006, the same Democratic Party leaders who previously joined the chorus of criminalization—such as Ted Kennedy and Hillary Clinton—rushed to the front of demonstrations to "speak for immigrants." They told the gathered crowds that the solution was not to build the movement in the streets, but rather to demobilize and vote Democrat. In other words, they urged immigrants to support the very same politicians and legislative proposals that would criminalize and segregate immigrant workers.

Even though he has cosponsored a bill that would create a second-class group of workers and expand the border crackdown on future migrants, Kennedy did not even blink at a massive April 10, 2006, rally in Washington, D.C., when he quoted Martin Luther King Jr.—calling on the nation to "let freedom ring" for immigrants.[33] So, as the immigrant working class goes about constructing a new civil rights movement aimed at democratizing society and winning equality for all workers, the Democrats have gone on the offensive to demobilize it.

When the movement coalesced into a national strike and boycott on May 1, 2006—in a direct confrontation with capital—the Democrats helped split the movement, and then turned their guns on those who joined the boycott. New Mexico's Democratic governor Bill Richardson joined a throng of other Democratic leaders when he called Monday's demonstrations "a distraction from what the real issue is, and that's the need for comprehensive immigration reform. And I would rather have those demonstrators go to each of the congressional offices ... and explain to their representatives how important this issue is."[34] In other words, the Democratic Party works to contain any self-activated protests of workers that operate outside of its control or challenge the absolute power of big business. In trying to demobilize immigrant workers, Democrats pass the initiative back to the Far Right.

The Right Wing Calls the Shots

Deteriorating fortunes in the war in Iraq have led the Bush administration to lean more heavily on the fear of a "terrorist threat" to counter growing discontent with its policies. While playing the "immigration threat" card has alienated some sections of capital, like the American Farm Bureau, the American Health Care Association, and the American Nursery and Landscape Association, it has distracted some within his base, and allowed him to retake some ground from critics within his own party.[1]

This shift has been aided and abetted by competing forces within the Republican Party. The Far Right—which is made up of cultural nationalists, religious and social conservatives, antitax groups, and sections of Bush's downwardly mobile, conservative middle-class voting base—has sought to mobilize against immigration (and a guest-worker program) on the grounds that it "dilutes American culture" and "burdens" the social welfare system. This racist component is omnipresent in the media and interlocks neatly with more acceptable economic alarmism. Racist elements—politicians like Tom Tancredo, CNN anchor Lou Dobbs, radio shock-jocks like California-based Michael Savage and Roger Hedgecock, and activist vigilantes like the Minutemen—have been able to gain national prominence and push the debate far to the right. Tom Tancredo, Republican congressman from Colorado's sixth district since 1999, has emerged as the champion of the anti-immigrant movement and has a long history of championing various right-wing causes.

His career began as a high school teacher whose attempts to redeem a "godless country" with a "truly Christian educational system" and tireless crusades against multiculturalism earned him positions in both Reagan's and Bush Sr.'s Department of Education (DOE). As a functionary in the DOE, Tancredo dedicated himself to the project of dismantling the department, in line with the then popular conservative goal of doing away with "big government."

From 1993 to 1998, Tancredo headed the Independence Institute, a right-wing think tank devoted to policy development that favored downsizing government spending on social services. According to the International Relations Center, collaborators included Jeff Coors of the Coors Brewing Company, a notorious right-winger whose own Castle Rock Foundation provoked a boycott of Coors products by the AFL-CIO for its overtly racist, homophobic, and antilabor practices and statements. While at the helm of the institute, Tancredo devoted himself to the "term limits" movement, which he abruptly abandoned when he decided to seek a fourth term to Congress in 2004.

As a congressman, Tancredo has sought to build his career around another cause: stopping immigration. He has proclaimed himself a disciple of Samuel Huntington's xenophobic "Clash of Civilizations" theory,[2] and reserves an animosity toward Muslims that borders on the lunatic. In an interview with RightWingNews.com, he characterized the "War on Terrorism" as one against all Muslims, stating, "I believe that what we are fighting here is not just a small group of people who have hijacked a religion, but it is a civilization bent on destroying ours."[3] Revealing his contempt for all non-European immigrants, he added, "If Western civilization succumbs to the siren song of multiculturalism, I believe we are finished." He later told Fox News that Muslim holy sites should be bombed in response to any further terrorist attacks. "If ... we determine that it is the result of extremist, fundamentalist Muslims, you know, you could take out their holy sites."[4] He has also advocated the restriction of all immigration and the deployment of U.S. troops on the border.

His hostility toward Mexican immigrants blends the political expediency of war with a racially based opposition to the cultural integration of Mexicans in the Southwest, predicated on the superiority of an illusory "Anglo-American" culture. In his personal war against Mexicans, Tancredo spares no one. When the *Denver Post* profiled an illegal immigrant high school student with a 3.9 grade point average (out of a possible 4.0), Tancredo tried to have the boy deported.[5]

In the self-delusional world of Tom Tancredo, Mexican immigrants, Muslims, and international crime syndicates are conspiring to destroy the "American way of life." In a *Newsweek* article, he referred to immigrants as a "scourge."[6] Whipping himself into a frenzy at an anti-immigrant rally, he spewed, "Yes, many who come across the border are workers. But among them are people coming to kill me and you and your children."[7] And finally, demonstrating his detachment from reality, he alleged in one interview that

> [Muslim fundamentalists] are recruiting in our prisons and in our inner cities. They are recruiting in Muslim communities that have branched out all over the world. There is a huge Muslim population in Calgary Canada. They are responsible for huge amounts of methamphetamines. They ship the components into the United States. They then cook them down here and they send the money back to the Muslim cartel in Calgary and they in turn support terrorist activities all over the world with the money.[8]

Despite the fact that Tancredo's wealthy suburban district is home to virtually no immigrants, he decided to make anti-immigration his primary focus in his climb to Congress. Linking immigration to the "War on Terror," Tancredo has built his career by exploiting domestic fears and painting the Bush administration as soft on terrorism and border enforcement. This has forced the balance of power within the party to shift to the right on immigration, with Bush now touting a "crackdown" on unauthorized immigration as a centerpiece of his administrative agenda.

Nevertheless, his crusade has put him on a collision course with those in Washington who are eager to institute a guest-worker program. Consequently, Tancredo has refashioned himself as a right-wing populist, appealing to the reactionary bases of the Republican Party and nativists such as the Minutemen (he was the keynote speaker at their inaugural event), the religious right, cultural supremacists, and anti-immigration policy institutes. Tancredo also cofounded the Team America Political Action Committee with Bay Buchanan. According to its mission statement, Team America aims to "make [immigration] a significant part of the national political debate and to identify, recruit, and help elect to public office individuals who are committed to enforcing our laws and securing our borders." As Tancredo put it himself, "I am intent on making this immigration issue part of the national debate during that [2006] Presidential election ... and I will do that any way I can."[9] In other words, Team America seeks to groom a generation of politicians dedicated to pushing the anti-immigrant agenda onto center stage, encouraging the paramilitary theatrics of the Minutemen, promoting dubious "studies" by pseudo-scientific think tanks such as the Center for Immigration Studies, and convincing working-class America to turn against its migrant counterparts.

While most opinion polls show that the American public does not share Tancredo's animosity toward immigrant workers, his efforts to legitimize racism and anti-immigrant hysteria have had an effect. In December 2005, Tancredo helped co-pilot the passage of the Sensenbrenner Bill (HR4437) through the House. Emboldened by his victory, Tancredo is now pushing to introduce legislation that would erase the practice of "birthright citizenship," embodied in the Fourteenth Amendment of the Constitution, which bestows citizenship to all children born on U.S. soil. The goal of this legislation is to prevent legal obstacles to the deportation of whole immigrant families, the endgame of the anti-immigrant movement.

Another voice from the Far Right is CNN's Lou Dobbs, who has devoted his news show to a spurious "exposé" on immigration. Entitled "Broken Borders," the program promotes every dubious sound bite that comes from the radical right and showcases the Minutemen and other anti-immigrant advocates as "authorities" on the subject. His "news reporting" is often indistinguishable from his editorializing. For example, he declared in an editorial that "U.S. immigration policy is a tragic joke at the expense of hard-working middle-class Americans."[10] His contempt for immigrants has led him to his open support for the Minutemen. He traveled to the border in 2005 to congratulate them for doing a great job of "patrolling" the border. In racist hyperbole that would make Minutemen founder James Gilchrist envious, he described the "conspiracy" behind immigration:

> In the United States, an obscene alliance of corporate supremacists, desperate labor unions, certain ethnocentric Latino activist organizations and a majority of our elected officials in Washington works diligently to keep our borders open, wages suppressed and the American people all but helpless to resist the crushing financial and economic burden created by the millions of illegal aliens who crash our borders each year.[11]

A study by FAIR (Fairness and Accuracy in Reporting) shows a long and nefarious record of immigrant bashing by Dobbs.

Dobbs' tone on immigration is consistently alarmist; he warns his viewers (3/31/06) of Mexican immigrants who see themselves as an "army of invaders" intent upon reannexing parts of the Southwestern U.S. to Mexico, announces (11/19/03) that "illegal alien smugglers and drug traffickers are on the verge of ruining some of our national treasures," and declares (4/14/05) that "the invasion of illegal aliens is threatening the health of many Americans" through "deadly imports" of diseases like leprosy and malaria. And Dobbs makes no effort to provide a nuanced or balanced picture of the issue; as he told CNN Reliable Sources host Howard Kurtz (4/2/06): "I'm not interested—are you interested in six or seven views, or are you interested in the truth? Because that's what I'm interested in; that's what my viewers are interested in."

The day of the massive immigrants' rights rallies across the country, he launched into a scornful tirade that seemed to even threaten violence against the peaceful protesters (4/10/06): "Once again, the streets of our country were taken over today by people who don't belong here.... Taxpayers who have surrendered highways, parks, sidewalks and a lot of television news time on all these cable news networks to mobs of illegal aliens are not happy about it.... America's illegal aliens are becoming ever bolder. March through our streets and demand your rights. Excuse me? You have no rights here, and that includes the right to tie up our towns and cities and block our streets. At some point this could all turn very violent as Americans become fed up with the failure of their government to address the most pressing domestic issue of our time." [12]

In May of 2005, anti-immigrant forces gathered in Las Vegas to call for stricter immigration legislation, including a campaign to prosecute businesses that hire the undocumented. Speakers at the event included Barbara Coe, a coauthor of California's Proposition 187, James Gilchrist, Tom Tancredo, and relatives of victims of the September 11 attacks, as well as several law enforcement agents, and Michael Cutler, a former agent in the INS. At times chants broke out at the rally, including "send them home." [13]

Anti-immigrant voices have also found expression in the Immigration Reform Caucus of the U.S. Congress. Seventy-one members of the House of Representatives (sixty-nine Republicans and two Democrats) comprise the Congressional Immigration Reform Caucus, which explicitly supports anti-immigrant projects like the Minutemen. Led by Tancredo, the caucus aims to shore up and register opposition to any expansion of rights for immigrants. [14] More than twenty congressmen attended a Minutemen rally and

six of those politicians actually signed up with [the] organization, strapped on handguns and participated in Minuteman patrols in October, along with Arizona Republican gubernatorial candidate Don Goldwater, nephew of archconservative one-time presidential contender Barry Goldwater ("Extremism in defense of liberty is no vice"). That same month, [Minutemen leader Chris] Simcox met with California Gov. Arnold Schwarzenegger and Texas Gov. Rick Perry. Both men have publicly endorsed Minuteman patrols in their states.[15]

The ultimate goal of these organizations is to permanently deny citizenship even to those with deep roots in a community, roots planted through work, friendship, familial connections, and participation in civic and social activities. They seek to strip children of the constitutional rights that strengthen all families residing in the United States by promoting legislation like the Sensenbrenner Bill and more than four hundred anti-immigrant bills on the state level.

> Nearly half of the undocumented population is women, most are in married couples and many have children, making them more likely to be enmeshed in American society through schools, churches and other organizations. Complicating matters, two-thirds of these children, or 3.1 million in 2004, are U.S.-born citizens, Pew estimates. This means that, even though their parents could be deported, these children have the legal right to be here and obtain social services and welfare benefits.[16]

While the bill passed the House, its passage in the Senate is unlikely, partly because the Senate represents more concentrated support for "business-friendly" proposals and partially because the immigrant rights movement has shifted the terms of the debate. Recognizing this, Tancredo said, "We know that not all of our ideas will become law, [but] our message today is clear: border security is too important and the chance for real reform is too rare to take any idea off the table."[17]

In other words, the bill was designed to "rally the troops," shift the debate further to the right, and secure a place at the negotiating table with the administration. Tom Tancredo and James Gilchrist are trying to capitalize on the discontent of the middle class. As right-wing populists, they direct their venom at both the poorest workers and the economic elite, swinging in all directions.

Knowing that they are powerless to resist the demands of big business, they seek to secure a larger share of limited social resources for themselves and their constituencies. The most extreme manifestations of their powerlessness and discontent are the vigilante movements, which propound cultural chauvinism and employ low-intensity violence to force the issue into public consciousness. As Mike Davis explains, "Like earlier anti-abortion protests (which culminated in right-wing terrorism), the vigilante movement offers a dramatic tactic for capturing press attention, galvanizing opposition to immigration, and shifting the balance of power within the national Republican Party."[18] The success of this method (due to the paucity of any worthwhile opposition from the Democrats) has become apparent. The Bush administration has attempted to coopt the symbolism and language of the Far Right into its own efforts. While Bush dismisses anti-immigrant "border watchers" as vigilantes, he will not lift a finger to stop them. The benefits that big business extracts from a steady flow of cheap labor can only be maintained as long as public opinion is kept tilted against immigrant rights. Therefore, big business tolerates (and in some cases, enables) the presence of far-right, anti-immigrant groups. Their hyperbole incites anger against immigrants, deflects attention away from systemic failures, and undermines the confidence of immigrant workers to participate in political processes.

The Far Right has made so much progress toward legitimacy that the commissioner of U.S. Customs and Border Protection, Robert C. Bonner, said in August 2005 that his agency would like to incorporate Minutemen-like vigilante groups into joint actions with the Border Patrol. While Bonner later backed off the idea, forty-seven members of Congress introduced House Bill 3622 to establish a "Border Protection Corps," which encourages "volunteer militant-vigilante-policemen in cities throughout the U.S. with the objective of reporting undocumented immigrants to collaborate with federal, state and local authorities."[19]

Celebrating the capture of the national spotlight, James Gilchrist proclaimed in the spring of 2005, "We have simultaneously brought national awareness to our national security crisis, of which porous borders and illegal alien and drug traffic are components. The Minuteman Project will take the next few months to reorganize, expand, and to become larger, better, stronger."[20]

The gains of the anti-immigrant movement are also being expressed in other areas. Open season against undocumented immigrants (and Latinos in general) has been declared across the country by those wishing to advance their interests at the cost of immigrant rights. In late 2005, a group of "out-of-state" college students (including two children of a wealthy, conservative former congressman) filed a lawsuit to overturn a 2002 California law that "allows students who attend at least three years of high school in California to qualify for the same in-state fee break given California citizens, regardless of their immigration status."[21] Even though only a small percentage of students apply for the fee break, and the majority are citizens, anti-immigrant opponents are seizing the opportunity to attack on all available fronts.

In another case, officials in Canyon County, Idaho, are trying to drive out undocumented workers by suing several local businesses under the Federal Racketeer Influenced and Corrupt Organization (RICO) Act. Usually reserved for the mafia, county officials claim local agribusinesses are acting like the mob by "conspiring to lower wages by hiring illegal immigrants."[22] These efforts are largely stop-gap measures aimed at slapping business on the wrist while driving immigrants from the public sphere.

Willfully encouraging racial profiling, Greyhound Lines issued a directive to its employees "that they could be arrested or fired for selling bus tickets to anyone they know or believe is an undocumented immigrant."[23] Meanwhile, the anti-immigrant group Connecticut Citizens for Immigration Control (CCIC) stoked the hysteria by producing and releasing a study that claims McDonald's disproportionately hires "Hispanic" workers in Connecticut. Paul Streitz, cofounder of CCIC, claims his study proves that "Hispanic immigrants—legal and illegal—are displacing other McDonald's workers."[24] Bordering on the absurd, Streitz revealed his utter contempt for all Latinos by referring to the fast-food chain as "Mexdonald's." Streitz, a Vietnam veteran and marketing director, took time from his busy schedule exposing McDonald's to join a Minutemen patrol, hunting immigrants along the border in Arizona.[25]

Characterizing his crusade against immigrants as a "war of attrition," executive director of the Center for Immigration Studies, Mark Krikorian, explained to the *Arizona Republic*,

> Ending this climate of impunity is the key to regaining control over immigration. What's needed is a policy of attrition of the illegal population through across-the-board enforcement. This would involve both conventional measures, like arresting and deporting more illegals. But an attrition strategy would also involve other measures—firewalls, you might say—to make it as difficult as possible for illegal aliens to live a normal life here. This would entice fewer to come in the first place and persuade millions who are already here to give up and deport themselves. That would mean no jobs for illegals, no driver's licenses, no bank accounts, no car loans, no mortgages, no business licenses, no access to state colleges.[26]

Anti-immigrant organizations such as the Federation for American

Immigration Reform and the Center for Immigration Studies have entered the American mainstream and are often cited and quoted as scientific, nonpartisan "think tanks" devoted to the issue of immigration. FAIR, which grew out of the "New Right" of the 1970s, is a membership organization dedicated to "ending illegal immigration."[27] They formed as a split from "Zero Population Growth" in 1979, as a more radical, activist anti-immigrant grouping. Their goal has been to arrest and roll back the gains of the civil rights movement, and especially to prevent an extension of civil rights to the migrant community. The leadership of FAIR is comprised of "former immigration agents, Border Patrol officers, and other law enforcement experts," and its founder, John Tanton, has set up a web of anti-immigrant formations that operate under one umbrella. These include U.S. English (1983), Center for Immigration Studies (1985), Social Contract Press (1990), Pro English (1994), and Numbers USA (1996). According to the International Relations Center, an organization that maps the movements of the Far Right,

> Along with a few other FAIR board members, Tanton founded a nationalist organization called WITAN—short for the Old English term *"witenagemot,"* meaning "council of wise men." In 1986 Tanton signed a memo that went to WITAN members that highlighted the supremacist bent of Tanton and FAIR. The memo charged that Latin American immigrants brought a culture of political corruption with them to the United States that that they were unlikely to involve themselves in civil life. He raised the alarm that they could become the majority group in U.S. society. What's more, he asked: "Can homo contraceptivus compete with homo progenitiva?" Answering his own rhetorical question, Tanton wrote that "perhaps this is the first instance in which those with their pants up are going to get caught by those with their pants down!" According to Tanton, "In California 2030, the non-Hispanic Whites and Asians will own the property, have the good jobs and education, speak one language and be mostly Protestant and 'other.' The Blacks and Hispanics will have the poor jobs, will lack education, own little property, speak another language and will be mainly Catholic." Furthermore, Tanton raised concerns about the "educability" of Hispanics. In 1988 the media published this Tanton memo, and caused a number of former supporters of U.S. English to cut ties with Tanton, including Walter Cronkite and eventually Linda Chavez, a right-wing analyst with the Equal Opportunity Center.[28]

Even the *Wall Street Journal* has condemned FAIR, CIS, and the other Tanton formations. In an article entitled "Borderline Republicans," the paper describes FAIR's agenda as having "less to do with immigration per se and more to do with environmental extremism and population-growth concerns influenced by the discredited claims of the 19th-century British economist Thomas Malthus."[29]

The desire to exclude immigrants is often packaged with a thinly veiled racial contempt and a mean-spirited cruelty that dehumanizes immigrants and thus deprives them of human rights. It also leads to the cultural oppression of Latinos in general. When anti-immigrant hysteria metastasizes, it transcends the borders of citizenship. Latinos across the country, citizens or not, are experiencing the intensification of an anti-Mexican backlash filtrating into their daily lives. Zach Rubio, a Mexican-American high school student in Kansas City, Kansas, was shocked when for no reason his principal suspended him from school. His parents were astounded to hear that his infraction and suspension were due to the use of Spanish in conversations with classmates.[30] In fact, the right-wing onslaught against immigrants takes no pains to distinguish between undocumented workers and children born in the United States who are citizens.

According to Washington, D.C., school board member Victor A. Reinoso, "There's a lot of backlash against the increasing Hispanic population. We've seen some of it in the D.C. schools. You see it in some cities, where people complain that their tax money shouldn't be used to print public notices in Spanish. And there have been cases where schools want to ban foreign languages."[31]

And according to the *Wall Street Journal*,

> Cases involving English-only policies are mounting at the EEOC, the federal agency that enforces antidiscrimination laws in the workplace, as well as at private law firms across the country. Complaints filed with the agency jumped to 155 in 2004 from 32 in 1996. More grievances— they usually involve Spanish—are likely being handled by private attorneys. Still, most instances of language discrimination go unreported because employees fear retaliation, such as job loss, or, if they are illegal immigrants, even deportation.[32]

Ironically, many of these same workers are hired specifically to communicate to a Spanish-speaking clientele while forbidden to converse with each other in Spanish.

Other forms of cultural racism are more subtle. For instance,

> The Nashville City Council considered a proposal by three of its members to ban taco trucks and other mobile food vendors. Supporters of the ban insisted that it was prompted by legitimate health concerns

and not by—as critics suggested—a cultural backlash against Hispanics who, according to the Associated Press, operate the majority of the mobile vending trucks in the city. But the council members had a tough time explaining why the ban did not apply to smaller street vendors, such as hot dog carts.[33]

Demonstrating how irrationally dangerous the debate has become, an opinion piece appearing in the newspaper of Georgetown College in Kentucky advocated the use of land mines to blow up migrant workers, stating "when it is plainly advertised that the area is mined, it causes a person to reconsider crossing the area." The author went on to justify this plan by stating, "I despise the idea of illegal immigrants, and all Americans should find it equally loathsome."[34] In the *Southwestern Sun*, the campus newspaper for the San Diego–based Southwestern College, one editor decried "illegal immigration" and compared migrants to "leeches" that need to be "burned off the system."[35]

It should not be too surprising that in an increasingly anti-immigrant climate, hostility would transform into violence. In fact, violence against all Latinos has been rising precipitously across the country. According to the Southern Poverty Law Center, "In the last year, the same period in which several Arizona ranchers made national news by 'arresting' at gunpoint illegal aliens who crossed their lands, three would-be border crossers have been killed in apparent vigilante violence."[36] In lashing out at immigrants, the Ku Klux Klan has latched on to a popular cause to revitalize its image. As David Lubell, director of the Nashville-based Tennessee Immigrant and Refugee Rights Coalition, put it, "All of a sudden it is acceptable to incite hatred of immigrants, whether Latino, or from Africa, or Asia or wherever." Referring to the violence against immigrants, including the 2005 beating death of five undocumented workers in Georgia, he said, "This is just a symptom of what has been anti-immigrant sentiment, much more freely used by radio talk show hosts, anti-immigrant groups and even politicians."

Chapter Twenty-Eight

Terrorists on the Border: The Minutemen Stalk Their Prey

Migrant workers' struggles for better wages and conditions are often followed by the rise of violent and racist nativist movements. Nativist movements (today characterized by groups like the Minutemen) are often drawn from the downwardly mobile middle-class and white-collar workers, but find boosters among the representatives of the elite. Their aim is to discipline "unruly workers" and restore power and confidence in the dominant capitalist class.

The most prominent of nativist groups, the Ku Klux Klan, demonstrates this connection. Made up mostly of poorer farmers and the white middle class (sheriffs, lawyers, judges, small businessmen), the KKK includes those kept socially sedentary or oppressed by big business and the land-owning oligarchy. The KKK has directed its violence primarily at Black workers. By terrorizing working-class Blacks, and any white workers that sympathize or unite with them, they helped to create a virtually insurmountable divide that has inhibited working-class organization across the South up to the present day.

With close to one-third of the nation's workforce, the South today has only one-sixth of its union members. Overall, the rate of unionization in the South is only 8 percent, compared to 18 percent of workers elsewhere. Four Southern states (South Carolina, North Carolina, Arkansas, and Virginia) register the lowest unionization rates overall.[1] Furthermore, working conditions and "labor flexibility laws" that favor corporations have induced companies to relocate to the South as a means to weaken or break existing unions. The Minutemen, while different in form from the KKK, are essentially drawn from the same substance.

As James Gilchrist posed before the news camera in the simmering Arizona Desert, he explained his group's border patrol routine to an apparently captivated media. "This thing was a dog and pony show designed to bring in the media and get the message out and it worked." His partner, Minutemen cofounder and Border Patrol reject Chris Simcox, added, "We are showing the government the model for homeland security. If they deployed 10,000 to 15,000 National Guard troops on the border, there would be nowhere else to funnel people."[2]

The reorganization of anti-immigrant groupings in the United States is currently being conducted under the umbrella of the Minuteman Project. Their aim is to create "citizens' patrols" on the border, capture national attention, and compel the government to take stricter measures to curb undocumented immigration. While they use the "Minuteman" name to evoke the populist iconography of American Revolutionary "patriotic citizen-soldiers," they are in fact a reconfiguration of the remnants of the right-wing, paramilitary formations that fragmented with the decline of the militia movement. Their media-staged border tours and migrant hunts attract a small throng of self-styled immigration foes from across the United States.

Their suburban counterparts, such as the Ventura County–based "Save Our State" (SOS), are an assortment of middle-aged activists who descend on workplaces, banks, and day-laborer sites frequented by undocumented workers. They are aided by reactionary AM radio shows such as the Murrietta, California–based *John and Ken Show* and the San Diego–based *Roger Hedgecock Show*. These shows have become the echo-chambers of the anti-immigrant movement, perpetuating every racist myth, stereotype, and sound bite ad nauseam. They also contribute airtime and resources to providing an organizing platform for targeted actions against immigrants.

The *John and Ken Show* devoted a series of shows to promoting a signature drive for the "California Border Police Initiative," a proposal to create a new state-run border-enforcement agency. Hedgecock called on his listeners to harass day laborers at pick-up sites, encouraging them to photograph the workers and their prospective employers and report them to immigration officials.

The strategy was shown recently in Lake Forest, Calif., when a white van eased into a liquor store parking lot and was swarmed by 30 Hispanic day laborers who began intense job negotiations with the driver. Within seconds, another wave of people descended on the van. Mostly white and middle aged, they snapped pictures as they cited federal labor laws. "If you hire illegal workers, we'll put your picture on the Internet," warned Robin Hvidston, a property manager who became an immigration activist after being alarmed by the number of Hispanics she saw in her Orange County community.[3]

These tactics amount to low-intensity terrorism, as the fear of incarceration and deportation are used as weapons to deprive migrant workers of the right to work.

The motley ranks of activists include gray-haired retirees, professionals, postal workers, marketers, property managers, failed right-wing politicos, and a further assortment of middle-class and white-collar discontents. Military veterans, camouflaged security guards, former cops, and border agents flock to their banners and are often the "lieutenants in the fields" for the border actions, adding a paramilitary veneer to their vigilante actions.

While they most resemble a group of weekend warriors, or a gun club of cranky malcontents and political opportunists, the Minutemen have gained national prominence by exploiting a volatile issue in a polarized environment. They, along with their collaborators in cities, present themselves as the only committed enforcers of "illegal immigrant" restriction. Although their core is comprised of marginal, fringe-right elements, they have orchestrated their actions for the popular consumption of the U.S.-born working class. In one interview, a spokesman referred to the group as "white Martin Luther Kings" fighting for the civil rights of the native-born.[4] By attempting to divide workers along national and racial lines, they hope to increase their negotiating power with capitalist politicians.

In other words, the Minutemen advance a right-wing populist agenda that aims to expose corporate America's appetite for cheap labor while also attacking labor's right to organize immigrants. By appealing to the disaffected middle class—those who mistakenly perceive that their lives would improve without immigrants—they hope to force politicians beholden to big business to negotiate concessions in immigration legislation that will criminalize immigration. While big business also benefits from disenfranchised labor, deportations in times of economic prosperity or labor shortages lead to divisions on the Right.

Simultaneously, the Minutemen's efforts reinforce anti-immigrant opposition and serve to buttress existing perceptions of all immigrant workers as "illegal." While they claim to oppose only "illegal immigration," their opposition is directed at Latinos as a whole. As one of the Minutemen said, in explaining his reasons for participation in the group, "When I drive down Bethany Home Road [a main Phoenix thoroughfare that runs through both predominantly Anglo and Hispanic neighborhoods] and read billboards in Spanish, when I walk into Wal-Mart and the signs are in Spanish, I feel threatened."[5]

Their broader constituencies are comprised of disaffected Anglo white-collar workers, middle-class professionals, and rural landowners. Compressed between the crushing dominance of corporate America on the one hand, and the decreasing availability of affordable housing, education, employment, and social services on the other, they direct their frustration toward the immigrant portion of the working class. One Minuteman group, in Herndon, Maryland, was profiled by the *Washington Post* in March 2006. Led by George Taplin, a computer software engineer and former sailor, his "little brigade" is described as

> Bill Campenni, the retired Air National Guard fighter pilot; his wife, Kathleen, the Canadian emigre who is now a U.S. citizen; Diane Bonieskie, the retired schoolteacher; Jeff Talley, who says he's losing his aircraft repair job because it's being outsourced to Mexico; and Joe, who won't provide his last name or say what he does because "who knows who might get the information."[6]

Taplin turned to politics after a failed career in technology and contracting, explaining "I was working at a job, and a promotion was coming up, and I was the most qualified, head and shoulders above everybody else.... One woman was chosen because she was black and female. It was a female-heavy group."[7]

He became an activist when he learned that the city was planning to devote funds to the construction of a day labor site, and when he heard a rumor that a "drunken Latino man" had made lewd comments to schoolchildren waiting at a bus stop. "The town's policy was to appease some people and ignore the rest of us."[8] He then devoted his spare time to rallying support against the town's Latino immigrants. After snapping photos of Latino workers gathering outside a local 7-Eleven store, Taplin and his cohorts blamed litter around the area on immigrants, claiming "It comes back to their culture.... When you come here, you're going to do what you did in your culture."[9]

As the offspring of the white, upwardly mobile generation of the postwar, pre–civil rights era, Minutemen formations like that in Maryland have concluded that the growth of immigrant and non-white communities and their access to citizenship benefits directly undermine their own privileged social position.

The emergence of anti-immigrant groups was prompted by a number of interrelated circumstances. The "War on Terrorism" electrified the "enemy amongst us" mentality and highlighted racial and national fault lines across the country. Also, traditional anti-Mexican sentiment has been revived alongside deep cuts to social spending and available state resources. The overall downsizing of the redistributive apparatus of the state has increased competition for scarce resources and intensified the sense of national and ethnic entitlement among more conservative layers of the middle classes. This has occurred at the same time that the tax burden has shifted increasingly from the richest to the rest of society, a process summarized by the *New York Times* as follows:

> So it appears that while it is easier for a few high achievers to scale the summits of wealth, for many others it has become harder to move up from one economic class to another. Americans are arguably more likely than they were 30 years ago to end up in the class into which they were born.

The *Times* report also noted that

> ... new research on mobility, the movement of families up and down the economic ladder, shows there is far less of it than economists once thought and less than most people believe. In fact, mobility, which once buoyed the working lives of Americans as it rose in the decades after World War II, has lately flattened out or possibly even declined, many researchers say [10]

And according to the *Chicago Sun-Times,*

> Middle-income workers suffer because the industrial jobs that were unionized and offered good wages, health care, pensions and security are disappearing. They are replaced increasingly by jobs in the service industry, too often nonunion, with no health care, pensions or security: the Wal-Mart economy that Vice President Dick Cheney says is the model company for America. America's companies trample labor laws and keep workers from organizing in those companies. So now profit is up, productivity is up, CEO salaries are up, but wages are down. [11]

Many white-collar recruits to the Minutemen have also fallen victim to outsourcing, in which their jobs are shifted to developing countries, where wages are lower. Under these circumstances, many go on to blame poor workers in the poorer countries, rather than the corporations or government officials that enable this process.

The yawning class divide, widened by the policies of the last successive neoliberal administrations, has begun the process of dismantling the "postwar social guarantees." It has also provided flammable kindling for those seeking to scapegoat immigrants. For instance, in one interview with the *Arizona Republic*, Gilchrist said that he was unable to get subsidized housing for his mother because the system was "flooded with requests from illegal aliens. I thought this was the United States of America, for U.S. citizens," he said. "But I realized slowly it wasn't. It was for whoever got here by whatever means necessary, whether they were legal or not."[12]

By acting as the flag-bearers of ultra-nationalism and xenophobic racism, groups like the Minutemen seek to reassert a false sense of entitlement, based on being white and native-born, and perpetuated by the subjugation of immigrants and communities of color. According to Robert Lovato of *Hispanic Vista Magazine*,

> Their main goal is not to "protect" the physical borders of the United States: their primary political objectives have more to do with protecting the borders of white privilege and the notions of citizenship that are being transcended by a global society. Their tactics also serve the interests of elites like George W. Bush and military industrialists as they wrap themselves with, and rally much poorer people around, the flag of extreme nationalism.[13]

Of course, the privilege of being white accrues only to the white elite, since white workers are made to suffer from racism and the divisions it creates in the working class. As Sharon Smith explains,

> Capitalism forces workers to compete with each other. The unremitting pressure from a layer of workers—be they low wage or unemployed—is a constant reminder that workers compete for limited jobs that afford a decent standard of living, The working class has no interest in maintaining a system that thrives upon inequality and oppression. All empirical evidence shows quite the opposite. Racism against blacks and other racially oppressed groups serves both to lower the living standards of the entire working class and to weaken workers' ability to fight back. Whenever capitalists can threaten to replace one group of workers with another—poorly paid—group of workers, neither group benefits.[14]

According to the logic of the Minutemen, by pushing out the undocumented and closing the borders, U.S. capitalism would correct itself, promote the native-born (in this case, the *white* native-born), and ensure them a larger piece of the economic pie. This illusion blinds the nativists to the real source of their own oppression. As corporate America exerts more control over wages, working conditions worsen and opportunity diminishes, and they are pushed farther down into the ranks that they are scratching and clawing to avoid.

As individuals, with no sense of collective power, they create enemies more vulnerable than themselves to rationalize their own impotence. In their blindness, they rage against sections of U.S. society that are even more oppressed by the same system. The more helpless they feel, the more they militate against immigrants. Ultimately, by attacking immigrants and creating racial and national divisions in the working class, they increase the power that corporate America wields over all. But the fact that federal policy has transformed the border region into a war zone only seems to validate their frustrations. For instance, while decent jobs have evaporated in southern Arizona (the home base of the Minuteman Project), "there [is] only one growth industry: the Border Patrol."[15]

While vehemently denying the racist character of their organizations, they can hardly contain their contempt for the negative effect "foreign" influence is having on "American culture." Their ideology combines racism with misguided economic theories, enabling a broad swath of forces to unite in common cause. During their inaugural expedition along the Arizona border, Gilchrist let slip what really bothers him about immigrants from Mexico. "It's a silent Trojan horse invasion that is eroding our culture," he told reporters.[16]

The notion of a "superior culture" is rooted in changes in the language used by white supremacists in the years since the civil rights era. Coined the "new racism" by sociologists, the exclusion of certain groups (non-Anglo, non-European cultures being the prime targets) on the basis of culture is perceived as a socially acceptable means to express racism without violating the linguistic norms institutionalized by the civil rights movement.[17] This new racism has also become fashionable among prominent social theorists such as Harvard scholar Samuel Huntington. His 2002 book, *The Clash of Civilizations,* describes the looming conflicts of the twenty-first century as a struggle between Western "civilization" and the cultures of the third world. This neocolonialist thesis aims to relegitimize the oppression of immigrants on the basis that their culture is incompatible with—and corrosive to—the American way of life.

The new racism runs throughout the nativist movements, which under the aegis of "opposing illegal immigration" declare total war on Mexican culture and Mexican people, documented or not. The same groups that have led the debate against immigration have been working for years to overturn bilingual education and multicultural programs, and have underwritten legislative proposals that seek to deny social services to all immigrants.

But good old-fashioned overt racism is rife in the anti-immigrant movement as well. Barbara Coe, director of the California Coalition on Immigration Reform (which played a key role in the passage of California's notorious Proposition 187), regularly refers to Mexican people as "savages." Chris Simcox consistently evokes racist stereotypes, alleging that immigrants are "trashing their neighborhoods, refusing to assimilate, standing on street corners, jeering at little girls walking on their way to school."[18]

The Minuteman Project also generally chooses to ignore the Canadian border and its sparsely protected seventy-nine points of entry, yet bleats about Mexico's thirty-seven heavily monitored points of entry. Some groups make no effort to hide their disdain for immigrants. The Web site for Save Our States (SOS) asks, "Aren't you tired of watching your state turn into a Third World cesspool right before your eyes?"[19] Joe Turner, the founder of SOS, describes the aim of the anti-immigrant movement as an idea

> predicated on a singular notion that Americans are fed up with illegal immigration and want to get involved with an outfit that is serious.... Eventually, we are going to have an activist presence that will intimidate and strike fear into our opponents' hearts. Not only because we will have the troop strength to evoke fear, but because of the manner in which we are active. We take our battles to the streets ... something no other organization in the movement has ever done with any consistency or persistence.[20]

The open contempt and the insinuation of the need for violence against immigrants have provided an opening for the active participation of fascist elements. Expressing his desire to take more direct action, James Garret, a "tactical officer" for the Arizona Minutemen, lamented to journalist Peter Lauffer, "We need a revolution [because] my government precludes me from fighting the Mexicans."[21] A member of the California Minutemen, James Chase, urged his followers to come prepared to the July 16, 2005, patrol in Campo, California, and bring "machetes, stun guns and baseball bats." This was urged in order "to protect our people against the monster, should they appear."[22]

Groups adopting the Minutemen mantra are springing up all over, some openly espousing fascist ideology. The Southern Law Poverty Center has documented the participation of the Neo-Nazi National Alliance in Minutemen activities in Arizona. Two days before staged actions, Alliance pamphlets were distributed across the Minutemen base town of Tombstone calling for extreme measures against immigrants.

Human rights groups have also documented the participation of such racists as Joe McCutchen, a member of the white supremacist organization Council of Conservative Citizens. Preparing for a border action, he described the immigrants they were there to hunt: "They've got tuberculosis, leprosy. I mean, you don't even want to touch them unless you're wearing gloves. So why the hell should we pay our taxes to cure them?" One participant summarized his relationship to the Minuteman Project in the following way: "We understand why Gilchrist and Simcox have to talk all this P.C. crap…. It's all about playing to the media. That's fine. While we're here, it's their game and we'll play by their rules. Once Minuteman's over, though, we might just have to come back and do our own thing."[23]

Neo-Nazi organizations have also appeared at SOS rallies in California. At a July 16, 2005, protest against immigrants at the Laguna Day Laborers Center in Orange County, members of the National Vanguard turned out, mixing with other SOS members, carrying an SOS banner and openly unfurling Nazi flags.[24] While some SOS members were alarmed at their presence, SOS founder Joe Turner chastised those who sought to disassociate themselves, stating, "So, if you are in [SOS] … accept this reality [of Nazis being at our events]. If you cannot accept this reality or feel uncomfortable about it, then it is time for you to bow out and move on to another organization. No hard feelings. No grudges."[25]

It is not a coincidence that the appearance of the Minutemen parallels a general increase of hate crimes against Latinos across the United States. Across the South, there has been a resurgence of Ku Klux Klan activity increasingly directed at Latino immigrants.[26] Concealing their former identities under the now acceptable Minutemen label, Klan and Nazi groups are finding a new lease on life, and a new target at which to direct their hate and violence.

Under current circumstances, they can both recruit opportunistic politicians eager to ride the anti-immigrant wave and attract followers at the grassroots level eager to take physical action to solve the "immigrant problem." As one racist cited on a neo-Nazi Web site said, "This is a movement every WN [white nationalist] should support and be active in. It moves in our direction even as it does not even acknowledge, or even know, that the WN movement exists. Anti-alien activism is a no-loose [sic] for WN."[27]

The appearance and growth of far-right hate groups in the present and future will depend on how immigrant rights activists respond. Left unchallenged, they present a façade of power and can further perpetuate a climate of hate and fear. Many on the Left have pinned their hopes on liberal politicians in the Democratic Party, hoping that electoral politics can counter the confident Right. But so far, the Democrats have been unable and unwilling to rise to the occasion, and the very nature of the party ensures that this will continue to be so.

Part V

¡QUEREMOS UN MUNDO SIN FRONTERAS!

Minuteman patrols receive instructions on the rules of engagement at morning orientation near Palominas Trading Post
before traveling to border watch stations. Palominas, Arizona,
April 2005.

Chapter Twenty-Nine

Human Rights Activists Confront the Far Right

When the Arizona Minutemen captured the national spotlight in April 2005, they were able to present themselves as a unified, national movement, acting on behalf of U.S. public opinion. Devouring it whole, the media presented the Minutemen as "concerned citizens." Because their "operations" and motives went unchallenged, they were able to create a political opening for themselves and attract opportunist politicians eager to take their cause to the national arena.

The effectiveness of this strategy led immigrant rights activists to draw an important conclusion about how to organize a counter-campaign. Armando Navarro, veteran human rights activist and scholar, gave expression to the emerging consensus, saying, "We have to be prepared much better and with a capacity to create a critical mass when these events take place."[1] Navarro and many other activists decided they needed to take the offensive. Grassroots coalitions began to form in communities and on campuses in order to confront the racist campaigns. Jesse Diaz Jr., an activist based in Los Angeles who became one of the national organizers of the May 1, 2006, national boycott, organized with local activists to confront the leader of the anti-immigrant Right, Jim Gilchrist, at his gated Aliso Viejo, California home.[2] Another key leader, Nativo Lopez, president of the Los Angeles–based Mexican-American Political Association (MAPA), helped organize a march on the mayor's office of Costa Mesa, California, after the mayor announced his support for the Minutemen along with plans to use local law enforcement to round up undocumented workers in the small coastal town. These kinds of confrontations gained national attention and took the initiative away from the small groups of well-funded and well-armed vigilantes.

Some activists remained divided on the question of tactics. For instance, many believed that the Minutemen were a "nuisance" that "should simply be ignored." Others argued that cultural and community events, far removed from the Minutemen's activities, were the best way to counter their racism. Nevertheless, a growing segment of activists were learning the value of confronting hate groups, to both undermine their confidence and delegitimize their activities.

In the aftermath of the "Arizona Patrols," members of SOS, beaming with confidence, tried to replicate that success by taking their message to the Latino community of Baldwin Park in Los Angeles. Their goal: removal of a sculpture by a popular Chicana artist that honors the area's Mexican and Native American history and culture. By going into the community and projecting a confident image of confrontation with the "illegal invaders," SOS sought to grow its base and attract more people to the cause of "driving immigrants out."

To the dismay of the twenty SOS members who showed up at the park, over five hundred activists and community members confronted them—defending the monument and their community in the process. SOS's confident and confrontational posture quickly deflated in the face of such a large outpouring of opposition. SOS members, clamoring for protection, were forced to flee the community with a police escort. Protest participant Randy Selenak told the *Los Angeles Times* that going to the Latino suburb of Los Angeles was "like going into a lion's den. I just want to get out of here in one piece."[3]

Buoyed by the praise California governor Arnold Schwarzenegger lavished on the Arizona Minutemen, a California faction of the group set up their own armed patrols. In July, the "Border Patrol Auxiliary" brought a motley assortment of armed vigilantes to the small rural town of Campo, just east of San Diego. Instead of having a media field day, filled with staged images of military discipline and bold, patriotic speeches, the two dozen mercenaries encountered nearly two hundred pro-immigrant activists who set up their own anti-Minutemen encampment in order to create a "racist-free zone" along the border.

Activists hounded the Minutemen's every move, frustrating their attempts to encounter and apprehend immigrants. At one point, about fifty protesters held up the whole group of vigilantes in the local Veterans of Foreign Wars hall, chanting "Racists, go home!" and "Brothers, sisters, you have nothing to fear, immigrants are welcome here!"

When Minutemen leader James Chase and his heavily armed cohorts tried to avoid confrontation by scurrying out under the cover of darkness, activists in four-wheel-drive vehicles dogged them with floodlights and loud music. These tactics proved successful, disrupting the "covert" actions and demoralizing many volunteers, who trickled away one by one into the night.

Frustrated, the self-proclaimed "peaceful citizens" threatened some activists with violence. On a videotape made by one group of counter-protesters, the vigilantes can be heard saying, "You come down here and you will be engaged in a firefight."[4] When James Gilchrist turned out in a show of solidarity, he was visibly shaken by the counterprotest and the confrontational actions of the activists, and issued an urgent communiqué to his followers:

> Reinforcements are needed in Campo, Ca. immediately to support Jim Chase's California Minutemen!... We witnessed the literal seige (sic) of VFW Post #2080 by about 60 belligerant (sic), death-threatening anti-Americans twice during that day.... Be warned that the roving gangs of adversaries engaging the California Minutemen WILL physically attack you if they outnumber you. I repeat, they WILL physically attack you.... One California Minuteman volunteer, Jim Woods, was physically assaulted by a gang of ten of Navarro's thugs as he sat in his car alone at a border outpost.... Stay in groups, and stay LEGALLY armed with pepper spray ... tasers ... etc. Sidearms are legal in certain areas in Campo.[5]

Despite the frantic hyperbole, activists were unarmed and there were no arrests as a result of the confrontations. But it was clear that the challenge to the Minutemen's ideology and the disruption of their racist activities had shaken Gilchrist's confidence. More proof of the effectiveness of confrontation came from the founder of SOS, who admitted the fragmentation of the group in the face of such tactics. After his group was driven out of an immigrant community, he stated,

> I have been seething with anger since the rally, analyzing and thinking about how to proceed with this organization.... After repeated contacts between myself ... and the police department in which we strongly asked for our group to be separated from the opposition.... [t]hey allowed the socialists/anarchists to scream, blow whistles and blare bullhorns in our ears. Literally, an inch from our ears. They allowed them to yell in our

faces ... within inches, so that spittle flew into our face (sic). They allowed the opposition to jostle us on the sidewalk.... It worked to some degree as some members could not locate our scattered group and proceeded to return home instead of facing the rabid opposition by themselves.[6]

In another victory for the movement, officials in Carlsbad, California (a small coastal town north of San Diego) cancelled a forum and rally entitled "The Illegal Immigration Crisis" scheduled to be held in a local high school with the aim of bringing together leaders of the Minutemen with local, state, and congressional sympathizers. Explaining why it was cancelled, school superintendent John Roach cited the surge of the immigrant rights movement and its challenge to the legitimacy of anti-immigrant hate speech. "Based on my understanding of the recent events in Garden Grove, Baldwin Park, and Campo [where anti-immigrant activists were confronted], it is my belief that the event ... planned poses exactly such a risk."[7]

As activist Yasser Giron concluded, "demonstrations and pickets are an effective way of confronting these groups. Not only do they bring attention to this type of hate, but they also show these racists that they cannot go anywhere unopposed. It was beautiful to see activists and community members unified on this issue, against racism."[8]

The Minutemen's ability to capture the media spotlight—and the hearts of anti-immigrant politicians and media pundits—has not been matched by massive interest among the native-born working class (their primary target). While anti-immigrant forces have succeeded in bringing the issue of illegal immigration to the fore, most people have not drawn punitive conclusions about what should be done. In fact, polls conducted amid the massive immigrant rights protests in March, April, and May 2006 show that public opinion has been resistant to the entreaties of the vigilante formations. According to *USA Today*, a majority of the U.S. population thinks undocumented immigrants within the country should have access to citizenship. Some telling statistics include:

> Those who are immigrants or have at least one parent who is an immigrant are more likely to support the idea; 71% do so, compared with 62% among those whose parents were native-born. Among Democrats, 68% support citizenship for illegal immigrants, as do 65% of independents. Among Republicans, a 55% majority endorse the idea. By region, those in the West are most favorable, at 67% support. Those in the Midwest are least supportive, at 57%.Women are more supportive than men, 67% vs. 58%.[9]

Opposition to the ideas of the Minutemen is also tangible when it comes to erecting barriers along the border. An April Associated Press-Ipsos poll showed that over two-thirds of the population opposed the idea of a border fence.[10]

A visible, growing opposition to the Minutemen, which has been confronting the group at every turn, combined with a general distrust of the politics of scapegoating among U.S. workers, has meant little tangible support for the Far Right. The failure of the Minuteman Project to build a mass base left them exposed and isolated when millions of immigrants took to the streets to oppose anti-immigrant legislation and racism in the spring of 2006. The movement pushed the Minutemen out of the spotlight and into the shadows, and sent far-right politicians running for cover. In fact, it wasn't until the Bush administration launched a series of national raids in late April 2006—detaining over a thousand undocumented workers in an attempt to sow terror into the hearts of marching workers—that the Minutemen found an opportunity to reemerge.[11]

In a desperate attempt to regroup a semblance of a movement, the Minutemen launched a national caravan through the South to rally support for their cause. Since their efforts have been called out as racially motivated by anti-Minutemen activists, they have changed tack, trying to put an African-American face on their cause. Their plan was to tap into the anger of Black workers over unemployment and living conditions and direct that anger against immigrants.

At the May 2006 kickoff rally of their caravan in Los Angeles, the Minutemen were able to enlist the support of the Reverend Jesse Lee Peterson, an African-American pastor opposed to undocumented workers gaining legality in the United States. They also enlisted Ted Hayes, a homeless advocate who believes immigrants hurt wages and housing prospects for Black workers. The two were promptly placed in front of the cameras to show "the multiracial face" of the Minuteman movement. The plan backfired. Within moments of the start of the rally, African-American protesters and anti-racist activists surrounded the small gathering, shutting down the event. As one participant explained: "The same system that wants to criminalize immigration is the same system that disproportionately imprisons black men." Chanting "Minutemen go home," the protesters angrily countered the assumption that these two Minutemen supporters spoke for the Black community. When

Najee Ali, a well-know South Central Los Angeles rights activist, confronted James Gilchrist, the Minuteman founder scrambled for safety, barking pseudo-military orders to his henchmen and bodyguards: "Minutemen, stand your ground. Do not fire unless fired upon, and if it's war [Ali] wants, then let it begin here." He was then whisked away from the boisterous crowd, leaving behind a tiny group of supporters to be overrun by counterprotesters and news personnel.[12]

The Minutemen's attempt to pit oppressed African-Americans against criminalized immigrant workers has foundered for the time being, but it shows they will attempt to use divide-and-conquer strategies in times of struggle. However, a common legacy of exploitation and resistance is encouraging new links between Black and brown workers. As the Reverend Jesse Jackson Sr. recently commented,

> Immigrants of previous generations, including African Americans, should see the new undocumented workers as allies, not threats. They share with African Americans a history of repression, of being subjected to back-breaking, soul deadening work—or to no work at all. They share a history of making a way where there was no way, creating community in often hostile environments, and fighting to carve out a better future for their children.
>
> This new immigrant freedom movement is being embraced by African Americans and today's movement for peace and social justice. Slowly, the hands that picked the cotton are joining with the hands that pick the lettuce, connecting barrios and ghettos, fields and plantations—working together for a more just and open society.[13]

Chapter Thirty

Unions and Immigrant Workers

W hen Karl Marx insisted that the emancipation of the working
class has to be the act of the working class itself, he recognized the complexities of class conflict in the modern world
and the need for an organization capable of harnessing and leveraging
the power of the working class to advance its own interests. Laws, bu-
reaucracies, and enforcement agencies do not exist above the competing
classes they regulate, but are rather *an integral feature* of class domination. While capitalist apologists view open class conflict as "aberrant" to
the functioning of democracy, it is in fact an indispensable feature of the
negotiation of power between the two main contending classes of society, and one that marks every progressive juncture of the historical landscape. For example, during the last half of the 1930s, when the American
working class launched the greatest strike wave and union drive of its
history,

> By organizing, protesting, sitting-in and voting as a progressive bloc,
> [workers] forced the federal government to begin acting as a guarantor
> of workers' right to organize, bargain collectively, and earn a decent
> wage, as well as of citizens' rights to livable housing and a secure re-
> tirement.... By challenging big business's political and economic dom-
> ination, workers extended the formal democracy of America's political
> system into their workplaces and communities.[1]

Though class struggle is an immutable feature of capitalism, immigration policies and social attitudes toward immigrants are fluid. Laws
and popular perceptions of immigrant workers reflect not only the

needs of capital and the attendant "ideological conditioning" of public discourse, but also migrant workers' own self-activity at the point of production and in the public arena.

The participation of Mexican workers in "American" class struggle has been instrumental in the formation of the labor movement. Mexican- and Mexican-American-based social movements in education, housing, and other areas of class struggle have superseded the barriers of exclusion based on race, class, and national origins. Despite the partial gains won by immigrant workers, the maintenance of the caste-labor system through the twin vectors of racism and nationalism remains a debilitating albatross around the neck of the whole working class. Divisions in the working class inhibit mass coordinated actions that could advance the interests of the class *as a class*, rather than advancing the individual interests of one or another nation's citizens. For the working class, the focus on citizens' rights merely serves to mask class divisions and increase atomization.

Marx illustrated the self-sabotaging nature of the conflict between "native-born" workers and immigrant workers in his analysis of the relationship between the English and Irish working classes.

> The ordinary English worker hates the Irish worker as a competitor who lowers his standard of life. In relation to the Irish worker, he feels himself a member of the *ruling nation* and so turns himself into a tool of the aristocrats and capitalists of his country *against Ireland*, thus strengthening their domination over himself. He cherishes religious, social and national prejudices against the Irish worker.... This *antagonism* is the *secret of the impotence of the English working class*, despite its organization. It is the secret by which the capitalist class maintains its power. And that class is fully aware of it.[2] [Emphasis in original.]

Inter-ethnic and international class solidarity, or lack thereof, has been a determinant of the progression, inertia, or regression of the American labor movement. When nationalist or chauvinist sentiments are strong, the working class is weak, demonstrating the deep penetration of ruling-class ideology into working-class consciousness.

Because the ruling ideas of any epoch are the ideas of the ruling class, workers have always needed organization to defend and express their interests. While growers merged into cartels and monopolies and transformed agriculture into a series of totalitarian fiefdoms, Mexican workers turned to labor organization and solidarity as a means to advance their interests and break the labor caste system. Though characterized by the business press as malleable and passive peons, many migrants were in fact seasoned veterans of the tumultuous struggles in Mexico at the turn of the century. As historian Devra Miller explains, "Many had joined rural uprisings, labor unions, and armed forces of the Mexican Revolution."[3]

This experience in class struggle influenced Mexican workers' ethnic and class consciousness in the United States. Mexican workers had organized strikes in the fields of California and Texas as early as 1903, and often sought solidarity with other workers. But immigration restrictions and racism within the established trade unions often crippled any reciprocity in kind. Mexican workers found themselves shunned by the American Federation of Labor—which adopted an anti-immigrant stance on the basis of protecting the narrow, sectional interests of the skilled, Anglo craftsman. In California, for instance, there was no mention of organizing farmworkers in the proceedings of the state AFL from 1919 to 1934. It was not until 1959, in fact, that the AFL-CIO (the AFL's successor) officially supported efforts to organize farmworkers in California.[4] As Jeremy Brecher explains, "The American Federation of Labor remained a collection of highly exclusive unions of skilled craftsmen, scornful of the unskilled and semi-skilled majority ... [seeking] to gain concessions while preserving the harmony between employers and employees."[5] Its sense of "privilege"—stoked by the prevalent racism introduced into labor relations and immigration policy—fueled an anti-immigrant disposition that strangled multi-racial solidarity in the crib of early industrialization.

The AFL went so far as to agitate for the exclusion and deportation of Mexican workers, often adopting the rhetoric of the nativists. In 1928, AFL president William Green declared, "There are too many Mexicans coming into the United States ... and restrictions must be placed upon them to protect American workers from competition just as they are protected from similar competition in other countries."

Trade union leaders joined politicians and the media in characterizing Mexican workers as "stupid and ignorant peons," and the Arizona State Federation of Labor warned that Mexican workers were "a positive threat to our most cherished industrial, political and social institutions." The racism against Mexicans embraced by union leaders politically aligned the AFL with such reactionary organizations as the American Legion, the Ku Klux Klan, Veterans of Foreign Wars, and other "patriotic" organizations seeking to purify the United States for "white Americans." Mexican workers were thus left alone by the AFL in waging Herculean struggles against their employers.

For example, in 1903, the "Japanese-Mexican Labor Association" grew out of wretched conditions and low pay in the fields of Oxnard, California. After a month-long strike and intense conflict—including the shooting death of one striker—the workers secured a favorable contract. The Sugar Beet and Farm Laborers' Union emerged from the conflict and sought affiliation with the American Federation of Labor. AFL president Samuel Gompers, displaying the racism that debilitated the union movement during this era, demanded that as a precondition, "your union must guarantee that it will under no circumstances accept membership of any Chinese or Japanese." The Mexican secretary of the union replied:

> We [Mexicans] are going to stand by men who stood by us in the long, hard fight which ended in victory over the enemy. We therefore respectfully petition the AFL to grant us a charter under which we can unite all the sugar beet and field laborers of Oxnard without regard to their color or race. We will refuse any other kind of charter except one which will wipe out race prejudices and recognize our fellow workers as being as good as ourselves.[6]

The union was denied a charter and ultimately disappeared against a much stronger opponent.

This hostility from union officialdom meant that when Mexican workers undertook unionization and strike efforts, they were often crushed, as bosses could rely on a united front of politicians, the media, and local law enforcement agencies to suffocate workers' efforts. For example, by 1928, Mexican workers had organized twenty-one chapters of the Confederación de Uniones Obreras, a union of migrant workers in different industries organized in California. When the union organized the great El Monte berry-picker's strike in California in 1933, it was virtually ignored by the AFL. Striking against "virtual peonage conditions," the strike drew the ire of the state's business community. As Dr. George P. Clements of the Los Angeles Chamber of Commerce warned, "Knowing the Mexican pretty well, my opinion is that unless something is done, this local situation is dangerous in that it will spread throughout the state as a whole.... This is the most serious break of the Mexican workers here."[7]

The strike spread into the vast cotton fields of the San Joaquin Valley, prompting growers, local officials, and the police to move in. By evicting families and arresting pickets, they effectively broke the strike. As one local deputy sheriff concluded after repressing the strikers to the point of mass starvation,

> We protect our farmers here in Kern County. They are our best people. They are always with us. They keep the country going. They put us in here and they can put us out again, so we serve them. But the Mexicans are trash. They have no standard of living. We herd them like pigs.[8]

Despite violent repression, strikes of Mexican workers raged through the 1930s. While in some cases they succeeded in pushing up wages, medieval-style repression ensured that no continuity or sustenance of union organization came out of the conflicts, and so wage gains were often wiped out over time.

The abandonment of migrant workers by organized labor, however, also opened the field to radical unions and organizations, whose internationalist philosophies meant they worked *against* racial and national divides within the working class. Organizers of the Industrial Workers of the World (IWW, also known as "the Wobblies"), for instance, immersed themselves in the totalitarian environs of western agriculture, often risking life and limb to build unions among the ethnically diverse farmworkers.

The philosophy of the Wobblies posited that any fundamental transformation of the conditions of work required a multiethnic, multinational union that brought all workers under one union banner. As an industrial union, they focused on the immigrant and unskilled workforce, a growing portion of the working class eclipsing the narrow, skilled craft unions of the day.

The organizing strategy of the Wobblies included a number of tactics, since basic freedoms granted by the Bill of Rights were voided in agriculture. Aside from direct organizing—often under violent conditions—IWW members initiated political struggles to demand freedom of assembly and free speech, in order to make subsequent organizing drives possible. IWW members were routinely arrested, beaten, and sometimes killed in their efforts to extend basic democratic rights into the political wastelands of agriculture.

Their commitment to multiethnic organizing led them to create "mixed locals" (unlike the segregated locals of the AFL), promote immigrant workers into positions of leadership, and hold and establish multilingual meetings and publications. For instance, Mexican IWW

members established a Spanish-language newspaper and were important leaders and organizers of the Los Angeles and San Diego IWW locals.
The IWW also aligned itself with the exiled Partido Liberal Mexicano,
led by the fiery anarchist Ricardo Flores Magon, as Mexico approached
the precipice of revolution in 1910. Together they organized Mexican
workers in the American Southwest, while supporting revolutionary efforts to democratize Mexico. The IWW also formed alliances with other
ethnic-based unions and organizations. For example, the Fresno, California, branch of the IWW "held a joint rally with representatives from
the two-thousand-member Japanese Labor League in 1909.... Here the
speakers, including Italian and Mexican Wobblies, advocated cross-ra-
cial and cross-ethnic worker solidarity." Furthermore,

> [The] Wobbly press frequently addressed the commonality of labor ex-
> periences amongst white, Asian, Hispanic and African-American work-
> ers. Whether reporting on the difficult working experiences of Mexican
> construction laborers in San Diego, the exploitation of white, Chinese
> and Japanese farm workers in California's central valleys, or the plight
> of impoverished white and African-American loggers in Louisiana's
> pine forests, the Wobbly press sought to encourage workers to see past
> race to their common struggle against the employer who controlled the
> means of production.[9]

But the Wobblies would face severe repression in the teens and
twenties, as their members were jailed or deported in a Red Scare that
swept the country. This fact, combined with the difficulties the Wobblies
faced in establishing a solid base among migratory workers, meant that
the project of organizing an internationalist union movement fell instead
to the American Communist Party (CP) in the 1920s and 1930s.[10]

The party, whose political imperative was to create "red unions"
to rival the conservative AFL, formed the Trade Union Unity League
in 1928, with the stated intention of winning workers to a new industrial, multiethnic, and multinational union confederation. While these
efforts produced minimal success in most established industries, they
broke new ground in agriculture, where the field was wide open and
ripe for organizing. When Mexican workers engaged in bare-knuckle
class war against California growers in the early 1930s, Communist organizers immersed themselves in the thick of the struggles.

The TUUL organized the Cannery and Agricultural Workers Industrial Union (C&AWIU) in 1930 in an attempt to coalesce the militancy of migrant workers into a national union. Like other efforts,

the fledgling union was ultimately crushed by a coalition of growers working hand in glove with the apparatus of the state. Nevertheless, the union "succeeded, briefly and with mixed outcomes, in bringing unionism to Mexican field workers. In 1933 the C&AWIU led 24 of the reported 37 agricultural strikes in California, and of those 24, 21 resulted in partial wage increases. Summarizing the experience of working with the militant Mexican farmworkers, C&AWIU organizer Dorothy Healey recalled that strikes 'usually broke out spontaneously and then the workers would come and find us.'"[11] Despite its failure to punch through the monolithic power of the agricultural oligarchy, the C&AWIU strengthened the tradition of struggle and furnished a new generation of alloyed organizers that would later rise to the challenge and help organize the next waves of class struggle.

The Great Depression plunged the labor movement into a deep crisis, and the ossified and conservative leadership of the AFL was unable to respond to the explosive radicalization among the rank and file, and unwilling to launch organizing drives in the industrial sector. "In fact, the militancy of … AFL members during 1933 and 1934 worried the AFL leadership. By 1934 hundreds of workers were striking against the wishes or consent of the national leadership."[12] Under these circumstances, the Congress of Industrial Organizations (CIO) emerged and split from the paralyzed AFL to transform the militancy of a growing sector of workers into a mass strike movement for industrial unionism, driven by the masses of unskilled workers. Communist and socialist workers provided leadership and a class-conscious, multiracial approach to organizing. First- and second-generation immigrants were the backbone of the new movement, a reality reflected by the fact that CIO unions "aimed to meet workers on their ethnic, or racial, ground and pull them into a self-consciously common culture that transcended those distinctions."[13] Mass militancy, often imbued with socialist ideology, created new confidence among workers to confront and overturn the prejudices of the past.

The leading role many immigrants played in the rising union movement—as well as the class consciousness that emerged through workers' collective struggles—smashed the putative segregation that had divided most workers on the basis of ethnic origins. The CIO represented the apex of working-class power, which redefined class relations and shifted the balance of power in U.S. politics. The working-class surge also spilled into the neglected countryside, where Mexican and Mexican-American workers had been isolated and left to their own devices.

The Communist Party, both independently and through CIO unionization efforts, recognized the importance of reaching out to rural Mexican workers and building multiracial solidarity. Mexican-American labor leader and Communist Emma Tenayuca (along with her husband Homer Brooks)

> concluded that although the ethnic Mexican people north of the border represented an "oppressed national group," they should still be considered an organic part of American society, rather than as a separate nation. [They] acknowledged that Mexican-Americans and Mexican immigrants had experienced social ostracism and de facto segregation for more than a century, [and] maintained that "their economic life inextricably connect[s] them, not only with each other, but with the Anglo-American population in each of these separated Mexican communities." "Therefore...their economic, and hence political interests are welded to those of the Anglo-American people of the southwest." [14]

Through the theoretical agency of Tenayuca, the Communist Party developed a political framework that recognized that the struggle for a multiethnic, international workers' movement had to address both the political and economic questions facing Mexican workers. In a progressive (and prescient) document authored by Tenayuca in 1939, the party called for a movement

> (1) Against economic discrimination [and] extra low wages; expropriation of small land holders.
>
> (2) For educational and cultural equality ... [including] the use of Spanish as well as English in the public schools.
>
> (3) Against social oppression—for laws making illegal the various forms of Jim Crowism (This struggle must be linked up with that of the Negro people)
>
> (4) Against political repression ... [and] the leading role will undoubtedly be played by the proletarian base of the Mexican population, its overwhelming majority. [15]

The party implemented this perspective through aggressive union organizing but also through "front organizations" (seemingly independent of the Communist Party, but actually controlled by it), set up to advance the particular political interests of oppressed nationalities. One such group, El Congreso del Pueblo que Habla Espanol (the Congress of Spanish-Speaking People), organized working-class Mexicans and

Mexican-Americans around the class issues that affected their daily lives. Popular campaigns included

> agitating against police abuse, enabling … access to low-cost housing, helping with residence and citizenship forms and job applications, affirming equality for women … guaranteeing equal education for Mexican youth, and supporting access for Spanish-speaking people to defense jobs and unionization.[16]

Another organization, the Asociación Nacional Mexico-Americana (ANMA), represented the party's attempts to break through the racial segregation affecting Mexican peoples in the United States. The organization, comprised of two thousand people (mostly CIO unionists affiliated through miner's unions) sought the political unification of Mexican workers in the United States and Mexico, and advocated for basic democratic rights, ethnic awareness, and solidarity. It fought the deportation of Mexican nationals, decrying such moves as a means to "consolidate a system of 'peonage and even semi-slavery.'"[17] It also mobilized its chapters around the country to provide material and legal support for Mexican detainees, and condemned the conditions of migrant farmworkers. Preceding the actions of César Chávez and the United Farm Workers (see the following chapter), the ANMA contrasted farmworkers' contribution to society with the continued poverty, unstable employment, and discrimination they faced. ANMA unsuccessfully appealed to the United Nations Commission on Human Rights to investigate the wretched conditions and racism farmworkers faced in the fields.[18]

Although led by Mexicans and Mexican-Americans, the ANMA emphasized its internationalist character, stressing that "any person or organization interested in the progress of 'el pueblo mexicano' could join the ANMA regardless of citizenship, nationality, color, religion or political affiliation."[19] The ANMA's unflinching opposition to anti-Mexican racism framed this racism as an abuse of all workers. In their analysis, they traced the orgins of racism "to the white ruling class, not to all whites, and certainly not to the working class. Indeed, ANMA found the solution to the ethnic Mexican population's problems in class cooperation—in ethnic Mexicans joining with white laborers to eradicate prejudice and improve working conditions. In short, the liberation of ethnic Mexicans required liberating all laborers."[20] The organization also advocated for "cultural liberation," stressing that Mexican-Americans and Mexicans had the right to "cultural democracy," rejecting the stifling and racist Anglo-centric assimilation policies that were foisted upon the peoples of the Southwest.[21] ANMA's fierce commitment to the rights of Mexican workers and its resolute opposition to the perpetual discrimination leveled against all Mexican-Americans made the ANMA a target for FBI infiltration and subsequent persecution. Members of the organization were harassed, jailed, and often targeted themselves for deportation.

The increasing frequency of politically motivated deportations inspired the Communist Party to launch the American Committee for Protection of Foreign Born in the early 1930s. The committee organized legal defense and public support for those singled out for deportation (often party members) because of their real or alleged sympathy for communism or participation in activities deemed radical by the State Department. This became urgent when Roosevelt expanded the mandate of the FBI and intensified surveillance operations against immigrants amid the increasing working-class militancy of the 1930s. The committee was instrumental in organizing opposition to anti-immigrant legislation and round-ups, and provided critical support for Mexican activists detained for their political activities.

The last mass workers' movement in the 1930s showed the potential for labor unions to challenge the orthodoxies of capitalist hegemony, such as the use of the border to stigmatize workers, the ability to deport those who spoke out, and the array of divide and conquer strategies deployed to control labor. Then, like now, it was immigrant workers who played a key role in forging an internationalist spirit that defied the confines of narrow, exclusionary politics rooted in nationalistic prejudices. It also exposed the governing administrations as both the promoters and saviors of big business. As Bert Corona concluded, "Labor in the thirties was a very vibrant and militant movement that took on the real power in America, which was found in General Motors, U.S. Steel, and other corporate giants."[22] While the labor movement was unable to break through the stultifying repression of the McCarthy era, it demonstrated the potential for a future without borders.

Chapter Thirty-One

Making Borders History

R adical immigrant women were a crucial part of building militant struggles during this period as well. Situated along the gendered division of labor within the U.S. economy, Mexican women were at the forefront of rank-and-file union organization within agriculture, the garment industry, and elsewhere. For instance, in the years 1930–50, women comprised up to 75 percent of all food-processing workers in agricultural industries. In California, the majority of these women were Mexican, both citizens and otherwise.

Rising out of the malaise of the Great Depression and emboldened by the mass militancy embodied in the CIO movement, Latina militants were instrumental in the formation of the United Cannery, Agricultural, Packing, and Allied Workers of America (UCAPAWA). This union, which became the seventh largest affiliate of the CIO, grew through the determined commitment of its Latina, Asian, and African-American organizers as they fanned out across the agricultural landscape. By 1938, for instance, UCAPAWA had 371 affiliated locals and 124,000 members.[1]

Through struggle, women in general across the country—and Latinas in particular in the U.S. Southwest—built the union from the ground up. According the Vicki Ruiz, "female canning and packing operatives filled 44 percent of their locals' principal offices as well as 65 percent of shop steward posts."[2]

The desire to forge a more inclusive, democratic union that reflected ethnic and national diversity—as well as the militancy of the working class—was enshrined in the preamble of UCAPAWA's constitution:

> Knowing full well that the old … forms of trade union organizations are
> unable to defend effectively the interests of the workers, THEREFORE,
> WE, THE WORKERS ENGAGED IN THE CANNING, AGRICULTUR-
> AL, PACKING AND ALLIED INDUSTRIES FORM AN ORGANIZA-
> TION which unites all workers in our industry on an industrial and
> democratic basis, regardless of age, sex, nationality, race, creed, color, or
> political and religious beliefs, and pursues at all times a policy of aggres-
> sive activity to improve our social and economic conditions.[3]

The expansion of industrial unionism and the ability to collectively confront the most preponderant sections of capital also transformed the union movement into a political instrument able to affect national politics and act as the voice for all its component elements. Living standards for the working class as a whole rose dramatically while poverty levels fell to their lowest point ever.[4]

Nevertheless, these gains were not spread out evenly. While unions served as a turnstile for many immigrants to become assimilated into the mainstream of U.S. society, this wasn't true for all immigrant workers. American business turned to migrant Mexican labor after World War II to glean greater profits. Since migrant workers were excluded from unions—through the stipulations of the Bracero Program or because they were undocumented, and thus excluded by the unions—they became a defenseless class of workers, exploitable through the formation of immigration policies that further segregated them.

The ultimate abandonment of agricultural labor embodied in most "New Deal" legislation and the persistence of de jure racial segregation across the South and Southwest halted the process of labor democratization.[5] Racial divisions and the agricultural-industrial dichotomy allowed for caste labor to be perpetuated in the form of the Bracero Program and the incorporation of unauthorized migrant flows into the U.S. labor pool that it conspicuously generated.

The Cold War era sounded the death knell for the forward progression of the labor movement and the internationalist tendencies of the CIO. The reactionary turn in U.S. politics in the late 1940s—posthumously called the era of "McCarthyism"—signaled the beginning of an employer's backlash on the political front. The arch-conservatism of the McCarthy era also emboldened the segregationist movement, which closed ranks with the federal government to counteract the civil rights movement, claiming it was communism to advocate "race equality." While McCarthyism was an offensive against "communist subversion" on many fronts, government repression was directed primarily at the labor movement as a means to extricate radicals from the movements they had built in the 1930s. Through anticommunist legislation, blacklists, imprisonment, physical intimidation, and firings, radicals were driven out of unions with government sanction.

> At the fall 1949 CIO Convention, CIO officials pushed through an amendment to the CIO Constitution to enable them to purge Communists from their midst, and during 1950 ... they subjected its Communist-led Internationals to pseudo-trials, threw them out, and went on to "cleanse virtually all the [other] unions in which Communist influence had been significant...." To the extent that the unions expelled had been the more militant and devoted advocates of racial justice, the cause itself lost much meaning and appeal.[6]

Having shed its radical origins, the CIO reunited with the AFL in 1955. While the new federation was much larger, it was denuded of its leading militants and devoid of the politics that would enable further advance of the democratization of labor. As one dissident explained, the return to the AFL represented a "surrender to the three R's of the AFL—racism, racketeering, and raiding.... The CIO's enlightened racial policies were ... replaced by the traditional racial practices of the major AFL affiliates."[7]

The removal of radicals—who had fought for unity and grassroots struggle—from the labor movement enabled union leaders to bring the movement back into the fold of national chauvinism. As a consequence, the AFL-CIO became ensconced within the Democratic Party, trading its independence for an illusory place at the negotiating table.

With the defeat of radicals in the labor movement, it would take many years to rebuild a fight against racism and xenophobia. The civil rights movement of the 1960s exposed how deeply entrenched racism in the United States was, and gave millions the confidence to fight back. Black urban protests against segregation ignited the aspirations of Mexicans and Mexican-Americans, long oppressed across the Southwest by immigration distinctions and Jim Crow racism. A new generation of the sons and daughters of Mexican immigrants, radicalized by events and their own experiences with racism, filled the ranks of the emerging Mexican-American wing of the movement. The Chicano movement, as it came to be called, drew parallels between the perennial exploitation of farmworkers and the persistence of racism against Mexican-Americans in the cities. One of the most significant leaders to emerge from this generation was a former farmworker himself, César Chávez.

Chávez and his supporters dedicated themselves to spreading the concept of civil rights to the most hostile and reactionary region of the country, the fields of the Southwest. The first significant victory for Chávez and the new generation of farmworker advocates, later organized into the United Farm Workers (UFW), was the dismantling of the Bracero Program in 1964.

In the context of the rising civil rights movement in the 1960s, César Chávez, UFW cofounder Dolores Huerta, and other union activists sought to build a new farmworkers' union modeled on a social movement that would link together a broad coalition of forces for support. Chávez painstakingly organized and enlisted the support of Chicano students, churches, and other labor unions.

Chávez extolled the virtues of pacifism and used religious icons to project the struggle as one of passivity and moral suasion. Influenced by Gandhi, he chose to emulate the experience of the farmworker by committing himself to a life of poverty and religious virtue. He viewed the struggle as a battle of perseverance and sought to appeal to civil society's sense of morality by focusing primarily on publicity through non-confrontational means. His personal opposition to radical politics and militancy fueled the intensification of religious mysticism and traditions, especially in times of crisis. His maintained an allegiance to the Democratic Party that never wavered and, in fact, only deepened when the social movements of the time began to attract the attention of high-profile liberals.

Despite his own philosophies, the UFW attracted many young militants who carried into the union the spirit of struggle that was radicalizing many in the civil rights movement. The militancy of the young UFW organizers and the farmworkers themselves had an effect on Chávez and the union, which was forced to move to more aggressive tactics in the face of the preponderant power and intransigence of the growers.

Chávez's goal was to break the isolation of the farmworkers and to win the basic right to organize unions. The UFW relied on a combined strategy of aggressive organizing, strikes, high-visibility marches, and boycotts to challenge the reactionary growers from the farm to the supermarket.

As in previous attempts to organize the farms, the UFW came up against a hostile and unified front of growers and the state. In 1973, a high point in strike activity, over thirty-five hundred farmworkers and UFW supporters were arrested for attempting to organize, while thousands more were harassed, beaten, and terrorized by local law enforcement, often in league with goon squads in the pay of the growers.

In a shameful chapter of U.S. labor history, the growers formed an alliance with the right-wing leadership of the International Brotherhood of Teamsters in order to preempt the UFW.[8] Phantom union contracts were signed with the Teamsters to lock out the UFW and on several occasions Teamsters armed with clubs and chains were brought in to break up picket lines.

Governmental indifference to (or actual complicity in) the repression reached the highest echelons. In 1973, Chávez traveled to Washington, D.C., to press for a federal investigation into the violence against farmworkers in California. William Ruckelshaus, acting director of the FBI, unctuously responded that his agency had no authority to conduct an investigation. Meanwhile, the FBI maintained a full-scale surveillance operation of leading UFW members and their picket lines.[9]

The tenacity and courage of UFW organizers and farmworkers led to key strike victories through the 1970s, which ultimately defeated the growers' most egregious opposition. The union became a force to be reckoned with. The UFW pressured California's Democratic governor of the time, Jerry Brown, to push through the Agricultural Labor Relations Act of 1975, a state version of Roosevelt's National Labor Relations Act of forty years prior.

The ALRA created a set of guarantees for union organizing in California and created an Agricultural Relations Labor Board to address the grievances of those involved in farm work. This victory inspired a mass organizing campaign that saw UFW membership rise to forty-five thousand by 1980.[10] Brown appointed pro-union board members who often ruled in favor of the UFW. This helped create a sense among farmworkers that, with a seemingly pro-union governor in office, the tide was finally turning in their favor. In reality, it was labor militancy in the fields that accomplished the elusive historic feat: the union had beaten the omnipotent growers and forced them to accept coexistence with the UFW. But how to seize the initiative and build on the momentum?

The idea that the Democratic Party could assist the farmworkers' struggle led Chávez in the early seventies to redirect the UFW's emphasis away from organizing, and toward supporting and funding Democratic candidates' campaigns. Chávez himself nominated Jerry Brown for president at the Democratic National Convention in 1976.[11] This strategy had a demobilizing effect. To placate mainstream political forces and appear more respectable and moderate, Chávez shifted UFW strategies to include such moves as attacking undocumented workers. As farm-worker advocate Frank Bardacke pointed out, "the U.F.W. sometimes supported the use of the *migra* against scabs, sacrificing long-term re-spect for a possible short-term gain."[12] Chávez also purged the union's leadership of radicals and concentrated power in his own hands. Those in the leadership who weren't fired resigned when it became clear that Chávez would have the final say over virtually everything.[13] The union's power deteriorated.

The success of the farmworkers in previous years had forced a split within the Democrats' ranks, with liberals courting the movement and promising support if the union moved away from confrontational tac-tics and endorsed Democratic candidates for office. Meanwhile, the right wing of the party—and especially those members of Congress who represented agricultural regions—moved to marginalize the influence of the UFW. Congressmen like Leon Panetta formed strategic alliances with Republicans to pass pro-grower legislation.[14] This alliance meant that even in California, liberals on the labor board were replaced with those aligned with the growers. It should be noted, however, that even during the tenure of the supposedly "pro-union" Democrats running the board, only 43 percent of union elections had resulted in an actual contract, as the growers simply flouted the results and the Democrats refused to put any real pressure on the growers.[15]

Disillusionment with the Democrats came out into the open within the UFW. In 1977, Chávez himself commented in frustration, "seventeen months after.the farm labor law went into effect, most farmworkers have yet to realize the promise and protection of this good law. Instead, for most, the law has been a cruel hoax."[16] The promise of reform through a strategy of alliance with the Democrats, who had always placed the interest of growers at the top of their list, had proven illusory.

When Republican Governor George Deukmejian came to office in 1983, Chávez used this as a "defensive" justification to further shift the union's resources into the Democratic Party and abandon the struggle in the fields altogether. Chávez saw this as the means to build on the gains of the movement, while others saw it as the tragic turn toward de-feat. Leading UFW member Marshall Ganz, for example, who resigned over this shift, commented, "I don't want to minimize the problems of

Deukmejian, but the fact is, we did build this union when Reagan was governor and Nixon was president."[17]

Nevertheless, the UFW continued to funnel money into Democratic Party campaigns with the hope that this could buy them a place at the negotiating table. Through the 1980s, the UFW funneled well over a million dollars away from organizing and into campaigns for Democrats.[18] The union's accompanying neglect of hands-on organizing allowed the balance of power to shift back in favor of the bosses, who gained the confidence to refuse to renegotiate expired contracts and rely more heavily on the antiunion labor contracting system. By the early 1990s, membership in the UFW had plummeted to about five thousand members.

As of 2006, according to an article in the *Los Angeles Times*, the UFW

does not have a single contract in the table grape vineyards of the Central Valley where the union was born. Nor does it have members in many other agricultural swaths of the state: The union Chávez built now represents a tiny fraction of the approximately 450,000 farmworkers laboring in California fields during peak seasons—probably fewer than 7,000."[19]

As an editorial in the *Sacramento Bee* lamented,

Despite the union organizing efforts of the legendary Chávez, despite the landmark legislation that created the Agricultural Labor Relations Board, despite the growing political clout of Hispanic legislators and despite labor-friendly Democratic majorities in both houses of the Legislature, little has been done to reform the system. Every year, bills to protect farm workers are smashed by agricultural interests, who distribute hundreds of thousands of dollars in campaign contributions.[20]

Undocumented workers, increasingly Mixtecs and other indigenous Mexican groups, again make up the majority in the fields. The conditions of work have largely reverted back to the conditions César Chávez faced in the early 1960s. Nevertheless, immigrants, undocumented or not, continue to provide the militant ranks for another wave of struggle. And the AFL-CIO, increasingly immobilized and factionalized by its inability to grow and organize resistance, has made a historic turn by reversing its traditional anti-immigrant policies. After a long history of lining up with the bosses on the question of immigration restrictions, the AFL-CIO reversed its position in 1999, calling for a general amnesty and the right of all workers, documented or not, to form unions. To back up its new policy, the AFL-CIO held a series of mass rallies—in Los Angeles, New York, Chicago, and Atlanta—for immigrant rights.

The largest, held in June 2000 in Los Angeles, drew twenty thousand people. Immigrant workers testified about how employers threatened to fire or deport them when they tried to organize. "Looking for a better future for our families is not illegal," said Seattle construction worker José Angel Juarez at the Los Angeles rally. Workers chanted, *"Aquí estamos y no nos vamos!"* (We are here to stay, and we are not leaving!). "Time after time," said AFL-CIO Vice President Linda Chavez-Thompson at the Los Angeles rally, "we see employers try to divide us from our sisters and brothers. They try to pit immigrants against non-immigrants, documented against undocumented, and try to drive down the wages and working conditions of all."[21]

The Immigrant Workers Freedom Rides [IWFR] in 2003 succeeded in mobilizing even larger numbers of people. Using the anti–Jim Crow Freedom Rides of the 1960s as their guide, activists, immigrant workers, and union officials set out on a cross-country trek with stops in all major cities. Their demands included amnesty and civil rights for the 8–11 million undocumented people in the United States, as well as better workplace protections for all workers—including the removal of employer sanctions.[22] They converged on New York City in a mass rally of a hundred thousand people.

With "big labor" supporting the rights of the undocumented workforce, the potential for amnesty grew precipitously by the end of 2003. The potential power of the AFL-CIO, even in a weakened state, can force big business to the negotiating table, especially if it is willing to use strikes to back up its demands. But by 2005, the AFL-CIO and its affiliates have largely abandoned their efforts to push for an amnesty. Fraught with internal dissension and stultified in the face of a generalized attack on its traditional sectors, the AFL-CIO has largely muted itself amid the rise of the anti-immigrant Right. Instead, many unions have opted to support the Kennedy-McCain Bill "with no discussion in union locals and among rank-and-file members over its impact on labor and immigrants."[23] This, in effect, lines the labor movement up with the Bush administration, and represents a huge step backward. A split within the AFL-CIO, producing the breakaway "Change to Win" coalition, has at least raised the question of organizing over lobbying, but any substantial break with "business unionism" or the emergence of real support for immigrant workers remains to be seen.

Since 2003 there has been no visible nationwide activity in the name of the

IWFR or its sponsors. But there have been many local struggles around the issues raised, such as fighting attempts to take away driver's licenses from immigrants without Social Security numbers. And since the Rides several unions, including especially those in what has become the Change to Win (CtW) group, but not only those, have been busy organizing new immigrant workers. They've also used the courts to secure millions in back pay for immigrant janitors cheated out of overtime and minimum wage by contractors working for national supermarket and other retail chains, and to stop the practice of locking them in the stores overnight.[24]

While these small battles are important, the big unions have yet to mobilize their members in the field of struggle, especially through workplace actions. And they are at odds about key questions that affect immigrant workers. For example, the AFL-CIO has rightfully come out against a guest-worker program. According to David Bacon,

> To Linda Chavez-Thompson, executive vice-president of the AFL-CIO, guest worker programs are like the old south's Jim Crow strictures. "There is absolutely no good reason," she says, "why any immigrant who comes to this country prepared to work, to pay taxes, and to abide by our laws and rules should be relegated to a repressive, second-class guest worker status."[25]

On the other hand, the Change to Win coalition, which includes unions with a high percentage of immigrant workers, has come out in support of a new guest-worker program.[26] The Service Employees International Union, a member of the coalition that has been focusing on organizing immigrant workers, supports the program, on the basis that it is the only acceptable option and that "realistic compromises" can be won.

Despite these contradictions, immigrants continue to fight for their rights at the point of production, filling the ranks of the union movement even during its overall decline. According to a study of the Migrant Policy Institute, 11 percent of the 17.7 million foreign-born workers in the U.S. are represented by unions, despite difficulties associated with citizenship. Reflecting changing attitudes in the unions and militancy among the workers themselves, the number of immigrants in unions has grown by 23 percent between 1996 and 2003.[27] The Service Employees Industrial Union (SEIU), with members primarily in the service and health care industries, as well as the public sector, has become the largest and fastest-growing labor union in the United States, claiming a membership of 1.8 million. Immigrant workers account for some two-thirds of that figure.[28] This reflects a willingness to fight back among many undocumented workers, even if the unions are lagging behind.

It also reflects a recognition among many immigrants that unions are their only means of advancement. According to a report by the American Federation of Teachers:

> In 2005, according to the BLS [Bureau of Labor Statistics], union members had median weekly earnings of $801, compared to $622 for nonunion workers, a 29 percent difference. A separate report released by the Center for American Progress shows the union advantage is even greater for Hispanic workers. The median weekly wage for Hispanic union members was $679 versus $428 for nonunion workers, a 59 percent advantage. Mexican-American women union members earn 70 percent more than their nonunion counterparts.[29]

According to Kate Bronfenbrenner of Cornell University, "Recent immigrants overall are more receptive to unions than native-born Americans, particularly those who had union experience in their own country" (apart from those countries where unions were controlled by repressive governments).[30] This receptivity is notable, given that these same workers face repression in the United States when they attempt to organize. In more than half of the organizing campaigns that involve undocumented workers, Bronfenbrenner found, employers use the threat of deportation to try and defeat the campaign.[31] According to Lance Compa, a former official of the NAFTA Labor Secretariat:

> Two things are true. One, many immigrants are afraid to organize because of fear of deportation, thus retarding union organizing in many workplaces and communities, and two, many immigrants are the most active, fearless organizers, bringing new unions to many workplaces and communities.[32]

Immigrant workers have been instrumental in union drives and strikes in service industries across the country in recent decades, and despite the harrowing climate in which they live and work, they will continue to be central to the future of the labor movement. As one undocumented worker concluded "The economy of this country would not be the same without us.... It's time *they* listened to *us*."[33]

A New Civil Rights Movement

T he challenges facing immigrant workers are challenges facing the working class as a whole. Neoliberalism, the war on unions, increased militarization of the border, and the intensification of racism in the form of restrictive and punitive immigration proposals serve to weaken the abilities of all workers to unite.

Immigrant workers have played a key role in advancing the labor movement historically, from the battle for the eight-hour day to the fight for industrial unionism within the CIO to the grassroots organizing of the United Farm Workers. In the modern era, they continue to fight. Through the 1990s, they led key strikes in the construction, hotel, and health care industries, and janitors led one of the most significant nationwide strikes of the last decade. At a time when the traditional strongholds of labor—such as airline workers and autoworkers—are in retreat, it is the least-paid and most vilified workers who are keeping the labor movement alive.

Despite victories among immigrant workers, though, capital has once again gained the upper hand. The "War on Terror," the bipartisan project to expand U.S. corporate power around the globe, is being used to beat back the working class. And new legislative proposals will intensify the state of siege immigrants live under. The current immigration debates—narrowly confined within the boardrooms of corporate America and the halls of Congress—consciously exclude the option of amnesty for undocumented immigrants.

The last time amnesty was granted to undocumented immigrants was in 1986, under the Immigration Reform and Control Act (IRCA). This led to legalization and citizenship for about 2.8 million immigrant workers, and was the product of struggle on a number of fronts. The first was within the labor movement, where the United Farm Workers led other unions in a fight against the Bracero Program, eventually winning an end to the use of guest workers in agriculture. In addition, unions like the International Ladies Garment Workers Union (ILGWU—which merged with another garment workers' union to form UNITE in 1995) had begun to organize undocumented workers starting in the early eighties, which helped to shift opinions within the movement as a whole in favor of organizing this group of workers. Demanding amnesty for the undocumented flowed logically from unionization drives by ILG-WU and others, since workplace raids by immigration authorities were devastatingly effective in getting rid of union sympathizers. However, the AFL-CIO at that time officially supported immigration restrictions, so there was a limit to how much pressure those unions who favored amnesty could marshall from the rest of the labor movement.

Second, social justice, Latino, and church organizations had played a significant role in advocating for migrant workers in the early eighties. They built a national "sanctuary movement," for instance, that aided and sheltered undocumented refugees from Central America during the civil wars there. This facilitated the rise of border-based human rights networks that advocated for migrant border crossers. A host of other organizations framed a national civil rights structure. As longtime immigrant-rights activist Bert Corona explained,

> We helped create a coalition … including groups such as the American Civil Liberties Union, various public welfare groups, the National Lawyers Guild, the American Immigrant Lawyers Association, the U.S. Catholic Conference, the National Coalition for Fair Immigration Laws and Practices, the National Council of Churches, and the National Conference of Catholic Bishops … as well as MAPA, LULAC and the National Council of La Raza.[1]

This alliance came together against a coalition that included Democrats and Republicans, big business, and an array of right-wing organizations seeking to combine criminalization of the undocumented with a revival of the Bracero Program.

In 1982, Democratic Congressman Romano Mazzoli joined with Republican Senator Alan Simpson to propose the Mazzoli-Simpson Bill.

This bill, which after several modifications became IRCA, introduced amnesty for undocumented workers in exchange for the introduction of sanctions against employers who hired undocumented workers, the reintroduction of a limited bracero-type program in agriculture, and increased militarization of the border.[2]

Because the labor movement and many liberal Latino organizations accepted the Right's premise of "securing borders" and "controlling immigration," the compromise set the stage for a further crackdown on migrant crossers. This shifted the focus of enforcement to the border and set the stage for Clinton's Operation Gatekeeper. But limited amnesty also set the stage for new organizing drives that built unions like SEIU, UNITE-HERE, and others. While many unions had been pushed onto the defensive during Ronald Reagan's reign in the 1980s, immigrant worker-led union drives revealed a great willingness to fight among the rank and file. This eventually led the AFL-CIO to support organizing drives among immigrants, including the undocumented, and it produced a growing demand among workers themselves for a new amnesty program.

This is the demand now emanating from the streets that is sending chills through corporate America. But this time around, the new movement must resist any compromising logic that legitimizes criminalization of the undocumented, or border militarization. And the movement has to reject the logic of border enforcement. Borders serve only to divide people and reinforce the power of capital over all workers.

Amnesty—in the form of immediate legalization and a real path to citizenship for the undocumented workforce—represents a threat to capital, since it would give immigrant workers leverage to form unions and use their collective power without fear of retribution. It would also allow for equal status with the rest of the working class, which would cut against the isolation that undocumented immigrants have historically suffered. It is also important to recognize that capitalism needs borders, but workers don't. Borders are designed to criminalize migration, not stop it. Open borders for workers would not only make it impossible to criminalize immigrants, they would also end deaths along the border, dangerous smuggling operations, and the separation of families that all occur solely for the sake of profits. It would equalize work and democratize participation, allowing for the increase in wages and working conditions for all workers.

The fight for unity between workers also raises the question of international solidarity, and the need to unite across borders. At a time when all workers are being squeezed globally, solidarity and unity are necessary for the advance of the working class as a whole. Since corporations have global reach, workers must begin to reject borders as well. Cross-border solidarity, opposition to neoliberalism, and ultimately the demilitarization and dismantling of the border are inextricably linked to the struggle for democracy and human rights for all working people.

In April 2001, a growing continent-wide fight against the Free Trade Area of the Americas (FTAA) brought workers and global justice activists together on both the U.S.-Mexico border and the U.S.-Canada border. In San Diego and Tijuana, twenty-five hundred activists demanded rights for workers, immigrants, and the indigenous, as well as environmental protections, standing together simultaneously on both sides of the border wall. These protests were the first step in internationalizing the struggle against corporate globalization and the walls that divide workers. Labor struggles on both sides of the border, often against multinational corporations based in both countries, have allowed for the creation of labor support networks such as the Coalition for Justice in the Maquiladoras and the Tijuana-San Diego Maquiladora Workers Support Network. Strategic alliances between unions have also developed, such as that between the U.S.-based United Electrical Workers (UE) and the Authentic Workers Front (FAT) in Mexico. These examples form part of the foundation that is growing for the fight against border militarization and for the freedom of movement, full rights, and equality for all workers of the Americas.

The struggles against neoliberalism and border militarization have illuminated the challenges that lie ahead. Nothing short of mass struggle within U.S. society will be required to advance the cause of labor and overcome the historic racial and national divides that influence daily life. Like the last civil rights movement, it will have to come from the grass roots.

The struggle is growing. Most significantly, the immigrant working class itself has entered the stage of history. In March 2006, a new civil rights movement exploded onto city streets across the country. After a protest of twenty thousand pro-immigrant activists converged on Washington, D.C., on March 7, 2006, a wave of protests shook the whole nation. Declaring "we are here and we are not leaving," about three hundred thousand immigrant workers and rights activists then poured into the streets of Chicago three days later. Workers walked off the jobs in droves, in what amounted to a spontaneous strike. As one activist noted, "No immigrant justice march like this has happened in Illinois history since some 80,000 immigrants marched down State Street demanding an eight-hour workday in 1886."[3]

The Chicago protests were followed by a groundswell of marches, with immigrant workers taking over the streets of at least fifty cities. 150,000 marched in Denver, 50,000 in Phoenix, and 30,000 in Milwaukee. This wave culminated in the massive protest of one million people in Los Angeles on March 25, 2006. A massive display of worker's power, solidarity, and the confidence to push back the anti-immigrant movement resonated throughout the day. The protests, organized against the notorious Sensenbrenner Bill, graduated into a new civil rights movement. In a matter of weeks, the movement evolved from a defensive struggle to one that is beginning to advance its own demands and push the working class forward.

It also demonstrated a visceral understanding among immigrant workers about their experience as international workers. As one participant, Plinio Castro, explained, "The treasury of Central America was taken by North Americans. That is why we are poor, why there is unemployment, poverty and hunger." Another marcher, Maria Sanchez, summarized the mood: "With this many people, we should demand legalization and amnesty."[4]

In the next few days, the sentiment spilled over among working-class students across the country. Over fifty thousand high school students poured out of their classes nationwide, organizing marches, taking over streets, and even blocking freeways. In a replay of the Chicano student movement, the walkouts demonstrated a mass awakening among the working class, a flowering of a new era in U.S. history. As student leader Nohelia Ramos Lozano explains about the student walkouts,

> Students are fed up. It's like the 60s in that it's an outlet for students, who have taken it upon themselves to participate in the *movimiento*. Most of those being activated with the walkouts are not able to vote, and so elections are not the ends to all means for millions of undocumented *raza* and youth. That is why the walkouts were so empowering: it showed that our power is in our numbers and the decisions we make, and that students have a role to play in this new civil rights movement.[5]

On May 1, the protests of March and April were overshadowed when over 3 million people went on strike, walked out of schools, boycotted, and marched in several hundred cities across the country. This massive turnout of working-class immigrants happened despite efforts by liberal organizations and union leaders to curtail work stoppages and the boycott. The overwhelming demand of the day was for full equality, amnesty, and no criminalization of the undocumented. An uncontainable desire to build and deepen the movement also ran through every protest. With entire neighborhoods shuttered and factories in many parts of the country closed down, workers' power was on display nationwide.

This power must be directed at fighting for a fundamentally different world. Militarized borders, starvation wages, unemployment, and the criminalization of workers whose only crime is seeking to escape grinding poverty will only be overcome if capitalism is overthrown. Socialism is the only solution to ending the tyranny of those at the top who have always sought to pit workers against one another on the basis of nationality. This is why socialists have a long and proud history of fighting immigration restrictions and the racism that undergirds them. As Kato Tokojiro, a Japanese socialist, said in 1907 while addressing a socialist conference on immigration:

> The Japanese are under the heel of capitalism just as much as are other peoples. It is only dire need that drives them from their homeland to earn their livelihood in a foreign land. It is the duty of socialists to welcome these poor brothers, to defend them, and together with them to fight capitalism. The founders of socialism, above all Karl Marx, did not address themselves to individual countries but to all humanity. Internationalism is inscribed in its banner. [6]

In the same discussion, Dr. Julius Hammer of the U.S. Socialist Labor Party argued, "There is no middle course in this question of immigration and emigration. Either you support restriction of immigration, or energetically combat it. Legal restriction of immigration must be rejected.... We must create a great nation of the exploited."[7]

In the fight for a borderless world, where freedom and democracy as well as equality for all workers trump the prerogatives of corporations and the super-wealthy, there will be many struggles along the way. Whether the struggle is for bilingual education, the right to a driver's license, or for better wages and conditions in the maquiladoras, they are all tied to the singular cause of improving the lives of all workers. In a civil rights movement, everyone has a role to play. This means taking the fight for immigrant rights and for socialism into every struggle, and every workplace, campus, and community. The fight can only conclude when a different, borderless world is constructed, one that puts the interests of human beings over corporations. Along the way, we must reject the language, legitimacy, and limitations of "illegality" and tear down the borders between us. *No one is illegal!*

Chapter Thirty-Three

Mass Mobilization Defeats Sensenbrenner-King (HR 4437)

"Y ou've kicked a sleeping giant." Perhaps no other sign from the million-strong immigrant rights march that shook the streets of Los Angeles on March 25, 2006, captured the mood and the magnitude of the emerging immigrant rights movement like this one did. By May 1, the historic day of recognition for the workers' movement internationally, demonstrations involving over three million people rolled through hundreds of cities across almost every state in the country. Immediately, the nondebate over immigration that had until then been the private domain of a narrow strata of Republicans in Congress was blown wide open, its contents scattering into the daily discussions of ordinary people and into a fight that will shape the future of labor in the United States.

The catalyst for the eruption was the draconian Sensenbrenner-King Bill, which passed the House of Representatives in December 2005 and, if passed by the Senate and signed by the president, would have made undocumented immigrants and those who assist them in any way felons.[1] Instead of driving immigrants deeper into the shadows, it sparked a mass outpouring of opposition and the materialization of millions of immigrant workers who had been previously confined to the social and political margins of national life. In large part, the first demonstrations were a spontaneous expression of anger, drawing out primarily Latino high school students, and workers and their families.

While local labor unionists played a role where they had roots and members in immigrant communities, the actions were not initiated by the labor movement or existing national networks.

The magnitude of the population and the integral role undocumented workers had come to assume within the U.S. economy forced the hand of the bill's Republican architects campaigning for a new era of immigrant persecution. Homemade signs at protests from San Diego to the Brooklyn Bridge reading, "We Are Not Criminals" and "*Amnistía Sí*" (Amnesty Yes!), reveal the depths of indignation, the willingness to come out of the shadows, and the desire to stand up and be seen and heard.

House approval of the reactionary Sensenbrenner bill, the passage of which would have turned twelve million undocumented immigrants and anyone who aided them into felons, gave impetus to the fledgling movement, pushing millions into opposition, flocking to protests called by small groups. Since no national structure existed that appeared capable of giving expression to such an outpouring, few were prepared for the size of the protests. In a flash, the masses had moved into motion, primarily in opposition to the Sensenbrenner bill, but the fight back has also raised the possibility for more far-reaching social change.

Following a series of smaller actions, a mass protest of twenty thousand took place in Washington, DC, on March 7, 2006.[2] This was followed by a monumental outpouring of at least three hundred thousand onto the streets of Chicago on March 10, 2006. The largest protest in Chicago history shut down the city, as workers walked off jobs, out of schools, and into the human streams that jammed several city blocks downtown. Entire families marched together, and the vast majority had clearly never been to a protest in their lives. "Middle-aged working-class men, young mothers pushing baby carriages, teens, retirees—every generation was represented" on the march.[3]

After Chicago, the dam broke. Mass protests of immigrant workers took place in more than fifty cities within two weeks. About 150,000 crowded onto Denver's streets, 50,000 marched through the streets of Phoenix, and over 30,000 took to the streets in Milwaukee. In Atlanta, more than 80,000 heeded a call to not go to work. In Tulsa, Oklahoma, 5,000 came out to oppose anti-immigrant legislation, 15,000 marched across the Brooklyn Bridge in New York, 3,000 took to the streets of Fort Smith, Arkansas, and thousands more clogged the downtowns in a constellation of other cities and towns across the country. The turnout reached new heights in Los Angeles, where over one million people transformed the downtown area into a human sea, with every open space commandeered by the otherwise hidden workforce of the city's vast street-level economy.

The March protests also spread to student actions. Sons and daughters of the Latino working class shut down schools across the country in protest of anti-immigrant racism. In California, tens of thousands of students walked out of classes across the state. In Dallas, four thousand walked out of school, another two thousand in El Paso, three thousand in Las Vegas, and one thousand in Aurora, Illinois. In Tucson, one thousand middle school students walked out of their schools, showing that even many young teens were keenly aware of what was at stake, and were making their voices heard.[4]

Some union organizations also got on board, joining with the National Council of La Raza and other civic and religious organizations calling for a day of protest on April 9 and 10. Half a million *more* came out in Dallas, one hundred thousand in San Diego, and twenty thousand in Salt Lake City on April 9. Protests also sprouted in smaller towns and in rural regions. Three thousand people converged on the small agricultural community of Garden City, Kansas. Thousands more turned out in South Bend, Indiana; Portland, Maine; Harrisburg, Pennsylvania; and Lake Worth, Florida.

On April 10, protests continued in ninety-four cities. Half a million came out in New York City, thirty thousand in Boston, and ten thousand in Madison, Wisconsin; ten thousand protested in Boston and in Omaha. The rolling protest movement culminated in the call for a general strike and economic boycott for May 1 — May Day, the international workers' holiday that commemorates the immigrant struggle for better working conditions in the United States over a century ago, which was effectively wiped from popular memory in the U.S. but celebrated in other countries. In 2006 it reemerged (without authorization) from across the border.

Calling May 1 "El Gran Paro Americano" (The Great American Boycott), organizers of the day of action called on all immigrants to stay away from work and school, close their businesses, refrain from buying and selling, and hold rallies at symbolic economic centers. Organizers explicitly rejected any bill in Congress that increased border enforcement or failed to grant full amnesty. For example, one press release stated:

We will settle for nothing less than full amnesty and dignity for the
millions of undocumented workers presently in the U.S. We believe
that increased enforcement is a step in the wrong direction and will
only serve to facilitate more tragedies along the Mexican-U.S. border in
terms of deaths and family separation.[5]

Millions of people responded to the call. Through word of mouth,
Spanish-language radio, email and text message, fliering, wheat-past-
ing, and other means, news of the boycott resonated in homes, schools,
and workplaces in immigrant communities across the country. Thousands of business shuttered—either in solidarity with the workers or
due to low anticipated turnout for the day's shifts. Whole industries or
sectors of industry were affected, from construction to agriculture to
food processing.

As one news report observed:

> Long Beach, the country's biggest port, 30 miles south of Los Ange-
> les, was reported to be quiet. Districts across the country with large
> Latino populations were said to be quieter than usual, and some large
> employers said they were shutting down for the day. Tyson Foods, the
> world's largest meat producer, closed about a dozen of its more than
> 100 plants.[6]

Furthermore, the protest had international dimensions. The San Di-
ego-Tijuana border, the busiest border crossing in the world, came
to a complete standstill. Mexican activists, including veterans of the
Bracero Program, blocked traffic crossing north, while five thousand
people from the San Diego side marched directly to the port of entry
to stand in solidarity.[7]

The boycott also spread from the point of production to that of
consumption. One poll cited on the Spanish-language news channel
Univision found that 65 percent of Latino participants did not work on
May Day, while 95 percent reported not buying anything on the boycott
day.[8] While the labor stoppages, disruption of commerce, and boycotts
did not amount to a nationwide shutdown, they do represent the largest
organized disruption of the U.S. economy by the working class in modern history. As commentators at the Center for Latin American and
Border Studies at New Mexico State University observed:

> Whatever the numbers, May Day was a spike in a new movement that
> remarkably, in only a couple months, turned the immigration reform
> debate in the US on its head, galvanized a new generation of youth ac-
> tivists, spread across borders, and even pumped new life into corporate

anti-globalization movements that declined in the wake of September 11, 2001. For the first time in decades, the idea of a general strike was popularized in the United States.[9]

Undocumented workers and their families, and legal immigrants and their native-born supporters came out in cities across the country. Although most of the estimated twelve million undocumented workers are from Mexico and Central America, an estimated three million are from countries outside Latin America, including Ireland, Russia, Poland, Canada, Haiti, Korea, India, China, and the Philippines. Hundreds of Irish workers joined marches in Chicago, Korean workers formed contingents in Los Angeles, and Filipino, Chinese, Caribbean, and Arab immigrant workers participated in San Francisco.[10] Solidarity between different ethnic groups has also developed in other ways. For example, the Council of Islamic Organizations of Greater Chicago has lobbied elected officials to support undocumented Latino immigrants. Affiliated mosques solicited donations from their members to help fund organizing efforts.[11]

A 2006 survey of several polls published in the *San Francisco Chronicle* measuring support for legalization in California (the state with the largest undocumented population) revealed that majorities of African Americans and Anglo American voters supported a path to citizenship for undocumented workers. According to Bernard Anderson, an economist and professor at the University of Pennsylvania, a lack of support for anti-immigrant politics amongst African Americans reveals a consciousness of their own historical oppression by the same forces: "The choice is to line up with right-wing reactionary forces under the claim that their action will benefit African Americans. . . . [B]ut those are the same forces that have been hell-bent on opposing civil rights, affirmative action and government programs for the less fortunate."[12] Active support from unions, religious institutions, and legal immigrants— interconnected through familial relationships and cultural organizations—has also contributed to the breadth and depth of the movement.

In a matter of weeks, the immigrant working class and their allies in the United States had made history. The most immediate tangible result of the upsurge was the defeat of the Sensenbrenner bill and a blow against the Far Right, who hitherto had been able to set the tone on the subject of "immigration reform." Shortly after the May Day strike and mass marches, the Senate announced that it would not vote on the bill, effectively killing it. It redrew the boundaries of the debate and broadened its scope. A discourse that had previously focused only on *the extent* to which undocumented immigrant workers would be persecuted *and not legalized* was now counterposed by the demand for amnesty, legalization, and access to citizenship *without punishment.*

These two polarized positions established the parameters in which the debate continued, but only shortly, as state repression against immigrant workers was unleashed in full force by the Bush administration, transforming the political landscape. On May 13, 2006, the Bush administration ordered the deployment of six thousand National Guard troops to the border to assist in immigration enforcement. In reality, the deployment did little to prevent crossings; rather, it signified the opening shots of a state-led massive crackdown on immigrant workers and the repression of immigrant-led labor mobilization.

Chapter Thirty-Four

State Repression
of Immigrant Workers

The immigrant workers' movement of 2006 to 2008 helped throw the Republican Party, already suffering from corruption scandals, an unpopular war in Iraq, and association with a faltering economy, into further disarray. Nevertheless, the right wing of the GOP continued to chart the course on immigration both within the party and on the national stage, seeking to unite and energize the party base around the issue of immigrant bashing. Enthusiastic bipartisan support for the putative "War on Terror" allowed the Right the operational space to ramp up national security rhetoric and turn it inward—coupling aggressive U.S. military interventions abroad with domestic immigration enforcement. The Democratic Party's complicity regarding the application of national security doctrine to unauthorized migration opened the gates for the further criminalization of migration and the militarization of enforcement.

The most intensive phase of state militarization of immigration policy began in the immediate aftermath of the attacks of 9/11. Within months, the Bush administration (with broad support from Democrats in the 107th Congress) created the Department of Homeland Security, a sweeping effort to bring twenty-two national agencies involved in domestic security enforcement into one centralized command with a common mission.[1] In its founding statement, the department identifies unauthorized immigration as one the "potential threats—both past and future—facing the nation" and pledges to "strengthen border security and interior enforcement and reform immigration processes."[2]

Immigration, a predominantly economic issue that is more appropriately adjudicated through government agencies overseeing trade or labor policy, has become the primary operation within repressive apparatus of the DHS, with an annual budget surpassing $64 billion in 2016.[3] As a result, the agency charged with overseeing the largest population of immigrants in the world has been retooled with a new mission. Instead of an emphasis on immigrant incorporation, the focus has become systematic expulsion. Through the DHS, immigration enforcement has become grounded in military doctrine, armed with an expansive body of shock troops and a sprawling complex of detention centers. The shift has been aided by the passage of laws that have dismantled constitutional rights previously afforded noncitizens on U.S. soil.

Since 9/11, the Bush and Obama administrations and their congressional allies have engineered the further deprivation of rights for immigrants. These include authorizing broad rules that permit immigration agents to conduct immigrant sweeps, dragnets, and raids without the need for a warrant; the denial of the right to a lawyer for detained immigrants facing deportation; and limited appeals and bail rights for immigrants languishing in detention.[4]

While entrusted to contain "domestic terrorism," the DHS has directed its energies toward undocumented workers. "Our interior enforcement efforts have focused on identifying, arresting and removing fugitives, criminals and illegal alien gang members in our country," Michael Chertoff said at a March 2008 congressional hearing on DHS oversight.[5] Since 2002, the federal government's efforts at immigration enforcement have been framed as a national security objective—aggressive efforts designed to prevent another 9/11 or worse. When the hunt for "domestic terrorists" yielded paltry results, enforcement efforts shifted to rooting out "criminal elements." This opened the door for the general persecution of undocumented workers, especially in the wake of the massive immigrant rights marches of May 1, 2006.

In 2006, the agency raised arrest quotas and eliminated a clause stating that three-quarters of those apprehended had to be criminals, allowing for nonfugitive "ordinary status violators" to be factored into their count. By 2007, immigrants with criminal records or deportation orders dropped to 9 percent of the total of those arrested and deported. Meanwhile, the number of nonfugitives increased to 40 percent.[6]

A subsequent report from the Migration Policy Institute has documented that despite expenditures of over $625 million over five years, 75 percent of the ninety-six thousand people apprehended under the National Fugitives Operation Program had committed no crime whatsoever other than being "out of status."[7]

Considering that more than 349,000 people were deported through various DHS efforts in 2008 alone, the corruption of enforcement policy has undoubtedly wrecked untold lives and separated thousands of families under false pretenses. For instance, Homeland Security inspector general Richard Skinner recently revealed that of the 2.2 million people deported from the U.S. between 1998 and 2007, more than 108,000 had U.S.-born citizen children.[8]

Despite the fact that researchers have concluded that as a group "undocumented workers are statistically less likely than native-born Americans to commit crimes," undocumented workers have received all the focus.[9] A May 2007 study released by Syracuse University concluded that "out of more than 800,000 cases filed in federal courts by the Department of Homeland Security (DHS) since 2004, only twelve were related to terrorism. Another 112 cases were filed using national security charges." All told, about 87 percent of those charged were undocumented workers and students. The report concluded,

> Despite the repeated statement by the DHS that stopping terrorism and preventing serious crime are its core missions, the record shows that since the DHS was established in the wake of 9/11/2001, most of the agency's actual work recorded in the Immigration Courts has focused on traditional immigration matters.[10]

The number of charges associated with "national security" and "terrorism" have actually dropped since the creation of the DHS. For fiscal years 1994 to 1996, national security charges made up 0.031 percent of all immigration charges. For fiscal years 2004 to 2006, such cases represented 0.014 percent. Regarding terrorism charges, the percentage of cases filed represented 0.009 percent during fiscal years 1994 to 1996. A decade later, that percentage also dropped, to 0.0015 percent.[11] Forged in the smoldering embers of the War on Terror against an illusory internal threat, the juggernaut of immigration enforcement was unleashed in full force against undocumented workers.

Despite the failure to identify and capture terrorists, immigration enforcement became an end itself in the eyes of the Bush administration.

By 2003, for example, the scope of "antiterror" enforcement was broadened to include the capture of the estimated six hundred thousand immigrant "fugitives"—that is, any undocumented immigrant with a criminal record or simply an outstanding deportation order.

Through paramilitary initiatives such as the National Fugitives Operation Program and Operation Return to Sender, money was pumped into the agency to set up more than a hundred "fugitive recovery teams" to carry out targeted roundups. Agents raided homes, apartment complexes, and neighborhoods across the U.S. But according to internal agency memos obtained through the Freedom of Information Act and subsequently published in the *New York Times*, ICE "changed the rules and the program increasingly went after easier targets. A vast majority of those arrested had no criminal record, and many had no deportation orders against them, either."[12]

As ICE declared open season on immigrants, arrest quotas to pad numbers and create the impression of success have become commonplace within other immigration enforcement agencies as well. A former Border Patrol officer in California revealed that constant demands to meet monthly arrest quotas led agents to cruise streets, bus stops, and even medical clinics looking for suspected undocumented immigrants.

According to an interview published in the *Los Angeles Times*, former agent Tony Plattel was fired for driving what he said were six dehydrated immigrants back to headquarters, despite orders to wait until his van was full. "We had to make eight apprehensions a day, and if we didn't meet that goal, we were pressured to get more the next day," he said. "I interfered with the quota, that's why I was fired." These "head counts" demanded from the top of the agency have demoralized some agents like Plattel, but most continue to racially profile and persecute undocumented workers with impunity.[13]

Targeted at the Workplace

Repression has proven an effective means of reducing the wages and social power of immigrant workers. According to the research of immigration experts Douglas Massey, Jorge Durand, and Nolan Malone, the wages of undocumented workers tended to be on par with native-born workers in similar industries prior to the onset of the first criminalization policies in the 1980s: "Research shows that there was little wage discrimination on the basis of legal status prior to 1986: documented and undocumented workers earned the same hourly wage once relevant background characteristics (such as education and experience) were controlled."[14] Wage differentials increased precipitously after 1986 with the implementation of the repressive aspects of IRCA (Immigration Reform and Control Act). This bill introduced amnesty for undocumented workers in exchange for the introduction of employer sanctions, the reintroduction of a limited guest-worker plan in agriculture, and the increased militarization of the border. In other words, the bill traded limited amnesty for the expansion of criminalization.[15]

From the employer's standpoint, the punitive aspects of IRCA were revealed to be a blessing and the amnesty a curse, factors that have since shaped contemporary debates over immigration reform. History shows that wages rose after the 1986 amnesty. Within five years, real wages of formerly undocumented workers increased by an average of 15 percent, according to the U.S. Department of Labor. Wages for many of these jobs had been declining prior to legalization. Wages also rose for native-born workers or legal immigrants who worked in similar jobs. A University of California Los Angeles study in 2001 estimated that if undocumented workers were legalized, wages for all workers would rise by about 5 percent in agriculture, 2.75 percent in services, and 2.5 percent in manufacturing.[16] Another UCLA study in 2011 found that legalization "would yield at least $1.5 trillion in added U.S. gross domestic product over 10 years" as wages increased, consumption increased, and more tax revenue was generated.[17] In the aftermath of the amnesty, criminalization was intensified against those undocumented workers that came after.

As a result of employer sanctions and other forms of repression increased after 1986, wages for undocumented workers (who did not qualify for the amnesty or those who came after) trended downward. Declining wages for these workers also pulled down wages for the recently documented migrants still working in the same industries. According to Massey, Durand, and Malone, by 1992 the average wages for all immigrant workers plummeted 13 percent overall as a result.[18] Nevertheless, enforcement tapered off, allowing the new arrangement to stabilize. From 1993 to 2003, the number of arrests at work sites nationwide dropped from 7,630 to 445, while the number of employer fines dropped from 944 to 124 over the same period.[19]

In this context enforcement efforts were greatly increased after 9/11 and especially after immigrant workers began to march for a new amnesty.

Migrant workers were subjected to an extensive campaign of repression in the wake of the May 1, 2006, mass immigrant rights protests. A seemingly arbitrary campaign of raids was conducted across the country in workplaces and communities populated with immigrant workers. Paramilitary in nature, with names like Operation Return to Sender, these, combined with the National Fugitive Operations Program, resulted in the deportation of more than two hundred thousand people by 2007.[20]

Since they began in 2003, these sweeps, allegedly to round up "criminal aliens" and those immigrants who have received deportation orders, have mostly netted laborers using false working papers and those who have committed no crime but were apprehended in the course of the raids and sweeps.[21]

By 2009, for instance, a Migration Policy Institute study found that from 2003 to 2008, 73 percent of those arrested in "fugitive recovery operations" had no criminal record or pending charges.[22] To date, ICE has reportedly removed 350,000 people through fugitive removal operations comprised of twenty-four Enforcement and Removal Operations field offices and 129 fugitive operations teams "that prioritize enforcement efforts toward aliens who present a heightened threat to national security and public safety, such as transnational gang members, child sex offenders, and aliens with prior convictions for violent crimes."[23] According to its own statistics, these more focused operations netted 59 percent "criminals" compared to 41 percent "non-criminal immigration violators" in 2015.[24] Nevertheless, of the 59 percent designated as "criminals," about 24 percent include those who only have an existing deportation order (without a criminal charge), those apprehended for "unlawful entry," and those charged with misdemeanors.[25] The remaining 35 percent are reflective of a shift in recovery tactics. According to Syracuse Trac Immigration,

> Most of these . . . apprehensions happened when ICE assumed custody of individuals held by another law enforcement agency. Many of these apprehensions occurred when ICE took individuals into custody from the prison or jail facility where they had been serving time for their criminal conviction.[26]

Rather than fulfill their stated purpose, targeted raids, systematic detention, and the institutionalized practice of selective and ongoing deportation are designed to instill fear in the immigrant community according to the "enforcement through attrition" strategy. The theory behind this doctrine is that undocumented people will be encouraged to "self-deport" if their lives are made sufficiently miserable through restrictive measures, selective punishments, and the constant fear of capture and detention. In practice, this program has become acceptable to most of the capitalist class because *migrants aren't self-deporting*; instead, raids and selective deportations are serving to hold the immigrant workers' movement in submission. The practice therefore fits the definition of state terrorism.[27]

Since 2005, increased workplace raids and deportations have ensnared an ever-growing number of workers. The pattern of the raids has seemed random, and tactics have varied. In July 2005, for instance, ICE arrested forty-nine workers at North Carolina's Seymour Johnson Air Force Base after luring them with a flier to what was advertised as a mandatory Occupational Safety and Health Administration meeting.[28] In April 2006, amidst the mass immigrant rights marches, authorities rounded up more than twelve hundred workers at IFCO Systems, a leading manufacturer of pallets, crates, and containers, at forty plants across the country.[29]

A similar raid was carried out a few months later in Stillmore, Georgia, which was reduced to a ghost town after ICE agents raided trailer parks and arrested 120 undocumented workers employed at the local poultry-processing plant.[30]

Swift & Company, the world's second-largest processor of fresh beef and pork, became the site of another workplace raid in December 2006, when thirteen hundred workers across Texas, Colorado, Nebraska, Minnesota, Iowa, and Utah were detained.[31] This was followed by a raid at the Smithfield pork slaughtering plant in Tar Heel, North Carolina, in January 2007, leading to the arrest of twenty-one workers. Smithfield, a large five-thousand-worker plant whose workers participated in the immigrant rights marches of 2006 and were on the verge of establishing union representation through the United Food and Commercial Workers Union.[32]

In April 2007, over 150 people were detained in a raid that was conducted in paramilitary fashion in the Latino business district of Chicago known as the "Little Village."[33] In Newport, Rhode Island, ICE agents raided restaurants, stores, and apartments in June 2008 during an orchestrated sweep and in some cases "appeared to be targeting people because they appeared foreign and were driving landscaping trucks."[34]

Another round of raids took place at meat-processing and manufacturing plants between 2007 and 2008. One hundred and sixty workers were arrested at Koch Foods chicken plant in Fairfield, Ohio; 390 workers were arrested at Agriprocessors in Postville, Ohio; and 400 were arrested at Pilgrim's Pride factories across the Midwest.[35] Fifty-seven workers at Mills Manufacturing (a third of its workforce) were rounded up after a raid at a parachute factory in Woodfin, North Carolina.[36]

In another large-scale raid, 595 of the 800 workers who showed up for work on August 25 at the Howard Industries electronics plant in Laurel, Mississippi, never made it home.[37] The rest of the detainees, mostly female workers with children left stranded at home and at school, were released only after having their ankles affixed with monitoring devices to ensure that they remained prisoners in their own homes pending eventual deportation hearings. Other raids nationwide raids have netted 63 taco-shop workers in San Francisco, 18 bakery workers in San Diego, 138 workers at a printer cartridge recycler in Los Angeles, 30 doughnut factory workers in Houston, 361 workers at a clothing manufacturer near Boston, 24 day laborers in Baltimore, 42 construction workers in Virginia, and many more detained in raids across the country.[38]

In 2007, the agency charged 863 people with criminal violations, such as identity theft, and 4,077 workers for allegedly being in the country illegally, while in 2002, ICE made only 25 criminal and 485 immigration-related arrests as a result of workplace raids. This represents an 800 percent increase.[39] Overall, raids targeting workers in 2007 were ten times what they were in 2002. By the summer of 2008, 3,077 workers had been detained in raids since the beginning of the year, with 1,755 arrested in the month of May alone.[40] At year's end, workplace raids had reached an all-time high with 6,287 arrests.[41]

While workplace raids decreased after the inauguration of Barack Obama, the incoming administration increased "workplace audits" as an alternative. These involve DHS investigating companies to identify and dismiss undocumented workers and to levy hefty fines against the employers who hire them. The threat of such an audit led the clothing manufacturer American Apparel to mass fire 1,500 workers in September 2009.[42] The administration also ramped up the use of the E-Verify system, a federal database used by employers to cross-check the status of would-be employees. Furthermore, the Obama administration continued the trend of increasing funding for border enforcement and militarization.

By 2009, there were 19,354 Border Patrol agents nationwide, an increase of 57 percent since the expansion of the border wall in September 2006. About 88 percent (17,011) were located in the nine Border Patrol sectors along the Southwest border. Another 4 percent were assigned to thirty-two permanent immigration checkpoints that flank the region, functioning like a second border.[43] The walling of the border has been further augmented by the increase in internal enforcement, although there is less vigorous enforcement along the country's northern boundary with Canada.

It is worth noting that the remaining 8 percent of the border patrol is assigned to the 5,525-mile U.S.-Canadian border. The 92 percent to 8 percent Mexico-Canada enforcement ratio established in 2009 reveals a stark contrast in the way the United States treats the two borders. According to Wayne Cornelius, director of the Center for Comparative Immigration Studies at the University of California, "Between the U.S. and Canada, there is almost no wall at all, nor any border line. . . . U.S. residents can go to Canada and return without any problem. Only at the border entries are there some clear border lines."[44]

The Mexico border strategy concentrated border agents and resources in populated areas, intentionally forcing undocumented immigrants to extreme environments and natural barriers that the government anticipated would increase the likelihood of injury and death. The stated goal was to deter migrants from crossing. But the deterrence strategy did not work. Migrants have died crossing the border every day, year after year. The Border Patrol has confirmed nearly seven thousand deaths between 1998 and 2016, while human rights groups estimate the number to be much higher based on missing persons reports and the tendency for remains to deteriorate rapidly or be dispersed by animals in the desert regions.[45] Meanwhile, enforcement through collaboration with local police departments was also expanded.

By 2009, over seventy local law enforcement agencies were participating in the DHS's 287(g) program. This arrangement, which was written into the Illegal Immigration Reform and Immigrant Responsibility Act of 1996 during the Clinton administration, began under the Bush administration and has been expanded by the Obama administration. It allows for individual police and sheriff departments to engage in local immigration enforcement as part of their other policing duties if they choose to affiliate.[46] As a result of this policy, immigration officials held a record 378,582 individuals in detention (61 percent of whom were Mexican nationals) by 2008.[47] They were detained in a vast complex of listed and secretive jails, holding centers, and field offices.[48]

The illegalization of movement for most Mexicans across the border has been augmented by the internal expansion of enforcement, which creates multiple "borders" throughout the interior. These include fixed immigration checkpoints, workplace raids and audits, "fugitive recovery teams," local sweeps involving local law enforcement (such as the 287[g] Program), and national citizenship databases—with the move away from the border shifting jurisdiction to ICE. The DHS has rapidly expanded its detention system and incarceration rate as a result. According to the website Detention Watch, the average daily population of detainees has skyrocketed from five thousand in 1994 to thirty thousand in 2009.[49] This vast webbing of immigration enforcement has developed in lieu of substantive change in immigration policy.

The enforcement focus on the U.S.-Mexico border and on unauthorized Mexican and other Latino immigrants is reflected in the growth of immigrant incarceration. Nonviolent, undocumented Latino immigrants are the fastest-growing segment of the prison population. By 2007, for instance, Latinos made up 40 percent of the estimated two hundred thousand prisoners in federal penitentiaries, which is triple their share of the total U.S. adult population and disproportionate to their representation in state and local jails (19 percent and 16 percent, respectively). Nearly half of the Latino population in federal prisons is immigrant, with 81 percent sentenced for entering or residing in the nation without authorization.[50]

Overall, accounting for all forms of raids in fiscal year 2008, ICE says it deported 349,041 undocumented immigrants. That's a nearly 20 percent increase over the 288,663 deported in 2007 and 100 percent more than 2004's 174,000 deportations.[51] It is also estimated that by 2008 about 280,000 people were being held on immigration violations at fifteen federal detention centers and more than four hundred state and local contract facilities nationwide.[52]

The federal government's campaign against undocumented workers has not been aimed at deporting all undocumented immigrants; after all, more workers continue to enter the United States annually (five hundred thousand) than have been deported.[53] In addition to appeasing the Far Right, the raids dovetail with what has become a bipartisan convergence to transform future migrants from "undocumented" (with limited freedom of movement, limited membership in unions, and limited permanent residence) into a class of noncitizen workers whose presence is regulated directly by the government (with no freedom of movement, no right to join unions, and no permanent residence). While this trajectory of immigration "reform" has been halted by the election of Trump, the latest round of repression serves the same purpose: to create a class of powerless and subservient laborers and to leverage the precarious status of undocumented workers in order to drive down wages and conditions for all workers. The multifaceted repression of immigration workers by federal agencies has further trickled down to state governments.

In 2007, more than 1,500 anti-immigrant laws were introduced in state legislatures across the country. In the first two months of 2008 alone, 350 immigration-related measures were announced.[54] The Oklahoma legislature passed the Oklahoma Taxpayer and Citizen Protection Act of 2007, which barred undocumented workers from obtaining jobs or state assistance and made it a felony to harbor or transport undocumented immigrants. The law's passage provoked a wave of terror across the Latino community. The ensuing crackdown caused thousands to flee to neighboring states, with as many as twenty-five thousand Latinos leaving northeastern Oklahoma, according to the Greater Tulsa Hispanic Chamber of Commerce. The law's fallout has also been felt in the economy, affecting local businesses and creating worker shortages and widespread fear among immigrants who say they are afraid to drive to church or the market because of racial profiling.[55]

By 2007, thirty small towns and midsize cities around the country had passed anti-immigrant ordinances at the local level that included banning rental housing, prohibiting business licenses for companies that hire undocumented workers, closing day labor pick-up sites, making English the "official language" of local government, and a host of other restrictive and punitive measures. In most cases, the efforts are not "homegrown" movements. Rather, they were often led by elected officials with right-wing leanings inspired by the success of the anti-immigrant movement elsewhere, and attempting to execute their own personal anti-immigrant crusade or seize upon the issue as a means to revive a flagging political career.[56]

The Immigrant Rights Movement at the Polls

As the negotiations over immigration reform reached an impasse in Congress after the defeat of HR 4437, national attention shifted to the election campaign of 2008. While the protest movement for legalization had decreased in size since 2006, it had broadened in scope. Ongoing efforts at the grassroots level have taken various forms, from the formation of support committees for detained workers, the picketing of ICE offices and detention centers, active support and solidarity for workplace struggles, voter registration drives, and community forums. Whether participating in the spectacular marches or union drives on the one hand, or being impacted by the fear, trepidation, and discrimination fueled by raids, vigilantes, checkpoints, and discrimination on the other, the collective experience deeply politicized Latino and immigrant voters and drove them to the polls. The Republican Party and its auxiliaries jockeyed to make immigration enforcement the centerpiece of their electioneering and the litmus test for both parties. The debate manifested itself through the 2006–2008 election cycle, providing a proving ground for each side to register its strength on the issue.

The immigrant workers' movement has politicized a whole generation, demoralized the Right, energized the Latino electorate, and shifted the political center of gravity leftward. The general public's distaste for the Far Right's anti-immigrant agenda has also came to the surface. From 2006 to 2008 opinion polls stayed largely consistent on the question of immigration, with a two-thirds majority of those polled consistently supporting legalization.[1] In California, the state with the largest population of undocumented immigrants in the nation, a Field Poll conducted in 2006 showed that 80 percent supported a path to citizenship.[2]

From the mid-term elections of 2006 to the presidential campaign of 2008, the Republican Party took a beating. Despite their success in saturating public discourse with anti-immigrant rhetoric, their efforts yielded little traction and failed to unify or mobilize their base in the way their opponents did. The focus on immigrants in the 2006 elections failed to marshal the xenophobic vote in substantial numbers. Not only did the Congressional Immigration Reform Caucus not grow, but ten of the most zealous congressional members *lost* their seats and Democrats gained control of both houses of Congress.[3] Diminishing support for the Right was revealed in the 2008 Republican presidential primaries and the increased isolation of racist vigilante groups.

In the Republican presidential primaries, Arkansas governor Mike Huckabee, an early front-runner, touted his "Secure America Plan," vowing to forcefully eject twelve million undocumented people and their families within 120 days. Massachusetts governor Mitt Romney and New York City mayor Rudy Giuliani joined the anti-immigrant frenzy, attacking each other's purported tolerance for migrant workers in their respective states and promising a heavy hand if elected. San Diego representative Duncan Hunter vowed to build two walls across the span of the U.S.-Mexico frontier. Others, including Texas congressman Ron Paul and Tennessee senator Fred Thompson, also joined the chorus and railed against migrant workers in line with the Republican script.

Rather than being the political holy grail, immigrant bashing provided no refuge for flagging Republican campaigns. Colorado congressman Tom Tancredo, the trumpeting figurehead of the anti-immigrant movement, ran such a feeble campaign that it sputtered out after he failed to muster more than 1 percent of the vote. Despite his routing, he relished the tenor of the primaries, blithely declaring that the campaign "has been wonderful because all I've heard is people trying to out-Tancredo Tancredo."[4] In short order, Republican voters proceeded to clear the field until only John McCain (considered a turncoat by the Far Right for his alleged moderation on the issue) was left standing. As it turned out, even 6 in 10 Republican voters disagreed with the far-right strategy.[5]

Another expression of a setback has been the isolation of the Minuteman Project and their cohorts. While the months following their highly publicized border spectacles led to a rapid growth of the movement, a counterprotest movement challenged violent tactics and racially motivated street actions that were largely unexamined in the media, and exposed the links that many of the Minuteman Project's members had to white supremacist organizations. While it received little attention from the media, the anti-vigilante protest movement forced the Minutemen on the defensive, compelling the all-white organization to seek Black and Latino allies and appealing more directly to white working-class voters to respond to the challenge they now faced.[6] The major test for white working-class support took place on January 19, 2006, when at the height of the Minuteman Project's growth they called for a protest in nineteen states to consolidate a national movement and offensive. As the Associated Press reported at the time, "only a smattering" turned out, exposing the limited support for their ideology and a dearth of followers outside of their own ranks.

When the Minutemen attempted to repackage themselves with a multiracial face, especially after the preventable catastrophe of Hurricane Katrina displaced thousands of low-income African Americans, few rallied to the cause.[7] The failure of the group to make inroads in working-class communities led to a series of internal squabbles, splits, and political divisions. In San Diego, where one of the largest Minutemen organizations could mobilize hundreds of supporters for actions in 2006, the group was in a state of disarray by late 2008. "We've lost the battle. . . . My intuition tells me . . . this entire movement will fizzle to nothing by the end of the year," said Minuteman Project founder Jim Gilchrist in May 2008, lamenting the national decline of the organization.[8] Despite the organization's setbacks, the Minutemen's efforts seeded the soil for other groups to take action.

From 2000 to 2007, the number of hate groups grew 48 percent (to over 880) in the United States while Klan chapters grew by 63 percent, directly attributable to the mainstreaming of immigrant bashing.[9] Between 2006 and 2008, over three hundred anti-immigrant hate groups sprouted across the country, inspired by the Minutemen's campaign to take armed action against migrant peoples.[10]

Even Gilchrist, the champion of the vigilante movement, was shocked by the violent elements he helped inspire and unleash. "There's all kinds of organizations that have spawned from the Minuteman Project and I have to say, some of the people who have gotten into this movement have sinister intentions," he concluded.[11] The Right fragmented and became polarized as the political climate shifted leftward in the lead-up to the 2008 presidential elections.

From 1970 to 2006 the Latino population in the U.S. grew from 9.6 million to 44.3 million. The majority are citizens, 9 million of whom are registered voters. In California, they had become one-third of all Democratic voters. In Texas, they comprised 25 percent of the electorate. Prior to the 2006 elections, polls showed that 76 percent of Latino voters believed that a growing anti-Latino climate should be blamed on Republican anti-immigrant policies. This translated into a shift toward Democratic candidates in the 2006 to 2008 election cycles. In the presidential primaries, Latino turnout for Democratic candidates was 300 percent higher than it was in 2004, and 78 percent of all Latinos who voted in the primaries have voted Democratic (compared to 40 percent who voted for Bush in 2004), leading to a massive Latino turnout for Democratic candidates in November of 2006 and 2008.[12]

The heated immigration debate that saw millions march in the streets also led millions to vote against the Right in the polls. "It was the immigration issue that drove the process," said Sergio Bendixen, a Miami-based pollster whose company exit-polled Latinos across the country in 2008, as a historic turnout of Latino and immigrant voters helped secure Barack Obama the presidency and the Democratic Party the biggest victory in a generation.[13] During the 2008 election campaign, the Obama team understood and adapted to the prevailing electoral winds, adopting the traditional Latino slogan of worker empowerment "Sí Se Puede" (We Can Do It) as a campaign slogan and criticizing the repression of immigrants. During one pivotal speech in front of a Latino caucus, Obama declared, "The system isn't working . . . when communities are terrorized by ICE immigration raids, when nursing mothers are torn from their babies, when children come home from school to find their parents missing."[14]

The Latino component of the Democratic landslide was highlighted by the fact that Latinos are concentrated in the western states that swung from Republican to Democratic in 2008. Seventy-three percent of Colorado's Latinos, 76 percent of Nevada's, and 69 percent of New Mexico's went for Obama. In California, 77 percent of Latinos voted for the Democrat, as did 57 percent of Florida's.[15] Latinos who were born outside the U.S. went for Obama by a slightly greater margin than native-born

Latino Americans, 78 percent to 76 percent.[16] The demographic and political shift in U.S. politics, registered with the Democratic victory, has shifted the immigration debate leftward. For many involved in immigrant rights, this now presents an opportunity for the movement to shift to the offensive—after a long, dark period of reaction.

As expectations for progressive change rose with the ascendancy of Obama and the Democrats, immigrant rights activists experienced their first setback with the new administration. During the Senate confirmation hearings for Obama's pick for the new secretary of homeland security, Janet Napolitano voiced support for a continuation of the Bush strategy, stating that under her watch "federal immigration agents would intercept illegal immigrants at the border . . . and would continue raiding businesses where they work." Furthermore, she said, "the Obama administration also would target employers who hire the immigrants on the gamble that their businesses won't be raided."[17] The move prompted activist groups around the country to pledge to continue to put pressure on the new administration for an end to raids and deportations and for a new program of legalization.

By 2008, the Democratic majority was propelled into office by a working majority eager for change. To their disappointment, the party did not break with the repressive enforcement policies of their predecessors or even disrupt the pro-corporate status quo on immigration as a form of labor procurement and control. The tenets of the Bush/Chertoff era passed to the Obama/Napolitano era with seamless continuity.

The Democratic Strategy: Let the Republicans Lead

Many who felt inspired by the mass immigrant rights marches of 2006 accepted the mantra of "today we march, tomorrow we vote." An empowered Latino and liberal-leaning electorate, coupled with a demoralized and divided Right, swept the Democrats into office. By 2006, the Democrats recaptured the House of Representatives, and by 2008 they also won a majority of the Senate and the presidency with Barack Obama.

Despite rhetorical support for legalization, in power the Democrats adopted large segments of the Republican program as their own, above all the "enforcement first" strategy. Despite making a major campaign promise, the Obama administration jettisoned plans for a legalization program by late April 2010, concluding that lawmakers lacked the "appetite" to get behind it. "I don't want us to do something just for the sake of politics that doesn't solve the problem," Obama was quoted as saying.[18]

Obama and the Democrats' looming failure on immigration reform was foreshadowed as far back as 2005. As a rising star in the party being groomed for 2008, Obama staked out a position that aligned him with Republican logic. Then a U.S. senator, Obama declared:

> To begin with, the agencies charged with border security require new technology, new facilities and more people to stop, process and deport illegal immigrants. But while security might start at our borders, it doesn't end there. . . . We need a guest-worker program to replace the flood of illegals with a regulated stream of legals who enter the U.S. after checks and with access to labor rights.[19]

Obama and the Democratic majority promised to pass legalization within his first one hundred days in office, but the party's framework for passing legislation guaranteed failure. By pledging not to support any legislation without "strong bipartisan commitment," Obama and the Democrats dispelled any illusion that they intended to challenge the status quo. As Charles Schumer, chair of the Senate Judiciary Subcommittee on Immigration and Obama administration front man on the issue, declared, "Unless we can convince Americans we're going to be really tough, then this is not going to work."[20]

The Democratic Party strategy under Obama was doomed from the start. It began with the party directive to bypass the House and push the issue through the Senate first. According to Democratic Speaker of the House Nancy Pelosi, this was carried out to ostensibly protect "vulnerable Democrats" who might lose in more conservative districts if they tangled with such a thorny issue. In reality, it was an effort to preempt and sideline efforts by Congressman Luis Gutierrez and the Congressional Hispanic Caucus to introduce a bill considered "too liberal" by Democratic leaders. Minutes before the Gutierrez bill was introduced at a press conference in a Washington, DC, Democratic Congressional Campaign Committee chair Chris Van Hollen (Maryland) made it very clear that it wouldn't see the light of day, stating to the press that "the Speaker's been very clear that the Senate would go first on an immigration bill."[21]

The Democratic leadership's vision for immigration policy followed a carefully worded script that would not allow for deviation. As with the health care debate, the Democrats wasted the opportunity to use their majority status in both houses of Congress to push for substantial reform and force the Republicans on the defensive. Instead, they conceded leadership to the minority-status Republicans through the illusory notion of "bipartisanship," a myth the Republicans were willing to dispense with immediately.

This set up the second premise of the strategy, which asserted that an immigration reform bill would have to be crafted jointly with Republicans. In practice, this meant that any form of legalization would have to be buried underneath a package of draconian enforcement measures in order to secure Republican support. This tack to the right was in fact already dovetailing with the Democratic leadership's own vision. As a presidential candidate, Obama had outlined the emerging Democratic Party strategy that would unfold under his administration. According to a campaign email, he believed that immigration reform must include a "three-pronged response":

1) strengthen border security;
2) establish a path to legalization that includes fines and adherence to the rule of law for immigrants and their families who may have entered the United States illegally but are now contributing and responsible members of society; and,
3) create a "guest worker" program whereby American businesses can temporarily recruit foreign workers for jobs that American workers cannot or refuse to fill.

This approach was theoretically crafted to reconcile the three main conflicting forces in motion around the immigration debate: the Republican Right, the immigrant rights movement and immigrant constituencies, and the sectors of big business eager to maintain access to migrant labor. But according to the Obama strategy, immigration reform could only begin with confirmed Republican support. The emphasis on a bipartisan approach is reflected in the positions of Senator Charles Schumer, the Obama team's point man in the Senate. Schumer is credited with pushing the party in a more conservative direction during his stint as chairman of the Democratic Senatorial Campaign Committee between 2005 and 2009 by promoting candidates who adopted Republican positions. This philosophy continues to inform his approach as chairman of the Senate Judiciary Committee's Subcommittee on Immigration. For instance, the *New York Times* quoted Schumer as saying, "Public sentiment about the proposed immigration overhaul that failed in the Senate two years ago was that it 'was too soft on illegal immigrants.'"[22]

This unilateral commitment to bipartisanship brought the Republican minority in through the front door of the process, despite the Democrats having substantial majorities in both the House and Senate. This was despite the fact that Republicans, running on an anti-immigrant platform, took heavy losses in the 2006 and 2008 elections, as well as the Republican presidential primaries. For example, the organization Immigration2006 tracked fifteen key congressional races in the 2006 elections, finding that pro-reform Democrats defeated Republicans running anti-immigrant campaigns in twelve of the contests. This helped produce a Democratic-controlled House.

An America's Voice study of the 2008 elections tracked sixteen competitive battleground races in which Republican candidates highlighted their Democratic opponent's purported positions in favor of immigration reform. In fourteen of the sixteen campaigns, the tactic failed. In the primaries, all of the candidates focusing on immigrant criminalization, from Tom Tancredo to Mike Huckabee to Mitt Romney, were handily defeated by John McCain, who was disparaged as being "pro-amnesty" by the other candidates. (McCain's position has shifted substantially since then.)

Taking their cues from the Republicans, the Democrats and their backers not only adopted the "enforcement first" strategy but developed their own vision for cracking down on immigrants. The Obama goal of "strengthening security" devolved into the primary focus of the plan. Democratic Party strategists and aligned think tanks began to push candidates and incumbents to take harder positions on immigration. For example, a policy brief entitled "Winning the Immigration Debate" was circulated through the Democratic Party by the Washington DC-based lobbying groups Center for American Progress and the Coalition for Comprehensive Immigration Reform (a coalition that includes the Service Employees International Union, the National Council of La Raza, America's Voice, and others).

The brief called on Democrats to co-opt punitive language when discussing immigration. Specifically, the report encouraged a shift from characterizing undocumented workers and their families as victims of scapegoating and harsh enforcement measures to lawbreakers who must be punished as part of any effort to regularize their status. *Huffington Post* cites a 2007 Obama campaign speech that demonstrates this subtle shift, in which the emphasis is on punishing fines and stringent requirements: "We want to have a situation in which those who are already here, are playing by the rules, are willing to pay a fine and go through a rigorous process should have a pathway to legalization. Most Americans will support that if they have some sense that the border is also being secured."[23]

The Schumer-led approach also reflects the desperate attempt to court intransigent Republicans by capitulating to their anti-immigrant rhetoric. In Schumer's "seven principles of immigration reform," he refers to immigrants as "illegal aliens" instead of undocumented workers. He calls on other Democrats to also make this shift, urging that "when we use phrases like 'undocumented workers,' we convey a message to the American people that their Government is not serious about combating illegal immigration, which the American people overwhelmingly oppose."[24]

Democrats Increase Repression

Rhetoric aside, the punitive measures against immigrant workers by the Obama administration were severe. The ideological framework was articulated by Department of Homeland Security (DHS) secretary Janet Napolitano, who stated in a *Houston Chronicle* editorial:

> The Obama administration's approach is to view border security, interior immigration enforcement, and counternarcotics enforcement as inextricably linked. . . . While enforcement at the border is critical, it's only effective if paired with smart enforcement of the immigration laws within our borders as well. That begins with a focus on apprehending criminals, whether they are employers who knowingly cultivate an illegal workforce, or criminal aliens who commit crimes that endanger lives.[25]

This set the stage for a multipronged approach to increased internal immigration enforcement through the DHS. This has included the expansion of the federal 287(g) program, which allows police to collaborate with agents in the apprehension and deportation of immigrants; the Secure Communities Initiative, which intensifies and streamlines the search and retrieval of undocumented immigrants in communities; the E-Verify database system, which allows employers to root out and fire workers without papers; and a federal system of personnel audits to punish companies that employ undocumented workers and encourage preemptive mass firings.

E-Verify has allowed for lower-profile, but no less pernicious, "sanction raids," in which the threat of employer sanctions forces some companies to turn out their undocumented workers without requiring the use of government resources such as high-powered rifles, ankle cuffs, and monitoring devices. It has also given employers more control over undocumented workers. Within Obama's first year in office, his

administration had "audited" 654 companies, leading to the termination of thousands of workers.[26] By 2010, these "audits" intensified. According to the *Los Angeles Times*:

> Federal officials are turning to some other familiar tactics, most notably
> the use of audits to check for illegal workers. Since July, the government
> has notified more than 1,600 companies nationwide of plans to audit
> their records. Hundreds of inspections are ongoing. In fiscal year 2010,
> which ends in September, the agency fined 109 companies a total of
> about $3 million, up from $675,000 in fines against 18 companies in
> fiscal year 2008. And so far this fiscal year, 65 employers have been ar-
> rested, compared to 135 in all of 2008.[27]

The administration also increased militarization and personnel
buildup along the U.S. border, and announced the deployment of 1,200
National Guard troops to the region within weeks of Arizona's passage of
the anti-immigrant SB 1070. As part of the strategy, the administration
also mandated that DHS ramp up deportations, establishing a quota of at
least four hundred thousand deportations per year by the end of 2010.[28]

The ratcheting up of enforcement under the Obama administration not only continued the policies of the Bush administration, but it
set a new standard in enforcement priority. According to the *San Francisco Chronicle*:

> The Department of Homeland Security unveiled a $56.3 billion bud-
> get [February 2010] that includes funding for the virtual border fence,
> E-Verify, and an increase in the number of border patrol officers and
> intelligence analysts along the southern border. In a year in which
> President Obama has spoken about the need to "save what we can"
> to combat record deficits, some federal agencies are seeing programs
> trimmed or eliminated entirely, but DHS escaped the budgeting pro-
> cess unscathed. Obama's budget, which must be approved by Congress
> before it takes effect, asks for $6 billion more for DHS than the depart-
> ment received in FY 2010.[29]

The culmination of this strategy took shape in the announcement
of the Democratic legislative framework—the Senate Democrats' proposal, under Schumer's leadership—for beginning the discussion of
immigration reform in early May 2010. This plan included a further
expansion of the Border Patrol, the tripling of fines against employers
who hire undocumented workers, and the development of biometric
identification cards that incorporate fingerprints, retinal scans, "vein
geometry," or "facial mapping" for all U.S. workers to be cross-checked
for eligibility with a federal database.[30]

The proposal was dead on arrival. So much had already been conceded to the minority Republican opposition without a fight that they had no need to make more overtures toward the Democrats and ditched any pretense of support for legalization. They could now beat the Democrats with the club they had been handed and use it as leverage in the upcoming elections. As the *Washington Post* reported:

> The plan's emphasis on "securing the border first" before taking steps to allow many of an estimated 11 million illegal immigrants living in the United States to pay fines and apply for legal status was plainly a gesture to Republicans. Even so, no Republican is supporting it, not even Sen. Lindsey O. Graham (R-S.C.), who has been working with Sen. Charles E. Schumer (D N.Y.) in bipartisan talks over the issue for months. The Democrats' shift underscores how, in the struggle between enforcement advocates and legalization backers, the former seem to be gaining.[31]

Despite being left at the altar, the Democratic leadership trudged on with the same strategy, supporting yet another increase in Border Patrol personnel in August. Obama and the Senate Democrats' call to add fifteen hundred agents to the bloated force of more than twenty thousand led the *Los Angeles Times* to conclude that only around border enforcement and militarization did the Senate find a "rare moment of bipartisan compromise in an otherwise divisive environment."[32]

In 2010, Republicans seized on the opportunity to energize and mobilize its base in response to the Democratic Party's failed strategy. Support for a campaign against immigrants offered benefits for a party that was being elegized as "a permanent minority" only a year after the sweeping victory of Obama and the Democratic Party's supermajority control of Congress in 2008. At that time of economic recession, shady financial bailouts, simmering anti-corporate sentiment, flagging imperial wars, and rapidly widening social inequality, anti-immigrant politics and racism offered the Republican Party a means to take the attention away from the failings of the capitalist system and its architects. Furthermore, Republicans believed that the substantial Latino, labor, and immigrant constituencies that helped propel the Democrats into office with high expectations for immigration reform would become demoralized by its failure, and stay home during the mid-term elections of November 2010. Their calculations were right. Latinos had a substantially lower turnout rate than all other ethnic groups.[33]

The failure of the Democratic Party's strategy is not just linked to faulty judgments. It is tied to the very nature of the party itself, especially its direct links to corporations. Legalization presents problems for big business, as legalized workers can fight for and negotiate higher wages and better working conditions with less fear of reprisal or state repression. As David Bacon pointed out in the *Progressive*:

> No one in the Obama or Bush administrations, or the Clinton administration before them, wants to stop migration to the U.S. or imagines that this could be done without catastrophic consequences. The very industries they target for enforcement are so dependent on the labor of migrants they would collapse without it. Instead, immigration policy and enforcement consigns those migrants to an "illegal" status, and undermines the price of their labor. Enforcement is a means for managing the flow of migrants, and making their labor available to employers at a price they want to pay.[34]

Because of their tendency to prioritize the needs of big business over labor and compromise over principle, the Democrats are more eager and willing to pursue enforcement than fight for legalization.

Passing the Initiative to the Right

The legalization component of Democratic Party strategy never materialized. Instead, the punitive measures and rhetoric shifted the immigration debate back into the terrain of the Far Right. This opening allowed the anti-immigrant wing of the Republican Party and extremists on its periphery to make a hard push on the issue, marginalizing moderates, sabotaging any attempts at reform, and continuing to force an anti-immigrant agenda to the forefront of national politics in the lead-up to the 2010 elections. *Politico* recognized this process unfolding in 2008, commenting, "Yet while Bush was passing the torch to McCain as the party's standard bearer, a half dozen conservative GOP senators were unveiling proposals dealing with deportation, making English the official language, revoking funds for 'sanctuary cities' and giving local police more immigration enforcement powers."[35]

Well-funded anti-immigrant lobby organizations and the anti-immigrant media circuit then sprang into action to do the heavy lifting at the state and local level. As the *Los Angeles Times* reported in June 2008:

> [Anti-immigrant] groups have begun working to hem in the future president. They have pushed for new city and state laws, helping spur hundreds of bills around the country in the last three months. They've held conferences to educate members nationwide and lobby local officials. And they're promoting the election of congressional candidates

who take a hard line on immigration. The strategy is to reshape the national political landscape to fend off future liberalization proposals.[36]

The broad-based anti-immigrant campaign swung the back door wide open for the inclusion of hate groups and the mainstreaming of racism. According to the Southern Poverty Law Center, the number of hate groups targeting immigrants grew by 33 percent between 2000 and 2005, while anti-Latino hate crimes increased 40 percent annually between 2003 and 2007. A May 2010 Associated Press–Univision poll revealed that 81 percent of Latinos believed that they experienced some or a lot of discrimination.[37] This growth of hate and violence has occurred in tandem with the crackdown on immigrants taking place across the country and has moved racism from the margins to the center of these campaigns. One hate group in particular, the pseudo-scientific, anti-immigrant Center for Immigration Studies, has advanced the theoretical framework of "enforcement through attrition" that now informs much of the efforts at criminalization. According to Tom Barry of the Center for International Policy:

> The Center for Immigration Studies (CIS) took the lead in developing this strategic framework. In April 2006 this restrictionist think tank published "Attrition through Enforcement: A Cost-Effective Strategy to Shrink the Illegal Population," which lays out the main components of a war of attrition against immigrants along with the estimated cost of a multi-front campaign to wear down immigrant residents and dissuade would-be immigrants. . . . Key components include: eliminating access to jobs through employer verification of Social Security numbers and immigration status; ending misuse of Social Security and IRS numbers by immigrants in seeking employment, bank accounts, and driver's licenses, and improved information sharing among key federal agencies, including the Internal Revenue Service, in the effort to identify unauthorized residents; increasing federal, state, and local cooperation, particularly among law enforcement agencies; reducing visa overstays through better tracking systems; stepping up immigration raids; and passing state and local laws to discourage illegal immigrants from making a home in that area and to make it more difficult for immigrants to conceal their status.[38]

By the end of the 2008 presidential campaign, Republican candidate John McCain had already changed tack on the issue, calling for heavy enforcement measures to be implemented before considering any form of legalization. After the election, Obama made the strategy his own. As the *New York Times* observed, "That approach brings Mr. Obama around to the position that his Republican rival, Senator John McCain of Arizona, espoused during last year's presidential campaign . . . [opening] a political rift with some immigrant advocacy and Hispanic groups whose voters were crucial to the Obama victory."[39]

Since Democrats had already adapted components of the "enforcement through attrition" strategy at the federal level, it became easier for Republicans to push the full agenda at the state and local level. For instance, Republican-controlled Arizona became the front edge of the national anti-immigrant crusade in 2010.

Arizona Republicans, emboldened by the Obama administration's abandonment of legalization, worked feverishly to pass a host of laws amounting to the most punitive and repressive restrictions to date. Right-wing and opportunist politicians across multiple states then followed suit, attempting to replicate the Arizona strategy of launching full-scale attacks on Latino immigrant populations. The rapid coalescence of political forces as part of the recalibration of xenophobic nativism encouraged the cross-fertilization of anti-immigrant ideology with both the reactionary libertarianism of the Tea Party movement and the racial identitarianism of the white supremacist movement.[40]

Rather than make a concerted push for immigrant legalization, which could have energized immigrant communities, unions, and the Democratic Party base, and which could have thrown Republican opponents on the defensive at time when they were weak, divided and vulnerable, the Democrats chose to prop up the Republican Party by claiming its strategy and abandoning all pretense of support for legalization during the apogee of their power. They not only squandered the best possible opportunity to administer the legalization of millions of immigrant workers and their families, but their timidity, capitulation, and failure opened the door to a reactionary backlash that has since arrested and reversed the momentum born out of the nationwide immigrant rights mobilizations of 2006. This backlash has included the incorporation of anti-immigration as a central issue within the revitalized right-wing Republican Tea Party movement in 2010, the passage of SB 1070 in Arizona, and the rehabilitation of Donald Trump as the champion of immigration restriction after an abysmal presidential campaign in 2012.

The Arizona Laboratory and SB 1070

Arizona's legislature passed SB 1070 in 2010, implementing the most sweeping series of immigration restrictions since the defeat of the Sensenbrenner-King Bill in 2006. The law empowered the police to check the immigration status of anyone encountered during "lawful stop, detention or arrest." It required all noncitizen people over the age of fourteen to register with the U.S. government and carry their legal documents at all times, or be subject to a misdemeanor charge for failure to show legal authorization to be in the country. Furthermore, the law contained the first "anti-sanctuary" provision, making it illegal for state or local officials to restrict or prevent their offices or agencies from collaborating with immigration agencies or complying with federal immigration requirements. It imposed harsh penalties for those sheltering, hiring, and transporting unregistered immigrants. In practice, SB 1070 became the full realization of the "enforcement through attrition" strategy, openly stating as much in the preamble to the law.[1]

Rewinding the reel of the Democrats' immigration debacle reveals that the passage of the law was wholly preventable. Ironically, by not advancing legalization at the federal level, the Obama administration and congressional Democrats allowed the Republican Party to seize the initiative at the state and local level and run aggressive crusade-like campaigns against immigrants to consolidate backing from a right-wing constituency and use fear, racism, and economic instability to drum up further support.

Arizona has been at the forefront of anti-immigrant racism and restriction. Through the activism of a coalition of right-wing groups, the anti-bilingual education Proposition 203 was passed in 1999, followed by the notorious Proposition 200, passed in November of 2004.[2] The intent of Prop 200 was to deny undocumented immigrants access to employment and all state and local benefits, including public housing, food assistance, college tuition, and employment benefits in a state where undocumented workers grew to comprise 16.2 percent of the workforce by 2010.[3]

The proposition, modeled on California's Prop 187, which passed in 1994 and was later killed in the courts, upped the ante by holding all state and local officials liable for reporting any undocumented immigrants who requested services. Prop 200 also made Arizona the first state in the country to require proof of citizenship to vote. The chairperson of the National Advisory Board for Proposition 200 was Virginia Abernethy, a self-described "white separatist" with a long and sordid career of racist activity, who has since allied with other anti-immigrant demagogues, organizations, and hate groups to export the effort to other states.[4]

Furthermore, the name of Sheriff Joe Arpaio was thrust into the national spotlight after he launched his own personal war against undocumented immigrants. Emboldened by the passage of Proposition 200 and through dubious interpretation the state's anti-human-smuggling laws, Arpaio turned Maricopa County into his own anti-immigrant fiefdom. He began arresting undocumented immigrants in March 2006, after cross-training 160 deputies to enforce immigration law and creating "citizen posses" to aid with traffic checkpoints, raids, and other forms of legally sanctioned vigilantism. In 2007, he enrolled the Maricopa County Sheriff's Department in the DHS's 287(g) program, which empowers local law enforcement agencies to participate in immigration enforcement.[5]

Other actions have included the launch of a hotline for people to report or turn in "suspected" undocumented immigrants and the creation of segregated, open-air tent jails for undocumented workers in the hot Arizona desert.[6] For his actions, Arpaio achieved celebrity status from the right-wing Fox Network, which awarded him his own short-lived reality show, which aired briefly in 2009. The media attention showered on Joe Arpaio led other like-minded sheriffs and electoral aspirants to try to replicate his approach in other counties and states.[7]

Republican and Democratic legislators in sixteen other states attempted to introduce similar bills into their legislatures.[8]

While Arizona Republicans took credit for the passage of SB 1070, it is actually a foreign import into the state. The law was the brainchild of Kris Kobach, an anti-immigrant lawyer on the payroll of the Federation for American Immigration Reform (FAIR). FAIR is a Washington DC-based lobbying group dedicated to promoting extreme measures against immigrants and is directly linked to the Center for Immigration Studies and the "enforcement through attrition" strategy. Kobach's origins are far from grassroots. According to the *Arizona Republic*:

> In 2001, just days after 9/11, Kobach got a job as chief adviser on immigration law and border security to John Ashcroft, who was in his first year as U.S. attorney general. Kobach oversaw Department of Justice efforts to tighten border security, including the design and implementation of a system that requires foreign nationals from certain nations to register with a program that tracks their movements in and out of the U.S. . . . When [SB 1070's sponsor in the Arizona Senate Russell] Pearce was ready to tackle state enforcement of federal immigration laws, he again called Kobach for help.[9]

In the preamble to SB 1070, the strategy of "enforcement through attrition" is clearly identified as the intention: "The legislature finds that there is a compelling interest in the cooperative enforcement of federal immigration laws throughout all of Arizona. The legislature declares that the intent of this act is to make attrition through enforcement the public policy of all state and local government agencies in Arizona."[10] The FAIR strategy was taken up wholeheartedly by Arizona's right-wing politicos as a way to capitalize on the anxiety and instability generated by economic recession and underlying racial tensions coming out into the open in the state. Others see it as a résumé builder, or the means to push through their own racist pet projects.

The border militarization strategy that began under Democrat Bill Clinton has rerouted a large percentage of migrant crossings through the state's southern desert region, providing the useful pretext for the onslaught against the immigrant and Latino community. Arizona politicians have used this to manufacture an "out-of-control border" scenario in order to soften and misshape public perceptions. For instance, in a 2010 speech from the Arizona Senate floor, moderate-turned-immigration-hawk John McCain bemoaned the failure to secure that border between Arizona and Mexico, which he said "has led to violence—the worst I have ever seen."[11] It was, in fact, the shooting death of South Arizona rancher Robert Krentz by an alleged undocumented immigrant that provided the grist for Governor Jan Brewer to justify signing SB 1070 into law. Even though it came to light shortly thereafter that an immigrant was not responsible for the shooting, the process moved forward anyway without so much as a murmur.[12]

In reality, government data had already dispelled the mythical "out-of-control border" scenario. According to 2009 data from the FBI Uniform Crime Reports cited in the *Arizona Republic*:

> While the nation's [undocumented] population doubled from 1994 to 2004, according to federal records, the violent-crime rate declined 35 percent. [Furthermore,] Arizona's violent-crime rate dropped from 512 incidents per 100,000 residents in 2005 to 447 incidents in 2008, the most recent year for which data is available. . . . Cochise County's crime rate has been "flat" for at least 10 years, the sheriff added. Even in 2000, when record numbers of undocumented immigrants were detained in the area, just 4 percent of the area's violent crimes were committed by [undocumented immigrants].[13]

This led Clarence Dupnik, the sheriff of Pima County, to conclude, "This is a media-created event. . . . I hear politicians on TV saying the border has gotten worse. Well, the fact of the matter is that the border has never been more secure."[14] Moreover, the FBI Uniform Crime Reports also found that the top four big cities with the lowest crime rates are all in border states: San Diego, Phoenix, El Paso, and Austin. Violent crime rates in Southwest border counties overall have been steadily dropping and are among the lowest in the country. Another study conducted by Customs and Border Protection found that Border Patrol agents face far less danger than their police counterparts in U.S. cities.[15]

Despite this trend, members of Congress from border states continue to push for more militarization. As immigrant advocate Isabel Garcia of the Tucson-based Derechos Humanos asserted in the *Arizona Daily Star*, "Politicians are hyping up this incredible fear across the country about the border, but these numbers show these are lies being perpetrated on the American public."[16] The impact of such fearmongering becomes apparent in the polls. A May 2010 CBS/*New York Times* poll that showed the percentage of U.S. respondents who considered immigration a "very serious problem" increased to 65 percent by the time the Arizona law had passed, compared to 56 percent in 2007 and

54 percent in 2006.[17] This despite all the indicators dispelling the various threats associated with immigration.

When the immigrant-as-criminal approach became too slippery to carry, the focus shifted to jobs and protecting Arizona's workers from the recession, a crisis also attributed to immigrant workers. According to the *Arizona Republic*, job opportunities for college graduates in the state plummeted during the recession. In 2007, only 51 percent of graduates found work; by 2009 the number had dropped to 20 percent.

The recession was especially tough on young workers. As the economy shed jobs by the thousands, many four-year college graduates had trouble launching careers and languished in lower-paying jobs. Historically, those with similar circumstances find it hard to get the same career opportunities and earn as much as those with college degrees who graduate in better times. Those with just a high-school education faced even more difficult challenges during this period.[18]

The linking of unemployment to the presence of immigrant workers was then taken up in opportunistic fashion by Arizona Republicans. Joe Arpaio, the notorious sheriff who has gained national attention for his "crime suppression sweeps" in Latino communities, chain gangs, tent-city prisons, and immigrant-hunting civilian posses, rebranded himself defender of Arizona's native-born workers. For example, speaking at a pro–SB 1070 rally in 2010, Arpaio boasted that his department had arrested or detained 38,000 undocumented workers, claiming that his actions created jobs. After a raid at a seafood processing plant, he declared, "We're going to continue business raids because you have to understand we have an unemployment problem."[19]

Arizona governor Jan Brewer forged a career out of criminalizing immigrants. As secretary of state of Arizona she promoted Proposition 200, which cut off the few, meager social services available to undocumented immigrants in the state and mandated that all voters show proof of citizenship at the polls. She investigated Arizona's welfare agencies to make sure they excluded all ineligible immigrants, and helped craft the final version of SB 1070. As a politician with a mediocre career record who only attained the governor's seat by constitutional succession after Janet Napolitano vacated it to work in the Obama administration, Brewer had faced an uphill battle to retain her post. This was observed by the *Arizona Republic*:

> "She is running in a primary that leans heavily to the right," [Maricopa County Supervisor Mary Rose] Wilcox said. "She had to outright the right, and that's what she did." Telephone polling since Brewer signed

SB 1070 suggests her decision sat well with would-be voters in the August Republican primary. Both her job-approval ratings and her lead over her opponents appeared to have gotten a boost in Rasmussen Reports surveys released over the past month.[20]

Seeking to salvage a flagging political campaign on the backs of undocumented immigrants became an increasingly popular sport in Republican circles in other states. The Republican governor's primary race in California between Meg Whitman and Steve Poizner, for instance, degenerated into a vitriolic slap-fight and a one-upmanship contest over who would restrict and deport more immigrants. According to the *Los Angeles Times*, Poizner sought to overcome Whitman's advantage by waving the "bloody red" shirt of anti-immigration:

> His campaign for governor on the ropes, Republican Steve Poizner has been blaming illegal immigration for the state's troubled schools, its crowded emergency rooms and some of its massive budget deficit. Last week he began airing ads accusing GOP front-runner Meg Whitman of mimicking President Obama in her positions on illegal immigration—specifically, a comment she made last year about envisioning "a path to legalization" for undocumented workers.[21]

Whitman won the primary by taking right-wing positions on immigration. These included a promise to end "sanctuary cities," referring to city governments that refuse to allow local police to engage in immigration enforcement, and declaring her opposition to any form of amnesty.[22] While she has said that she opposed SB 1070, she also believed that it "should stand now that it has passed."[23] Shamelessly, after winning, she reached out to Latino voters with a flurry of ads in Spanish that emphasized her opposition to SB 1070 and California's 1994 Proposition 187, which would have denied education, health, and other services to undocumented families if it had passed. None of her ads reminded "voters that her campaign chairman is former Gov. Pete Wilson, a top proponent of Proposition 187 and still an unpopular figure among state Latinos."[24]

SB 1070 opened the door wide enough for other reactionary laws and policies linking anti-immigration to the broader Latino community. The passage of HB 2281 followed, for instance, which banned ethnic studies courses in K–12 schools under the pretense that they advocate "race and class resentment" and promote "ethnic solidarity." A pet project of State Superintendent of Public Instruction Tom Horne, the bill targeted a successful ethnic studies program in the Tucson Unified School District that has been linked to higher student performance. Horne had been advocating the upending of the ethnic studies program since 2007, when he published "An Open Letter to the Citizens of Tucson," unsuccessfully urging them to abolish the program.[25] When this failed, he turned to conservative lawmakers in the Arizona legislature and found a hearing. Horne used the passage of this law as a rallying point for his successful campaign for Arizona state attorney general in 2011.

The attack on education also opened the door for SB 1070 supporters to go after Latino teachers. Republican partisans within the Arizona Department of Education used the crackdown as an opportunity to establish a policy that required "heavily accented teachers" and those "lacking fluency" to be removed from developmental English classes throughout Arizona's school districts. Qualifications are to be ostensibly determined by school officials, even though English proficiency was theoretically a condition of the original hiring process. In practice, this empowered administrators to remove "undesirable" teachers based on individually determined characteristics. It also made the whole community of Latino and immigrant teachers suspect and vulnerable at a time when many were already taking a stand for their academic rights and the civil rights of their immigrant students. As the *Wall Street Journal* pointed out:

> The teacher controversy comes amid an increasingly tense debate over immigration. Arizona Gov. Jan Brewer this month signed the nation's toughest law to crack down on illegal immigrants. Critics charge that the broader political climate has emboldened state education officials to target immigrant teachers at a time when a budget crisis has forced layoffs. "This is just one more indication of the incredible anti-immigrant sentiment in the state," said Bruce Merrill, a professor emeritus at Arizona State University who conducts public-opinion research.[26]

This kind of institutional targeting of Latinos and their civil and political rights increased as the immigration debate devolved into the mainstreaming of racial animus. According to Steven Nuño, assistant professor in the Department of Politics and International Affairs at Northern Arizona University, the racialization of immigration enforcement in Arizona represents a demographic and generational conflict in a state where a conservative and entrenched white political structure feels threatened.

Latinos in Arizona are quite young, averaging twenty-six years old and comprising 44 percent of all K–12-aged children, while the non-Hispanic white population is in their electoral prime, averaging forty-six years old.[27] The outcome of this demographic reality, combined with Latinos' higher birthrates, is that Latinos are simply pushing non-Hispanic whites out the back door, and the institution is fighting back, as hopeless as it is.

Citizenship status remains the greatest structural barrier to participation for Latinos. More than a third of Latinos in Arizona are not citizens, and therefore they are ineligible to vote. However, even among citizens, Latinos in Arizona lag behind their non-Hispanic white counterparts, with only 37 percent of Latino citizens voting in 2008 and 52 percent of eligible residents registered to vote. While Latinos make up 14 percent of those registered to vote in Arizona, they only made up 12 percent of Arizona's voters in 2008. If Latinos participated at the same rates as non-Hispanic whites, they would make up 21 percent of Arizona's voters, nearly double their 2008 numbers. Even more daunting to the system, if noncitizens were given a clear pathway to citizenship and participated at the same rate, they would make up more than 32 percent of Arizona's voters. Rolling out the welcome mat to Latinos may result in doubling their participation rates, and favorable citizenship laws could result in tripling the current electoral power of Latinos. Arizonans seem unwilling to do either without a fight.[28]

In the anti-immigrant frenzy unleashed in Arizona, overt acts of racism are increasingly crawling out into the open—and open racists are feeling emboldened to act. For example, the central Arizona city of Prescott gained national attention when artists from the Downtown Mural Project were asked to "whiten" the faces of children they were painting in a mural at Miller Valley Elementary School. As artist R. E. Wall told the *Arizona Republic*:

> "We consistently, for two months, had people shouting racial slander from their cars. . . . We had children painting with us, and here come these yells of (epithet for Blacks) and (epithet for Hispanics)." Wall said school Principal Jeff Lane pressed him to make the children's faces appear happier and brighter. "It is being lightened because of the controversy," Wall said.[29]

Neo-Nazi and other unabashed hate groups have become so comfortable operating under the Arizona sun that they are no longer seeking the anonymity of the crowd, so much so that even less extreme anti-immigrant groups such as the Americans for Legal Immigration PAC have tried to distance themselves from some recent pro–SB 1070 rallies. According to a recent article in *Mother Jones*, "[t]he group says it is withdrawing its support from any rallies supporting the Arizona law next month 'due to the discovery of racist group involvement and the actions of former Congressman Tom Tancredo.'"[30]

Merely a few weeks after Arizona governor Jan Brewer made the wildly false and dangerous claim that the "majority of the illegal trespassers that are coming into the state of Arizona are under the direction and control of organized drug cartels and they are bringing drugs in," a reputed neo-Nazi in southern Arizona took that as his cue.[31] Jason "J. T." Ready and the "National Socialist Movement" took matters into their own hands, organizing armed patrols and "declaring war on 'narco-terrorists' and keeping an eye out for illegal immigrants."[32]

While the Obama administration filed an eleventh-hour legal challenge to prevent implementation of SB 1070, and as other Democrats lamented the hard-right shift in immigration politics, they had little to offer that was different. From 2012 to 2016, the Democrats further increased their own brand of immigrant repression, opening the door further to a right-wing regroupment within the Republican Party behind Donald Trump and the resurgence of the neo-fascist street movement, both claiming the mantle of anti-immigration.

Chapter Thirty-Seven

S. 744: The Degeneration of "Comprehensive Immigration Reform"

The Border Security, Economic Opportunity and Immigration Modernization Act of 2013, known as S. 744, is a proposal that only corporate America should love. Although the bipartisan "Gang of Eight" senators who drafted it, like their counterparts in the House of Representatives, present S. 744 as a reasonable and measured approach to legalization, an in-depth read of the 844-page document tells a different story. It is laden with punitive measures, disqualifications and exclusions, and ramped-up enforcement. It is so prohibitive that it should be seen, in its current form, as the continuation of the attack on immigrant workers, not a genuine—or even partial—reform.

The proposal does represent a consensus among the ruling class to move forward with the restructuring of immigration policy. This can be attributed to the defeat of the "enforcement-only strategy"—in the streets and at the polls in 2012—that has been dominant over the last several years. Nevertheless, S. 744 does not break with the underlying policy doctrines that have continued from George W. Bush to Barack Obama to Donald Trump. This includes the treatment of immigration and the border as a national security issue in the context of the War on Terror, encouraging the militarization of enforcement and the criminalization of migrants. It also strongly reflects a continuation of the effort to further subordinate workers' rights to the needs of big business.

Thus, while partisan debates over details have begun in various congressional committees, there is a high level of agreement about the principal components: increased spending on the enforcement apparatus, at the border and in the interior, to control current and future migration flows; the development of a substantial noncitizen, low-wage workforce through expansion of a guest-worker program; a merit-based visa system; and a long and arduous legalization process designed to disqualify any who speak up, step out of line, or stop working.

Expanding the War on Immigrants, Yet Again

At the heart of the proposal is the requirement that before any legalization for the estimated eleven million undocumented can be considered, border-enforcement agencies must achieve an effective apprehension rate of 90 percent or higher in all high-risk border sectors by the end of a five-year period. Despite the tide turning in favor of legalization, this was a preemptive concession to Republicans.[1] While it wasn't exactly clear what criteria would be used to determine this "effectiveness rate," three current aspects of border reality belie the urgency to "take control of the border."

First, according to the Pew Hispanic Research Center, net cross-border migration fell to *zero* in 2011.[2] In other words, an equal number of migrants were returning to Mexico as coming in. Second, though the drop in migration has been attributed to increased enforcement, the economic recession is the primary reason.[3] Even the Border Patrol acknowledges that the recession played a key role, while still inventing convoluted formulations to "prove" that their work has been a success and to justify their bloated budgets.[4] Third, economic and demographic trends point to decreased migration from Mexico into the foreseeable future.[5]

Since the implementation of the North American Free Trade Agreement in 1994, millions of workers have been economically displaced as the treaty opened up Mexico's economy to foreign capital. Direct competition with U.S., European, and Asian multinational corporations wiped out small farmers, many domestic producers, and Mexico's teetering state-owned sector. At least one million economic refugees left Mexico each year until the recession hit.[6] As a result, the country is now experiencing a generational gap—the population of young workers most likely to migrate has rapidly declined because many are already in the U.S.

At the same time, substantial foreign investment has fueled the growth of Mexico's economy, along with increased rates of inequality and deep poverty.[7] Nevertheless, declining wages in the United States have narrowed the wage gap between the two countries. Increased demand for labor in Mexico as a result of a labor shortage, alongside declining wages in the U.S., will reduce future migration flows.[8]

To achieve its stated goals on enforcement, S. 744 calls for adding $6.5 billion more per year to the $18 billion already spent on border measures in 2012. This additional spending would be slated to go toward increased surveillance and detection hardware, double- and triple-layer fencing, mobile surveillance equipment, command centers and other infrastructure, forward-operating bases and vehicles, as well as more drones, helicopters, and fixed-wing aircraft. The legislation would add an additional 3,500 Border Patrol agents to the 21,790 already in the field in 2013, eventually reaching 38,400 with full implementation.[9]

Anticipating the border budget engorgement, defense companies expanded their repertoire of border-adaptable military-grade wares to feed from the potential trough. According to the New York Times:

> [M]ajor military contractors, including Raytheon, Lockheed Martin and General Dynamics, are preparing for an unusual desert showdown here this summer, demonstrating their military-grade radar and long-range camera systems in an effort to secure a Homeland Security Department contract worth as much as $1 billion.[10]

Northrop Grumman, meanwhile, had pitched to Homeland Security officials an automated tracking device—first built for the Pentagon to find roadside bombs in Afghanistan—that could be mounted on aerial drones to find illegal border crossers. And General Atomics, which manufactures the reconnaissance drones, doubled the size of the fleet under a DHS-awarded contract worth $443 million.[11]

To assist in the project, the bill contains language to allow for the activation of the National Guard to participate in all aspects of border enforcement. This includes surveillance, communications, deployment of drones, construction of checkpoints, and direct assistance for operations on a full-time basis. There are already seventy-one traffic checkpoints and thirty-two permanent checkpoints in eight of the nine border region sectors, but the bill proposes more.[12]

The increased border militarization packaged in the most recent immigration proposal would only intensify the warlike atmosphere that already defines the Southwest border region. Far from making the country safer, it will produce more rampant racial profiling, detention and incarceration, deportations, and, more grimly, increased deaths.

Despite the decreased migration rates of the past few years, the rate of deaths of migrants crossing the border has increased. For instance, 2012 saw the highest recorded number of migrant deaths in Texas (271) and the second-highest number on record in Arizona (142).[13] While border deaths dipped slightly to an average of 368 documented deaths per year between 2013 and 2015, they have ticked up once more with 232 documented deaths in the first seven months of 2017.[14]

From the Border to the Workplace

The expansion of enforcement extends beyond the border region and into the interior of the country, demonstrating the comprehensive approach to controlling migrant labor, from border to workplace. To accomplish internal control, the bill mandates nationwide use of E-Verify by all employers (Title 3, Section 3101). E-Verify is a federal database system used by employers to determine the legality of their workers, based on the Employment Eligibility Verification Form, or Form I-9. The section of the bill about E-Verify also requires the collection of biometric data on all immigrant workers and contains language that could extend the requirement to all workers seeking employment, regardless of citizenship status. This would necessitate the establishment of a national biometric database, an alarming prospect in light of the contemporary revelations of increased NSA spying on U.S. citizens revealed by Edward Snowden.[15]

By early 2013, only about 7 percent of the six million employers in the U.S. used E-Verify, which is notoriously prone to error.[16] According to an independent government audit in 2009, E-Verify had an error rate of 4.1 percent. If applied nationally, this would negatively affect the employment of millions of workers.[17]

Furthermore, the study doesn't even take into account how E-Verify would "incentivize discrimination" against Latino/a workers.[18] Recent experience with E-Verify suggests that employers have used the program to racially profile, harass, and push out Latino/a workers. This was illustrated in San Diego in 2013 when nine hotel workers employed at the Hilton Mission Valley were fired because of E-Verify. As some of the workers had been employed at the hotel for as long as fifteen years, they didn't believe that it was a coincidence that their removal by the new, incoming management coincided with their support for a union organizing drive led by UNITE HERE.[19]

The national implementation of E-Verify would likely lead to mass firings, since many undocumented workers won't qualify for the "legalization" component of S. 744. Employers will have up to four years to comply, giving them the power to determine the pace of implementation and removal. The removal of thousands of ineligible workers would likely create a new layer of the underground economy, where the industries most dependent on cheap labor will find or develop mechanisms to avoid the program—pushing wages down even further.[20]

Furthermore, anyone caught using, buying, or distributing a false or duplicate Social Security number for the purpose of employment faces a maximum five-year prison term and a fine (Section 3102). Given the likelihood of future unauthorized immigration from different regions of the globe, the further criminalization of something so essential for the undocumented will almost certainly lead to increased incarceration and further growth of the ranks of the undocumented living precariously in the shadows.

The vast, vulnerable pool of undocumented workers that this bill would create would make it harder to unionize immigrant workers, currently one of the most dynamic sectors of union growth.[21] Once the new interior measures for exclusion are in place, future migrants caught in the U.S. would face draconian punishments reminiscent of the notorious Sensenbrenner-King Bill, known as HR 4437, that was defeated in 2006.

If an undocumented crosser is apprehended, they will face up to a year in prison and a fine ranging from $250 to $5,000. For a second offense, the prison term increases to up to three years, and the fine is doubled. If the violation occurs after the migrant has committed three misdemeanors or one felony, the individual could be locked up for ten to fifteen years. Those re-entering after deportation would face up to two years in prison, and anyone caught producing, selling, or distributing fake passports could face up to twenty years in prison (Section 3704).

Despite the emphasis on cracking down on labor "traffickers," the vague wording of the bill will likely result in the targeting of end users of false documents, since they are commonly needed by undocumented workers to obtain employment. This was the basis for the military-style workplace raids that began in 2006.

Legalization without Rights

When you look at the fine print, the promise of "legalization" that sponsors of S. 744 talk about betrays the meaning of the word. Millions of workers would be able to transition to a "legal" status—but it is very far from full or even partial citizenship. It can be better understood as a carefully crafted strategy to create a subclass of workers *without* rights, made perpetually vulnerable by an austere and rigid set of immigration rules and regulations.

For the first step in the "legalization" process, qualified migrants are placed into a specially created category of legal laborer: Registered Provisional Immigrant (RPI) status. Under this status, immigrants begin a minimum ten-year period during which they must work consistently, pay all taxes, be disqualified from publicly funded services and benefits (including Obamacare), register for the Military Selective Service, and pay up to two thousand dollars in fines (Section 2101).

To qualify—and to remain qualified for the duration of the long process—migrants must have been present in the U.S. before December 31, 2011, and must not have committed a felony or three misdemeanors (excluding traffic violations) before or during the period.

Perhaps most revealing about how this bill is designed to control immigrant labor, RPIs "must be regularly employed throughout the period of admission . . . allowing for brief periods lasting not more than 60 days," according to the bill. In other words, workers who don't maintain consistent employment or who quit or get fired from their jobs for any reason can be disqualified. This will make workers fearful and dependent on their employers, who can then leverage this power to keep wages low, and harass or intimidate workers.

Workers can also be disqualified if they fall into poverty, even while working. According to the bill, workers must be able to "demonstrate average income or resources that are not less than 125 percent of the Federal poverty level throughout the period of admission as a registered provisional immigrant." This also reinforces dependency on employers, who will have an incentive to goad workers into hyperproductivity to maintain the minimal threshold of income.

Not only will this arrangement be profitable for employers, who can still keep wages low, but it will also be lucrative for the state. Since these workers will have to pay taxes, they will continue to subsidize the U.S. economy and fill government coffers without the right to get benefits from government programs. This is already the experience for the undocumented. For instance, a 2013 study revealed that immigrants contributed an estimated $115.2 billion more to Medicare than they took out in the years 2002–2009.[22]

After immigrant workers complete ten years under this status—and if the border control effectiveness rate of 90 percent is achieved—they can then apply for Legal Permanent Residence. After three years in this secondary status, they can then apply for citizenship. The whole process amounts to thirteen-plus years of walking a tightrope without a single slip-up—guaranteeing a stable, low-wage, noncitizen workforce into the next generation.

No Relief for Undocumented Youth

While the proposal allows for shorter waiting periods for undocumented youth, they must still endure a long delay. Young people who were eligible under the DREAM Act proposal and under Barack Obama's Deferred Action for Childhood Arrivals executive order can also transition to Registered Provisional Status. If they acquire a high school diploma, or complete two years of college or four years of military service, they can get five years off the waiting period (Section 2103). Still, for youth to have to wait eight years to become eligible for citizenship is a step backward from the growing momentum and high level of support, gained through several years of high-profile and heroic activism, for expedited citizenship for undocumented youth.[23]

Blue Card Status: Indentured Servitude for the Twenty-First Century

Another form of labor subjugation embedded in the bill is the Blue Card status of the Agriculture Worker Program. To deal with the persistent labor shortages wracking U.S. agriculture due to stringent internal immigration enforcement and perpetually low wages, the bill creates a special classification, under which agricultural workers will be bound to growers. Under this program, agricultural workers who have engaged in agriculture for at least two years prior to the legislation *and* who agree to work in agriculture for at least a hundred days a year for five years can qualify for permanent legal residence at the end of that five-year period. After three more years of residency, they can apply for citizenship.

Since agricultural workers must show consistent documentation of farm work provided by employers, this makes them beholden to growers.

Reminiscent of indentured servitude in the days when America was a colony ruled by Britain, the Blue Card status is designed to keep a cheap and exploitable workforce in place and bound to employers, especially during harvesting season, in exchange for being allowed to apply for citizenship. This will perpetuate a largely unorganized agricultural workforce and ensure that farm work continues to be the lowest-paying and most dangerous work in the U.S. economy—for the benefit of agriculture profits.[24]

High-Tech Exploitation

As for future migration, the bill would overhaul the visa system in favor of those with higher levels of education and technical skills, aligned with the needs of the U.S. economy. The new "merit-based system" for determining who gets into the U.S. would allow for up to 250,000 visas, distributed based on a point system. The most points would go to those with the highest levels of education, to entrepreneurs, to those who speak English fluently, to the young, and to those with skills in "high-demand industries." Unlike the Registered Provisional Immigrants, these "top-tiered" immigrants would enter immediately as Legal Permanent Residents.

This provision can be understood as a concession to the high-tech industry, exemplified by the lobbying group FWD.us. Fronted by Facebook founder Mark Zuckerberg and including industry heavies like Microsoft, Google, and Intel, FWD.us describes itself as "a diverse group of leading innovators, job creators, business owners and founders from Silicon Valley's tech sector."[25]

In reality, say critics of this program, high-tech companies face a dwindling pool of U.S. workers with the requisite skills, and so they want the merit-based system as a way to expand the current, more limited version of the H-1B visa system. According to the *Washington Post*:

> [S]ome experts say these big firms have been using the system to pay foreign-born employees less than their American counterparts, and that immigrant workers with H-1B visas end up being completely beholden to their employers. The path to a green card that confers permanent legal residence can take years, and workers in the middle of the process are often loath to switch companies—an enormous advantage for companies that want to retain workers.[26]

A second track of merit-based visas favors employment-based applicants (along with their families) whose applications have been pending five years or more under the current system.

While the merit-based visa system will expand the number of skilled workers getting visas, the number of family-based visas will remain the same (480,000). The legislation also removes the category for sibling-based family migration and for married sons or daughters of U.S. citizens who are over thirty years of age.

Workers who are not tech-savvy, highly educated, or wealthy get bumped into lower "non-immigrant" temporary worker categories. This includes the W visa and the Non-Immigrant Agricultural Worker Program, which are also referred to as "guest worker" programs.

You Can Work, but You Can't Stay

Working-class immigrants employed in manual labor jobs make up the largest proportion of immigrants in the U.S. They are concentrated in low-wage industries and have been historically excluded from legal paths to immigration, making them the largest proportion of the undocumented population since they tend to find long-term employment—two-thirds of undocumented workers have been in the U.S. for over ten years—and establish family roots.[27]

The exclusion of pathways to citizenship for working-class undocumented immigrants will continue in the form of a new guest-worker program. This will allow for the creation of a vast army of noncitizen labor, used by employers to expand the low-wage sectors of the economy.

The W visa program (Section 7401) and Non-Immigrant Agricultural Worker visa (Section 2232) are based on the needs of industries that employ "unskilled" workers. These industries can petition the government on the basis of what they describe as labor shortages, with caps varying by industry but expandable.

To qualify, workers must apply in their home country and can be granted a renewable three-year work permit. With the W visa, guest workers can only work for registered employers. Although they can leave an employer and seek work elsewhere, it must be with another registered company. With the NAIW visa, workers must have three years of previous experience in U.S. agriculture, and they can be as young as sixteen. Agricultural workers entering through a contract with an employer can only work for that employer for the duration of the contract, and the employer also has the right to terminate the contract unilaterally. "At-will workers" can be admitted but must work for registered employers.

In reality, there is no shortage of "unskilled" labor in the U.S. Employers, with the complicity of the state, have leveraged the vulnerabilities of undocumented workers to create lower wage floors in multiple sectors of the economy, such as agriculture, food service, landscaping, construction, and domestic service. Nevertheless, immigrant worker mobility and the willingness of some to fight for better wages, conditions, and union representation are clearly a threat to employers in these sectors.[28]

That's why they look to the bipartisan immigration "reform" proposal. With these guest-worker programs, industries can count on a permanent stream of workers bound to their industries, without the right to establish roots or engage in political activities. What's more, workers cannot be unemployed for longer than sixty consecutive days. If they cannot find work, they must leave voluntarily or be subject to forced removal. Like the old-fashioned Bracero programs, this places power in the employer's hands to determine wages, conditions, and length of employment.

The Limits of Reform under Neoliberal Capitalism

Repressing people's movement and restricting their ability to work, participate in the political process, and integrate into society serves only the interests of big business. Immigrant workers have historically subsidized the economic development and expansion of the U.S. economy, and today is no different. S. 744 is designed to continue this process while at the same time hurtling society backward by introducing new forms of segregation and exclusion through the cynical manipulation of citizenship.

Immigrant workers have historically used a human rights and labor rights framework to advance their own vision for social inclusion. The mass marches, strikes, boycotts, and sit-ins for immigrant rights over the last decade have demonstrated this with slogans emphasizing unconditional legalization, family unification, and full and equal rights.

Because of immigrant rights activism, the most reactionary pieces of immigration legislation—like the Sensenbrenner bill—have been defeated. But sustained action culminating in an alternative platform for unconditional legalization has not materialized. Instead, elections and the empty promises of Democratic Party politicians have drawn activists away from the streets and into electoral strategies that have hit a dead end.

This most recent manifestation of "comprehensive immigration reform" illustrates the problem. Without an immigrant rights–based social movement to push the process forward, toward a more just and humane resolution, anti-immigrant reactionaries have felt confident to push the whole process off the rails.

Immigrant Rights at a Crossroads

To try to make sense out of why immigration reform has failed to materialize since the election of Barack Obama and the Democratic congressional majority in 2008, we have to look beyond the oversimplification that Washington partisanship is solely to blame. The onset of economic recession transformed the landscape, with immigration politics being pushed into the background and pre-2008 political alignments and arrangements wiped away.

Instead of a comprehensive restructuring of immigration policy providing a path to citizenship, a new consensus has taken shape within the U.S. ruling class—expressed through both political parties—that real reform be taken off the table. Instead of providing a path to legalization, the preferable modus operandi in the context of a crisis of capitalism is keeping immigrant workers mired in the conditions of social marginalization.

In other words, the status quo has been the best-case scenario for maximum profitability at a time of economic instability, since the maintenance of a persecuted section of the working class can be used to leverage lower wages and working conditions against other sections of the labor force. This became especially possible after the repression and decline of immigrant worker organizing, which coincided with the movement's organizational leadership (unions, liberal nongovernmental organizations, and so forth) leading the movement into the Democratic Party, which in turn subordinated it to the needs of capital. Economic instability and persistent unemployment during and after the recession and ten years of persistent state repression have severely weakened and subdued the immigrant workers' movement.

This can explain why both political parties have closed ranks to endorse the "enforcement-only" approach to immigration ("enforcement through attrition"), while at the same time maintaining a sizeable undocumented worker population. If right-wing demagogues had been unsuccessful in efforts to pass more extremist measures at the congressional level by 2016, it is because the politics of immigrant scapegoating have failed to find a hearing with a large majority of the U.S. working class.

This is why the anti-immigrant movement has since shifted efforts to more conservative states where traditions of Jim Crow racism still infect the body politic. At the same time, the electoral strategy that linked immigrant rights to campaigning for the Democratic Party has also hit a dead end, demoralizing many Latino supporters of the Obama administration and rights activists who believed meaningful reform would quickly emerge from a Democratic congressional majority in 2008.[1] The failure and unwillingness of the Democratic Party leadership to present an alternative to the neoliberal and enforcement-only approach more cogently pursued by the Republican Party demoralized the voters who turned out in 2008.[2] This can help explain why the anti-immigrant right wing was able to regroup within the Republican Party as part of the Tea Party insurgency in 2010. It can also explain why in 2016 Trump could appropriate the mantle of anti-immigration, and reanimate and mobilize the previously weakened and demoralized right wing to the polls.

In the era of Trump, anti-immigration politics have elevated a right-wing demagogue and Congress, who now have access to the vast machinery of immigrant worker oppression that developed in a bipartisan way. Meanwhile, the targeting of immigrant workers continues under the aegis of the Department of Homeland Security (DHS) and state governments across the country. While the immigrant rights movement had demobilized by 2008, the potential for rebuilding the mass movement has been rekindled by substantial opposition to Trump and the Right.

Popular Opinion in Support of Immigrants

Current immigration policy is limited to enforcement-only measures, which have been largely moved out of the public eye. To understand why immigration politics have been toned down, it is necessary to examine two significant and overlapping factors. First, there is the lack of substantial support on a national level for an intensive campaign against immigrants. In other words, a majority of working people see the failing economy, unemployment, and widening inequality as the main source of their hardship, not immigrants. Secondly, a substantial, contained population of undocumented workers have become indispensable and highly profitable for U.S. capital, even more so at a time of economic stagnation. The disconnect between public opinion and the representatives of the two capitalist parties is reflected in polls over the last ten years. Furthermore, the mass mobilizations not only shifted public opinion but also demoralized the Far Right. This has been reflected in a substantial deterioration of support for anti-immigrant organizations after 2006.

Polls have demonstrated two trends over the last several years: a consistent level of support for legalization and a decline in scapegoating of immigrants for the economy's problems. A 2009 Pew Research Center poll showed that 63 percent of the population supported a "path to citizenship" for the nation's undocumented workforce.[3] A May 2009 CNN poll found that two out of three respondents supported legalization.[4] A May 2010 CNN/Opinion Research Corporation poll found that while there is a substantial increase in support for enforcement measures (reflecting the enforcement-only trajectory in the media and politics), 81 percent of respondents nationally support "creating a program that would allow illegal immigrants already living in the United States for a number of years to stay here and apply to legally remain in this country permanently if they had a job and paid back taxes."[5] A December 2011 Fox News poll found that 66 percent of national respondents (including 57 percent of Republicans) supported a path to citizenship, leading even Fox to concede "the GOP candidates are largely at odds with voters of their party."[6]

While a consistent majority supports legalization, there is less of an appetite to focus on immigration enforcement, a theme that Republican presidential candidates have rehashed on the campaign trail. A January 2012 *Washington Post*/ABC News poll showed that 51 percent of respondents believed that politicians should focus on jobs and the economy, with only 1 percent believing that immigration was their main presidential issue.[7] A January 2012 Pew poll revealed a decreasing percentage of potential voters who believed that "illegal immigration" was a top priority (55 percent in 2007, 39 percent in 2012), whereas the desire for a focus on job creation increased from 57 percent to 82 percent over the same period.[8]

By 2016, on the eve of the election of Donald Trump, 88 percent of respondents to a national Gallup poll believed that undocumented immigrants living in the U.S. should have the chance to become citizens if they met requirements. Sixty-six percent opposed or strongly opposed the deportation of undocumented people, while the same percentage, 66 percent, opposed the expansion of the border wall.[9]

In California, which has the largest immigrant population in the nation, the numbers are also revealing. Seventy-five percent of California respondents to a USC–*Los Angeles Times* poll believed that undocumented immigrants already in the U.S. should have the right to remain in the country, increasing to 90 percent amongst those aged eighteen to twenty-nine.[10] After the election of Trump, Californians reversed their majority sentiment opposing "sanctuary cities," now shifting in favor. A poll in 2015, for instance, showed that 74 percent of respondents to a UC Berkeley study opposed the practice of some cities refusing compliance with federal immigration enforcement. A 2017 poll, carried out by the same research institution, found that 70 percent of Californians *supported* sanctuary policies.[11]

This sample of polls reveals the dissonance between common people and the representatives of capital and the Far Right. As the large-scale mobilizations of the Occupy movement of 2012 and significant public support for the protests and encampments showed, the crisis of capitalism was directing popular sentiment against corporate greed and rising inequality, not toward immigrants.[12] This was validated in electoral defeats for the Far Right in Arizona and in the 2012 presidential elections.

In the 2012 Republican primaries, far-right candidate Michele Bachmann called for sealing the U.S.-Mexico border with a double wall. Not to be outdone, Herman Cain called for a deadly electrified fence backed by military personnel armed with live rounds. Mitt Romney chastised Rick Perry for supporting a Texas law that allows undocumented college students to pay in-state tuition rates. Perry, for his part, accused Romney of employing undocumented landscapers on his property as a means to tarnish his credentials. The pile-up on immigration stood in stark contrast to the fact that more people were much more concerned with the economy. According to an October 2012 Gallup poll, for instance, only 2 percent saw immigration as their main concern.[13]

After Mitt Romney won the nomination, he pursued the same course, making anti-immigration a central plank of his platform. He hired the architect of the "attrition through enforcement" doctrine, Kris Kobach, to advise his campaign. As he stated in a January 2012 presidential debate how he would address the issue of immigration, Romney expressed his intention to continue repressing undocumented immigrants until they "self-deported" as a whole, claiming:

> The answer is self-deportation, which is people decide they could do better by going home because they can't find work here because they don't have legal documentation to allow them to work here.[14]

The right-wing lurch by Romney failed to generate a surge at the polls, instead turning out a larger number of Latinos to vote against him. Nevertheless, the reelection of Barack Obama did little to advance the cause of legalization, which was largely scrapped while the "enforcement through attrition" approach was tacitly embraced.

At the federal level, the harshest anti-immigrant efforts failed for lack of support. Legalization, albeit broadly supported, failed due to the lack of political appetite and effort amongst Democrats once in office. The locus of immigration politics shifted away from the national legislative forum and into less representative arenas. The Obama administration ramped up enforcement measures through DHS directives, and anti-immigrant partisans shifted tack to focus on passing anti-immigrant measures piecemeal through conservative state legislatures, where these politics could be propelled forward with less opposition.

Nevertheless, even in the most reactionary environments, the anti-immigrant Right also suffered setbacks. Russell Pearce, Arizona State Senate president and the national anti-immigrant lightning rod who orchestrated the passage of anti-immigrant legislation SB 1070, became the first state lawmaker in Arizona history and the first Senate president of any state to be recalled. Latino voters, most of whom supported the recall effort, accounted for 13 percent of the recall electorate. Since Pearce's Republican rival, Jerry Lewis, won 53.4 percent to 45.3 percent, a large segment of his own base voted against Pearce. According to the *Arizona Republic*, a conservative-leaning newspaper, "Poll respondents who voted against Pearce said they chose to recall the legislator, who was the state Senate president, because they felt that their representatives needed to focus less on immigration and more on jobs and the economy."[15] The outcome even led anti-immigrant demagogue Tom Tancredo to conclude that the outcome could have a "chilling effect" on like-minded (anti-immigrant) politicians in the short term.[16]

Declining Material Support for Anti-Immigrant Organizations

A third way of understanding public attitudes toward immigration politics has to do with the level of material support for anti-immigrant organizations. National trends during and after the Great Recession show a substantial decrease in both active members and monetary donations. During this period, popular sentiment and frustration was focused on economic instability and social inequality.[17] This is illustrated by the fact that nearly 60 percent of Americans supported the anti-corporate Occupy Wall Street movement at the same time that there was declining support for anti-immigrant organizations.[18] According to the Institute for Research and Education on Human Rights:

- The membership of the anti-immigrant Federation for American Immigration Reform fell by 58 percent from a high in 2007 to its lowest membership in 2011.
- The total gross receipts for ten established nativist organizations fell by 28 percent from 2008 to 2009.
- The number of Minuteman organizations dropped by more than half, down from 115 local chapters in 2010 to fifty-three local groups in 2011.
- The number of active local anti-immigrant groups fell 62 percent, from 320 in 2010 to 121 in 2011.[19]

The failure of the nativist movement to develop a substantial base in the working class has caused the hard core of the movement to change its strategy. Anti-immigrant organizers, funders, and demagogues have moved the focus of their campaigns out of the streets and into Tea Party electoral formations, where they have found a welcome home for their racial politics. Since they have not been able to cultivate a mass movement, they have shifted to the ballot box where there is more passive support.

The space opened up by the far right-wing Tea Party movement has allowed the nativists to push their agenda into state politics, especially in those areas where Jim Crow racism is still prevalent. Since the Tea Party is funded by the right-wing sections of the capitalist class and supported by a small but highly mobilized base of middle-class supporters, this relationship has allowed anti-immigrant politics to proceed at the state level where these formations wield more influence.[20] This has driven conflict over immigration into the heart of the Republican Party in these regions, where some sections of big business, especially agriculture and construction, have been adversely affected by the diminished pool of immigrant labor.[21]

For example, despite the declining public support for anti-immigrant politics, the National Conference of State Legislators reports that state lawmakers introduced more than 1,600 bills and resolutions relating to immigration and immigrants in 2011, up from about 1,400 in 2010.[22] If a survey of electoral trends shows that the majority of the population does not perceive anti-immigrant politics in their interest, at least at this point, then why do these measures advance? The dominant narrative attributes the impasse to partisan gridlock.[23]

Despite this conventional wisdom of Washington beltway politics, there are plenty of legislative techniques for bypassing gridlock. Even with legislative opposition, Obama could have halted deportations or suspended Homeland Security's various enforcement programs through an executive order pending legislative resolution. The fact is that immigration reform was never even brought onto the floor of either house of Congress for debate, a process that could have opened up a wider discussion and encouraged mobilization of public opinion. Obama himself revealed why he dropped his first major policy proposal. According to the Associated Press:

> Immigration reform was an issue Obama promised Latino groups that he would take up in his first year in office. But several hard realities—a tanked economy, a crowded agenda, election-year politics and lack of political will—led to so much foot-dragging in Congress that, ultimately, Obama decided to set the issue aside.[24]

The lack of a political appetite to advance immigration reform can be at least partially attributed to the changing priorities of the U.S. ruling class when the economy entered into recession in 2007–2008. Despite campaign promises for immigration reform to the Latino community, the Democratic Party quickly abandoned the issue, especially after the effects of the 2008 recession deepened. Instead, the war on all workers was accelerated, with immigrant workers the softest target.

Sustaining a criminalized segment of the workforce has proven instrumental for the 1 percent in sustaining higher profits through increased exploitation of immigrant labor. Since immigrant workers are integrated into many industries across the economy, maintaining this population in subjugation works to hold down other workers. Furthermore, anti-immigrant politics have served as a useful tool for conservative politicians in states like Arizona, Alabama, and Georgia to cut social spending under the guise of immigration enforcement.

The repression of immigrant workers takes place against the backdrop of an intensification of class warfare, especially against those segments of workers organized into unions and where collective resistance has been the strongest. For example, Republican governors across the Midwest have been pushing laws to abolish or weaken both public and private unions.[25] This is now being promoted at the national level under the Trump administration. Democratic governors have also done their part, pushing savage budget cuts, cutting pensions, and serving up mass layoffs of public-sector, unionized workers.[26] The demobilization of immigrant workers has become a key aspect of this strategy.

Capitalist Crisis and Immigration

During the Great Recession, roughly 2007 to 2010, an average of about 150,000 Mexican workers crossed the border into the United States each year, compared with 500,000 annually during the first half of the last decade.[27] Capitalist crisis, more than any border-enforcement policy, explains the decline in immigration, even as restrictionist politicians tried to take credit for the immigration slowdown. According to Juan Luis Ordaz, senior economist for the Bancomer Foundation, "The arrests on the border are moving like the U.S. economic cycle."[28] In other words, there was a decline in migration as the recession decreased the number of job opportunities. Because of their social marginalization and vulnerable economic position, the capitalist crisis has hit migrants in the United States the hardest. Despite the fluctuations, the criminalization and "strategic" deportation of immigrant workers continued unabated.

The poverty rate for Latino immigrants increased as low-income jobs dried up and those at the bottom were squeezed the hardest by unemployment. For example, especially hard hit in the economic downturn were the home-building and construction industries, which employ a large percentage of undocumented workers. According to migration scholar German Vega of the Colegio de la Frontera Norte in Tijuana, "Migration has decreased because employment opportunities in the United States are not good. Fewer migrants have full-time jobs. Hours are reduced. Wages are lower. The amount of money they send home is less."[29] Their vulnerable status under capitalism, which has been reinforced by punitive political policy, has suppressed Latino/a immigrant wages and working conditions.

Nationally, Latinos in general have the highest poverty rates, while most poverty is concentrated in Latino immigrant families. According to the Pew Hispanic Center, Latinos have seen the greatest decline in household wealth, compared to other racial or ethnic groups, as a result of recession. From 2005 to 2009, median household wealth among Latinos fell by 66 percent, compared with a drop of 53 percent among Blacks and 16 percent among whites.[30] According to the Bureau of Labor Statistics, the unemployment rate among Latinos in December 2011 was 11 percent, up from 6.3 percent at the start of the Great Recession in December 2007. Over the same period, the national unemployment rate increased from 5 percent to 8.5 percent.[31] Between 2006 and 2010, the poverty rate among Latinos increased nearly 6 percentage points, more than any other group, from 20.6 percent to a high point of 26.6 percent.[32] Latino children now have the highest rate of poverty, reaching 30 percent in 2010, and 36 percent by 2015.[33]

East of San Diego, the border community of El Centro typifies this effect. More than 80 percent of the city's 42,500 residents are Latino, with a large percentage of Latino immigrant workers concentrated in agriculture and construction. Since these two industries have been hard hit by the recession, the unemployment rate has climbed to 28 percent, one of the highest in the country for a city of that size.[34] The degrading of immigrant workers extends beyond systemic economics. Employers also exploit their vulnerabilities in other, more direct ways.

Over two-thirds of low-wage immigrant workers experienced "at least one pay-related violation" in the work week reported, according to a 2011 survey conducted by the Center for Urban Economic Development, the National Employment Law Project, and the UCLA Institute for Research on Labor and Employment. Furthermore, 26 percent of workers were paid less than the legal minimum wage; 76 percent of employees who worked overtime were not paid the legally required overtime rate;

70 percent of workers who performed work outside of their regular shifts did not receive any pay for this work; and 30 percent of tipped workers were not paid the tipped minimum wage.[35]

So what is the result of such efforts to drive down the standard of living of immigrants? Sociologists Doug Massey and Julia Gelatt of Princeton University reveal that the result is higher profitability. According to their research, "the average wages of Mexican-born immigrants in the U.S., adjusted for inflation, were no higher in 2007, on the eve of the Great Recession, than they were in the early 1960s." Furthermore, the research shows that

> between 1950 and 1970—a more welcoming era for immigrants in the US—the average hourly wages of Mexican-born workers rose in tandem with the wages of native-born whites and Mexican Americans, though immigrant wages were lower overall. But from 1970 to 1990, it shows, the wages of native-born Mexicans in the US dropped to early 1960s levels (about $15 per hour in today's dollars), and have been stuck there ever since.[36]

Massey and Gelatt point out that the intensification of enforcement, beginning in 1986 with the passage of the Immigration Reform and Control Act under President Ronald Reagan and continuing in bipartisan fashion through to the Obama administration, is to blame for the stagnant wages of Mexicans in the United States.

> The structural shift, we argue, stems substantially from the rising share of undocumented migrants and increasing exploitation and exclusion on the basis of legal status during the 1990s, followed by increasing marginalization of all immigrants in the context of a deteriorating economy after 2000.[37]

They conclude:

> [A] plausible account . . . is that US immigration policy evolved to generate a larger population of people without labor rights in the United States, inducing scrupulous employers to exclude undocumented migrants as well as those who look like they might be undocumented, while at the same time providing unscrupulous employers with new leverage to increase exploitation of all workers, both documented and undocumented.[38]

Like the relationship between capital investment and displacement, migration and criminalization are integrated parts of the profit equation.

This fits into the larger patterns of capital accumulation in recent years. There has been a concerted effort over the past few decades to increase the rate of profitability by pushing down wages and the standard of living for all workers in the United States. This is a response to increased competition internationally and a declining share of the world market for U.S. corporations. According to the McKinsey Global Institute:

> In 1999, the web of cross-border investments centered on the United States, which was partner to 50 percent in all outstanding international financial positions. By 2009, the US share of total cross-border investments had shrunk to 32 percent. . . . Prior to the 2008 financial crisis, cross-border investments between Latin America, emerging Asia, and the Middle East were growing at 39 percent annually—roughly twice as fast as these regions' investments with developed countries.[39]

The investigative website Remapping Debate illustrated how the Obama administration adhered to this policy, even as the president appeared to strike a populist tone in the run-up to the 2012 elections. As part of an effort to decelerate outsourcing and increase manufacturing, the administration promoted a study that shows a trend of increasing productivity and declining wages as a favorable development. This, combined with rising labor costs in China, holds out the possibility that U.S. corporations might "return home" if labor costs continue to plummet. The study, produced by the Boston Consulting Group,

> claimed that rising labor costs in China combined with the fact that the United States "is becoming a lower-cost country" would "virtually close the cost gap" between the two countries for many goods. It went on to say that "when all costs are taken into account, certain US states, such as South Carolina, Alabama, and Tennessee, will turn out to be among the least expensive production sites in the industrialized world."[40]

In fact, U.S. productivity has been outpacing wage increases consistently since 1970.[41] The other faces of labor suppression, from the full-frontal assault on workers' rights in Wisconsin, Indiana, and other states, to the repression of immigrant workers through the aegis of law enforcement, connect the different facets of the war on workers that is raging in U.S. society. In each case, the 1 percent and its enforcers aim to divide the working class amidst the economic crisis, by turning workers against each other.

But the ratcheting up of immigration enforcement is doing nothing to alleviate the economic crisis for other workers. In fact, it is deepening the crisis. As previously mentioned, Arizona became a flashpoint for the repression of immigrants. It was also one of the states hardest hit by the recession. Under the conditions of crisis, high unemployment, and a visible migrant population, anti-immigrant politics found a hearing. For this reason, anti-immigrant groups like the Minutemen flocked to Arizona, and reactionary and opportunistic Republicans launched political careers off the backs of undocumented workers and their families, attempting to generate public antipathy toward an immigrant presence.

Even though a broad array of anti-immigrant policies had been implemented in Arizona, it has done nothing to improve conditions for citizens. According to the *Arizona Republic*, job opportunities for college graduates in the state have continued to plummet even amidst the crackdown on immigrants. In 2007, 51 percent of graduates found work; by 2009 this number had dropped to 20 percent.[42] After waging a public campaign to purge undocumented immigrants from state welfare rolls, Governor Jan Brewer then proceeded to cut the state's Medicaid program by $500 million, pushing an estimated 100,000 low-income Arizonans off the program rolls.[43]

In 2010, Arizona had the second-highest foreclosure rate in the nation with 1 in 17 housing units, or 5.73 percent, receiving at least one foreclosure filing. The state had a total of 155,878 foreclosures. By 2010, more than 50 percent of the homeowners in the Phoenix area owed more than their home was worth and were "underwater" on their mortgages.[44]

In Alabama, another anti-immigrant law (HB 56, the so-called Hammon-Beason Alabama Taxpayer and Citizen Protection Act) allowed for local police to check the immigration status of people detained, required public school officials to collect data on the number of undocumented children enrolling, and forbade undocumented immigrants from entering into private contracts or conducting any business with the state.[45] The first assessment of the law has shown its harmful effects. The fear of arrest sowed terror in the immigrant community, which fled in droves.[46] It also exposed the hollowness of the idea that the expulsion of immigrants would create jobs for citizens. Instead, the law could cost Alabama up to $11 billion in GDP and nearly $265 million in state income and sales tax (since fewer than nine of every hundred of the eighty thousand jobs vacated were being filled by unemployed legal residents and citizens), according to Dr. Samuel Addy of the Center for Business and Economic Research.[47]

The crisis of capitalism and continued attacks on the standard of living of most Alabamans, Arizonans, and other working and poor people across the country sets the backdrop for the further criminalization of immigrants.

Continuity of Enforcement through Attrition in the Obama Years

The conditions of economic downturn and intensifying competition internationally have exerted greater pressures on the U.S. capitalist class to extract even more surplus value from workers. The suppression of the immigrant segment of the working class is one important facet of this overall strategy.

As fewer immigrants have entered the United States during the recession, even fewer have returned to their country of origin since then.[48] The average undocumented worker has spent at least ten years in the United States, developed roots, and is often raising U.S.-born children.[49] Many have little incentive to return to their country of origin, especially Mexico and Central America, where the crisis has been even harder felt.[50] For example, a February 2012 National Autonomous University of Mexico report has documented that the cost of living for the Mexican working class has risen while wages have dropped precipitously over the years 2001 to 2011. For example:

> Mexican workers earning the daily minimum wage had to toil 11.38 hours in December 2011 to buy a basic basket of commodities, compared with the 9.55 hours of work necessary to buy the same group of products in December 2001. . . . The study reported that the daily minimum wage in Mexico lost 24.42 percent of its consumer punch in the ten-year period analyzed. . . . In sum, more than 60 percent of Mexican workers struggle to get by on wages that hover between $5 and $15 each day.[51]

Under the successive administrations of Bush and Obama, and now under Trump, there has been no attempt to create a workable policy that addresses economic displacement stemming from trade policies. This increases the likelihood of future displacement and migration into the United States, especially as neoliberal policies are intensified on a regional scale.[52] Instead, the emphasis continues to be placed on enforcement only. This has included expanding the border wall, the incorporation of military technology and tactics, increases in enforcement personnel, and the expansion of immigration enforcement into the domestic sphere.

The U.S. government currently spends about $66 billion annually on immigration and border enforcement, totaling more than $400 billion spent between the years 1987 and 2016.[53] The greatest increase occurred between the Bush and Obama administrations. A DHS report outlining the Obama administration's accomplishments in "securing the Southwest border" bragged that the number of Border Patrol agents increased "from approximately 10,000 in 2004 to more than 21,000 today with nearly 18,500 'boots on the ground' along the Southwest border," deploying "dual detection canine teams as well as non-intrusive inspection systems, Mobile Surveillance Systems, Remote Video Surveillance Systems, thermal imaging systems, radiation portal monitors, and license plate readers to the Southwest border."[54]

The United States has also added 413 miles of new fencing to its southern boundary since 2006, raising to 650 miles the total length of border.[55] The Customs and Border Protection agency has also added a fleet of Predator drones and high-tech blimps that it now uses for border surveillance.[56] Since the border is designated as a War on Terror conflict zone, new military technologies have been incorporated into enforcement, and in some cases the border provides a useful testing ground.

Within the United States, the machinery of enforcement and detention has been greatly expanded. Immigration and Customs Enforcement (ICE), for example, extracts individuals or small groups of immigrants from their communities, homes, schools, workplaces, parks, public transit, supermarkets, and other sites with such tactical stealth so as not to alarm the public, attract the media, or disrupt business as usual. Deportations reached record levels under President Obama, rising to an annual average of nearly four hundred thousand since 2009 (with that number now the quota)—about 30 percent higher than the annual average during the second term of the George W. Bush administration and about double the annual average during his first term.[57]

During Obama's tenure, the total number of deportations under him topped 3.1 million people, surpassing the total of George W. Bush by one million.[58] What's more, most of the people deported had no criminal records. Of the 344,354 people deported in his final year of 2016, for example, 85 percent of those deported in 2016 had not been convicted of a crime or had criminal charges pending other than the violation of entering without authorization.[59] The ratcheting up of deportations was enabled by the expansion of ICE operations within the country during Obama's tenure. By 2012, the ICE budget as a portion of immigration enforcement spending increased from $3.1 billion to $6.3 billion. Total enforcement personnel increased from 41,001 to over 61,354, and there was a vast expansion of ICE offices, field operations, and detention centers throughout the interior of the country.[60]

Deportation targets a large section of the workforce for the sole reason of working without documents. For example, in California 53 percent of deportation proceedings in 2011 were based solely on that violation, up more than two thousand cases statewide from 2010. Meanwhile, the share of those deported charged with an aggravated felony has remained consistent at about 4 percent or less.[61]

The intensification of detention and deportation under the Obama administration was highlighted during a massive immigrant roundup at the end of March 2012. ICE agents detained 3,168 undocumented immigrants over the course of six days in a national operation across all fifty states, three territories, Puerto Rico, and the District of Columbia.[62] Dubbed Operation Cross Check, it was the largest single coordinated immigration sweep in U.S. history.

These national raids are taking place concurrently with the systematic, mass firings of undocumented workers through workplace "immigration audits," which began under the Obama administration in 2009. An audit requires an employer to verify employee documentation with ICE agents, and to fire those without papers or risk fines and penalties. There were over 2,300 companies audited in 2011.[63] There have been some recent instances of employers "self-auditing" at a time when their workers have tried to form or join unions, effectively using the audit as a union-busting tool.[64]

In practice, enforcement policy has done little to alter the realities of immigration. Rather, it leads to the increased isolation and oppression of immigrant workers. As a result, elements of Jim Crow era segregation are reinstituted in communities, cruel and unusual forms of punishment are invented, and federal immigration agents target, detain, and deport thousands of individuals each day across the border in an extrajudicial manner. Without legalization, immigrant workers have limited means to leverage their legal rights to challenge low wages and poor working conditions. Intensified internal enforcement, along with the conditions of vulnerability in a recessionary period, means that most workers will remain on the job but in conditions that breed fear and underconfidence. Under these conditions a substantial exploitable workforce can be maintained. This has led immigration expert Douglas Massey to conclude that "discrimination against a large number of Mexicans is mandated by federal law."[65]

Class Determines Mobility

While workers are persecuted, the wealthy move freely around the globe without fear of detention or deportation. For example, NAFTA reduced or eliminated restrictions for the free movement of capital, and by extension the owners of capital. U.S. investors have since extended their reach deep into the Mexican economy, owning or controlling large shares in many sectors of that country's industries. Large numbers of U.S. citizens have since followed, with little or no restriction on their movement.[66]

Investment in Mexico has been very profitable, while the extension of global production and distribution networks (vis-à-vis corporate supply chains) into previously sheltered markets has also been destructive. Not only have high productivity rates and low wages in Mexico provided a boon for U.S. investors, but illicit outflows to the sum of $50 billion a year have skyrocketed since NAFTA was implemented.[67]

According to a report from the Washington-based anti-corruption advocacy group Global Financial Integrity, at least $872 billion has flowed out of Mexico illegally between 1970 and 2010. Of that, $642.9 billion, or about 74 percent, result from so-called trade mispricing, such as companies manipulating export and import invoices.[68] NAFTA facilitated the siphoning off of vast quantities of wealth, much of it leaving Mexico in repatriated profits (legal and illegal). This helps explain the dramatic boom in out-migration, which becomes a second source of profitability as U.S. business exploits undocumented workers.

One of NAFTA's unstated aims was to attract displaced, cheap labor into the United States as a means to aid in the restructuring of the U.S. economy, asserts Ricardo Delgado Wise, director of development studies at the Universidad Autonoma de Zacatecas.[69] This form of "restructuring" is a euphemism for lowering wages and weakening unions to increase profitability. His studies on Mexican labor migration further reveal that Latino immigrant labor, through its high productivity and low wages, contributed 17 percent of total U.S. economic growth between 2000 and 2007. These immigrants receive about 30 percent less than they should receive in comparison to what they contribute.[70]

On the other hand, those with money can purchase mobility. The international 1 percent (the wealthiest of the wealthy) amounts to 185,795 individuals worldwide, with *at least* $30 million net worth each, and with a combined bank account of $25 trillion (38.5 percent of global household wealth), spread out in various forms and investments across the globe.[71] The global 1 percent and their capital know no boundaries. In fact, a person's legal mobility is determined by where he or she fits in the hierarchy of wealth. Money buys entry in various forms: assets, education, employment, and potential investments are all keys. The richest maintain properties in multiple nations, but they are not called immigrants. Others find gateways through privileged visas, trade agreements, or other means associated with their wealth or position.

In Britain, for instance, overseas "super-investors" who keep £5 million in a UK bank account are to be given the right to stay indefinitely in Britain after only three years, two years faster than the five-year wait imposed on every other migrant.[72] In the United States, the EB-5 visa program allows foreign investors to attain a green card for themselves and their families if they invest a minimum of $500,000 in a U.S.-based enterprise. Between fiscal years 2012 and 2013, more than eleven thousand immigrant investors provided a combined $5.8 billion in capital through the EB-5 visa program, up from $845 million in 2010. Many more investors arrive with other variants of the E-series visas, available to immigrants who make substantial investments (generally more than $100,000) in a business venture, which provides them with cross-border mobility.[73]

For example, in 2010 the State Department issued 1,965 E1 and E2 visas to wealthier Mexicans, a 49 percent increase since 2005. Furthermore, the number of Mexicans with college degrees working in the United States more than doubled between 2005 and 2010 to 1.1 million.[74] In 2009, 13.1 million Mexicans traveled to the United States, representing almost a quarter of the total foreign arrivals to the country (second only to Canada) and spending $8.3 billion, according to the U.S. Commerce Department.[75] Most come on business or tourist visas. According to a BBVA Bancomer research study on migration, 20 percent of people with doctoral degrees born in Mexico live in the United States. This number is greater than the number of researchers attached to Mexico's National System of Researchers.[76] This represents the mobility of Mexico's business and middle classes, whose education and dollars are valuable to U.S. capitalism through legal access, compared to the labor of the working classes, whose profitability is increased with persecution. While the recession has meant that fewer immigrants have entered the United States since 2008, those within the country have faced increased poverty.

Notes

Preface to the 2018 Edition. Trump and the Failure of Neoliberal Immigration Reform

1. See W. W. Chattanooga, "Divide and Conquer," *Economist*, July 8, 2015. Available online at http://www.economist.com/blogs/democracyinamerica/2015/07/donald -trumps-xenophobia?fsrc=scn/tw/te/bl/ed/divideandconquer.
2. From the text of "Executive Order Protecting the Nation from Foreign Terrorist Entry into The United States," White House Press Office, March 6, 2017. Available online at https://www.whitehouse.gov/the-press-office/2017/03/06/executive-order-protecting -nation-foreign-terrorist-entry-united-states.
3. See Molly Hennessy-Fiske and W. J. Hennigan, "U.S. Acknowledges Airstrike in Mosul, Where More Than 200 Iraqi Civilians Died," *Los Angeles Times*. March 25, 2017. Available online at http://www.latimes.com/world/middleeast/la-fg-iraq-mosul-airstrike -20170325-story.html.
4. See their report: "A Culture of Cruelty: Abuse and Impunity in Short-Term U.S. Border Patrol Custody," No More Deaths, 2011. Available online at http://forms.nomoredeaths .org/wp-content/uploads/2014/10/CultureOfCruelty-full.compressed.pdf
5. See "Deaths by Border Patrol since 2010 (as of September 2017)," Southern Border Communities Coalition. Available online at http://www.southernborder.org/deaths _by_border_patrol.
6. "Our Values on the Line: Migrant Abuse and Family Separation at the Border," Kino Border Initiative, 2015. Available online at http://jesuits.org/Assets/Publications /File/REPORT_2015_Our_Values_on_the_Line.pdf.
7. See Fernanda Santos, "She Showed Up Yearly to Meet Immigration Agents. Now They've Deported Her," *New York Times*, February 8, 2017. Available online at https://www.nytimes.com/2017/02/08/us/phoenix-guadalupe-garcia-de-rayos.html.
8. See Christine Hauser, "Woman Detained after Speaking about Deportation Fears Is Released," *New York Times,* March 10, 2017.
9. See Matt Hamilton, Richard Winton, and James Queally, "Border Patrol Detains 22-Year-Old Cal State L.A. Student Activist; Her Lawyer Says It Is Retaliation," *Los Angeles Times,* May 19, 2017. Available online at http://www.latimes.com/local/lanow /la-me-ln-immigration-activist-20170518-story.html.

10. See Kathleen Masterson, "Federal Judge Releases 2 Vermont Migrant Activists Arrested By ICE," WBUR News, March 27, 2017. Available online at http://www.wbur.org /news/2017/03/27/vermont-immigration-rights-activists-ice.

11. Michael D. Shear and Ron Nixon, "New Trump Deportation Rules Allow Far More Expulsions," *New York Times*, February 21, 2017. Available online at https://www .nytimes.com/2017/02/21/us/politics/dhs-immigration-trump.html.

12. See "Hate Groups Increase for Second Consecutive Year as Trump Electrifies Radical Right," Southern Poverty Law Center, February 15, 2017. Available online at https://www.splcenter.org/news/2017/02/15/hate-groups-increase-second-consecutive -year-trump-electrifies-radical-right.

13. Mark Berman and Samantha Schmidt, "He Yelled 'Get Out of My Country,' Witnesses Say, and Then Shot 2 Men from India, Killing One," *Washington Post*, February 24, 2017. Available online at https://www.washingtonpost.com/news/morning-mix /wp/2017/02/24/get-out-of-my-country-kansan-reportedly-yelled-before-shooting-2 -men-from-india-killing-one/?utm_term=.845d88e39f0b.

14. Damian Paletta, "Trump Pulls Back Threat to Shut Down Government over Border Wall—for Now," *Washington Post*, September 1, 2017. Available online at https://www .washingtonpost.com/news/wonk/wp/2017/09/01/trump-pulls-back-threat-to -shutdown-government-over-border-wall-for-now/?utm_term=.543e9e852265.

15. For a full list and description of U.S. free trade agreements, see Office of the United States Trade Representative, available online at https://ustr.gov/trade-agreements/free -trade-agreements.

16. For a full discussion of the origins, development, and effects of neoliberal policy in the U.S. and abroad, see David Harvey, *A Brief History of Neoliberalism* (New York: Oxford University Press, 2005).

17. See Natasha Lycia Ora Bannan, "Puerto Rico's Double Devastation: Hurricanes and Austerity," *Huffington Post*, September 26, 2017. Available online at https://www .huffingtonpost.com/entry/puerto-ricos-double-devastation-hurricanes-and-austerity _us_59ca850fe4b0cdc7733531b0.

18. As an example, Wal-Mart was found paying millions in bribes to Mexican politicians. See David Barstow and Alejandra Xanic von Bertrab, "The Bribery Aisle: How Wal-Mart Got Its Way in Mexico," *New York Times*, December 17, 2012. Available online at http://www.nytimes.com/2012/12/18/business/walmart-bribes-teotihuacan.html ?pagewanted=all.

19. Dave Gilson, "Overworked America: 12 Charts That Will Make Your Blood Boil," *Mother Jones*, July/August 2011. Available online at http://www.motherjones.com /politics/2011/06/speedup-americans-working-harder-charts.

20. "Union Membership Rate 10.7 Percent in 2016," Bureau of Labor Statistics, February 9, 2017. Available online at https://www.bls.gov/opub/ted/2017/union-membership-rate -10-point-7-percent-in-2016.htm.

21. "244 Million International Migrants Living Abroad Worldwide, New UN Statistics Reveal," United Nations: Sustainable Development Goals. Available online at http://www .un.org/sustainabledevelopment/blog/2016/01/244-million-international-migrants -living-abroad-worldwide-new-un-statistics-reveal/.

22. "Labor Force Characteristics of Foreign-Born Workers Summary," Bureau of Labor Statistics, May 19, 2016. Available online at https://www.bls.gov/news.release/forbrn.nr0.htm.

23. See Jie Zong and Jeanne Batalova, "Mexican Immigrants in the United States," Migration Policy Institute, March 17, 2016. Available online at http://www.migrationpolicy .org/article/mexican-immigrants-united-states; and Gabriel Lesser and Jeanne Batalova, "Central American Immigrants in the United States," Migration Policy Institute, April 5,

2017. Available online at http://www.migrationpolicy.org/article/central-american-immigrants-united-states#2.

24. See Walter Ewing, Daniel E. Martínez, and Rubén G. Rumbaut, "The Criminalization of Immigration in the United States," American Immigration Council, July 13, 2015. Available online at https://www.americanimmigrationcouncil.org/research/criminalization-immigration-united-states.

25. See Daniel González, "Obama Exceeds 2 Million Mark in Deportations," *Arizona Republic*, April 4, 2014.

26. See Jerry Markon, "Fewer Immigrants Are Entering the U.S. Illegally, and That's Changed the Border Security Debate," *Washington Post*, May 27, 2015. Available online at https://www.washingtonpost.com/politics/flow-of-illegal-immigration-slows-as-us-mexico-border-dynamics-evolve/2015/05/27/c5caf02c-006b-11e5-833c-a2de05b6b2a4_story.html; also Jie Zong and Jeanne Batalova, "Mexican Immigrants in the United States," Migration Policy Institute, March 17, 2016. Available online at http://www.migrationpolicy.org/article/mexican-immigrants-united-states.

27. Most calculations of "criminal immigrants" include nonviolent minor infractions or include those charged with "illegal re-entry," referring to those arrested after being deported. For examples, see Ana Gonzalez-Barrera and Jens Manuel Krogstad, "U.S. Deportations of Immigrants Reach Record High in 2013," Pew Research Center, October 2, 2014. Available online at http://www.pewresearch.org/fact-tank/2014/10/02/u-s-deportations-of-immigrants-reach-record-high-in-2013/; Elliot Young, "The Hard Truths about Obama's Deportation Priorities," *Nation*, March 1, 2017. Available online at http://www.huffingtonpost.com/entry/hard-truths-about-obamas-deportation-priorities_us_58b3c9e7e4b0658fc20f979e. Since Trump has taken office, see Hari Sreenivasan, "Half Targeted by ICE Had Traffic Convictions or No Record," *PBS News Hour*, April 30, 2017. Available online at http://www.pbs.org/newshour/bb/half-targeted-ice-traffic-convictions-no-record/.

28. For a breakdown of Trump's far-right base, see Nicholas Carnes and Noam Lupu, "It's Time to Bust the Myth: Most Trump Voters Were Not Working Class," *Washington Post*, June 5, 2017. Available online at https://www.washingtonpost.com/news/monkey-cage/wp/2017/06/05/its-time-to-bust-the-myth-most-trump-voters-were-not-working-class/?utm_term=.6ab46f356d81. For his big financial backers, see "Top Contributors, Federal Election Data for Donald Trump, 2016 Cycle," Center for Responsive Politics. Available online at Shttps://www.opensecrets.org/pres16/contributors?id=n00023864. See also Carrie Levine and Michael Beckel, "Billionaires and Corporations Helped Fund Donald Trump's Transition," Center for Public Integrity, February 23, 2017. Available online at https://www.publicintegrity.org/2017/02/23/20711/billionaires-and-corporations-helped-fund-donald-trumps-transition.

29. Small and middle-sized businesses profit immensely from the exploitation of immigrant labor, from food service to in-home health care to construction. Low wages allow for a rate of exploitation that allows stability in the middle class through the extraction of more surplus value than that extracted from citizen workers. Without this workforce, these businesses might otherwise lose market share against their larger competitors. Furthermore, their low-cost labor allows them to buy consumer goods more cheaply. As one study reported, "More [immigrant] workers also benefit Americans by lowering the prices of goods and services. By leaving more money in the pockets of consumers, Americans can buy more elsewhere in the economy, which creates demand for jobs in those areas." See David Bier, "How Immigration Benefits America's Middle Class," *The Hill*, March 9, 2015. Available online at http://thehill.com/blogs/pundits-blog/immigration/235003-how-immigration-benefits-americas-middle-class. For an example of how corporations exploit immigrant vulnerability, see Nina Bernstein, "Companies Use Immigration Crackdown

to Turn a Profit," *New York Times*, September 27, 2011. Available online at http://www.nytimes.com/2011/09/29/world/asia/getting-tough-on-immigrants-to-turn-a-profit.html.

30. For an example, see Joseph Hincks, "CEOs from More Than 400 Leading U.S. Companies Urge Trump to Keep DACA," *Fortune*, September 5, 2017. Available online at http://fortune.com/2017/09/05/daca-trump-dreamers-business-leaders/. For a state perspective, see also David Dyssegaard Kallick, "AZ Business Leaders: An Anti-immigrant Reputation Hurts Our Economy," *Huffington Post*. Available online at http://www.huffingtonpost.com/david-dyssegaard-kallick/az-business-leaders_b_5155368.html.

31. See "Consideration of Deferred Action for Childhood Arrivals (DACA)," U.S. Citizenship and Immigration Services, described online at https://www.uscis.gov/humanitarian/consideration-deferred-action-childhood-arrivals-daca.

32. See Priya Krishnakumar, Joe Fox, and Ally Levine, "What's Next for DACA and the Nearly 800,000 People Protected by It," *Los Angeles Times*, September 6, 2017. Available online at http://www.latimes.com/projects/la-na-pol-daca-future/.

33. On immigrant labor's contribution to the economy, see Daniel Costa, David Cooper, and Heidi Shierholz, "Facts about Immigration and the U.S. Economy," Economic Policy Institute, August 12, 2014. Available online at http://www.epi.org/publication/immigration-facts/.

34. See Eric Lipton, "Corporations Push for Immigration Legislation," *New York Times*, October 26, 2013. Available online at https://thecaucus.blogs.nytimes.com/2013/10/26/corporations-push-for-immigration-legislation/?_r=0; also Julia Preston, "The Big Money behind the Push for an Immigration Overhaul," *New York Times*, November 14, 2014. Available online at https://www.nytimes.com/2014/11/15/us/obama-immigration-policy-changes.html.

Preface

1. Marjorie Berry, "San Diego Speaks Out: '¡Sí Se Puede!'" *Socialist Worker*, April 14, 2006.

Part I. Introduction

1. Carey McWilliams, *North from Mexico* (Philadelphia: J.B. Lippincott Co., 1948), p. 175. See also Devra Weber, *Dark Sweat, White Gold: California Farm Workers, Cotton, and the New Deal* (Berkeley: University of California Press, 1994), pp. 97–98.

2. Cletus Daniel, "Labor Radicalism in Pacific Coast Agriculture" (PhD diss., University of Washington, 1972), p. 224.

Chapter One. Pinkertons, Klansmen, and Vigilantes

1. Robert Ingalls, *Urban Vigilantes in the New South: Tampa, 1882–1936* (Knoxville: University of Tennessee Press, 1988), p. xv.

2. Robert Goldstein, *Political Repression in Modern America, from 1870 to 1976* (Boston: Two Continents Publishing Group, 1978), p. 3.

3. Partial exceptions would include landowner violence in the Mezzogiorno and employer-hired assassins in Barcelona (1917–21).

4. Goldstein, *Political Repression*, p. 12.

5. In the same period, seven Blacks were lynched in the Northeast, seventy-nine in the Midwest, and thirty-eight in the far West. See W. Fitzhugh Brundage, *Lynching in the New South: Georgia and Virginia, 1880–1930* (Champaign-Urbana: University of Illinois Press, 1993), p. 8.

6. Stewart Tolnay and E. Beck, *A Festival of Violence: An Analysis of Southern Lynchings*,

1882–1930 (Urbana: University of Illinois Press, 1995), p. 100.

7. Ingalls, *Urban Vigilantes*, p. xviii.

8. Ibid., p. xvii.

9. E. Beck and Stewart Tolnay, "The Killing Fields of the Deep South: The Market for Cotton and the Lynching of Blacks, 1882–1930," *American Sociological Review* 55 (1990), pp. 526–39; and Tolnay and Beck, *A Festival of Violence*, p. 251.

10. Carey McWilliams, *Factories in the Field* (Boston: Little, Brown and Co., 1939), p. 137.

11. Quoted in Donald Fearis, "The California Farm Worker, 1930–1945" (PhD diss., UC Davis, 1971), p. 117.

12. W. Fitzhugh Brundage, "Introduction," in Brundage, ed., *Under Sentence of Death: Lynching in the South* (Chapel Hill: University of North Carolina Press, 1997), p. 4.

13. Ingalls, *Urban Vigilantes*, p. 206.

14. Ray Abrahams, *Vigilante Citizens: Vigilantism and the State* (Cambridge: Polity Press, 1998), p. 158.

15. Richard Brown, *Strain of Violence: Historical Studies of American Violence and Vigilantism* (New York: Oxford University Press, 1975), pp. 97 and 111.

16. It is important to emphasize, however, that a similar strain of plebian self-interest was evident in parts of the South, where "land-hungry white farmers also adopted terrorist methods as a means to shore up their increasingly vulnerable economic status.... By driving away black tenants [through lynchings and terror] and ostracizing the white farmers who rented to them, they hoped to create a labor shortage and force white landowners to employ only whites" (Brundage, *Lynching in the South*).

Chapter Two. White Savages

1. John Boessenecker, *Gold Dust and Gunsmoke* (New York: John Wiley, 1999), p. 113.

2. Cormac McCarthy, *Blood Meridian, or, The Evening Redness in the West* (New York: Random House, 1985). See the important discussion by Neil Campbell, "Liberty beyond Its Proper Bounds; Cormac McCarthy's History of the West in *Blood Meridian*," in Rick Wallach, ed., *Myth, Legend, Dust* (New York: Manchester University Press, 2000).

3. Richard Street, *Beasts of the Field* (Stanford, CA: Stanford University Press, 2004), p. 148.

4. Quoted in James Rawls and Walton Bean, *California: An Interpretative History* (Boston: McGraw-Hill, 2003), p. 153.

5. Kevin Starr, *California: A History* (New York: Modern Library, 2005), pp. 86–87.

6. Leonard Pitt, "'Greasers' in the Diggings," in Roger Daniels and Spencer Olin, eds., *Racism in California: A Reader in the History of Oppression* (New York: Macmillan, 1972), pp. 195–97.

7. Boessenecker, *Gold Dust*, pp. 68–69.

8. Ibid., p. 130. Boessenecker, a defender of the Anglo version of these events, is dogmatic that Flores, Daniels, and others were "pillagers, not patriots" (p. 133).

9. Ibid., p. 131.

10. Arthur Quinn, *Rivals: William Gwin, David Broderick, and the Birth of California* (New York: Crown Publishers, 1994), p. 108.

11. Robert Senkewicz, *Vigilantes in Gold Rush San Francisco* (Stanford, CA: Stanford University Press, 1985), p. 80.

12. Ibid., pp. 172–73.

Chapter Three. The Yellow Peril

1. Royce Delmatier, et al., *The Rumble of California Politics, 1848–1970* (New York: John

Wiley, 1970), p. 77.

2. William Locklear, "The Celestials and the Angels: A Study of the Anti-Chinese Movement in Los Angeles to 1882," *Southern California Quarterly* 42 (September 1960), pp. 239–54.

3. Alexander Saxton, *Indispensable Enemy: Labor and the Rise of the Anti-Chinese Movement in California* (Berkeley: University of California Press, 1971).

4. Pierton Dooner, *The Last Days of the Republic* (San Francisco: Amo Press, 1880), p. 257.

5. Cf. Victor Davis Hanson, *Mexifornia* (San Francisco: Encounter Books, 2003); Daniel Sheehy, *Fighting Immigration Anarchy* (Bloomington, IN: RoofTop Publishing, 2006); and Tom Tancredo and Jon Dougherty, *In Mortal Danger* (Nashville: WND Books, 2006).

6. Street, *Beasts of the Field*, pp. 311 and 319.

7. Saxton, *Indispensable Enemy*, p. 264.

8. Ibid.

9. Ibid., pp. 348–51.

10. Saxton, *Indispensable Enemy*, p. 205. On the formidable defenses of Chinatown, see p. 149.

11. Ibid., pp. 377–86.

12. As one Hayward grower observed during the debate on exclusion: "Our orchards and vineyards are the product of Chinese labor. Had not such labor been at our command, there would not now be one fruit tree or grapevine in the state … there would have been no fruit or canning factories, nor any immense wineries." Quoted in Fearis, "The California Farm Worker," pp. 51–52.

Chapter Four. "Swat a Jap"

1. Quoted in Thomas Walls, "A Theoretical View of Race, Class and the Rise of Anti-Japanese Agitation in California" (PhD diss., University of Texas, 1989), p. 215.

2. Saxton, *Indispensable Enemy*, pp. 251–52.

3. Kevin Starr, *Embattled Dreams: California in War and Peace: 1940–1950* (New York: Oxford University Press, 2002), p. 43; and Philip Fradkin, *The Great Earthquake and Firestorms of 1906* (Berkeley: University of California Press, 2006), pp. 297–98.

4. McWilliams, *Factories in the Field*, p. 112.

5. Ibid., pp. 113–14.

6. George Mowry, *The California Progressives* (Berkeley: University of California Press, 1951), p. 155.

7. Starr, *Embattled Dreams*, p. 49.

8. Ibid., p. 97.

9. Ibid., p. 105.

Chapter Five. The Anti-Filipino Riots

1. Quoted in H. Brett Melendy, "California's Discrimination against Filipinos, 1927–1935," in Daniels and Olin, *Racism in California*, p. 141.

2. Virtually all subaltern laboring groups in California have been victims of sexualized calumnies at one time or another. Carey McWilliams, for example, cites the case of Punjabi farmworkers in Live Oak in 1908 who were beaten and driven from their camp by local vigilantes for the supposed offense of "indecent exposure." The Chinese, Japanese, Armenians, IWWs, Okies, African-Americans, Arabs, and Mexicans were all portrayed by their enemies as "sexually depraved." See McWilliams, *Factories in the Field*, pp. 139–40.

3. Melendy, "California's Discrimination against Filipinos," in Daniels and Olin, *Racism in California*, pp. 144–45.

4. McWilliams, *Factories in the Field*, pp. 133 and 138.

5. Richard Meynell, "Little Brown Brothers, Little White Girls: The Anti-Filipino Hysteria of 1930 and the Watsonville Riots," *Passports* 22 (1998). Excerpts available at http://www.modelminority.com/article232.htlml, n.p.

6. Ibid.

7. Howard DeWitt, *Anti-Filipino Movements in California* (San Francisco: R and E Research Associates, 1976), p. 48.

8. Meynell, "Little Brown Brothers."

9. Ibid.

10. DeWitt, *Anti-Filipino Movements,* pp. 49–51.

11. Melendy, "California's Discrimination against Filipinos," in Daniels and Olin, *Racism in California,* pp. 148–51.

Chapter Six. The IWW versus the KKK

1. Quoted in Philip Foner, *The Industrial Workers of the World, 1905–1917* (New York: International Publishers, 1965), p. 191.

2. Ibid., p. 186.

3. McWilliams, p. 157.

4. The best short account of the San Diego Free Speech fight is in Jim Miller, "Just Another Day in Paradise?" in Mike Davis, Kelly Mayhew, and Jim Miller, *Under the Perfect Sun: The San Diego Tourists Never See* (New York: New Press, 2003).

5. Philip Foner, ed., *Fellow Workers and Friends: IWW Free-Speech Fights as Told by Participants* (Westport, Conn: Greenwood Press, 1981), pp. 140–41.

6. Kevin Starr, *Endangered Dreams: The Great Depression in California* (New York: Oxford University Press, 1996), p. 38. My niggling criticisms aside, this remains a magnificent, one-volume history of California's waterfront and harvest wars, written from a staunchly pro-labor perspective that may surprise some readers of earlier installments of his "Americans and the California Dream" series.

7. Foner, *The Industrial Workers of the World,* p. 198.

8. Starr, *Endangered Dreams.*

9. John Townsend, *Running the Gauntlet: Cultural Sources of Violence against the IWW* (New York: Garland, 1986), pp. 50–51.

10. Foner, *The Industrial Workers of the World,* p. 202.

11. Ibid., p. 211; and Foner, ed., *Fellow Workers,* p. 141.

12. Melvyn Dubofsky, *We Shall Be All: A History of the IWW* (Chicago: Quadrangle Books, 1969), p. 439.

13. See discussion of the law's origins in Hyman Weintraub, "The IWW in California: 1905–1931" (master's thesis, UCLA, 1947), pp. 162–64.

14. Ibid., p. 168.

15. Philip Foner, *The T.U.E.L. to the End of the Gompers Era* (New York, International Publishing, 1991), p. 32.

16. Goldstein, *Political Repression,* p. 156.

17. Weintraub, "The IWW in California," pp. 228.

18. Foner, *The T.U.E.L. to the End of the Gompers Era,* p. 38.

19. Ibid., pp. 39–50.

20. Ibid., p. 236.

21. Louis Perry and Richard Perry, *A History of the Los Angeles Labor Movement, 1911–1941* (Berkeley, Calif: University of California Press, 1963), pp. 190–91.

22. Ibid.

Chapter Seven. In Dubious Battle

1. Starr, *Endangered Dreams*, p. 159.
2. Fearis, "The California Farm Worker," p. 85; and Gilbert Gonzalez, *Mexican Consuls and Labor Organizing* (Austin: University of Texas Press, 1999).
3. Fearis, "The California Farm Worker," pp. 95–97.
4. Paul Scharrenberg quoted in Camille Guerin-Gonzales, *Mexican Workers and American Dreams* (New Brunswick, N.J.: Rutgers University Press, 1996), p. 124.
5. Daniel, "Labor Radicalism," pp. 135–36.
6. Ibid., p. 210.
7. Fearis, "The California Farm Worker," p. 105.
8. Daniel, "Labor Radicalism," p. 272.
9. Gonzalez, *Mexican Consuls*, p. 174.
10. Ibid., p. 178.
11. Ibid., p. 263.

Chapter Eight. Thank the Vigilantes

1. Fearis, "The California Farm Worker," p. 238.
2. Starr, *Endangered Dreams*, p. 109.
3. Mike Quinn, *The Big Strike* (Olema, CA: Olema Publishing Company, 1949), p. 160.
4. Ibid., p. 161.
5. Urban vigilantes were also an integral part of the violent response to the great Teamsters' struggle in Minneapolis in 1934. For a magnificent account, see Charles Rumford Walker, *American City: A Rank-and-File History* (New York: Farrar & Rinehart, 1937).
6. Quinn, *The Big Strike*, p. 169.
7. McWilliams, *Factories in the Field*, p. 228.
8. Ibid., p. 231.
9. Ibid., pp. 232–33.
10. David Selvin, *Sky Full of Storm: A Brief History of California Labor* (Berkeley: University of California Press, 1966), pp. 62–63.
11. McWilliams, *Factories in the Field*, p. 234.
12. Ibid., pp. 240–42 and 249–53.
13. Carey McWilliams, *California: the Great Exception* (New York: Current Books, Inc., 1949), p. 163.
14. Fearis, "The California Farm Worker," p. 133.
15. McWilliams, *Factories in the Field*, pp. 256–58.
16. Starr, *Endangered Dreams*, p. 183.
17. Starr, *Endangered Dreams*, pp. 187–88.
18. Quoted in ibid.
19. Dorothy Ray (Healy) quoted in Susan Ferris and Ricardo Sandoval, *The Fight in the Fields: Cesar Chavez and the Farmworkers Movement* (San Diego: Harvest/HBJ Books, 1997), p. 31.
20. McWilliams, *Factories in the Field*, pp. 259–60.
21. Starr, *Endangered Dreams*, p. 190.
22. Fearis, "The California Farm Worker," p. 111. Also see in Fearis the entirety of chapter VI ("The Farm Workers and the Government"), an unexcelled analysis of how farm labor was politically marginalized in the 1930s.
23. Fearis, "The California Farm Worker," pp. 271–74.
24. Patrick Mooney and Theo Majka, *Farmers' and Farm Workers' Movements: Social Protest in American Agriculture* (New York: Twayne, 1995), pp. 143–44.

25. Enough Okies stayed in the fields of the San Joaquin, however, to be the protagonists of the unsuccessful 1949 strike against DiGiorgio, discussed in a later section.

26. Quoted in Goldstein, *Political Repression*, pp. 223–24.

Chapter Nine. The Zoot Suit Wars

1. G. Edward White, *Earl Warren: A Public Life* (New York: Oxford University Press, 1982), pp. 69–74.

2. Quoted in Roger Daniels, *Prisoners Without Trial: Japanese Americans in World War II* (New York: Hill and Wang, 1993), p. 36.

3. House Select Committee Investigating National Defense Migration, *Hearings before the Select Committee*, 77th Congr., 2nd sess., 1942, pp. 11017–18.

4. "No one knows the real worth of the property lost by the Japanese-Americans. As economists have pointed out, the true losses should take into account not just the 1942 value of the property but also the lost economic opportunities in a time when most Americans were enjoying wartime prosperity, and the tremendous increase in land values on the Pacific Coast." Daniels, *Prisoners Without Trial*, pp. 89–90.

5. Cited in Thomas Sugrue, *The Origins of the Urban Crisis* (Princeton: Princeton University Press, 1996), p. 29.

6. David Kennedy, *Freedom from Fear: The American People in Depression and War, 1929–1945*, vol. 9, *Oxford History of the United States* series (New York: Oxford University Press, 2005), p. 768.

7. See Serge Durflinger, "The Montreal and Verdun Zoot-Suit Disturbances of June 1944," in Serge Bernier, ed., *L'Impact de la Deuxieme Guerre Mondiale sur les Societes Canadienne et Quebecoise* (Montreal: McGill University Press, 1997).

8. I generalize here from readings of contemporary New York, Chicago, and Los Angeles newspapers in the course of research on street gangs. Authorities' perceptions of a new kind of minority youth problem in the 1939–41 period deserves a serious exploration.

9. McWilliams, *North from Mexico*, p. 215.

10. Eduardo Pagan, *Murder at the Sleepy Lagoon* (Chapel Hill: University of North Carolina Press, 2003), p. 163.

11. McWilliams, *North From Mexico*, p. 221.

12. Ibid., p. 224.

13. Ibid., p. 231.

Chapter Ten. Beating the UFW

1. Clementina Olloqui, quoted in Ferris and Sandoval, *The Fight in the Fields*, p. 182.

2. Mooney and Majka, *Farmers' and Farm Workers' Movements*, p. 166.

3. Ibid., p. 186.

4. Ibid., p.170.

5. Ibid., p. 163.

Chapter Eleven. The Last Vigilantes?

1. John Steinbeck, *The Grapes of Wrath* (New York: Viking Critical Library, 1972), pp. 385–86.

2. Associated Press, "After Praising Border Patrols, Schwarzenegger Calls Self 'Champion of Immigrants,'" April 29, 2005.

Part II. Introduction

1. Roger Daniels, *Coming to America: A History of Immigration and Ethnicity in American Life* (New York: Harper Collins, 1990), p. 3.
2. "Migration and Globalization," a fact sheet from *The Globalist* online magazine, July 13, 2005, http://www.theglobalist.com/DBWeb/StoryId.aspx?StoryId=4174.
3. James D. Cockroft, *Outlaws in the Promised Land: Mexican Immigrant Workers and America's Future* (New York: Grove Press, 1986), p. 143.
4. For a more complete discussion of neoliberalism, see Eric Toussaint, *Your Money or Your Life*, 3rd ed. (Chicago: Haymarket Books, 2005).
5. Since World War II, many undeveloped nations (what some would later call "Third World nations") attempted to build up their economies through state-centered initiatives to industrialize and modernize the means of production in key sectors. The logic of these initiatives dictated that through tariffs, protectionism, and massive reinvestment into national industries, and by promoting their own "comparative advantage," poor countries could attain "first world" status. By seeking a greater share of the world market, they aimed to break out of their status as underdeveloped backwaters that were constantly exploited by the world's powers. For a complete description of why these policies were not successful, see Toussaint, *Your Money or Your Life*.
6. For instance, much migration into wealthier countries comes from previous colonies, or countries dominated by capital from the "host country."
7. Statistics from "Migration and Globalization" fact sheet.
8. Basan Sev, "Legalized Human Trafficking," *Z Magazine*, April 2006, pp. 11–14.
9. Quoted in Juan F. Perea, *Immigrants Out! The New Nativism and the Anti-Immigrant Impulse in the United States* (New York: New York University Press, 1997), p. 226.
10. Isaac Shapiro and Joel Friedman, "Tax Returns: A Comprehensive Assessment of the Bush Administration's Record on Cutting Taxes," Center on Budget and Policy Priorities Web site, April 23, 2004, http://www.cbpp.org/4-14-04tax-sum.htm.
11. "Minimum Wage: Frequently Asked Questions," fact sheet on the Economic Policy Institute Web site, January 2006, http://www.epinet.org/content.cfm/issueguides_minwage_minwagefaq.
12. "Economic Snapshots: When Do Workers Get Their Share?" fact sheet on the Economic Policy Institute Web site, May 27, 2004, http://www.epinet.org/content.cfm/webfeatures_snapshots_05272004.
13. Tom Regan, "Report: Iraq War Costs Could Top $2 Trillion," *Christian Science Monitor*, January 10, 2006.
14. Mike Allen and Peter Baker, "$2.5 Trillion Budget Plan Cuts Many Programs," *Washington Post*, February 7, 2005.
15. Quoted in Katrin Bennhold, "Chirac Urges Calm as Suburban Riots Spread," *International Herald Tribune*, November 3, 2005.
16. "Sarkozy to Introduce Immigration Bill," United Press International, February 6, 2006, www.upi.com/InternationalIntelligence/view.php?StoryID=20060206-072907-3174r.
17. Mark Stevenson, "Few Protections for Migrants to Mexico," Associated Press, April 19, 2006.
18. See Saskia Sassen, *Globalization and its Discontents: Essays on the New Mobility of People and Money* (New York: New Press, 1999), xxviii.

Chapter Twelve. Conquest Sets the Stage

1. While Manifest Destiny was merely a term coined by a newspaper editor to describe the feeling that American expansionism was a natural process, it embodied the ideological

justification promoted by the ruling class of the day that the territorial integrity of Native Americans and Mexicans was invalid and not recognized within the "community of nations," due to their purported "inferiority."

2. Reginald Horseman, *Race and Manifest Destiny: The Origins of Anglo-Saxonism* (Cambridge: Harvard University Press, 1981), pp. 1–2.

3. Merrill D. Peterson, *Thomas Jefferson and the New Nation* (New York: Oxford University Press, 1970), p. 746.

4. The availability of land proved illusory after the opening up of the Southwest. For an in-depth discussion of how land became concentrated in the hands of industrial and agricultural interests, see Carey McWilliams, *Factories in the Fields* (Berkeley: University of California Press, 2000).

5. Richard Griswold del Castillo, *The Treaty of Guadalupe Hidalgo: A Legacy of Conflict* (Norman, OK: University of Oklahoma Press, 1990), p. 51.

6. For instance, California's first constitution revoked the right of most Mexicans to vote, stating that only "white Mexicans" were entitled to the franchise. The California Land Settlement Act of 1851 forced Mexican land-holders to "prove" their titles in court. Many had no titles or were unable to cover the long-term litigation costs of the legal process, and had to sell their lands as a result.

7. Horseman, *Race and Manifest Destiny: The Origins of Anglo-Saxonism*, p. 211.

8. Ibid., p. 212.

9. Daniels, *Coming to America*, p. 124.

10. Roger Daniels, *Guarding the Golden Door: American Immigration Policy and Immigrants* (New York: Hill and Wang, 2004), p. 8.

11. Sharon Smith, *Subterranean Fire: A History of Working Class Radicalism in the United States* (Chicago: Haymarket Books, 2006), pp. 6–7.

12. For a thorough discussion of this process, see Angie Debo, *A History of the Indians of the United States* (Norman, OK: University of Oklahoma Press, 1983) and Dee Brown, *Bury My Heart at Wounded Knee* (New York: Bantam, 1970).

13. It also helped produce the ultimate showdown for economic supremacy between the North and the South, that is, between the plantation system and industrial capitalism.

14. Thomas Torrans, *Forging the Tortilla Curtain: Cultural Drift and Change Along the United States-Mexico Border from the Spanish Era to the Present* (Fort Worth: Texas Christian University Press, 2000), p. 4.

15. Cockroft, *Outlaws in the Promised Land*, p. 43.

16. See Adolfo Gilly, *A People's History of the Mexican Revolution* (New York: New Press, 2005).

17. V. I. Lenin, *Imperialism: The Highest Stage of Capitalism* (New York: International Publishers, 1990), p. 68.

18. John Ross, *The Annexation of Mexico: From the Aztecs to the IMF* (Monroe, ME: Common Courage Press, 1998), p. 53.

19. David Lorey, *The U.S.-Mexican Border in the Twentieth Century* (Wilmington, DE: SR Books, 1999), pp. 40–42.

20. Devra Miller, *Dark Sweat, White Gold: California Farmworkers, Cotton and the New Deal* (Berkeley: University of California Press, 1994), p. 50.

21. See Gilly, *A People's History*.

22. For a useful discussion on the legacy of the Mexican Revolution, see Dan La Botz, *Democracy in Mexico: Peasant Rebellion and Political Reform* (Boston: South End Press, 1995).

23. Tom Barry, *Zapata's Revenge: Free Trade and the Farm Crisis in Mexico* (Cambridge: South End Press, 1995), p. 12.

24. Ibid., p. 20.

25. The nationalization of oil in 1938 was one such reform, which occurred during a mass

strike movement in Mexico at the time. See Dan La Botz, *The Crisis of Mexican Labor* (New York: Praeger Publishers, 1988).
26. Judith Adler Hellman, *Mexico in Crisis* (New York: Holmes and Meier, 1988), p. 93.

Chapter Thirteen. Neoliberalism Consumes the "Mexican Miracle"

1. In the era of deindustrialization, beginning in the 1970s, migration into the cities fed an ever-expanding informal sector, spawning populations of every type of street vendor, performer, "car-watcher," and window washer, to name just a few occupations.
2. Hellman, *Mexico in Crisis*, p. 108.
3. Barry, *Zapata's Revenge*, p. 27.
4. Cockroft, *Oulaws in the Promised Land*, pp. 172–73.
5. Cockroft, *Mexico's Hope: An Encounter with Politics and History* (New York: Monthly Review Press, 1998), p. 210.
6. Ross, *The Annexation of Mexico*, p. 168.
7. Much like landless Americans who poured across the frontier onto Indian lands to escape the virtual land monopoly by the colonial elite, Mexican out-migration has become an integral feature of the Mexican economy, one that is acknowledged and encouraged in order to prevent social rebellion. Otherwise, more of the wealth produced by the Mexican working class (but concentrated in the hands of the very rich) would have to be reinvested in social welfare and other forms of redistribution.
8. For a complete discussion on the failure of Mexico's import substitution industrialization, see Cockroft, *Mexico's Hope*, Chapter 5, and La Botz, *Crisis of Mexican Labor*.
9. The rise of neoliberalism in Mexico was mirrored by the rise of a new group of intellectuals referred to as the "Tecnicos." U.S.-educated and intellectually bound to the neoliberal, free-market theories of Milton Friedman and the Chicago School, they came of age through the Party of Institutional Revolution (PRI) and gained preeminence in the administration of Carlos Salinas de Gortari (1988–94) and through the passage of the North American Free Trade Agreement.
10. Despite Mexican regulations prohibiting foreign majority ownership of key industrial sectors of the Mexican economy, there were a number of ways around this. For some examples and the statistics cited here, see Cockroft, *Outlaws in the Promised Land*, p. 186.
11. Major oil discoveries in the 1970s helped boost the economy and increase oil exports dramatically, which led to the hope that "black gold" would solve Mexico's financial woes.
12. Ross, *The Annexation of Mexico*, pp. 171–72.
13. Ibid., p. 175.
14. Toussaint, *Your Money or Your Life*, p. 119.
15. Ibid., p.135.
16. Devaluations of the peso have been as great as 40 percent, bankrupting working families and small farmers almost instantly.
17. David Bacon, *Children of NAFTA: Labor Wars on the U.S.-Mexico Border* (Berkeley: University of California Press, 2004), p. 53.
18. World Bank, "Mexico Country Brief," April 2006, http://web.worldbank.org/WBSITE /EXTERNAL/COUNTRIES/LACEXT/MEXICOEXTN/0,,menuPK:338407~pagePK :141132~piPK:141107~theSitePK:338397,00.html.
19. Manuel Gonzales, *Mexicanos: A History of Mexicans in the United States* (Bloomington: Indiana University Press, 2000), p. 225.
20. David Bacon, "Showdown Coming in Mexico over Privatization," ZNet, February 23, 2003, http://www.zmag.org/content/showarticle.cfm?ItemID=3108.

Chapter Fourteen. From the Maquiladoras to NAFTA: Profiting from Borders

1. Altha J. Cravey, *Women and Work in Mexico's Maquiladoras* (Lanham, MD: Rowman and Littlefield, 1998), p. 15.
2. "U.S.-Mexico Border 2012 Framework," United States Environmental Protection Agency Web site, March 6, 2006, http://www.epa.gov/usmexicoborder/intro.htm.
3. "Frequently Asked Questions," Made in Mexico, Inc. Web site, http://www.madeinmexicoinc.com/FAQs.htm.
4. "What is a Maquila?" Twin Plant News Web site, http://www.twinplantnews.com/whatIs.htm.
5. Avery Wear, "Class and Poverty in the Maquila Zone," *International Socialist Review* 23 (May–June 2002).
6. Alfredo Mena, "More Tax Breaks for Maquiladoras," *El Diario de Juarez*, January 21, 2006.
7. Cockroft, *Outlaws in the Promised Land*, pp. 168–69.
8. "What is a Maquila?" Twin Plant News Web site.
9. Mexico Solidarity Network, "Maquiladora Employment Reaches New High," *MSN News*, January 23–29, 2006.
10. Cravey, *Women and Work*, p. 57.
11. Ibid., p. 49.
12. David Bacon, "Stories from the Borderlands," *NACLA* 39, no. 1 (July–August 2005).
13. Based on a personal interview May 10, 2006 in San Diego, Calif.
14. David Bacon, Presentation at San Diego City College, San Diego, CA, March 8, 2006.
15. Myriam Garcia and editorial staff, "While West Looks East, East Looks to the Border," *Frontera NorteSur News*, June 14, 2005.
16. Wear, "Class and Poverty in the Maquila Zone."
17. Lorey, *The U.S.-Mexican Border*, pp. 2–3.
18. Migration Policy Institute staff, "A New Century: Immigration and the U.S.," *Migration Information Source* Web site, February 2005, http://www.migrationinformation.org/Profiles/display.cfm?ID=283.
19. Shannon McMahon, "Mexican Consumers Pour Billions Annually into San Diego's Economy," *San Diego Union-Tribune*, August 7, 2005.
20. Quoted in La Botz, *Crisis of Mexican Labor*, p. 146.
21. Cockroft, *Mexico's Hope*, p. 314.
22. Cited in Bacon, *Children of NAFTA*, p. 45.
23. Barry, *Zapata's Revenge*, pp. 54–55.
24. Bureau of Western Hemisphere Affairs, "Background Note: Mexico," U.S. Department of State Web site, December 2005, http://www.state.gov/r/pa/ei/bgn/35749.htm.
25. "Mexico: Trade Summary," Office of the U.S. Trade Representative, http://www.ustr.gov/assets/Document_Library/Reports_Publications/2005/2005_NTE_Report/asset_upload_file467_7483.pdf.
26. A. Ellen Terpstra, "The Benefits of NAFTA for U.S. Agriculture," U.S. Department of Agriculture presentation, April 20, 2004, http://www.fas.usda.gov/itp/Policy/NAFTA%20Presentation.ppt.
27. Eric Green, "Mexico Leads Latin America in Attracting Foreign Investment," U.S. Department of State Web site, April 13, 2006, http://usinfo.state.gov/wh/Archive/2006/Apr/13-262517.html.
28. Richard Boudreaux, "NAFTA 10 Years Later: New Opportunities, New Struggles," *Los Angeles Times*, January 7, 2004.
29. Peter Andreas, *Border Games: Policing the U.S.-Mexico Divide* (Ithaca, NY: Cornell Uni-

NO ONE IS ILLEGAL

versity, 2000), p. 105.

30. "Youth Migration on the Rise," Frontera NorteSur News, January 10, 2006, http://www
    .immigrantsolidarity.org/cgibin/datacgi/database.cgi?file=Issues&report=SingleArticle
    &ArticleID=0399.
31. Bureau of Western Hemisphere Affairs, "Background Note: Mexico," U.S. Department
    of State Web site, December 2005, http://www.state.gov/r/pa/ei/bgn/35749.htm.
32. Gonzales, Mexicanos, p. 226.
32. Cockroft, Mexico's Hope, p. 315.
33. Bacon, Children of NAFTA.
34. Cockroft, Mexico's Hope, p. 315.
35. Mary Dalrymple, "House Hands Bush Narrow Victory on CAFTA," Associated Press,
    July 28, 2005.

Chapter Fifteen. Mexican Workers to the Rescue

1. Lorey, The U.S.-Mexican Border, p. 71.
2. Daniels, Guarding the Golden Door, p. 52. The way they implemented this was by ex-
   empting nations from the Western hemisphere from immigration quotas.
3. Mark Reisler, By the Sweat of Their Brow: Mexican Immigrant Labor in the United
   States, 1900–1940 (Westport, CT: Greenwood Press, 1976), p. 11.
4. Reisler, Sweat of Their Brow, p. 6.
5. Mae M. Ngai, Impossible Subjects: Illegal Aliens and the Making of Modern America
   (Princeton: Princeton University Press, 2004), p. 133.
6. Reisler, Sweat of Their Brow, p. 39.
7. Ibid., p. 96.
8. Ibid., pp. 96–7.
9. Zaragosa Vargas, Proletarians of the North: A History of Mexican Industrial Workers in Detroit and the Midwest, 1917–1933 (Berkeley: University of California Press, 1993), p. 21.
10. Lorey, The U.S.-Mexican Border, p. 59.
11. Maggie Rivas-Rodriguez, Mexican-Americans and World War II (Austin, TX: Univer-
    sity of Texas Press, 2005), p. 273.
12. Vickie L. Ruiz, Cannery Women, Cannery Lives: Mexican Women, Unionization, and the
    California Food Processing Industry, 1930–1950 (Albuquerque: University of New Mex-
    ico Press, 1999), p. 14.
13. Rivas-Rodriguez, Mexican-Americans, pp. 250–55.

Chapter Sixteen.
Segregated Workers: Class Struggle in the Fields

1. Ngai, Impossible Subjects, p. 129.
2. McWilliams, Factories in the Field, p. 56.
3. Justin Akers, "Farmworkers in the U.S.," International Socialist Review 34 (March–
   April 2004).
4. Ibid.
5. McWilliams, Factories in the Field, p. 98.
6. Ibid., p. 97.
7. Ronald Takaki, A Different Mirror: A History of Multicultural America (New York-Bos-
   ton: Little, Brown and Company, 1993), p. 252.
8. McWilliams, Factories in the Field, p. 118.
9. Ibid., p. 100.

10. Black farmworkers often faced conditions of bonded labor, which denied them free movement. See Robin Kelley, *Hammer and Hoe: Alabama Communists During the Great Depression* (Chapel Hill: University of North Carolina Press, 1990) and Daniel Rothenberg, *With These Hands* (Berkeley: University of California Press, 1998).

11. Powerful corporations often use front groups, or privately funded "think tanks," to provide a veneer of "scientific credibility" for the demands of corporate sponsors. For instance, the American Meat Institute (AMI), while promoting itself as the watchdog of healthy meat policy, is actually comprised of the biggest meat and poultry producers in the country, and is primarily concerned with sponsoring and lobbying for legislation favorable to meat producers. Through the American Meat Institute, for instance, the largest meat and poultry corporations are promoting a new guest-worker program. See http://www.meatami.com/ for more information on the AMI.

12. The Chinese Exclusion Act of 1882 was "passed by the 47th Congress," and "suspended immigration of Chinese laborers for ten years; permitted those Chinese in the United States as of November 17, 1880, to stay, travel abroad, and return; prohibited the naturalization of Chinese; and created a 'Section 6' exempt status for teachers, students, merchants, and travelers. These exempt classes would be admitted upon presentation of a certificate from the Chinese government." From "Chinese Exclusion Laws: Background," U.S. National Archives online, http://www.archives.gov/pacific/education/4th-grade /chinese-exclusion.html. The Geary Act was the first significant instance of the state policing existing immigrant populations in the United States. It allowed for the deportation of undocumented Chinese, and it created the machinery for further deportations.

13. Miriam J. Wells, *Strawberry Fields: Politics, Class and Work in California Agriculture* (Ithaca, NY: Cornell University Press, 1996), p. 66.

14. Rodolfo Acuña, *Occupied America: A History of Chicanos*, 4th ed. (New York: Longman, 2000), p. 182.

15. Art Preis, *Labor's Giant Step: The First Twenty Years of the CIO: 1936–1955* (New York: Pathfinder Press, 1994), p. xv.

16. According to historian Barton J. Bernstein, "The liberal reforms of the New Deal did not transform the American system; they preserved and protected American corporate capitalism, occasionally by absorbing parts of threatening programs." See Elizabeth Cobbs Hoffman and Jon Gjerde, *Major Problems in American History*, vol. 2, *Since 1865: Documents and Essays* (Boston: Houghton Mifflin, 2002), p. 237.

17. McWilliams, *Factories in the Field*, p. 215.

18. Rothenberg, *With These Hands*, p. 246.

19. Mike Davis, Kelly Mayhew, and Jim Miller, *Under the Perfect Sun: The San Diego Tourists Never See* (New York: New Press, 2003), p. 199.

20. Charles D. Thompson Jr. and Melinda F. Wiggins, eds., *The Human Cost of Food: Farmworkers' Lives, Labor and Advocacy* (Austin: University of Texas Press, 2002), p. 141.

Chapter Seventeen.
The Bracero Program: A Twentieth-Century Caste System

1. Kitty Calavita, *Inside the State: The Bracero Program, Immigration, and the INS* (New York: Routledge, 1992), p. 21.

2. Ernesto Galarza, *Farm Workers and Agri-Business in California, 1947–1960* (Notre Dame: University of Notre Dame Press, 1977), p. 31.

3. Ernesto Galarza, *Merchants of Labor: The Mexican Bracero Story* (Santa Barbara: McNally and Lofton, 1964), p. 24.

4. Manuel G. Gonzales, *Mexicanos: A History of Mexicans in the United States* (Bloomington: Indiana University Press, 2000), p. 172.

5. Galarza, *Merchants of Labor*, p. 223.
6. Galarza, *Farm Workers*, p. 33.
7. Quoted in Rivas-Rodriguez, *Mexican-Americans*, p. 275.
8. Ibid., p. 32.
9. Ibid., p. 83.
10. Cockroft, *Outlaws in the Promised Land*, p. 71.
11. Gonzales, *Mexicanos*, p. 167.
12. Cockroft, *Outlaws in the Promised Land*, p. 78.
13. Ngai, *Impossible Subjects*, p. 139.
14. Ibid., p. 29.
15. Galarza, *Farm Workers*, p. 82.
16. Even George Bush uses this idea to advance a guest-worker program. See "President Tours Border, Discusses Immigration Reform in Texas" press release on the White House Web site, November 29, 2005, http://www.whitehouse.gov/news/releases /2005/11/20051129-2.html.
17. The fund never materialized. It wasn't until 2005 that the Mexican government agreed to compensate former braceros for these lost wages. See Hiram Soto, "Mexico to Compensate for Long-Forgotten Fund," *San Diego Union-Tribune*, January 3, 2006.
18. Galarza, *Merchants of Labor*, p. 55.
19. Calavita, *Inside the State*, pp. 33–34.
20. Ngai, *Impossible Subjects*, pp. 142–54.
21. Cockroft, *Outlaws in the Promised Land*, p. 70.
22. Nigel Harris, *National Liberation* (Reno: University of Nevada Press, 1990), p. 50.
23. Bill Ong Hing, *Defining America through Immigration Policy* (Philadelphia: Temple University Press, 2004), p. 122.
24. Ibid., p. 128.
25. Calavita, *Inside the State*, p. 28.
26. David Reimers, *Still the Golden Door: The Third World Comes to America* (New York: Columbia University Press, 1992), p. 208.
27. Cockroft, *Outlaws in the Promised Land*, p. 72.

Chapter Eighteen. Poverty in the Fields: Legacy of the Bracero Program

1. Rothenberg, *With These Hands*, p. 26.
2. Stephen Magagnini, "Struggling in El Norte, Mixtec Indians Seek a Better Life in the U.S.," *Sacramento Bee*, October 20, 2002.
3. Ibid.
4. Leopold Center for Sustainable Agriculture at Iowa State University report, http://www.leopold.iastate.edu/pdfs/FarmSect.pdf.
5. "United States Farmworker Fact Sheet," Student Action With Farmworkers Web site, http://cds.aas.duke.edu/saf/factsheet.htm.
6. Some 328,000 farming and ranch-related jobs are expected to be lost during this decade. "Employment Decline in Selected Occupations, 2000–2010," *Occupational Outlook Quarterly* (Winter 2001–2002), http://www.bls.gov/opub/ooq/2001/winter/art03.pdf.
7. Bill Christison, "Family Farms and U.S. Trade Policy," *In Motion Magazine*, July 14, 1998, http://www.inmotionmagazine.com/bruss.html.
8. Anuradha Mittal and Mayumi Kawaai, "Freedom to Trade? Trading Away American Family Farms," *Backgrounder* 7, no. 4 (Fall 2001), http://www.foodfirst.org/pubs /backgrdrs/2001/f01v7n4.html.

9. Anuradha Mittal, "Giving Away the Farm: The 2002 Farm Bill," Food First Web site, Summer 2002, http://www.foodfirst.org/pubs/backgrdrs/2002/s02v8n3.html.
10. "Facts About Farmworkers," fact sheet on the National Center for Farmworker's Health Web site, http://www.ncfh.org/docs/fs-Facts%20about%20Farmworkers.pdf.
11. Estimates run as high as eight hundred thousand. "United States: Failure to Protect Child Farmworkers," fact sheet on the Human Rights Watch Web site, http://www.hrw.org/campaigns/crp/farmchild/facts.htm.
12. Thompson and Wiggins, Human Cost of Food, pp. 6–7.
13. Ibid., p. 7.
14. Rothenberg, With These Hands, p. 25.
15. Thompson and Wiggins, Human Cost of Food, pp. 208–10.
16. "United States: Failure to Protect Child Farmworkers," fact sheet on the Human Rights Watch Web site, http://www.hrw.org/campaigns/crp/farmchild/facts.htm.
17. Thompson and Wiggins, Human Cost of Food, p. 234.
18. Alan M. Kraut, Silent Travelers: Germs, Genes and the "Immigrant Menace" (New York: Basic Books, 1994), pp. 270–71.
19. For a complete breakdown of rules and regulations governing child labor in agriculture, visit the Department of Labor's Web site at http://www.dol.gov/esa/programs/whd/state/agriemp2.htm.
20. Editorial, "Supersize Picker's Pay," The Minnesota Daily, April 19, 2006.
21. "Immokalee Tomato Pickers Win Campaign against Taco Bell," Democracy Now! March 10, 2005.

Chapter Nineteen.
Immigrant Workers Continue to Build America

1. Pierrette Hondagneu-Sotelo, Domestica: Immigrant Workers Cleaning and Caring in the Shadows of Influence (Berkeley: University of California Press, 2001), pp. 17–18.
2. Barry, Zapata's Revenge, p. 196.
3. Jeffrey Passel, "Unauthorized Migrants: Numbers and Characteristics," Pew Hispanic Center Web site, June 14, 2005, http://pewhispanic.org/files/reports/46.pdf.
4. S. Mitra Kalita, "Illegal Workers' Presence Growing," Washington Post, March 8, 2006.
5. Hondagneu-Sotelo, Domestica, p. 3.
6. Roben Farzad, "The Urban Migrants," New York Times, July 20, 2005.
7. S. Mitra Kalita, "Illegal Workers' Presence Growing," Washington Post, March 8, 2006.
8. Peter Prengaman, "Study Gives Snapshot of Day Laborers," Associated Press, January 22, 2006.
9. Brian Grow et al., "Embracing the Undocumented," BusinessWeek, July 13, 2005.
10. Hondagneu-Sotelo, Domestica, p. 17.
11. Blanca Villaseñor and José Moreno Meña, "Women Migrants on the Move," Frontera NorteSur News, January 11, 2006.
12. Soledad Jarquin Edgar, "A Town of Women Migrants," Frontera NorteSur News, October 11, 2005.
13. "Latin America Border Series: The Century of the Woman Migrant," Frontera NorteSur News, March 7, 2006.
14. "Myths and Facts in the Immigration Debate," American Immigration Lawyers Association, March 7, 2005, http://www.aila.org/content/default.aspx?docid=17242.
15. "Hispanics Now One-Seventh of U.S. Population," Associated Press, June 10, 2005.
16. "Turning Boomers into Boomerangs," special report in The Economist, February 16, 2006.
17. "California's Changing Demographics At-a-Glance," Associated Press, November 23, 2005.

18. Rakesh Kochhar, Roberto Suro, and Sonya Tafoya, "The New Latino South: The Context and Consequences of Rapid Population Growth," Pew Hispanic Center Web site, July 26, 2005, http://pewhispanic.org/files/reports/50.1.pdf.

19. Center for Continuing Study of the California Economy, "The Impact of Immigration on the California Economy," a report of the California Regional Economies Project 2005, September 2005, http://www.labor.ca.gov/panel/impactimmcaecon.pdf.

20. Cited in "The Globalist Quiz: Immigration Havens," *San Jose Mercury News*, February 5, 2006.

21. Amy M. Traub, "Principles for an Immigration Policy to Strengthen and Expand the American Middle Class," The Drum Major Institute for Public Policy Web site, http://www.drummajorinstitute.org/library/report.php?ID=21.

22. Sonya Geis, "Shortage of Immigrant Workers Alarms Growers in West," *Washington Post*, November 22, 2005.

23. American Farm Bureau Federation—Economic Analysis Team, "Impact of Migrant Labor Restrictions on the Agricultural Sector," February 2006, http://www.fb.org/news/nr/nr2006/02-07-06/labor%20study-feb06.pdf.

24. Sonya Geis, "Shortage of Immigrant Workers Alarms Growers in West," *Washington Post*, November 22, 2005.

25. Jeffrey Passel, "Unauthorized Migrants: Numbers and Characteristics," Pew Hispanic Center Web site, June 14, 2005, http://pewhispanic.org/files/reports/46.pdf.

26. Martin Hüfner, "Immigration–What Europe Can Learn from the United States," *The Globalist*, February 22, 2005, http://www.theglobalist.com/StoryId.aspx?StoryId=4369.

27. Center for Continuing Study of the California Economy, "The Impact of Immigration."

28. Jeffrey Passel and Roberto Suro, "Rise, Peak, and Decline: Trends in U.S. Immigration 1992–2004," Pew Hispanic Center Web site, September 27, 2005, http://pewhispanic.org/reports/report.php?ReportID=53.

29. Center for Continuing Study of the California Economy, "The Impact of Immigration."

30. Edward Iwata, "Immigrant Businesses Can Have Wide Economic Impact," *USA Today*, November 17, 2005.

31. Lance Selfa, "The Lies They Tell about Immigrants," *Socialist Worker*, June 17, 2005.

32. Benjamin Powell, "The Pseudo Economic Problems of Immigration," *San Diego Union-Tribune*, December 22, 2005, http://independent.org/newsroom/article.asp?id=1641.

33. Cited in "Hispanic Impact," *Winston-Salem Journal*, January 6, 2006, http://www.hispanic5.com/hispanic_impact.htm.

34. Jonathan Higuera and Daniel González, "Immigrants: Boom or Bane," *Arizona Republic*, October 17, 2005.

35. Shannon McMahon, "Mexican Consumers Pour Billions Annually into San Diego's Economy," *San Diego Union-Tribune*, August 7, 2005.

36. Lisa Takeochi Cullen and Darin Fonda, "What It Means For Your Wallet," *Time* magazine, April 10, 2006.

37. Mike Davis, *Magical Urbanism: Latinos Reinvent the U.S. Big City* (New York: Verso, 2000), p. 52.

38. Amy M. Traub, "Principles for an Immigration Policy to Strengthen and Expand the American Middle Class," The Drum Major Institute for Public Policy Web site, http://www.drummajorinstitute.org/library/report.php?ID=21.

39. Haya El Nasser, "New Urbanism Embraces Latinos," *USA Today*, February 15, 2005.

40. Anna Gorman, "Illegal Immigrants Can Be Legal Homeowners," *Los Angeles Times*, Auguest 8, 2006.

41. Gayle Pollard-Terry, "Where It's Booming," *Los Angeles Times*, December 23, 2005.

42. Alexander Dworkowitz, "In Northeast, a City's Tale of Turnaround," *Christian Science*

Monitor, July 28, 2005.

43. Brian Grow et al., "Embracing the Undocumented," *BusinessWeek*, July 13, 2005.

44. "Top Ten Migration Issues of 2005: Remittances Reach New Heights," Migration Information Source Web site, December 1, 2005, http://www.migrationinformation.org /Feature/display.cfm?id=355.

45 "Migration, Remittances and Development," Organization for Economic Cooperation and Development Web site, March 21, 2005, http://www.oecd.org/document/34/0,2340 ,en_2649_201185_35744418_1_1_1_1,00.html.

46. "Legislators Go After Remittance Monies," Frontera NorteSur News, February 19, 2006.

47. "According to Laura Velasco Ortiz, a researcher with Tijuana's Colegio de la Frontera Norte, more than 60 percent of the estimated $20 billion in remittances received by Mexico is now sent by women, as opposed to about 39 percent sent by men." From "Latin America Border Series: The Century of the Woman Migrant," Frontera Norte-Sur News, March–April 2006, http://www.nmsu.edu/~frontera/immi.html.

48. Kent Patterson, "Remittances Driving Central American Economies," Frontera Norte-Sur News, April 17, 2006.

49. Roberto Gonzalez Amador, "Migrant Dollars Drive Mexico's Economy," Frontera NorteSur News, March–April 2006, http://www.nmsu.edu/~frontera/comm.html.

50. Toussaint, *Your Money or Your Life*, pp. 175–77.

51. Roberto Gonzalez Amador, "Migrant Dollars Drive Mexico's Economy."

52. "Legislators Go after Remittance Monies," Frontera NorteSur News, Frontera Norte-Sur News, February 19, 2006.

53. "Myths and Facts in the Immigration Debate," fact sheet on the American Immigration Lawyers Association Web site, August 23, 2005, http://www.aila.org/Content/default.aspx?docid=17242.

54. "The Immigrants: Myths and Reality," Intelligence Report on the Southern Poverty Law Center Web site, Spring 2001, http://www.splcenter.org/intel/intelreport/article.jsp?sid=173.

55. Tim Annett, "Illegal Immigrants and the Economy," *Wall Street Journal*, April 13, 2006.

56. Eduardo Porter, "Illegal Immigrants Are Bolstering Social Security with Billions," *New York Times*, April 5, 2005.

57. Ibid.

58. Ben Ready, "Help or Harm: Illegal Immigration's Effect on the Economy a Contentious Issue," *Daily Times-Call*, December 30, 2005.

59. Lisa Takeuchi Cullen and Daren Fonda, "What it Means For Your Wallet," *Time* magazine, April 10, 2006.

60. Amy M. Traub, "Principles for an Immigration Policy to Strengthen and Expand the American Middle Class," The Drum Major Institute for Public Policy Web site, http://www.drummajorinstitute.org/library/report.php?ID=21.

61. Billy House, "Bill Bars Migrants from Social Security Pay," *Arizona Republic*, June 26, 2005.

62. Anna Gorman, "Illegal Immigrants Can Be Legal Homeowners," *Los Angeles Times*, August 8, 2006.

63. Anna Gorman, "Here Illegally, but Choosing to Pay Taxes," *Los Angeles Times*, April 17, 2006.

64. "Affordable Health Care for All: Moving Beyond Political Deadlock," Universal Health Care Action Network presentation, available at http://www.uhcan.org/files/SJHC /AHCSlides.ppt#279,1.

65. Hilary Abramson, "Latinos Feel Brunt of Job-Based Insurance Drop," *Pacific News Service*, August 25, 2005.

66. Daniel Yi, "Most ER Patients Are Insured, Study Says," *Los Angeles Times*, March 29, 2006.

67. "U.S. Hazardous to Health of Mexican Entrants," Reuters, October 16, 2005.

68. Nina Bernstein, "Recourse Grows Slim for Immigrants Who Fall Ill," *New York Times*, March 3, 2006.

69. Ibid.

70. Anthony DePalma, "For Hispanic Immigrants in U.S., What Future?" *New York Times*, May 27, 2005.

71. Jeffrey Passel, "Unauthorized Migrants: Numbers and Characteristics," Pew Hispanic Center Web site, June 14, 2005, http://pewhispanic.org/files/reports/46.pdf.

72. Dana Bartholomew, "Child Poverty Soars In LA," *Los Angeles Times*, August 26, 2004.

73. Lisa Friedman, "Immigration Debate Has Familiar Ring," *Whittier Daily News*, December 31, 2005.

74. Miriam Jordan, "Once Here Illegally, Mexican Family Savors Children's Success," *Wall Street Journal*, July 20, 2005.

75. Center for Continuing Study of the California Economy, "The Impact of Immigration."

76. James McKinley Jr., "In Mexico, Burying Soldiers Killed in a U.S. War," *New York Times*, March 23, 2005.

77. "Easing Path to Citizenship for 'Green Card Soldiers,'" legislation summary on the National Immigration Forum Web site, http://www.immigrationforum.org/DesktopDefault.aspx?tabid=233.

Chapter Twenty.
Immigration Policy as a Means to Control Labor

1. Hoffman and Gjerde, *Major Problems in American History*, vol. 2, p. 80.

2. Quoted in Hal Draper, *Karl Marx's Theory of Revolution*, vol. 2, *The Politics of Social Classes* (New York: Monthly Review Press, 1978), p. 66.

3. Kitty Calavita, *U.S. Immigration Law and the Control of Labor: 1820–1914* (London: Academic Press, 1984), p. 39.

4. Ibid., p. 41.

5. John Higham, *Strangers in the Land: Patterns of American Nativism, 1860–1925* (New Brunswick: Rutgers University Press, 1988), p. 14.

6. Calavita, *U.S. Immigration Law*, p. 122.

7. Ibid., p. 25.

8. For empirical research on the benefits of union membership, see Lawrence Mishel and Matthew Walters, "How Unions Help All Workers," Economic Policy Institute Briefing Paper #143, August 2003, http://www.epinet.org/content.cfm/briefingpapers_bp143.

9. Calavita, *U.S. Immigration Law*, p. 27.

10. Ibid., p. 49.

Chapter Twenty-One. The Race and Class Construction of Immigration Restrictions

1. Takaki, *A Different Mirror*.

2. Philip S. Foner, *History of the Labor Movement in the United States*, vol. 3, *The Policies and Practices of the American Federation of Labor 1900–1909* (New York: International Publishers, 1981), p. 266.

3. Founded in 1849, it was also called the American Party. It was called the Know-Nothing Party because of its secretive character and the commonly used response, "I don't know," when members were questioned about their activities.

4. For a complete discussion of Irish radicalism in the United States, see David A. Wilson, *United Irishmen, United States: Immigrant Radicals in the Early Republic* (Ithaca, NY:

Cornell University Press, 1998).

5. Hoffman and Gjerde, *Major Problems in American History*, vol. 2, p. 155.

6. William H. Tucker, *The Science and Politics of Racial Research* (Urbana, IL: University of Illinois, 1994).

7. Jon Gjerde, *Major Problems in American Immigration and Ethnic History: Documents and Essays* (Boston: Houghton Mifflin, 1998), p. 279.

8. Cited in Lance Selfa and Helen Scott, *No Scapegoats, Why Immigrants Are Not to Blame* (Chicago: Bookmarks, U.S., 1995), p. 17. Available online at http://www.isreview.org /issues/46/Immigrationpamphlet.pdf.

9. Hoffman and Gjerde, *Major Problems in American History*, vol. 2, p. 183.

10. Matthew Frye Jacobson, *Whiteness of a Different Color: European Immigrants and the Alchemy of Race* (Cambridge: Harvard University Press, 1998), p. 43.

11. Calavita, *U.S. Immigration Law*, p. 106.

12. Gjerde, *Major Problems in American Immigration*, p. 317.

13. David Montgomery, *Workers' Control in America: Studies in the History of Work, Technology, and Labor Struggles* (New York: Cambridge University Press, 1979), p. 97.

14. Higham, *Strangers in the Land*, p. 229

15. Ibid., pp. 229–31.

16. Calavita, *U.S. Immigration Law*, p. 86.

17. For the most comprehensive demolition of scientific racism, see Stephen J. Gould, *The Mismeasure of Man* (New York: W. W. Norton & Company, 1996).

18. Edwin Black, *War Against the Weak: Eugenics and America's Campaign to Create a Master Race* (New York: Thunder's Mouth Press, 2004), p. 23.

19. Ibid., p. 75.

20. Ibid., p. 99.

21. "People and Discoveries: Eugenics Movement Reaches its Height, 1923," article on PBS Web site, http://www.pbs.org/wgbh/aso/databank/entries/dh23eu.html.

Chapter Twenty-Two. Constructing the "Illegal" Mexican Worker: Racism and Mexican Labor

1. For instance, Mexicans developed much of the cultural and economic foundation of "the West" (cowboy culture, cattle ranching, mining, etc.) that would later be not only expropriated by Anglo historians and filmmakers, but redefined and romanticized as part of the "American experience" in taming the "Wild West" as well.

2. California Constitution of 1849, art. 2, sec. 1.

3. For instance, the Foreign Miner's Tax and the Federal Land Act deprived Mexicans of their claims to mines and lands, respectively.

4. Reisler, *Sweat of Their Brow*, p. 208.

5. Acuña, *Occupied America*, p. 221.

6. John Box, "Immigration Restriction," on the Digital History Web site, http://www .digitalhistory.uh.edu/mexican_voices/voices_display.cfm?id=92.

7. Acuña, *Occupied America*, p. 222.

8. Cited in Francisco Balderrama and Raymond Rodriguez, *Decade of Betrayal: Mexican Repatriation in the 1930's* (Albuquerque: University of New Mexico Press, 1995), p. 7.

9. Balderrama and Rodriguez, *Decade of Betrayal*, p. 9.

10. Cockroft, *Outlaws in the Promised Land*, p. 77.

11. Zaragosa Vargas, *Major Problems in Mexican-American History* (Boston: Houghton Mifflin, 1999), pp. 280–81.

12. Selfa and Scott, *No Scapegoats*, p. 23.

13. "INS Grants Deportation Relief to Minneapolis Immigrant Workers Fired for Union Activities," *Immigrants Rights Update* 14, no. 3, June 6, 2000. Available on the National Immigration Law Center Web site, http://www.nilc.org/immsemplymnt/wkplce _enfrcmnt/wkplcenfrc012.htm.

Chapter Twenty-Three. Immigration Double Standards

1. Reimers, *Still the Golden Door*, p. 25.
2. Ibid., p. 36.
3. *Shifting Borders: Rhetoric, Immigration, and California's Proposition 187* (Philadelphia: Temple University Press, 2002), pp. 45–46.
4. Reed Ueda, *Postwar Immigrant America: A Social History* (Boston-New York: Bedford/ St. Martin's, 1994), p. 46.
5. Claudine LoMonaco, "Push Is on for Faster Immigration," *Tucson Citizen*, July 4, 2004.
6. Ibid.
7. Sergio Bustos, "Backlog Keeps Immigrants Waiting Years for Green Cards," Gannet News Service, July 27, 2004.

Chapter Twenty-Four.
Militarizing the Border: Death Warrant for Migrant Workers

1. Perea, *Immigrants Out!*, p. 223.
2. William Langewiesche, *Cutting for Sign* (New York: Pantheon, 1993). Cited in "Immigration: Crossing the Line," an article on the Texas State Comptroller Web site, http://www.window.state.tx.us/border/ch11/ch11.html.
3. Carlos Rico, "Migration and U.S.-Mexican Relations," in Christopher Mitchell, ed., *Western Hemisphere Immigration and U.S. Foreign Policy* (University Park, PA: Penn State University, 1991). Cited in "Immigration: Crossing the Line," an article on the Texas State Comptroller Web site, http://www.window.state.tx.us/border/ch11/ch11.html.
4. Timothy J. Dunn, *The Militarization of the U.S.-Mexico Border, 1978–1992: Low-Intensity Conflict Doctrine Comes Home* (Austin, TX: CMAS Books, 1996), pp. 37–38.
5. Nevins, *Operation Gatekeeper*, p. 67.
6. Dunn, *Militarization of the U.S.-Mexico Border*, p. 2.
7. Nevins, *Operation Gatekeeper*, p. 68.
8. "Bill Clinton on Immigration," OnTheIssues Web site, http://www.issues2000.org /Celeb/Bill_Clinton_Immigration.htm.
9. Francis Harris, "Bush Vows to Expel All Illegal Migrants," *The Telegraph* (UK), December 20, 2005.
10. Nedra Pickler, "Bush Vows Crackdown on Illegal Immigrants," Associated Press, November 28, 2005.
11. "Members of Congress Introduce Comprehensive Border Security and Immigration Reform Bill," press release on Senator Edward Kennedy's Web site, May 12, 2005, http://kennedy.senate.gov/~kennedy/statements/05/05/2005512A04.html.
12. Carrie Kahn, "Illegal Entry," National Public Radio, *Morning Edition*, April 19, 1999, http://www.npr.org/templates/story/story.php?storyId=1049435.
13. Jim Abrams, "Little Consensus on Immigration Policy," Associated Press, December 1, 2005.
14. Mitch Tobin, "Guardians of the Line," *Arizona Daily Star*, November 27, 2005.
15. See http://www.stopgatekeeper.org/English/index.html for the names of the fallen migrants.
16. Leslie Berestein, "Posters on Fence Tell of 3,600 Found Dead in 11 Years," *San Diego Union-Tribune*, December 1, 2005.

17. Andreas, *Border Games.*
18. Debbie Nathan, "Border Geography and Vigilantes," *NACLA* 34, no. 2 (September–October 2000), p. 5.
19. Leslie Berestein, "Posters on Fence Tell of 3,600 Found Dead in 11 Years," *San Diego Union-Tribune,* October 1, 2005.
20. Quent Reese, "Nightmare in Texas," *Socialist Worker,* May 23, 2003.
21. American Civil Liberties Union, "UN Human Rights Panel Asked to Investigate Migrant Deaths on U.S. Border," April 14, 1999, http://www.aclusandiego.org/UNCHR.htm.
22. Giovanna Dell'orto, "14 Mexicans Die in Border Crossing," *Washington Post,* May 24, 2001.
23. Claudia E. Smith, "Operation Gatekeeper Resolves Nothing," California Rural Legal Assistance Foundation's Border Project, http://www.stopgatekeeper.org/English/oped1.htm.
24. Ibid.
25. National Center for Policy Analysis, "Mexican Immigrants Go Home," Public Policy Institute of California study, http://www.ncpa.org/pd/immigrat/pdimm/pdimm3.html.
26. Amnesty International, "Human Rights Concerns in the Border Region with Mexico," May 20, 1998, http://web.amnesty.org/library/Index/engAMR510031998.
27. Debby Nathan, "Border Geography and Vigilantes."
28. Tom Barry, Harry Browne, and Beth Sims, *Crossing the Line: Immigrants, Economic Integration, and Drug Enforcement on the U.S.-Mexico Border* (Albuquerque: Inter-Hemispheric Resource Center Press, 1994), p. 42.
29. Janine Zuniga, "City Sees a Transformation," *San Diego Union-Tribune,* July 11, 2004.
30. "Operation Gatekeeper Fact Sheet," April 30, 2001, California Rural Legal Assistance Foundation's Border Project, http://www.stopgatekeeper.org/English/facts.htm.
31. Joe Cantlupe, "Arrests Up Since 1994, Crackdown at Border: Costly Effort Fails to Deter Illegal Flow," *San Diego Union-Tribune,* February 20, 2001.
32. Nic Paget-Clarke, "U.S. Border Patrol in Southern California Developing Deadly but Ineffective Operation Gatekeeper," interview with Roberto Martinez, *In Motion Magazine,* June-August 1999, http://www.inmotionmagazine.com/rm99.html.
33. Ruben Martinez, *Crossing Over: A Mexican Family on the Migrant Trail,* (New York: Picador Press, 2001), p. 109.
34. "Operation Gatekeeper Fact Sheet," April 30, 2001, California Rural Legal Assistance Foundation's Border Project, http://www.stopgatekeeper.org/English/facts.htm.
35. Joe Cantlupe, "Arrests Up Since 1994, Crackdown at Border: Costly Effort Fails to Deter Illegal Flow," *San Diego Union-Tribune,* February 20, 2001.
36. "Southwest Border Apprehensions," U.S. Department of Homeland Security Web site, March 24, 2006, http://www.uscis.gov/graphics/shared/aboutus/statistics/msrmar06/SWBORD.HTM.
37. Douglas S. Massey, "The Wall That Keeps Illegal Workers In," *New York Times,* April 4, 2006.
38. Nathan, "Border Geography and Vigilantes."
39. Anna Gorman, "Employers of Illegal Immigrants Face Little Risk of Penalty," *Los Angeles Times,* May 29, 2005.
40. Eduardo Porter, "The Search for Illegal Immigrants Stops at the Workplace," *New York Times,* March 5, 2006.
41. Ibid.
42. Ibid.
43. Jordan Rau, "Drivers License Bill Gains," *Los Angeles Times,* June 16, 2004.
44. Andreas, *Border Games,* p. 75.
45. "Border Patrol Agents Accused of Smuggling," Frontera NorteSur News, February–March 2006, http://www.nmsu.edu/~frontera/Mexicalinews.html.

46. Ken Ellingwood, *Hard Line: Life and Death on the U.S.-Mexico Border* (New York: Pantheon Books, 2004), p. 85.

47. Jose Palafox, "Militarizing the Border," *Covert Action Quarterly* 56 (Spring 1996), http://mediafilter.org/CAQ/CAQ56border.html.

48. Marisa Taylor, "Border Agent Accused of Taking Bribes," *San Diego Union-Tribune*, September 26, 2000.

Chapter Twenty-Five. Inventing an Invisible Enemy: September 11 and the War on Immigrants

1. In the aftermath of the September 11 attacks, over twelve hundred people were interned and investigated as "potential terrorists" throughout the United States. The U.S. government also restricted immigration from twenty-five Arab and Muslim countries (and alleged "terrorist states"), and now requires registration with immigration officials of all male tourists aged sixteen to forty-five. See John N. Pader and Peter W. Singer, "America Slams the Door (On Its Foot): Washington's Destructive New Visa Policies," *Foreign Affairs* (May/June 2003), http://www.foreignaffairs.org/20030501facomment11216 /john-n-paden-peter-w-singer/america-slams-the-door-on-its-foot-washington-s -destructive-new-visa-policies.html.

2. For an in-depth analysis of such groups, see Tom Barry, "Whose Side Are You On?: The Immigration Debate," *CounterPunch* online, June 3, 2005, http://www .counterpunch.org/barry06032005.html.

3. Andreas, *Border Games*, p. 9.

4. Eric Lichtblau, "Prosecutions in Immigration Doubled in Last Four Years," *New York Times*, September 29, 2005.

5. Ibid.

6. Elaine Hagopian, ed., *Civil Rights in Peril: The Targeting of Arabs and Muslims* (Chicago: Haymarket Books, 2004), p. 28.

7. Mark Dow, *American Gulag: Inside U.S. Immigration Prisons* (Berkeley: University of California Press, 2004), p. 26.

8. Janet Hooks, "Border Security an Issue for GOP," *Los Angeles Times*, November 27, 2005.

9. Ron Hutcheson, "Bush Tries to Straddle Divide over Illegal Immigration to U.S.," Knight-Ridder News Service, November 29, 2005.

10. "U.S. Ends Undocumented Immigrant Stings," Associated Press, May 29, 2005.

11. From an e-mail announcement by the anti-immigrant group Save Our State. Web site available at www.saveourstate.org.

12. Janet Hooks, "Border Security an Issue for GOP," *Los Angeles Times*, November 27, 2005.

13. "The Immigration Debate: The Politics of Fear Do Not Always Carry the Day," National Immigration Forum Web site, November 21, 2005, http://www.immigrationforum.org /DesktopDefault.aspx?tabid=773.

14. Nicholas Riccardi, "States Take on Border Issues," *Los Angeles Times*, January 16, 2006.

15. Michael Kunzelman, "U.S. Judge Raps Congressmen Over Deportation Act," *Boston Globe*, July 13, 2005.

16. Deborah Barfield Berry, "The Coming Battle over Immigration," *Newsday*, May 11, 2005.

17. Alan Elsner, "Lawmakers Seek to Crack Down on Undocumented Immigrants," Reuters, June 24, 2005.

18. Nick Guroff and Singeli Agnew, "The 'Paper Ceiling'—Undocumented Youths Face Barriers at the Brink of Adulthood," *New America Media*, January 12, 2006, http://news.newamericamedia.org/news/view_article.html?article_id =a9616e3389ea916e0d83dda9e9ce76ef.

19. "United States: Failure to Protect Child Farmworkers," fact sheet on the Human Rights Watch Web site, http://www.hrw.org/campaigns/crp/farmchild/facts.htm.

20. Pam Belluck, "Town Uses Trespass Laws to Fight Illegal Immigrants," *New York Times*, July 12, 2005.

21. Ibid.

22. Gregory Alan Gross, "Roving Patrols by Border Agents Net 300 Arrests, Stir Controversy," *San Diego Union-Tribune*, June 15, 2004.

23. Tram Nyugen, ed., *We Are All Suspects Now: Untold Stories from Immigrant Communities After 9/11* (Boston: Beacon Press, 2005), pp. 100–1.

24. Carla Marinucci, "'Close the Borders,' Schwarzenegger Says," *San Francisco Chronicle*, April 20, 2005.

25. Carla Marinucci and Mark Martin, "Schwarzenegger Condemns Sign: Praises Minutemen and Immigration Reform Movement," *San Francisco Chronicle*, April 29, 2005.

26. "Governor's Approval Rating Plummets," Associated Press, June 21, 2005.

27. "Making Immigration Enforcement Work: What Will It Take?" press release on the Migration Policy Institute Web site, December 6, 2005, http://www.migrationpolicy.org/ITFIAF/1206_releases.php.

28. Complete budget for the Department of Homeland Security may be viewed at http://www.epic.org/privacy/surveillance/spotlight/0505/dhsb06.pdf.

29. Nevins, *Operation Gatekeeper*, p. 167.

30. Dow, *American Gulag*, p. 9.

31. Alisa Solomon, "Detainees Equal Dollars," *Village Voice*, April 14–20, 2002.

32. Dow, *American Gulag*, p. 10.

33. Adam Liptak, "Courts Criticize Judges' Handling of Asylum Cases," *New York Times*, December 26, 2005.

34. Both quotes in Dow, *American Gulag*, p. 10.

35. "Corrections to House Immigration Detainees," Associated Press, December 21, 2005.

36. Rachel L. Swarns, "Halliburton Subsidiary Gets Contract to Add Temporary Immigration Detention Centers," *New York Times*, February 4, 2006.

37. Armando Carrasco, "HMLA 267 Marines Help Secure Texas Border," U.S. Marines Web site, August 19, 2005, http://www.marines.mil/marinelink/mcn2000.nsf/main5/A099DDB2919D78B68525705B001618AE?opendocument.

38. Alonso Urrutia Enviado, "Lista, la Sofisticada Caza de Migrantes en EU," *La Jornada*, June 15, 2004.

39. Nicholas Riccardi, "States Take on Border Issues," *Los Angeles Times*, January 16, 2006.

Chapter Twenty-Six. The Bipartisan Segregationists of Labor

1. David Bacon, "Talking Points on Guest Workers," *Truthout*, July 6, 2005, http://www.dsausa.org/DavidBacon/guest%20workers.html.

2. Peter Wallsten and Nicole Gaouette, "President George Bush to Build Immigration Reform Coalition to Court Hispanics," *Los Angeles Times*, July 24, 2005.

3. June Kronholz, "Guest-Worker Proposals Prove Divisive," *Wall Street Journal*, November 9, 2005.

4. "Business Group Supports Bipartisan Innigration Reform Bill," press release on the Essential Worker Immigration Coalition Web site, May 12, 2005, http://www.ewic.org/press/05172005.html.

5. Nicole Gaouette, "Immigration Linked to Security Revamp," *Los Angeles Times*, July 14, 2005.

6. Holly Bailey, "Tom Tancredo Is Pulling the Immigration Debate to the Right—and

Away from Bush," *Newsweek*, April 3, 2006.

7. June Kronholz, "Guest-Worker Proposals Prove Divisive," *Wall Street Journal*, November 9, 2005.

8. Ron Harris, "Illegal Immigration Concerns Could Split Both Parties," *St. Louis Post-Dispatch*, December 20, 2005.

9. For an outstanding description of how this process worked during the civil rights era, see Ahmed Shawki, *Black Liberation and Socialism* (Chicago: Haymarket Books, 2006).

10. Alan Maass, "Anybody But Bush?" *International Socialist Review* 30 (July–August 2003).

11. Roger Daniels, *Guarding the Golden Door*, p. 65.

12. Ibid., p. 180.

13. Perea, *Immigrants Out!*, p. 229.

14. Alisa Solomon, "Detainees Equal Dollars," *Village Voice*, April 14–20, 2002.

15. Michael Welch, *Detained: Immigration Laws and the Expanding I.N.S. Jail Complex* (Philadelphia: Temple University Press, 2002), p. 64.

16. Feinstein was a fierce advocate of immigration restrictions even before September 11. For a summary of the various proposals she has supported, see "Congressional Immigration Reform," Migration News Web site; http://migration.ucdavis.edu/mn/more.php?id=610_0_2_0.

17. Michael Doyle, "Feinstein Gets Tougher on Immigration," *Sacramento Bee*, June 5, 1994.

18. Charles Hurt, "Hillary Goes Conservative on Immigration," *Washington Times*, December 13, 2004.

19. Ibid.

20. Leslie Casmir and Leo Standora, "Hil: Border Needs Wall," *New York Daily News*, April 23, 2006.

21. "Transcript: Third Presidential Debate," *Washington Post*, October 13, 2004, http://www.washingtonpost.com/wp-srv/politics/debatereferee/debate_1013.html.

22. Nicholas Riccardi, "States Take on Border Issues," *Los Angeles Times*, January 16, 2006.

23. "Bush Turns Focus To Immigration," *CBS*/AP, November 28, 2005, http://www.cbsnews.com/stories/2005/11/28/politics/main1080957.shtml.

24. For a full discussion of the proposal, see American Immigration Lawyers Association, "Secure America and Orderly Immigration Act: Section-by-Section Analysis," http://www.aila.org/content/default.aspx?docid=16719.

25. "Members of Congress Introduce Comprehensive Border Security and Immigration Reform Bill," press release on Senator Edward Kennedy's Web site, May 12, 2005, http://kennedy.senate.gov/~kennedy/statements/05/05/2005512A04.html.

26. Patrick McGreevy, "Latinos, Flexing Political Muscle, Come of Age in LA," *Los Angeles Times*, June 27, 2005.

27. "Border Emergency Declared in New Mexico," *CNN*, August 13, 2005.

28. Nicholas Riccardi, "States Take on Border Issues," *Los Angeles Times*, January 16, 2006.

29. John Rice, "Nuñez Visits Mexico to Talk Immigration," Associated Press, August 26, 2005.

30. Tom Baxter, "Illegal Immigration Hot Issue in Legislatures Nationwide," *Cox News Service*, February 20, 2006.

31. Katrina vanden Heuvel, "Toward a Sensible Immigration Policy," *The Nation*, January 21, 2006.

32. Sharon Smith, "The Making of a New Movement," *Socialist Worker*, March 17, 2006.

33. Andy Sullivan and Thomas Ferraro, "Immigration Rallies Sweep U.S.," Associated Press, April 10, 2006.

34. Carolyn Lochhead, "Protests Could Cause Political Problems for Backers of Balanced Approach," *San Francisco Chronicle*, May 1, 2006.

Chapter Twenty-Seven. The Right Wing Calls the Shots

1. Warren Vieth, "Businesses Cast Cloud over Bush's Immigration Plans," *Los Angeles Times*, November 21, 2005.

2. In his book, *The Clash of Civilizations,* Samuel Huntington posits that the future of global conflict will be shaped not by ideology, but by culture and religion. Anti-immigrant politicians like Tancredo use this theory to characterize Mexican migrants as "waging a cultural war" against the "American way of life."

3. Tom Tancredo, interview by John Hawkins, *Right Wing News*, http://www.rightwingnews.com/interviews/tancredo.php.

4. Associated Press, "Tancredo: If They Nuke Us, Bomb Mecca," Fox News, July 18, 2005, http://www.foxnews.com/story/0,2933,162795,00.html.

5. Michael Crowley, "Border War," *New Republic*, March 28, 2005.

6. Holly Bailey, "Tom Tancredo Is Pulling the Immigration Debate to the Right—and Away From Bush," *Newsweek,* April 3, 2006.

7. Marc Cooper, "Showdown on Immigration," *The Nation*, April 3, 2006.

8. Tom Tancredo, interview by John Hawkins, *Right Wing News*, http://www.rightwingnews.com/interviews/tancredo.php.

9. Adam Schrager, "Tancredo Considers Presidential Run to Spotlight Immigration Issue," *9News-NBC*, July 1, 2005, http://www.hispanicvista.com/HVC/Opinion/Commentary/071105Lcomm.htm.

10. Lou Dobbs, "U.S. Policy on Immigration Is a Tragic Joke," *The Arizona Republic*, August 28, 2005.

11. Ibid.

12. "CNN's Immigration Problem: Is Dobbs the Exception—or the Rule?" Fairness and Accuracy in Reporting Web site, April 24, 2006, http://www.fair.org/index.php?page=2867.

13. Jennifer Delson and Anna Gorman, "Immigrant Activists Gather," *Los Angeles Times*, May 29, 2005.

14. Steven K. Paulsen, "Hispanic, Islamic Groups Want Tancredo Out," Associated Press, July 26, 2005.

15. Susy Buchanan and David Holthouse, "Minuteman Leader Has Troubled Past," Southern Poverty Law Center Web site, http://www.splcenter.org/news/item.jsp?pid=166.

16. Daniel González, "Families Sink Roots in Arizona," *Arizona Republic*, October 16, 2005.

17. Holly Yeager, "Republicans Ready to Turn the Screw on Immigration," *Financial Times*, December 14, 2005.

18. Mike Davis, "Vigilante Man," *Tom Dispatch*, May 6, 2005, http://www.tomdispatch.com/index.mhtml?pid=2378.

19. Eduardo Juarez, "The Future Looks Ominous for Immigrants," *El Diario/La Prensa*, August 4, 2005.

20. David Kelly, "Border-Watch Group to Stop Patrols," *Los Angeles Times*, April 21, 2005.

21. Juliet Williams, "Lawsuit Challenges College Fee Break for Illegal Immigrants," *San Diego Union-Tribune*, December 15, 2005.

22. "Anti-Mafia Law Used to Fight Illegal Immigrants," *Fox News*, September 21, 2005, http://www.foxnews.com/story/0,2933,169970,00.html.

23. Daniel Gonzalez, "Greyhound Ticket Policy Biased, Latino Groups Say," *Arizona Republic*, September 24, 2005.

24. Edward Crowder, "Hispanic Hiring Practices Queried in Connecticut," *Connecticut Post*, September 29, 2005.

25. Don Michak, "Anti-Immigration Group 'MexDonald' Author Hit by Pie," *Manchester Journal-Inquirer*, September 29, 2005.

26. Mark Krikorian, "Immigration Problem Needs an Attrition Policy," *Arizona Republic*,

August 28, 2005.

27. "Profile: Federation for American Immigration Reform," Right Web, July 14, 2004, http://rightweb.irc-online.org/profile/1467.

28. Ibid.

29. Editorial, "Borderline Republicans," *Wall Street Journal,* June 17, 2004.

30. T. R. Reid, "Spanish at School Translates to Suspension," *Washington Post,* December 9, 2005.

31. Ibid.

32. Miriam Jordan, "Employers Requiring Workers to Speak English Face Suits," *Wall Street Journal,* November 9, 2005.

33. Rubén Navarette Jr., "From Irrational to Illogical on Immigration," *San Diego Union-Tribune,* December 25, 2005.

34. John Sosbe, "Desperate Times Call for Drastic Measures," *The Georgetonian,* November 2, 2005.

35. Southwestern College is a 60–70 percent Latino college ten miles from the Mexican border. Consequently, upwards of 25 percent of the students are from Mexico. To read about the racist op-ed, and the reaction to it, see Hector Carreon, "'Immigrant Bashing' by a Campus Newspaper," Immigrant Solidarity Network, January 8, 2005, http://www.immigrantsolidarity.org/cgi-bin/datacgi/database.cgi?file=Issues&report =SingleArticle&ArticleID=0152.

36. Southern Poverty Law Center, "Intelligence Report, Blood on the Border," http://www. splcenter.org/intel/intelreport/article.jsp?aid=230.

37. Bill Poovey, "Hispanics New Target of Hate Groups," Associated Press.

Chapter Twenty-Eight. Terrorists on the Border: The Minutemen Stalk Their Prey

1. For a complete discussion of these and other states' unionization rates in 2005, see U.S. Department of Labor, "Union Members in 2005," Bureau of Labor Statistics Web site, January 20, 2006, http://www.bls.gov/news.release/union2.nr0.htm.

2. David Kelly, "Border Watchers Capture Their Prey—the Media," *Los Angeles Times,* April 5, 2005.

3. Peter Prengaman, "Day-labor Employers New Target of Activists," *Arizona Daily Star,* December 12, 2005.

4. David Kelly, "Border Watchers Capture Their Prey—the Media," *Los Angeles Times,* April 5, 2005.

5. Judd Slivka, "On Patrol with the Minutemen," *Slate,* April 6, 2006, http://www.slate .com/id/2139399/entry/2139400/.

6. Michael Leahy, "Crossing the Line," *Washington Post,* March 19, 2006.

7. Ibid.

8. Ibid.

9. Ibid.

10. Janny Scott and David Leonhardt, "Class Matters: Shadowy Lines That Still Divide," *New York Times,* May 15, 2005.

11. Jesse Jackson, "U.S. Economic Divide Swells," *Chicago Sun-Times,* June 21, 2005.

12. Cited in Joe Anthony, "Vigilantes Patrol U.S. Border: The Politics of the Minuteman Project," World Socialist Web site, May 20, 2005, http://www.wsws.org/articles/2005 /may2005/minu-m20.shtml.

13. Robert Lovato, "Minutemen Mobilize Whites Left Behind by Globalization," *Hispanic Vista Magazine,* December 22, 2005.

14. Smith, *Subterranean Fire,* p. 45.
15. Nicholas Riccardi, "Some Border Patrol Agents Take a Chance on Love," *Los Angeles Times,* December 26, 2005.
16. David Kelly, "Border Watchers Capture Their Prey—the Media," *Los Angeles Times,* April 5, 2005.
17. Anthony Giddens, Mitchell Duneier, and Richard P. Appelbaum, *Introduction to Sociology,* 4th ed. (New York: W. W. Norton & Company, 2003), available at http://www.wwnorton.com/giddens4/chapters/chapter11/welcome.htm.
18. Susy Buchanan and David Holthouse, "Minuteman Leader Has Troubled Past," Southern Poverty Law Center Web site, http://www.splcenter.org/news/item.jsp?pid=166.
19. Sarah Knopp, "Racist Network of Right-Wingers," *Socialist Worker,* July 8, 2005.
20. Cited in Sarah Knopp, "Racist Network of Right-Wingers," *Socialist Worker,* July 8, 2005.
21. Peter Lauffer, *Wetback Nation: The Case for Opening the Mexican-American Border* (Chicago: Ivan R. Dee, 2004), p. 118.
22. Susy Buchanan and David Holthouse, "Playing Rough," Southern Poverty Law Center Web site, http://www.splcenter.org/intel/intelreport/article.jsp?pid=953.
23. "Nazis, Racists Join Minutemen Project," Southern Poverty Law Center Web site, April 22, 2005, https://secure.splcenter.org/intel/news/item.jsp?aid=13.
24. To see photo evidence on Indymedia, go to http://sandiego.indymedia.org/en/2005/07/110247.shtml. Also see Susan Gill Vardon and Elizabeth Brotherton, "Day Labor Site Protested," *Orange County Register,* July 31, 2005.
25. Post #9 on the "Strategies, Ideas and Accomplishments" thread, in the forums section of the Save Our States Web site, http://www.saveourstate.org/forums/index.php?showtopic=3897&hl=.
26. Bill Poovey, "Hispanics New Target of Hate Groups," Associated Press, July 29, 2005.
27. "Immigration Protesters Joined by Neo-Nazis in California," Southern Poverty Law Center Web site, http://www.splcenter.org/intel/news/item.jsp?aid=16.

Chapter Twenty-Nine.
Human Rights Activists Confront the Right

1. Brock N. Meeks, "Minutemen Opposition Organizes Resistance," *MSNBC,* June 15, 2005.
2. See Ashley Powers, "Activist's Persistence a Driving Force in Boycott," *Los Angeles Times,* May 1, 2006.
3. David Pierson and Patricia Ward Biederman, "Protest Over Art Forces Police to Draw a Line," *Los Angeles Times,* May 15, 2005.
4. Lance Newman, "Protesters Challenge Vigilantes," *Socialist Worker,* July 22, 2005.
5. "Minutemen Calling for Reinforcements in Campo CA," letter from Gilchrist posted on the Americans for Legal Immigration Web site, July 18, 2005, http://www.alipac.us/article549.html.
6. Post #1 on the "Strategies, Ideas and Accomplishments" thread, in the forums section of the Save Our States Web site, http://www.saveourstate.org/forums/index.php?showtopic=3928.
7. Phillip K. Ireland, "Carlsbad Schools Chief Cancels Forum on Immigration," *North County Times,* August 4, 2005.
8. Bruce Cooley, "Protesters Run Over by Bigot in LA," *Socialist Worker,* June 3, 2005.
9. Susan Page and Kathy Kiely, "Public Divided Over How to Treat Illegals," *USA Today,* April 11, 2006.
10. Susan Decker, "Graham Says Republicans Risk 'Political Suicide' on Immigration," Bloomberg News Service, April 2, 2006.
11. Nicole Gaouette, "Nationwide Raids Intensify Focus on the Employment of Illegal Im-

migrants," *Los Angeles Times,* April 21, 2006.

12. Hemmy So, "Minutemen Get Cold Reception From Blacks," *Los Angeles Times,* May 3, 2006.

13. Jesse L. Jackson Sr., "'Si Se Puede' Means 'We Shall Overcome,'" BlackNews.com, May 13, 2006, http://www.blacknews.com/pr/overcome101.html.

Chapter Thirty. Unions and Immigrant Workers

1. American Social History Project, *Who Built America: Working People and the Nation's Economy, Politics, Culture, and Society* (New York: Pantheon Press, 1992), pp. 421–22.

2. Harris, *National Liberation,* p. 45.

3. Devra Miller, *Dark Sweat,* p. 49.

4. Cockroft, *Outlaws in the Promised Land,* p. 71.

5. Jeremy Brecher, *Strike!* (Cambridge: South End Press, 1997), p. 116.

6. Juan Gómez-Quiñones, *Mexican-American Labor, 1790–1990* (Albuquerque: University of New Mexico Press, 1994), p. 77.

7. Reisler, *Sweat of Their Brow,* pp. 238–39.

8. Ibid., pp. 239–40.

9. Greg Hall, *Harvest Wobblies: The Industrial Workers of the World and Agricultural Workers in the American West, 1905–1930* (Corvallis, OR: Oregon State University Press, 2001), pp. 58–59.

10. For a full discussion of the successes and failures of the IWW, see Philip S. Foner, *History of the Labor Movement in the United States,* vol. 4, *The Industrial Workers of the World* (New York: International Publishers, 1997).

11. Paul Buhle and Dan Georgakas, *The Immigrant Left in the United States* (Albany: State University of New York Press, 1996), pp. 27–28.

12. Rhonda F. Levine, *Class Struggle and the New Deal: Industrial Labor, Industrial Capital, and the State* (Lawrence: University of Kansas Press, 1988), p. 132.

13. Ruth Milkman, *Organizing Immigrants: The Challenge for Unions in Contemporary California* (Ithaca, NY: Cornell University Press, 2000), p. 4.

14. David Gutierrez, *Walls and Mirrors: Mexican Americans, Mexican Immigrants, and the Politics of Ethnicity* (Berkeley: University of California Press, 1995), p. 108.

15. Buhle and Georgakas, *The Immigrant Left,* p. 29.

16. Ibid., p. 31.

17. Ibid., p. 31.

18. Mario T. Garcia, *Mexican Americans* (New Haven: Yale University Press, 1989), p. 212.

19. Ernesto Chavez, *"¡Mi Raza Primero!" Nationalism, Identity and Insurgency in the Chicano Movement in Los Angeles 1966–1978* (Berkeley: University of California Press, 2002), p. 16.

20. Ibid., p. 16.

21. Ibid, p. 16

22. Mario T. Garcia, *Memories of Chicano History: The Life and Narrative of Bert Corona* (Berkeley: University of California Press, 1994), p. 257.

Chapter Thirty-One. Making Borders History

1. Ruiz, *Cannery Women,* pp. 45–46.

2. Ibid., p. xvii.

3. Ibid., p. 44.

4. Ibid., p. 5.

5. The segregation of African-Americans was a key component of this, but a thorough

discussion of this is beyond the scope of this book. See Manning Marable, *How Capitalism Underdeveloped Black America* (Boston: South End Press, 1983), for a detailed analysis of this process.

6. Judith Stephan-Norris and Maurice Zeitlan, *Left Out: Reds and America's Industrial Unions* (New York: Cambridge University Press, 2003), p. 265.

7. Ibid., p. 265.

8. The Teamster president at the time, Frank Fitzsimmons, endorsed the presidential campaign of Richard Nixon in exchange for several pardons of convicted Teamsters, including Jimmy Hoffa Sr. See Susan Ferris and Ricardo Sandoval, *Fight in the Fields: Cesar Chavez and the Farmworkers Movement* (San Diego: Harcourt Brace and Company, 1997).

9. Ferris and Sandoval, *Fight in the Fields*, p. 184.

10. Ibid., p. 221.

11. Ibid., p. 208.

12. Frank Bardacke, "Cesar's Ghost: Decline and Fall of the U.F.W.," *Nation*, July 1993.

13. Wells, *Strawberry Fields*, p. 95.

14. Ferris and Sandoval, *Fight in the Fields*, p. 276.

15. Jim Wasserman, "Governor Davis Signs Farmworker Mediation Bills," Associated Press, September 30, 2002.

16. Ferris and Sandoval, *Fight in the Fields*, p. 209.

17. Ibid., p. 95.

18. Ibid., p. 224.

19. Miriam Pawel, "UFW: A Broken Contract, Farmworkers Reap Little as Union Strays from Its Roots," *Los Angeles Times*, January 8, 2006.

20. Editorial, "'Honored' by Neglect: Will State Again Ignore Farm Workers' Plight?" *Sacramento Bee*, May 22, 2001, http://www.sacbee.com/static/archive/news/projects/workers/20010522_editorial.html.

21. "20,000 Mobilize for Immigrant Workers' Rights," *Asheville Global Report* 74 (June 15–21, 2000), http://www.agrnews.org/issues/74/labor.html.

22. Alan Maass, "Freedom Ride for Immigrant Rights," *Socialist Worker*, October 3, 2003.

23. David Bacon, "Unions at War," *San Francisco Bay Guardian*, August 10–16, 2005.

24. Andrew Pollack, "Immigrant Workers and the Split in the AFL-CIO," *Labor Standard*, http://www.laborstandard.org/AFLCIO/aflcio_split_and_immigrants.htm.

25. David Bacon, "Equality, or Not," *Truthout*, March 3, 2006, http://www.truthout.org/docs_2006/030306S.shtml.

26. "Statement of Change to Win Chair Anna Burger on the Immigration Reform Bill Approved by the Senate Judiciary Committee," press release on the Change to Win Web site, March 29, 2006, http://www.changetowin.org/pdf/BurgerImmig032906.pdf.

27. "Immigrant Union Members: Numbers and Trends," Fact Sheet #7, Migration Policy Institute, May 2004, http://www.migrationpolicy.org/pubs/7_Immigrant_Union_Membership.pdf.

28. Peter Costantini, "A New Internationalism Rising," IPS News Service, January 9, 2006.

29. "As Income Inequality Grows, Union Advantage Increases," American Federation of Teachers Web site, http://www.aftguild.org/News%20Items/AS%20INCOME%20INEQUALITY%20GROWS,%20UNION%20ADVANTAGE%20INCREASES.htm.

30. Peter Constantini, "A New Internationalism Rising," Inter-Press News Service, January 9, 2006.

31. Ibid.

32. Ibid.

33. Eduardo Stanley, "Where Are the Immigrants in the Immigration Debate?"

Chapter Thirty-Two. A New Civil Rights Movement

1. Garcia, *Memories of Chicano History*, p. 316.
2. For a full discussion of IRCA, see David Reimers, *Still the Golden Door*, chapter 7.
3. Lee Sustar, "We're Here and We're Not Leaving!" *Socialist Worker*, March 17, 2006.
4. Ty Coronado et al., "We Want to Be Equal," *Socialist Worker*, March 31, 2006.
5. From a personal interview, conducted in San Diego on May 20, 2006.
6. Quoted in *Lenin's Struggle for A Revolutionary International: Documents: 1907–1916*. (New York: Monad, 1984), p. 19.
7. Quoted in *Ibid.*, p. 19–20.

Chapter Thirty-Three.
Mass Mobilization Defeats Sensenbrenner-King (HR 4437)

1. House Resolution 4437: Border Protection, Antiterrorism and Illegal Immigration Control Act of 2005 was introduced by Republican cosponsors: Representative James Sensenbrenner (R-WI) and Representative Peter King (R-NY). For a full description of its components, see http://www.ncsl.org/research/immigration/summary-of -the-sensenbrenner-immigration-bill.aspx.
2. For a timeline of the marches, see Clare Bayard, "Immigrant Justice Rising: A Chronology of Immigrant-Led Mobilizations, Spring 2006," *Left Turn*, September 1, 2006. Available online at http://www.leftturn.org/immigrant-justice-rising-chronology -immigrant-led-mobilizations-spring-2006.
3. Lee Sustar, "We're Here and We're Not Leaving," *Socialist Worker*, March 17, 2006.
4. Alan Maass, "Week of the Walkouts," *Socialist Worker*, April 7, 2006.
5. From the May 1 protest Web site as of April 2006: www.nohr4437.org.
6. Dan Glaister and Ewen MacAskill, "US Counts Cost of Day without Immigrants," *Guardian*, May 1, 2006. Available online at https://www.theguardian.com/world/2006 /may/02/usa.topstories3.
7. "1 Million March for Immigrants across U.S.," NBC News, May 1, 2006. Available online at http://www.nbcnews.com/id/12573992/ns/us_news-life/t/million-march -immigrants-across-us/
8. Poll cited in Frontera NorteSur online, "Mayday 2006: Initial Assessments," Center for Latin American and Border Studies, New Mexico State University, May 10, 2006.
9. Ibid.
10. Tyche Hendricks, "Irish Join Battle over Illegal Immigration," *San Francisco Chronicle*, March 15, 2006.
11. Oscar Avila, "Activists Unite, Push for Immigrant Rights," *Chicago Tribune*, November 20, 2005.
12. Leslie Fulbright, "Polls, Leaders Say Many Blacks Support Illegal Immigrants," *San Francisco Chronicle*, April 13, 2006.

Chapter Thirty-Four. State Repression of Immigrant Workers

1. Created through the Department of Homeland Security Act of 2002 (November 2002).
2. From the Department of Homeland Security's "Six Point Agenda" available on its Web site at http://www.dhs.gov/xabout/history/editorial_0646.shtm.
3. By 2016, the budget of Homeland Security reached about $64 billion. See "Budget-in-Brief Fiscal Year 2016," United States Department of Homeland Security. Available online at https://www.dhs.gov/sites/default/files/publications/FY_2016_DHS_Budget_in_Brief.pdf.

4. See Julia Preston, "No Need for a Warrant, You're an Immigrant," *New York Times*, October 14, 2007; and Matt O'Brien, "Last-Minute Bush Administration Immigration Changes Could Affect California," *Contra Costa Times*, January 9, 2009.

5. Testimony of Secretary Michael Chertoff before the House Committee on the Judiciary, March 5, 2008.

6. Ibid.

7. Margot Mendelson, Shayna Strom, and Michael Wishnie, "Collateral Damage: An Examination of ICE's Fugitive Operations Program," Migrant Policy Institute, February 2009.

8. Suzanne Gamboa, "Report: Over 100,000 Deportees Had Children in US," Associated Press, February 13, 2009.

9. Sebastian Mallaby, "The Low Risk from Immigrants: Off-Target Priorities for Home-land Defense," *Washington Post*, May 28, 2007.

10. "Immigration Enforcement: The Rhetoric, the Reality," TRAC Immigration, Syracuse University, May 28, 2007. Available online at http://trac.syr.edu/immigration/reports/178/.

11. Norberto Santana Jr., "Report Questions DHS Focus on Immigration," *Orange County Register*, May 28, 2007.

12. Nina Bernstein, "Target of Immigrant Raids Shifted," *New York Times*, February 3, 2009.

13. David Kelly, "Fired Border Patrol Agent Alleges Quota Pressure in Inland Empire," *Los Angeles Times*, February 6, 2009.

14. Douglas S. Massey, Jorge Durand, and Nolan J. Malone, *Beyond Smoke and Mirrors: Mexican Immigration in an Era of Economic Integration* (New York: Russell Sage Foundation, 2002), p. 62.

15. For a full discussion of IRCA, see David Reimers, *Still the Golden Door: The Third World Comes to America* (New York: Columbia University Press, 1992), chapter 7.

16. For a summary of the study, see Dean Calbreath, "Undocumented Workers Carry Big Stick," *San Diego Union Tribune*, September 5, 2006.

17. See Raúl Hinojosa Ojeda, "The Economic Benefits of Comprehensive Immigration Reform: General Equilibrium Approach," *Cato Journal* 32, no. 1 (Fall 2011), 2. Available online at http://www.naid.ucla.edu/uploads/4/2/1/9/4219226/a53_hinojosa_2012_cato_091511 .pdf_published.pdf.

18. Massey, Durand, and Malone, *Beyond Smoke and Mirrors*, 121.

19. Anna Gorman, "Employers of Illegal Immigrants Face Little Risk of Penalty," *Los Angeles Times*, May 29, 2005.

20. See Department of Homeland Security, "An Assessment of United States Immigration and Customs Enforcement's Fugitive Operations Teams," March 5, 2007. Available online at http://www.dhs.gov/xoig/assets/mgmtrpts/ OIG_07-34_Mar07.pdf.

21. An estimated one-third of arrests are "collateral." See Sandra Dibble, "Religious Leaders Want End to Raids' 'Collateral Arrests,'" *San Diego Union Tribune*, April 6, 2007.

22. See Mendelson, Strom, and Wishnie, *Collateral Damage*, 1.

23. From ICE's website. See "Fugitive Operations," available online at https://www.ice.gov /fugitive-operations#wcm-survey-target-id.

24. "ICE Enforcement and Removal Operations Report: Fiscal Year 2015," U.S. Immigration and Customs Enforcement, December 22, 2015, 2. Available online at https:// www.ice.gov/sites/default/files/documents/Report/2016/fy2015removalStats.pdf.

25. Ibid., 4.

26. See "ICE Immigration Raids: A Primer," TRAC Immigration, Syracuse University, February 13, 2017. Available online at http://trac.syr.edu/immigration/reports/459/.

27. For an interesting analysis of terrorism, see "The Definition of Terrorism," *Guardian*, May 7, 2001.

28. See "49 Undocumented Workers Detained At Seymour Johnson," WRAL.com, July 7, 2005. Available online at http://www.wral.com/news/local/story/118273/.

29. See "1,200 Caught in Immigration Raids at IFCO Systems Plants," *USA Today*, April 20, 2006. Available online at https://usatoday30.usatoday.com/money/companies/2006-04 -20-ifco-raids_x.htm.

30. Patrik Jonsson, "Crackdown on Immigrants Empties a Town and Hardens Views," *Christian Science Monitor*, October 3, 2006. Available online at https://www.csmonitor .com/2006/1003/p01s01-ussc.html.

31. "Swift Raids," *New York Times*, December 18, 2006. Available online at http://www .nytimes.com/2006/12/18/opinion/18mon1.html.

32. David Bacon, "The Story of the Smithfield Raid," *Truthout*, May 18, 2007. Available online at http://www.truth-out.org/archive/item/70682:david-bacon--the-story-of-the -smithfield-raid.

33. "Raid Outrage: Crowd Protests Federal Raid at Little Village Shopping Plaza," *Chicago Tribune*, April 27, 2007. Available online at http://articles.chicagotribune.com/2007-04 -25/news/0704250739_1_afternoon-raid-illegal-immigration-agents.

34. Karen Lee Ziner, "Immigration Sweep Nets 42, Provoking Outcry," *Providence Journal*, June 14, 2008.

35. See Andrea Hopkins, "Immigration Raids Koch Foods Ohio Chicken Plant," Reuters, August 28, 2007. Available online at https://www.reuters.com/article/us-immigration -koch/immigration-raids-koch-foods-ohio-chicken-plant-idUSN2825845020070828; "Immigration Raid at Meat Processing Plant in Iowa Largest Ever in US," *New York Daily News*, May 13, 2008. Available online at http://www.nydailynews.com/latino /immigration-raid-meat-processing-plant-iowa-largest-article-1.332576; and "Immi- gration Agents Detain Hundreds at Poultry Plants," CNN.com, April 17, 2008. Avail- able online at http://www.cnn.com/2008/US/04/17/immigration.raid/index.html.

36. "Immigration Raid at Parachute Plant Nets 57," *Mountain Express News* (Asheville, North Carolina), August 12, 2008. Available online at https://mountainx.com/news /community-news/immigration_raid_at_parachute_plant_nets_57/.

37. See Adam Nossiter, "Nearly 600 Were Arrested in Factory Raid, Officials Say," *New York Times*, August 26, 2008. Available online at http://www.nytimes.com/2008/08/27 /us/27raid.html.

38. See Heather Knight, "Immigration Raids at 11 El Balazo Restaurants—63 Seized," *San Francisco Chronicle*, May 3, 2008. Available online at http://www.sfgate.com/restaurants/ar- ticle/Immigration-raids-at-11-El-Balazo-restaurants-3285437.php; Kristina Davis, "French Gourmet Case a Cautionary Tale about Workplace Immigration Enforcement," *San Diego Union Tribune*, March 4, 2017. Available online at http://www.sandiegouniontribune.com /news/immigration/sd-me-french-gourmet-20170304-story.html; "114 Employees File Complaints over ICE raids" *Los Angeles Daily News*, April 26, 2008. Available online at http://www.dailynews.com/2008/04/26/114-employees-file-complaints-over-ice-raids/; James Pinkerton, "20 Arrested in Immigration Raid at Houston Shipley Do-Nuts," *Houston Chronicle*, April 16, 2008. Available online at http://www.chron.com/news/article/20 -arrested-in-immigration-raid-at-Houston-1664461.php; "Mass. Factory Closed, Site of '07 Immigration Raid," *Twin Cities Pioneer Press,* May 9, 2009. Available online at http://www .twincities.com/2009/05/29/mass-factory-closed-site-of-07-immigration-raid/; Nick Madi- gan, "Man Suing Government over Raid at 7-Eleven Fled to U.S. because of Death Threat," *Baltimore Sun*, June 25, 2011. Available online at http://www.baltimoresun.com/news /maryland/politics/bs-md-alvarez-raid-20110613-story.html; N.C. Aizenman, "42 Workers Detained in ICE Raid at Dulles," *Washington Post*, August 14, 2008. Available online at http:// www.washingtonpost.com/wp-dyn/content/article/2008/08/13/AR2008081303649.html.

39. Emily Bazar, "West Coast Mayors Decry Immigration Raids," *USA Today*, June 19, 2008.
40. Stewart M. Powell, "Bush Administration Steps Up Immigration Raids," *Houston Chronicle*, June 1, 2008.
41. Rogelio V. Solis, "Immigration Raid Spotlights Rift of Have-Nots," Associated Press, January 24, 2009.
42. Richard Stana, "Immigration Enforcement Controls over Program Authorizing State and Local Enforcement of Federal Immigration Laws Should Be Strengthened," testimony by the director of homeland security and justice issues presented before the Committee on Homeland Security, House of Representatives, March 4, 2009. Report prepared by the United States Government Accountability Office.
43. Dzung Do, "The Border, the Wall and a Post-9/11 World," *AlterNet*, December 30, 2008.
44. Maria Jimenez, "Humanitarian Crisis: Migrant Deaths at the U.S.-Mexico Border," *Report of the American Civil Liberties Union of San Diego and Imperial Counties and Mexico's National Commission of Human Rights*, October 2009.
45. See "Stopping Migrant Deaths," National Network for Immigrant and Refugee Rights. Available online at http://www.nnirr.org/drupal/stopping-migrant-deaths. A similar figure is cited in Manny Fernandez, "A Path to America, Marked by More and More Bodies," *New York Times*, May 4, 2017. Available online at https://www.nytimes.com/interactive/2017/05/04/us/texas-border-migrants-dead-bodies.html.
46. Kristen McCabe and Jeanne Batalova, "Immigration Enforcement in the United States," Migration Policy Institute, November 2009.
47. Jacqueline Stevens, "America's Secret ICE Castles," *Nation*, December 16, 2009.
48. Mark Hugo Lopez, "A Rising Share: Hispanics and Federal Crime," Pew Hispanic Center, February 18, 2009. Available online at http://pewhispanic.org/reports/report.php?ReportID=104.
49. United States Government Accountability Office, "Border Patrol Checkpoints Contribute to Border Patrol's Mission, but More Consistent Data Collection and Performance Measurement Could Improve Effectiveness," Report to Congressional Requesters, August 31, 2009.
50. Mark Hugo Lopez, "A Rising Share: Hispanics and Federal Crime," Pew Hispanic Center, February 18, 2009. Available online at http://pewhispanic.org/reports/report.php?ReportID=104.
51. See the Web site for Immigrations and Customs Enforcement for data at www.ice.gov.
52. Marisa Taylor, "Immigration Officials Detaining, Deporting American Citizens," *McClatchy Newspapers*, January 24, 2008.
53. Ginger Thompson, "Fewer Reported Entering U.S. Illegally," *New York Times*, October 3, 2008.
54. Howard Witt, "Immigration Issue Rerouted to State Level as National Interest Wanes," *Chicago Tribune*, March 23, 2008.
55. Justin Juozapavicius, "Oklahoma Feels Effects of Strong Law Targeting Undocumented Immigrants," Associated Press, January 28, 2008.
56. David Fried, "Local Illegal Immigration Laws Draw a Diverse Group of Cities," *North County Times*, September 3, 2006.

Chapter Thirty-Five. The Immigrant Rights Movement at the Polls

1. See Kathy Kiely, "Public Divided over How to Treat Illegals," *USA Today*, April 11, 2006. See also Julia Preston and Marjorie Connelly, "Majority Favor Changing Immigration

Laws, Poll Says," *New York Times*, May 24, 2007.

2. John Marelius, "California Voters Support Comprehensive Approach," *San Diego Union Tribune*, July 27, 2006.

3. For a detailed breakdown of the 2006 vote, see David L. Leal, Stephen A. Nuño, Jongho Lee, and Rodolfo O. de la Garza, "Latinos, Immigration, and the 2006 Midterm Elections," *PS: Political Science Journal* 41, no. 2 (April 2008), 309–17.

4. Justin Akers Chacón, "Candidates Close Ranks Against Immigrants," *San Diego Union Tribune*, December 21, 2007.

5. Tamar Jacoby, "Immigration Bomb Is a Dud," *Arizona Republic*, February 3, 2008.

6. For example, see the following example of how protesters weakened Minuteman efforts: Leslie Berestein, "Protesters, Turnout Shake Up Organizer," *San Diego Union Tribune*, September 19, 2005.

7. For examples, see Peter Prengaman, "Minuteman Caravan to Capitol Hill Launches amid Black Divisions," Associated Press, May 3, 2006; and Leslie Fulbright, "Polls, Leaders Say Many Blacks Support Illegal Immigrants," *San Francisco Chronicle*, April 13, 2006.

8. Kerry Lester, "Could Infighting End Minuteman Movement?," *Daily Herald* (Chicago), May 19, 2008.

9. "Illegal Immigration Fears Fuel Klan Growth," Associated Press, February 12, 2007.

10. David Holthouse and Mark Potok, "2007: A Year Marked by Staggering Levels of Racist Hate," Southern Poverty Law Center, *Intelligence Report*, March 1, 2008. Available online at https://www.splcenter.org/fighting-hate/intelligence -report/2008/2007-year-marked-staggering-levels-racist-hate.

11. Amy Taxin, "Minutemen Leader Laments Path of Anti-Illegal Immigration Groups," *Orange County Register*, June 25, 2008.

12. See David Almager, "Hispanic Voters Can Flex Their Muscles in Texas," *Amarillo Globe-News*, February 24, 2008; Jeanne Cummings, "Hispanic Voters Shift Allegiance to Democrats," *Wall Street Journal*, November 8, 2006; and Joe Mathews, "Voting Like It's Mañana," *Los Angeles Times*, February 24, 2008.

13. Leslie Berestein and John Marelius, "Immigration Steered Latinos to Obama," *San Diego Union Tribune*, November 7, 2008.

14. John Marelius and Leslie Berestein, "Obama Tells La Raza That Immigration Reform Is a Priority," *San Diego Union Tribune*, July 13, 2008.

15. See Tim Rutten, "L.A.'s Political Predictor—the Latino Vote," *Los Angeles Times*, November 12, 2008. Available online at http://articles.latimes.com/2008/nov/12/opinion /oe-rutten12.

16. Tim Rutten, "L.A.'s Latinos Are a Sign of Things to Come," *Los Angeles Times*, November 12, 2008.

17. Stewart M. Powell, "Napolitano Signals Shift in Worksite Raids," *Houston Chronicle*, January 15, 2009.

18. Suzanne Gamboa, "Obama Takes Immigration Reform off Agenda," Associated Press, April 29, 2010.

19. See "Obama Fence Statement: Border Security," video, C-Span, https://www.c-span.org /video/?c4652652/obama-fence-statement.

20. See Ginger Thompson and David M. Herszenhorn, "Obama Set for First Step on Immigration Reform," *New York Times*, June 24, 2009. Available online at http://www .nytimes.com/2009/06/25/us/politics/25immig.html.

21. Jared Allen, "Speaker Pelosi to Shield Vulnerable Members from Controversial Votes," *The Hill*, December 16, 2009.

22. Thompson and Herszenhorn, "Obama Set for First Step."

23. Sam Stein, "Confidential Study Suggests Tougher Words for Dems on Immigration," *Huffington Post*, February 29, 2008. See: http://www.huffingtonpost.com/2008/02/29 /confidential-study-sugges_n_89077.html.

24. Posted on Schumer's Web site: https://www.schumer.senate.gov/new_website/record .cfm?id=314990.

25. Janet Napolitano, "U.S. Pursuing Integrated Strategy for Border Problems," *Houston Chronicle*, August 14, 2009.

26. The actual number of those fired or who quit to avoid identification is impossible to know for sure, although it likely reached into the thousands. See Julia Preston, "Immigration Crackdown with Firings, Not Raids," *New York Times*, September 29, 2009. Available online at http://www.nytimes.com/2009/09/30/us/30factory.html.

27. Richard Marosi and Anna Gorman, "Immigration Agency Targets Upscale San Diego Restaurant," *Los Angeles Times*, May 25, 2010.

28. Spencer S. Hsu and N. C. Aizenman, "DHS Corrects Report That Overstated ICE Deportations under Obama," *Washington Post*, March 8, 2010.

29. Meredith Simons, "Obama Beefs Up Border Security in 2011 Budget," *San Francisco Chronicle*, February 1, 2010.

30. See Schumer's Web site for full description of the "seven principles" of immigration reform.

31. Spencer S. Hsu, "Senate Democrats' Plan Highlights Nation's Shift to the Right on Immigration," *Washington Post*, May 2010.

32. Lisa Mascaro, "Senate Sends Last-Minute Bills to the House before Recess," *Los Angeles Times*, August 6, 2010.

33. Jens Manuel Krogstad, "Hispanics Punch below Their Weight in Midterm Elections," Pew Research Center, April 2, 2014. Available online at http://www.pewresearch.org /fact-tank/2014/04/02/hispanics-punch-below-their-weight-in-midterm-elections/.

34. David Bacon, "Firing Immigrants," *Progressive*, December 2009/January 2010.

35. See Patrick O'Connor, "Immigration Split Still Hangs over McCain and Republicans," *Politico*, March 5, 2008.

36. Nicole Gaouette, "An Immigration End Run around the Next President," *Los Angeles Times*, June 23, 2008.

37. Alan Fram, "Poll: Hispanic Discrimination High," Associated Press, May 20, 2010. Available online at http://www.nbcnews.com/id/37263388/ns/us_news-life/t/poll -hispanic-discrimination-high/#.WdhKGzBryUk.

38. Tom Barry, "Planning the War on Immigrants," Americas Program, Center for International Policy (CIP), December 13, 2007.

39. Julia Preston, "Firm Stance on Illegal Immigrants Remains Policy," *New York Times*, August 3, 2009.

40. As an example, the notorious anti-immigrant sheriff Paul Babeu of Pinal County, Arizona, spoke on a white nationalist radio show. See Brahm Resnik, "Pinal County Sheriff: Obama near 'Borderline' of Treason," *Arizona Republic*, July 23, 2010.

Chapter Thirty-Six. The Arizona Laboratory and SB 1070

1. In 2012, the U.S. Supreme Court struck down several clauses, ruling the federal law preempted state law on the matter. These included the requirement that immigrants carry documentation at all time, restrictions on the ability of police to be able to arrest people without a warrant, and the provision that workers without federal authorization be denied the right to work. Nevertheless, the other provisions were retained although they have rarely been enforced after numerous lawsuits. See Nigel Duara, "Arizona's

Once-Feared Immigration Law, SB 1070, Loses Most of Its Power in Settlement," *Los Angeles Times*, September 15, 2016. Available online at http://www.latimes.com/nation /la-na-arizona-law-20160915-snap-story.html.

2. For more on Proposition 203, see Jeff Bale, "The Fight for Bilingual Education," *International Socialist Review* 69 (January 2010). Available online at http://isreview.org /issue/69/fight-bilingual-education.

3. Randal C. Archibald, "Arizona Is Split over Hard Line on Immigrants," *New York Times*, December 14, 2007. See also John Schmitt, "Unions and Upward Mobility for Immigrant Workers," Center for Economic and Policy Research, March 2010. Available online at http://cepr.net/publications/reports/unions-upward-mobility-immigrant-workers.

4. "Extremist Leads New Arkansas Anti-Immigration Group," Southern Poverty Law Center, January 25, 2005. Available online at http://www.splcenter.org/intel/news/item .jsp?aid=8. See Department of Homeland Security, "An Assessment of United States Immigration and Customs Enforcement's Fugitive Operations Teams," March 5, 2007. Available online at http://www.dhs.gov/xoig/assets/mgmtrpts/.

5. Delegation of Immigration Authority Section 287(g), Immigration and Nationality Act. According to the DHS: "The Illegal Immigration Reform and Immigrant Responsibility Act (IIRAIRA), effective September 30, 1996, added Section 287(g), performance of immigration officer functions by state officers and employees, to the Immigration and Nationality Act (INA). This authorizes the secretary of the U.S. Department of Homeland Security (DHS) to enter into agreements with state and local law enforcement agencies, permitting designated officers to perform immigration law enforcement functions, pursuant to a Memorandum of Agreement (MOA), provided that the local law enforcement officers receive appropriate training and function under the supervision of sworn U.S. Immigration and Customs Enforcement (ICE) officers." Available online at http://www .ice.gov/partners/287g/Section287_g.htm.

6. Judi Villa and Yvonne Wingett, "Sheriff Unveils Migrant Hotline," *Arizona Republic*, July 21, 2007.

7. As an example, Joe Arpaio went to San Diego, California, in November 2009 to campaign for county sheriff candidate Jay LaSuer, who boasted that he would run the county in a similar way. See Stephen Lemons, "Joe Arpaio Stumps Southern California for Conservative Sheriff Wannabes Jay LaSuer and Bill Hunt," *Phoenix New Times*, October 2, 2009. Available online at http://www.phoenixnewtimes.com/blogs/joe-arpaio -stumps-southern-california-for-conservative-sheriff-wannabes-jay-lasuer-and -bill-hunt-6500796.

8. Seth Freed Wessler, "Bills Modeled after Arizona's SB 1070 Spread through States," *Colorlines*, March 2, 2011. Available online at http://www.colorlines.com/content /bills-modeled-after-arizonas-sb-1070-spread-through-states.

9. Alia Beard Rau, "Arizona Immigration Law Was Crafted by Activist," *Arizona Republic*, May 31, 2010.

10. Senate Bill 1070.

11. Dennis Wagner, "Violence Is Not up on Arizona Border," *Arizona Republic*, May 2, 2010.

12. Dennis Wagner, "Slaying of Arizona Rancher Is Still a Mystery," *Arizona Republic*, November 24, 2010. Available online at http://archive.azcentral.com/news/politics /articles/20131123arizona-border-robert-krentz-unsolved.html.

13. Wagner, "Violence Is Not Up."

14. Ibid.

15. See Tim Padgett, "The 'Dangerous' Border: Actually One of America's Safest Places," *Time*, July 30, 2010.

16. Martha Mendoza, "Border Is Relatively Safe, Gov't Data Show," Associated Press, June

4, 2010.

17. Stephanie Condon, "Poll: Most Still Support Arizona Immigration Law," CBS News, May 25, 2010.

18. Betty Beard, "Arizona Jobs Outlook for Recent College Graduates Bleak, but Improving," *Arizona Republic*, June 6, 2010.

19. Salvador Rodriguez, "15 Arrested during Raid of Phoenix Meat-Packing Business," *Arizona Republic*, October 12, 2010. Available online at http://archive.azcentral.com /news/articles/2010/10/12/20101012phoenix-sheriff-immigration-raid-abrk.html.

20. Ginger Rough, "Signing Arizona Immigration Law Was Never a Question for Governor," *Arizona Republic*, June 1, 2010.

21. Cathleen Decker, "Steve Poizner Zeros In on an Untimely Issue," *Los Angeles Times*, March 28, 2010.

22. Teddy Davis, "Meg Whitman Alters Immigration Rhetoric," ABC News Online, March 16, 2010.

23. "Whitman: Arizona Immigration Law OK for Arizona," *Sacramento Bee*, July 29, 2010.

24. Jack Chang, "Meg Whitman Courts Latinos with Spanish-Language TV Ads," *Sacramento Bee*, June 18, 2010.

25. Text of the letter available here: http://www.faculty.umb.edu/lawrence_blum/courses /CCT627_10/readings/horne_open_letter_tucson.pdf.

26. Miriam Jordan, "Arizona Grades Teachers on Fluency," *Wall Street Journal*, April 30, 2010.

27. According to 2014 statistics. See "Demographic Profile of Hispanics in Arizona, 2014," Pew Research Center. Available online at http://www.pewhispanic.org/states/state/az/.

28. Stephen A. Nuño, "Is Arizona 2010 Like California 1994?," Latino Decisions, May 24, 2010.

29. Dennis Wagner, "Altered Mural Fuels Racial Debate in Prescott," *Arizona Republic*, June 4, 2010.

30. Suzy Khimm, "Anti-Immigration Group Claims Neo-Nazis Involved in Tancredo Rally," *Mother Jones*, May 19, 2010.

31. Paul Davenport, "Brewer Claims Most Illegal Immigrants Are Smuggling Drugs," Associated Press, June 26, 2010.

32. Michelle Price, "Reputed Neo-Nazi Joins Border Action," Associated Press, July 18, 2010.

Chapter Thirty-Seven. S. 744: The Degeneration of "Comprehensive Immigration Reform"

1. CNN Political Unit, "CNN Poll: Most See Pathway to Citizenship," April 16, 2013. Available online at http://politicalticker.blogs.cnn.com/2013/04/16/cnn-poll-most-see -pathway-to-citizenship-2/.

2. Jeffrey S. Passel, D'Vera Cohn, and Ana Gonzalez-Barrera, "Net Migration from Mexico Falls to Zero—and Perhaps Less," Pew Research Center: Hispanic Trends, April 23, 2012. Available online at http://www.pewhispanic.org/2012/04/23/net-migration-from -mexico-falls-to-zero-and-perhaps-less/.

3. "Top 10 of 2010 - Issue #1: Evidence from the Great Recession Is In: Migration Flows Dropped, Unemployment among Certain Immigrants Rose," Migration Policy Institute, December 2, 2010. Available online at http://www.migrationpolicy.org/article/top-10 -2010-issue-1-evidence-great-recession-migration-flows-dropped-unemployment-among/.

4. See the report "Border Patrol: Goals and Measures Not Yet in Place to Inform Border Security Status and Resource Needs," United States Government Accountability Office, February 26, 2013. Available online at http://www.gao.gov/assets/660/652331.pdf.

5. See Andrew Selee, "The New Reality at the Border," *Los Angeles Times*, April 2, 2013.

Available online at http://articles.latimes.com/2013/apr/02/opinion/la-oe-0402-selee
-immigration-Mexico-20130402.

6. See Demetrios Papademetriou and Aaron Terrazas, "Immigrants in the United States
    and the Current Economic Crisis" Migration Policy Institute, April 1, 2009. Available
    online at http://www.migrationpolicy.org/article/immigrants-united-states-and-current
    -economic-crisis/.

7. Javier Rojo and Manuel Perez-Rocha, "NAFTA at 20: The New Spin," Foreign Policy in
    Focus, March 14, 2013. Available online at http://fpif.org/nafta_at_20_the_new_spin/.

8. See Kevin G. Hall, "U.S. Workers Endure 'Lost Decade' of Declining Wages," *McClatchy
    Newspapers*, November 15, 2012. Available online at http://www.mcclatchydc.com
    /news/nation-world/national/economy/article24740389.html.

9. See "On a Typical Day in FY2012," U.S. Customs and Border Protection Web site, avail-
    able online at https://www.cbp.gov/newsroom/stats/on-typical-day-fy2012; and Leigh
    Ann Caldwell, "The U.S. Already Spends Billions on Border Security," NBC News,
    August 31, 2016. Available online at https://www.nbcnews.com/politics/2016-election
    /trump-s-wall-would-add-billions-u-s-spends-border-n640251.

10. Eric Lipton, "As Wars End, a Rush to Grab Dollars Spent on the Border," *New York
    Times*, June 6, 2013. Available online at http://www.nytimes.com/2013/06/07/us
    /us-military-firms-eye-border-security-contracts.html?pagewanted=all.

11. Ibid.

12. See "Border Patrol: Checkpoints Contribute to Border Patrol's Mission, but More Con-
    sistent Data Collection and Performance Measurement Could Improve Effectiveness,"
    U.S. Government Accountability Office, August 31, 2009. Available online at http://
    www.gao.gov/assets/300/294558.html.

13. See "A Continued Humanitarian Crisis at the Border: Undocumented Border Crosser
    Deaths Recorded by the Pima County Office of the Medical Examiner, 1990–2012,"
    Binational Migration Institute, The University of Arizona, June 2013. Available online
    at http://bmi.arizona.edu/sites/default/files/border_deaths_final_web.pdf.

14. See Jean Guerrero, "Death at the Border: Threat of Trump's Wall Intensifies Search for
    Dying Migrants," KPBS, December 13, 2016. Available online at http://www.kpbs.org
    /news/2016/dec/13/death-border-threat-trumps-wall-intensifies-search/; and Amanda
    Holpuch, "Migrant Deaths at US-Mexico Border Increase 17% This Year, UN Figures
    Show," *Guardian*, August 5, 2017. Available online at https://www.theguardian
    .com/us-news/2017/aug/05/migrants-us-mexico-border-deaths-figures.

15. Glenn Greenwald, Ewen MacAskill, and Laura Poitras, "Edward Snowden: The Whis-
    tleblower behind the NSA Surveillance Revelations," *Guardian*, June 11, 2013. Available
    online at https://www.theguardian.com/world/2013/jun/09/edward-snowden-nsa
    -whistleblower-surveillance.

16. Sara Murray and Mark Peters, "E-Verify Would Gain in Immigration Overhaul," *Wall
    Street Journal*, April 10, 2013. Available online at https://www.wsj.com/articles
    /SB10001424127887323741004578415012503635342.

17. "Findings of the E-Verify® Program Evaluation," U.S. Department of Homeland Security,
    Washington, DC, December 2009. Available online at https://www.uscis.gov/sites
    /default/files/USCIS/E-Verify/E-Verify/Final%20E-Verify%20Report%2012-16-09_2.pdf.

18. See David Bier, "Will E-Verify Have Discriminatory Results?," *Huffington Post*, June 26,
    2013. Available online at http://www.huffingtonpost.com/david-bier/will-everify
    -have-discrim_b_3165193.html.

19. See Doug Porter, "The Starting Line: Mission Valley Hilton Hotel Management Tactics
    Prompt Employee Hunger Strike," *San Diego Free Press*, April 5, 2013. Available online
    at http://sandiegofreepress.org/2013/04/the-starting-line-mission-valley-hilton-hotel

-management-tactics-prompt-employee-hunger-strike/.

20. See Brad Plumer, "The $2 Trillion Shadow Economy Is the Recession's Big Winner," *Washington Post*, April 23, 2013. Available online at https://www.washingtonpost.com /news/wonk/wp/2013/04/23/americas-2-trillion-shadow-economy-is-the-recessions -big-winner/.

21. Jennifer Medina, "Immigrant Workers Give New Direction to Los Angeles Unions," *New York Times*, May 23, 2013. Available online at http://www.nytimes.com/2013 /05/18/us/los-angeles-labor-leader-puts-focus-on-immigrants.html?pagewanted=all.

22. See Leah Zallman, Steffie Woolhandler, David Himmelstein, David Bor, and Danny Mc-Cormick, "Immigrants Contributed an Estimated $115.2 Billion More to the Medicare Trust Fund Than They Took Out in 2002–09," *Health Affairs*, May 2013. Available online at http://content.healthaffairs.org/content/early/2013/05/20/hlthaff.2012.1223.full.

23. Matt Barreto, "Why the DREAM Act Will Matter in the 2012 Election," Latino Decisions, February 28, 2012. Available online at http://www.latinodecisions.com /blog/2011/02/28/why-the dream-act-will-matter-in-2012/.

24. "United States Farmworker Factsheet," North Carolina Farmworker Institute. Available online at http://saf-unite.org/sites/default/files/SAF_Fact_Sheet_US07_0.pdf.

25. See their Web site at https://www.fwd.us/.

26. Jia Lynn Yang and Craig Timberg, "Tech Industry Poised to Win in Immigration Debate," *Washington Post*, April 12, 2013. Available online at https://www.washingtonpost .com/business/economy/tech-industry-poised-to-win-in-immigration-debate /2013/04/12/c735d758-a38c-11e2-82bc 511538ac90a4_story.html.

27. See Ed Stoddard, "Exclusive: Over a Million Immigrants Land U.S. Jobs in 2008–10," Reuters, January 20, 2011. Available online at http://www.reuters.com/article/us-usa -immigrants-employmentexclusive-idUSTRE70J37P20110120; Papademetriou and Terrazas, "Immigrants in the United States"; Jeffrey S. Passel, "Unauthorized Immigrants: How Pew Research Counts Them and What We Know About Them," Pew Research Center, April 17, 2013. Available online at http://www.pewresearch.org/2013/04/17/unauthorized -immigrants-how-pew-research-counts-them-and-what-we-know-about-them/; Jeffrey S. Passel, and D'Vera Cohn, "A Portrait of Unauthorized Immigrants in the United States," Pew Research Center, April 14, 2009. Available online at http://www.pewhispanic. org/2009/04/14/a-portrait-of-unauthorized-immigrants-in-the-united-states/.

28. See Demetrios G. Papademetriou, Will Somerville, and Madeleine Sumption, "The Social Mobility of Immigrants and Their Children," Migration Policy Institute, June 2009. Available online at www.migrationpolicy.org/pubs/soialmobility2010.pdf; Elizabeth Grieco, "Immigrant Union Members Numbers and Trends," Migration Policy Institute, May 2004. Available online at http://www.migrationpolicy.org/research/immigrant-union-members -numbers-and-trends?pdf=7_immigrant_union_membership.pdf.

Chapter Thirty-Eight. Immigrant Rights at a Crossroads

1. Ray Sanchez, "Latino Voters 2012: Exhilaration over President Obama Turns to Dread and Disappointment," *Huffington Post*, January 17, 2012.

2. Perry Bacon Jr., "Low Turnout by Young Voters Hurts Democrats in Midterm Elections," *Washington Post*, November 3, 2010. Available online at http://www.washingtonpost .com/wp-dyn/content/article/2010/11/03/AR2010110304486.html.

3. Scott Keeter, "Where the Public Stands on Immigration Reform," Pew Research Center, November 23, 2009.

4. CNN Wire Staff, "CNN Poll: Support for Border Crackdown Grows," CNN, May 26, 2010.

5. "CNN Poll: Should Illegal Immigrants Be Allowed to Stay?," CNN, July 29, 2010. Avail-

able online at http://politicalticker.blogs.cnn.com/2010/07/29/cnn-poll-should-illegal
-immigrants-be-allowed-to-stay.
6. Elizabeth Llorente, "On Immigration, Polls Show Most GOP Voters Share Gingrich
   Stance," Fox News Latino, December 14, 2011, available online at http://www.foxnews
   .com/politics/2011/12/14/on-immigration-polls-show-most-gop-voters-share-gingrich
   -stance.html#ixzz1gWDArQq8.
7. January 2012 Washington Post–ABC News Poll available online at http://www.washing-
   tonpost.com/wp-srv/politics/polls/postabcpoll_011512.html.
8. America's Voice Online, "Republicans, Fenced in by Immigration: 20 Pro-Reform Candidates
   Beat Hard-Liners in 22 Battleground House and Senate Races," January 25, 2010. Available
   online at https://americasvoice.org/content/republicans_fenced_in_by_immigration.
9. "Immigration Polls," 2016 numbers, Gallup. Available online at http://www.gallup.com
   /poll/1660/immigration.aspx.
10. Kate Linthicum, "Most California Voters Think Illegal Immigration Is a Problem, but
    Don't See Mass Deportation as the Answer," Los Angeles Times, March 31, 2016. Avail-
    able online at http://www.latimes.com/politics/la-pol-ca-latimes-immigration
    -california-primary-poll-20160331-story.html.
11. Mike McPhate, "California Today: A Big Swing on Sanctuary Cities," New York Times,
    April 24, 2017. Available online at https://www.nytimes.com/2017/04/24/us/california
    -today-sanctuary-cities.html.
12. For an example of the convergence between Occupy and pro-immigrant sentiment,
    see Kent Paterson, "For Immigrant Groups and Occupy Movement, Issues Converge,"
    NMPolitics.net, May 4, 2012. Available online at http://nmpolitics.net/index/2012/05
    /for-immigrant-groups-and-occupy-movement-issues-converge.
13. Lydia Saad, "Economy Is Dominant Issue for Americans as Election Nears," Gallup,
    October 22, 2012. Available online at http://www.gallup.com/poll/158267/economy
    -dominant-issue-americans-election-nears.aspx.
14. See Frank Sherry, "One Year Ago Today, Mitt Romney Said 'Answer Is Self-Deportation,'
    Setting Stage for His Loss in November," America's Voice, January 23, 2013. Available
    online at http://americasvoice.org/blog/on-this-day-in-history-mitt-romney-said-answer
    -is-self-deportation-one-year-ago-today-setting-the-stage-for-his-loss-in-november/.
15. Elizabeth Llorente, "Poll: Latinos Were Key Factor in Arizona Recall Vote," Fox News
    Latino, November 15, 2011.
16. Alia Beard Rau, "Russell Pearce Recall May Indicate New Political Climate," Arizona
    Republic, November 12, 2011.
17. See Jeffrey M. Jones, "Economy Is Paramount Issue to U.S. Voters," Gallup, February 29,
    2012. Available online at http://www.gallup.com/poll/153029/economy-paramount
    -issue-voters.aspx; see also Drew Desilver, "U.S. Income Inequality, on Rise for De-
    cades, Is Now Highest since 1928," Pew Research Center, December 5, 2013. Available
    online at http://www.pewresearch.org/fact-tank/2013/12/05/u-s-income-inequality
    -on-rise-for-decades-is-now-highest-since-1928/. Lastly, nearly half the population
    thought social inequality was a serious concern. See Bruce Stokes, "The U.S.'s High
    Income Gap Is Met with Relatively Low Public Concern," Pew Research Center, De-
    cember 6, 2013. Available online at http://www.pewresearch.org/fact-tank/2013/12/06
    /the-u-s-s-high-income-gap-is-met-with-relatively-low-public-concern/.
18. See Matt Cooper, "Poll: Most Americans Support Occupy Wall Street," Atlantic, Octo-
    ber 9, 2011. Available online at https://www.theatlantic.com/politics/archive/2011/10
    /poll-most-americans-support-occupy-wall-street/246963/.
19. Devin Burghart and Leonard Zeskind, "Beyond FAIR: The Decline of the Established
    Anti-Immigrant Organizations and the Rise of Tea Party Nativism," Institute for

Research & Education on Human Rights (IREHR), January 17, 2012. Available online at www.irehr.org.

20. See Frank Rich, "The Billionaires Bankrolling the Tea Party," *New York Times*, August 28, 2010.

21. Miriam Jordan, "Alabama Immigrant Law Irks Business," *Wall Street Journal*, August 24, 2011.

22. See National Conference of State Legislators, "Immigration Policy Report," September 19, 2011. Available online at www.ncsl.org.

23. For example, see Rachel Rose Hartmann, "Obama Blames Republicans for Failure of Immigration Reform, Says Increase in Deportations Is Misleading," Yahoo News, September 28, 2011.

24. Suzanne Gamboa, "Obama Takes Immigration Reform Agenda Off Table," Associated Press, April 29, 2010.

25. Tom LoBianco, "Indiana Governor Signs Right-to-Work Bill," *Associated Press*, February 1, 2012.

26. See Wyatt Buchanan, "Democrats OK Big Cuts to California's Safety Net," *San Francisco Chronicle*, March 4, 2011.

27. Elizabeth Aguilera, "Illegal Immigration from Mexico Continues Decline," *San Diego Union Tribune*, July 7, 2011.

28. Nick Miroff and William Booth, "Border Arrests See Big Decline," *Washington Post*, December 4, 2011.

29. Ibid.

30. Rakesh Kochhar, Richard Fry, and Paul Taylor, "Hispanic Household Wealth Fell by 66% from 2005 to 2009," Pew Hispanic Center, July 26, 2011.

31. Paul Taylor, Mark Hugo Lopez, Gabriel Velasco, and Seth Motel, "Hispanics Say They Have the Worst of a Bad Economy," Pew Hispanic Center, January 26, 2012.

32. Carmen DeNavas, Bernadette D. Proctor, and Jessica C. Smith, "Income, Poverty, and Health Insurance Coverage in the United States: 2010," US Census Bureau.

33. Mark Hugo Lopez and Gabriel Velasco, "Childhood Poverty among Hispanics Sets Record, Leads Nation," Pew Hispanic Center, September 28, 2011; and "Children in Poverty by Race and Ethnicity," Annie Casey Foundation Data Center. Available online at http://datacenter.kidscount.org/data/tables/44-children-in-poverty-by-race-and-ethnicity#detailed/1/any/false/573,869,36,868,867/10,11,9,12,1,185,13/324,323.

34. Jennifer Medina, "Economic Downturn Holds Fierce Grip on Border Town," *New York Times*, March 16, 2011.

35. Matt Hilburn, "Wage Theft Shatters American Dream for Many Low-Income Immigrants," Voice of America, December 28, 2011. Available online at www.voanews.com.

36. These findings by Massey and Gelatt ae summarized in Melinda Burns, "Why Mexican Immigrants Can't Get Ahead," *Pacific Standard*, December 22, 2011.

37. Douglas S. Massey and Julia Gelatt, "What Happened to the Wages of Mexican Immigrants? Trends and Interpretations," *Latino Studies* 8 (2010), 328–54.

38. Ibid.

39. Charles Roxburgh, Susan Lund, and John Piotrowski, "Mapping Global Capital Markets 2011," McKinsey Global Institute, August 2011.

40. Mike Alberti, "On Manufacturing Policy, White House Remains in Grip of 'Ratchet-Down' Consultants," Remapping Debate, January 18, 2012. Available online at www.remappingdebate.org.

41. Mike Alberti, "Producing More, Earning Less," Remapping Debate, January 25, 2012.

42. Betty Beard, "Arizona Jobs Outlook for Recent College Graduates Bleak, but Improving," *Arizona Republic*, June 6, 2010.

43. Mary K. Reinhart, "Arizona Supreme Court Lets AHCCCS Cuts Stand," *Arizona Republic*, February 15, 2012.

44. Susanna Kim, "2010 Had Record 2.9 Million Foreclosures," ABC News, January 11, 2011.

45. Some aspects have since been blocked by federal courts. For a good analysis of the law, see Shaun Harkin and Nicole Colson, "Resisting Juan Crow in Alabama," *International Socialist Review* 81, January–February 2012. Available online at https://isreview.org/issue/81/resisting-juan-crow-alabama.

46. For instance, see Campbell Robertson, "After Ruling, Hispanics Flee an Alabama Town," *New York Times*, October 3, 2011. Available online at http://www.nytimes.com/2011/10/04/us/after-ruling-hispanics-flee-an-alabama-town.html.

47. Samuel Addy, "A Cost-Benefit Analysis of the New Alabama Immigration Law," Center for Business and Economic Research, University of Alabama, January 2012. Available online at https://cber.cba.ua.edu/New%20AL%20Immigration%20Law%20-%20Costs%20and%20Benefits.pdf.

48. See Ana Gonzalez-Barrera, and Jens Manuel Krogstad, "What We Know about Illegal Immigration from Mexico," Pew Research Center, March 2, 2017. Available online at http://www.pewresearch.org/fact-tank/2017/03/02/what-we-know-about-illegal-immigration-from-mexico/.

49. Jens Manuel Krogstad, Jeffrey S. Passel, and D'Vera Cohn, "5 Facts about Illegal Immigration in the U.S.," Pew Research Center, April 27, 2017. Available online at http://www.pewresearch.org/fact-tank/2017/04/27/5-facts-about-illegal-immigration-in-the-u-s/.

50. Immigration Policy Center, "Mexican Migration Patterns Signal a New Immigration Reality," August 1, 2011.

51. Frontera NorteSur online, "Mexican Workers Pulverized," Center for Latin American and Border Studies, New Mexico State University, February 9, 2012.

52. The piecemeal privatization of Mexico's oil industry has now led to Mexico becoming a net importer of U.S. fuel. These structural changes, many of which happened in other industries under the North American Free Trade Agreement, will likely increase unemployment as the state oil company PEMEX is restructured and cut into state oil revenues, which fund much of Mexico's social spending. See Laurence Iliff, "Oil-Rich Mexico Becomes Net Importer of U.S. Petroleum Goods," *Wall Street Journal*, May 14, 2014. Available online at https://www.wsj.com/articles/oil-rich-mexico-becomes-net-importer-of-u-s-petroleum-goods-1400104955; and Tracy Wilkinson, "Mexico, Which Depends Largely on Oil Revenue, Cuts Public Spending," *Los Angeles Times*, January 30, 2015. Available online at http://www.latimes.com/world/mexico-americas/la-fg-mexico-budget-20150130-story.html.

53. See Doris Meissner, "Border Budget Is Already Enormous," *New York Times*, January 31, 2013. The total of $219 billion was calculated by 2013, with the budgets for 2014, 2015, and 2016 added. Available online at https://www.nytimes.com/roomfordebate/2013/01/31/is-the-border-secure-enough-1/border-budget-is-already-enormous; see also U.S. Department of Homeland Security, "Budget-in-Brief, Fiscal Year 2016." Available online at https://www.dhs.gov/sites/default/files/publications/FY_2016_DHS_Budget_in_Brief.pdf; and U.S. Department of Homeland Security, "Budget-in-Brief, Fiscal Year 2017." Available online at https://www.dhs.gov/sites/default/files/publications/FY2017BIB.pdf.

54. Department of Homeland Security, "DHS' Progress in 2011: Southwest Border," press release, January 23, 2012. Available online at www.dhs.gov.

55. Marshall Fitz, "Safer Than Ever: A View from the US–Mexico Border: Assessing the Past, Present, and Future," Center for American Progress, August 2011. Available online at www.americanprogress.org.

56. William Booth, "More Predator Drones Fly US-Mexico Border," *Washington Post*, December 21, 2011.

57. Mark Hugo Lopez, Ana Gonzalez-Barrera, and Seth Motel, "As Deportations Rise to Record Levels, Most Latinos Oppose Obama's Policy," Pew Hispanic Center, December 28, 2011.

58. See Muzaffar Chishti, Sarah Pierce, and Jessica Bolter, "The Obama Record on Deportations: Deporter in Chief or Not?," Migration Policy Institute, January 26, 2017. Available online at http://www.migrationpolicy.org/article/obama-record-deportations -deporter-chief-or-not.

59. Ibid.

60. See Doris Meissner, Donald M. Kerwin, Muzaffar Chishti, and Claire Bergeron, "Immigration Enforcement in the United States: The Rise of a Formidable Machinery," Migration Policy Institute, January 2013. Available online at www.migrationpolicy.org /pubs/pillars-reportinbrief.pdf.

61. Ryan Gabrielson, "Fewer Face Deportation Because of Criminal Charges, Data Shows," California Watch, December 11, 2011.

62. Jorge Rivas, "ICE Arrest 3k Immigrants in 6 days, Largest Roundup Ever," *Colorlines*, April 3, 2012.

63. Miriam Jordan, "Immigration Audits Drive Illegal Workers Underground," *Wall Street Journal*, August 15, 2011.

64. Emma Roller, "Firing of Workers Who Failed to Provide Documents Divides Pomona College," *Chronicle of Higher Education*, February 12, 2012.

65. Burns, "Why Mexican Immigrants Can't Get Ahead."

66. See Justin Akers Chacón, "The US-Mexico Border: Free Trade without Free People," *International Socialist Review* 73 (September–October 2010).

67. "Mexico Loses $50 Bln/Year in Illegal Outflows—Report," Reuters, January 30, 2012.

68. Ibid.

69. Michael Graybeal, "Mexico's Economic Policy and Migration," Center for Strategic and International Studies, May 2011.

70. Ibid.

71. "Credit Suisse: Global Wealth Has Soared 14% since 2010 to USD 231 Trillion with the Strongest Growth in Emerging Markets," press release, October 19, 2011. Available online at www.credit-suisse.com.

72. See Alan Travis, "Super-Rich to Be Given Fast-Track to Settle in Britain," *Guardian*, March 15, 2011; Qian Chen, "The 'Golden Visa' Program into the US Is Set to Expire, and That's Worrying Many in China," CNBC, April 28, 2017. Available online at https://www.cnbc.com/2017/04/28/eb-5-visa-and-china-the-golden-visa-program -into-the-us-is-expiring.html.

73. See Lornet Turnbull, "Wealthy Immigrants Can Invest Way to Visas," *Seattle Times*, December 10, 2011.

74. Jeremy Schwartz, "Austin Beginning to Compete with Other Texas Cities for Wealthy Immigrants from Mexico," *Statesman*, June 6, 2011.

75. Juan Carlos Ruiz, "Mexico: Travel Trends to the United States," U.S. Department of Commerce, December 2010.

76. BBVA Research, "Mexico Migration Outlook," press presentation, October 25, 2010. Available online at www.bbvaresearch.com.

Index

About the Authors

Justin Akers Chacón is a professor of U.S. History and Chicano Studies in San Diego, California. He has contributed to the *International Socialist Review* and the book *Immigration: Opposing Viewpoints*.

Mike Davis is a historian, activist, and author of many books, including *City of Quartz, The Monster at Our Door*, and *Planet of Slums*. Davis teaches in the Department of History at the University of California at Irvine.

Julián Cardona was born in 1960 in Zacatecas, Mexico, and migrated to the border city of Juárez with his family as a small child. He worked as a technician in the maquiladora industry before becoming a photojournalist in 1993. In 2004, Cardona received a Cultural Freedom Fellowship from the Lannan Foundation.

About Haymarket Books

Haymarket Books is a radical, independent, nonprofit book publisher based in Chicago.

Our mission is to publish books that contribute to struggles for social and economic justice. We strive to make our books a vibrant and organic part of social movements and the education and development of a critical, engaged, international left.

We take inspiration and courage from our namesakes, the Haymarket martyrs, who gave their lives fighting for a better world. Their 1886 struggle for the eight-hour day—which gave us May Day, the international workers' holiday—reminds workers around the world that ordinary people can organize and struggle for their own liberation. These struggles continue today across the globe—struggles against oppression, exploitation, poverty, and war.

Since our founding in 2001, Haymarket Books has published more than five hundred titles. Radically independent, we seek to drive a wedge into the risk-averse world of corporate book publishing. Our authors include Noam Chomsky, Arundhati Roy, Rebecca Solnit, Angela Y. Davis, Howard Zinn, Amy Goodman, Wallace Shawn, Mike Davis, Winona LaDuke, Ilan Pappé, Richard Wolff, Dave Zirin, Keeanga-Yamahtta Taylor, Nick Turse, Dahr Jamail, David Barsamian, Elizabeth Laird, Amira Hass, Mark Steel, Avi Lewis, Naomi Klein, and Neil Davidson. We are also the trade publishers of the acclaimed Historical Materialism Book Series and of Dispatch Books.